Emily French (seated), circa 1912
(see list of illustrations for details)

i

Mr. Edward C. Randall, circa 1904
(see list of illustrations for details)

# THE FRENCH REVELATION

Voice to Voice Conversations With The Living Dead
Through the Mediumship of

## Emily S. French

Witnessed and Documented by the Famous Buffalo Attorney

## Edward C. Randall

### *The Most Complete Study of Objective Psychic Phenomena of the 20th Century*

The Complete Works
Compiled, Researched & Edited
by
## N.Riley Heagerty

Copyright 1995. N.Riley Heagerty

ISBN: 0-9703914-0-4

Library of Congress Control Number: 00-91247

THIS STORY IS TRUE–THE CHARACTERS ARE REAL

Printed in the United States by
Morris Publishing • 3212 East Highway 30 • Kearney, NE 68847
1-800-650-7888

In the beginning, one of my co-workers in the life beyond said:

"I find about you, Mr. Randall, a crowd of earnest spirit people who are bending all their thought upon this which you are about to undertake. They will help you, when writing, by their suggestions, and, as the little book begins its journey to find the hearts of men, they will open many doors, and guide it to many darkened homes. The light illuminating every page will be the beacon for many in distress, and we in spirit do most sincerely thank you for your efforts to bring these great truths to all people.

"We see so many entering spirit-life who have lived and died ignorant of this natural law, and we know so well the importance of knowing and living according to that law, that we rejoice over this book of knowledge and we will speed it on its helpful journey with eagerness and with pleasure."

—Spirit quote preceding first chapter of The Future of Man, the second published work of Edward C. Randall, 1908.

# THE FRENCH REVELATION

*To Those Splendid Minds In The Spheres of Progression Who, Voice to Voice, Have Told Me To What Life Leads, I Dedicate This Book.*

—Edward C. Randall. From His First Work, *Life's Progression*, 1906.

*To Emily S. French, Edward C. Randall and All of The Celestial Visitors Whose Combined Patience, Perseverance and Persistence Brought These Great Truths To The World I Dedicate This Complete Work.*

—N.Riley Heagerty, Compiler and Editor, 1995.

# ACKNOWLEDGMENTS

However large or small their contribution to *The French Revelation*, thanks are due to the following for their help along the way.

The Oswego Public Library—Carol, Martha and the staff, Oswego, New York; Penfield Library at Oswego State University, Mrs. Mary Bennett; Edward A. Mervine, Attorney at Law, Oswego, New York; Onondaga County Public Library, Syracuse, New York, Mr. Chris Cox, I.L.L.; Buffalo and Erie County Public Library—William H. Loos, Curator/Grosvenor Rare Book Room, Buffalo, New York, who supplied me with, over the years, invaluable biographical information on Edward C. Randall; Buffalo and Erie County Historical Society; University of Rochester, Rochester, New York; Rochester Public Library—Local History Division; Rochester Historical Society; Erie County Surrogate's Court, Buffalo, New York; Middle Earth Books, Paul B. Hudson, Michigan; The Lily Dale Spiritualist Assembly and The National Spiritualist Association of Churches, Lily Dale, New York; Library of Congress—Rare Books and Special Collections Division, Washington, D.C.; The Eileen Garrett Library, Joanne D.S. McMahon, PhD., Parapsychology Foundation, New York, New York; University of Buffalo—Charles B. Sears Law Library; Allegheny College—Lawrence Lee Pelletier Library, Meadville, Pennsylvania; Stanford University Libraries, Elizabeth Green, Stanford, California; The New York State Library, Cultural Education Center, Henry Ilnicki, Albany, New York; The American Society of Psychical Research, New York, New York; The Blue Dragon Bookshop, Ashland, Oregon; Berry Hill Book Shop, Deansboro, New York; Chester Valley Old Books, Frazer, Pennsylvania; The Book Mark, Rittenhouse Square West, Philadelphia, Pennsylvania; Yankee Peddler Bookshop, Rochester, New York; Bettman Archive, New York, New York; Health Research, Mokelumne Hill, California (original store), and now Ben Roberts and Nikki Jones, Pomeroy, Washington;

## Acknowledgements

Mrs. Ellie Tritchler, genealogist, Buffalo, New York; Mr. Roy D. Goold, genealogist, Brockport/Rochester, New York; The National Archives Trust Fund, Washington, D.C.; Virginia W. Common, granddaughter of Edward C. Randall; Mrs. Marylyn Graham, wife of the late Thomas H. Graham, grandson of Edward C. Randall, Joanna Haney, Oswego, New York for her help in editing the introduction, and lastly, the home circle; **England**: The Noah's Ark Society for Physical Mediumship, the committee, staff, mediums and members; The Society for Psychical Research, London; Harry Price Library, University of London; College of Psychic Studies, London; Marion Hancock, Bookseller; The Spiritualist National Union, Essex, Publication Committee, for permission to use the quotes of Arthur Findlay from 'On The Edge of The Etheric,' and 'Looking Back.'; **Australia**: The University of New England, Department of Psychology, Armidale; Melbourne Theosophical Society, Melbourne, Victoria; The Australian Institute of Parapsychological Research; La Trobe University, Dr. Al Babay, Department of Humanities, Bendigo, Victoria; State Library of New South Wales, Sidney; State Library of Victoria, Melbourne, Victoria. The rare, elusive unpublished material of Edward C. Randall could not have been located and included in this work were it not for some good old-fashioned determination and the help of my Australian friends.

# LIST OF ILLUSTRATIONS

Illustration 1: Frontispiece photograph of Emily S. French (seated), circa 1912, taken shortly before her death, with her daughter Ella French Oberst (1855-1940), standing to her left dressed in white; her granddaughter Louise Oberst Augell (1882-1958), standing behind her and, on her lap, her grandson Alan Scott Augell (1909-1963); four generations represented.

Illustration 2: Frontispiece photograph of Edward Caleb Randall, Men of Buffalo portrait, circa 1904.

In center of book:

Illustration 3: Photograph of Edward C. Randall, the Courier Express, circa 1934.

Illustration 4: Photograph of Emily Sophia McCoy French, age 40 years, taken in 1871, seven years after the untimely death of her husband Lieu't James H. French (see appendices), and nineteen years before meeting Edward C. Randall. As a symbol of her state of mourning over the loss of James in 1864 and her young son William H. French, "Willie" as he was called, at age 26 in 1881, Mrs. French wore the color black until her death in 1912.

Illustration 5: The house at West Ferry Street, city of Buffalo, New York; former home of the Edward C. Randall family as seen in modern times, where the psychic experiments with Emily S. French took place. The *Tower Room* was built into a remote section of the third story of this stately home, used specifically for their seances. The Randall family was in residence at this location from 1899 to 1921.

Illustration 6: The little headstone marking the final resting place of the psychic wonder of the world, at Mt. Hope Cemetery, Rochester, New York. Hardy mums planted yearly, compliments of the editor.

# Table of Contents

# APPENDICES

# Editor's Postscript

## A Call From Emily

The one main discouragement that I constantly faced throughout the entire process of putting together *The French Revelation* was that I had never obtained an actual photograph of the principal character of the story, Emily S. French, and Mr. Randall—for whatever reason—had never included one in any of his books. After I had completed the manuscript, I was "inspired" to make one last-ditch effort to locate a photograph and contacted a genealogist from Rochester. This individual had never heard of Emily S. French or her work with Edward C. Randall but said she would look into the matter and get back to me. Forty-eight hours later I received a phone call from another genealogist who knew the first genealogist I contacted. She asked me if the name Emeline Sophia French meant anything to me. (I had never come across Mrs. French being referred to as Emeline before, nor had I known that her middle name was Sophia.) It turned out that at that very moment she had been conducting an extensive genealogical search for a gentleman named Thomas Chesrown, the great-great grandson of none other than Emily French herself, I wonder, is that what the word "coincidence" means?

Aside from the photographs which I used for the book, there was also sent to me a posed military photograph of her husband James H. French, another four-generation shot of Emily with her daughter, granddaughter and grandson, a photo of her daughter Ella, her father William C. McCoy, her mother Elizabeth C. Pierpont McCoy, a photo of Ella when she was very old, and Fidel B. Oberst, the husband of Ella. I was also able to find out the exact birth date of Mrs. French, 10 July, 1831.

Thanks to Mr. Thomas Chesrown who supplied me with these invaluable photographs, I can now say, at last, that *The French Revelation* stands complete.

For Caroline,
my shining light

# Introduction

*Nothing is too wonderful to be true.* –Faraday

Audacious, startling and incredible would be mild characterizations of the assertions that were contained within the first published work of Edward C. Randall entitled *Life's Progression; Research in Meta-psychics* (Henry B. Brown Company: Buffalo, New York, 1906.), which he suddenly and unexpectedly dropped like an atom bomb of controversy into the religious world. His announced object in publishing the work, which he said represented fifteen years' research in meta-psychics, a comparatively unknown field of study, was to illuminate, but he also knew that it would produce a fire storm of heat as well as light.

"There is no death; there are no dead."

These words stood out on the cover of the book, and in its foreword he asserted the following: "I have no need of creeds nor use for faiths. Positive knowledge has displaced them both and I have come to know there is no death; there are no dead. That change is one step only in life's progression, in the unceasing march of evolution, in which neither identity nor individuality is lost, and that life goes on and labor continues as the soul works toward perfection, for progress is an absolute law that nothing can resist."

His words were a direct challenge to orthodox thinking and through all the pages of his work ran this disconcerting challenge to those whose idea of God, of heaven, hell and a future life were based strictly on the Bible. If there is no death, if there are no dead, what then would become of the resurrection morn; where shall we look for the great White Throne, where for the One who shall intercede for the sinful; where shall the separation of the goats and

1

sheep take place; where are the streets made of gold? Mr. Randall's findings annulled these widely-accepted teachings. He was convinced that every man must, and will, stand as his own redeemer. He was not inferring by his statements that he did not believe in the life hereafter, nor in the universal power and controlling force which is denominated God and which is thought by some to be clothed with a personality and by others considered the essence of good; the true spirit of love, only not embodied. He did not contend the existence of these things. He did believe in a heaven, not a heaven of idleness and exclusiveness, but a heaven peopled by active, progressive and hard-working spirits. Mr. Randall likewise believed in hell, only it was not a hell where punishment is meted out in an atmosphere of flames and sulfurous fumes. In this modern day, belief in a hell of fire and brimstone may seem outmoded, but there are some, rest assured, who still look upon hell as a place of physical torment. Many conceive hell to be a place apart from heaven where the wicked have gained admission by their actions while on earth. There is also the steadily growing belief that hell is a state of remorse of the spirit, and this view comes extremely close to Mr. Randall's hell.

The author of *Life's Progression* published four more, equally startling books which together embodied the results of his psychic research. The works were the outcome of what Mr. Randall termed his positive knowledge, yet he never claimed that he was the only one that knew or could know. This certainty, in the year 1906, was remarkable of psychic literature. Many books had been written previously about the life hereafter; men of many minds had reasoned from many viewpoints as to what might be seen beyond death's mysterious door. These speculations began in the very early ages and have continued right up until this present day, but at the turn of the century, few books, if any, had been written which purported to give exact and definite knowledge of the life that is beyond the Everlasting line.

And where did Mr. Randall get his information? His answer, always direct and without equivocation, was: "From those that are living that life"; he said, "from spirits with whom I have talked voice to voice, for many years," and he meant "voice-to-voice" very literally. Commenting on the reasons for publishing his research, he further stated: "I do so in the hope that the fear of death may pass, that those who mourn may find consolation, and that all may find understanding. All the facts that we know and can gather—the miracle of death; each new birth; all teachings from the great beyond, and here; all discoveries and inventions; all the wondrous paintings, miracles of form and color; the marvelous marbles that seem to live and breathe; the secrets told by winding stream and desert sand; the record of all events evidence a *Directive Force* that we call God, that finds expression not only on this poor earth of ours, but in the planes beyond, where all at last must go. I have come to know something of the plan, purpose and operation of the Directive Force, not only here, but in the planes beyond. Having come into touch with those who live there, we have discussed these questions, and their teachings, faithfully recorded, I have given to you as they were given to me unaltered and unchanged."

The world seemed to stand at attention when Mr. Randall made public the results of his research and soon after, his works attracted the following of the two foremost American psychic researchers at the time, Dr. Richard Hodgson and Prof. James Hyslop, and also, England's leading experts of psychic research, J. Arthur Findlay and Vice-Admiral W. Usborne Moore (see Appendices and Reading List). This was, after all, no ordinary man making these astonishing assertions concerning the very nature of man's destiny; Mr. Randall was an esteemed member of the highest echelon of society, one of the most powerful leaders of business in the United States, and, furthermore, a celebrated trial lawyer, well known for his abilities of sifting evidence and interrogation of witnesses on the stand. His very presence within this body of research was, in itself, a proclamation of its seriousness.

Edward Caleb Randall was born in Ripley, New York, in 1860 and obtained his preliminary education in the district school and academy of his native place. He was prepared for college under private tutorship and he pursued his classical studies at Allegheny College in Meadville, Pennsylvania. In 1883 he was admitted to the bar, having been practicing at Dunkirk since 1879. He married Maria Howard of Buffalo in 1897. At the time of his death in 1935, he was the president of the American Super Power Corporation, Super Power Syndicate Inc., Niagara Terminals Buildings Inc., Cataract Development Corporation, South Buffalo Gas Corporation, vice-president of Eureka Smelting Company, and director of Prest Air Corporation.

Mr. Randall stated when he began his investigations into psychic research, he had absolutely no place in his mind for even a conception of a spiritual existence, or for any agencies in the universe other than matter and force. For this famous trial lawyer and astute businessman, his days of agnosticism and conjecture ended and a wondrous journey of transformation began with his introduction to a quiet little woman who lived on Tremont Street in Rochester, New York. She was a psychic medium; her name, Mrs. Emily S. French.

## Mrs. Emily French And the Direct-Independent Voice Phenomena

*"For to one is given by the Spirit the word of wisdom; to another the word of knowledge by the same Spirit... To another the working of miracles; to another prophecy; to another discerning of spirits..."*

—1 Corinthians12: 8-10

Arthur Findlay, in his classic book entitled *On the Edge of the Etheric*, published in 1931, mentions that when he visited Mr. Randall in 1923 and asked him how he became interested in the phenomena of Direct-Voice, Mr. Randall responded by saying that in 1890 he had been approached by a number of his associates who requested him to investigate the practices of a lady named Mrs. French since, reportedly, she was a magician of the highest class and the cleverest fraud in America. It was assumed that Mr. Randall, being a master of detecting fraud on any level, was the last person who could be bamboozled by any charlatan, especially one pretending to be contacting the so-called dead. So began his association with the elderly, frail and gentle Emily French, whose aspect hardly resembled that of your stereotypical conniving trickster. He quickly realized that the accusations made previously by his associates were nothing less than absurd. Without exception, Mrs. French was held in the highest regard by her acquaintances and never a penny did she receive for her services, ever. That she inspired trust is evident in the astonishing reports about her, some of which are given by those with weighty names and marks of scholarship. Mr. Randall was to eventually consider this unassuming woman from Rochester the greatest living psychic in America, if not in the entire world. His deep and unalterable conviction of the extraordinary nature of the case led him to experiment with and investigate the phenomena attending Mrs. French for twenty-two consecutive years; phenomena so marvelous that such occurrences would be impossible to apprehend unless an individual be familiar with the experience itself or the literature which deals with it.

In the presence of the medium, Mrs. French, but quite apart from her, *voices*, claiming to be those of deceased people would speak, and, when replied to, would answer back intelligently, which proved that not only was a mind behind the voice, but also

4

that the speaker was able to hear as well as speak. Isolated voices manifesting from space without visible source of agency; could something be too wonderful to be true? Absolutely not, according to Mr. Randall. The proof, he said, was incontrovertible and conclusive, brought about by the sheer weight of evidence resulting from his many sittings and exacting experiments in which he tested the powers of Mrs. French in every conceivable way he could devise. The evidence was spoken; it was established through the attestations of men, women and children who had experienced the drama of death and who had come back by way of the direct-independent voice to share their experiences with those still living in the physical world.

From Edward Randall's book, *The Dead Have Never Died*, published in 1917, comes the following spirit description spoken in the direct-independent voice, concerning the mechanics of speech:

"There are in our group," the spirit replied [after being asked by Mr. Randall to tell of the conditions which enabled them to speak], "seven people, —all expert in the handling of the electric and magnetic forces, and when you and the psychic, Mrs. French, meet, the vital force that emanates from her personality is gathered up. We also take physical emanations—substances—from you and the others with you, while we contribute to the mass a certain spirit force. Now, that force, which we gather and distribute, is just as material as any substance that you would gather for any purpose; it is simply higher in vibration. We clothe the organs of respiration of the spirit who is to speak, so that his voice will sound in your atmosphere, and when this condition is brought about, it is just as natural for a spirit as it is for you. You then have what is known as the direct or independent voice, that is, the voice of a spirit speaking as in earth life."

Although very little information is obtainable on the early life and biographical background of Mrs. French and, as of yet, no existing photograph of her that I know of, some insight into her person and practices may be gleaned through the following passages.

This information was taken from a letter written by the secretary of the Rochester Art Club, Mr. A.W. Moore, dated 1905:

With a newspaperman's soul, I found out something about the lady's antecedents. She belongs to the American branch of the Pierrepont family, the head of which is the Earl of Manvers, whose principle estate is at Holme Pierrepont, Nottinghamshire, England. I borrowed a book giving the history of the American branch, in which there is a list of the members of the family then living in the United States. In the list I found the name of the late Judge Pierrepont, one time minister to the Court of Saint James, London, and at the very end, I found the names of Mrs. French and her only child, Mrs. D. Oberst. Mrs. French is the widow of the late Lieut. French of the United States Volunteers, who lost his life during the war of the Rebellion. She draws a pension of an officer's widow. For many years she has made her home with her daughter, and her chief pleasure in life is administering to the comfort and education of her grandchildren. She is a lady of refinement and possesses the charming, unassuming and gentle manners of a well-born race.

From *The Encyclopedia of Psychic Science*:

Mrs. Emily French (1831-1912), of Rochester, a relation of President Cleveland, excellent American direct-voice medium. She was investigated for more than twenty years by Edward C. Randall of Buffalo. Isaac K. Funk and Prof. Hyslop [see Part III and appendices] also conducted remarkable experiments and proved that the voices did not originate in the vocal organs of the medium. "Red Jacket", her Indian guide, had an exceedingly loud, masculine voice which could have easily filled a hall with a seating capacity of two thousand people. The medium at that time, was a frail old woman, with a weak and irregular heart and very deaf. Yet the communicators—the spirits—could hear every remark of the sitters at the seances.

As a superb example of a completely spontaneous situation involving the phenomena attending Mrs. French and one with the highest evidential value, I include the testimony of Mrs. French's personal physician and friend, Dr. Jane M. Frear, who lived at 21 Orton Place, Buffalo, New York; it is dated 1907:

. . . My father [and I] at one time were talking with her, we standing on opposite sides of a doorway. The light from the next room made Mrs. French's face plainly visible to me. I was looking at her and talking to her when the loud voice known as "Red Jacket" spoke to us from the top of the stairway, which was in the dark. I have also heard a voice beginning to speak while she was talking. This has happened on several occasion, while I was chatting with her—her deafness prevented her from catching the first vibrations of the other voice or voices. I have also heard two voices singing at the same time—she does not sing. These voices were male voices.

Emily French was 80 years, 11 months and 12 days old when she quietly passed away on June 22, 1912 at her home at 227 Tremont Street in Rochester, where she had spent most of her adult life. She was buried in Mt. Hope cemetary in that city.

## The French Revelation:
## The Complete Work of Edward C. Randall

*Seek, and you will find; for you have aids from Nature for the discovery of Truth. But if you are not able yourself, by going along those ways, to discover that which follows, listen to those who have made the enquiry.* —Epictetus

Ninety years after his first published work startled the world, I present to a new audience as one edition, the complete meta-psychic research of Edward Randall with the spiritual medium, Mrs. Emily S. French. Included are his five books, published between 1906 and 1922, and unpublished rare excerpts from his last unfinished manuscript, written in 1926, which I was fortunate enough to locate in Melbourne, Australia. All of Mr. Randall's work has been carefully condensed. Only the occasional instances of repetition (occuring mostly in the later works as a result of the compilation) are eliminated. The majority of chapter material has been retained, thus maintaining the structural format and intellectual integrity of Mr. Randall's original works.

*The French Revelation* is presented in four parts. An idea of the scope of the volume will be gathered by a brief summary of its contents.

## Part I

This first section encapsulates the philosophy of Edward Randall. It is a compilation of all the forwards of his books where he outlines in his compelling style the certainty of his beliefs. Modern readers, steeped in the new language of science and cosmology, may find some of his deductions archaic and speculative. It is true that Mr. Randall expressed his descriptions of the afterlife in terms of the physics of his day. The spirits themselves constantly affirm that they are always progressing and learning what the afterlife is like; they can only describe it as they have experienced it and this is the case now, as well as at the time of Mr. Randall's speech with them. His refuge of certainty, wherein lies the value of his work, is in the basing of his beliefs on information transferred through the mediumship of Emily French by the voices which attended her. His writings were conveyances of the vast knowledge taught him by the higher intelligences; the "hundreds, yea, thousands" that came and spoke to him in their own voices over a period of more than two decades. Mr. Randall's meta-psychic philosophy, culled from all of his works, exhibits the broad scope of his learning and his deep love for the progress of humanity. Taken altogether, these writings are a masterpiece of psychic literature and nothing less.

## Part II

The nine chapters that comprise this section present Mr. Randall's stenographic records of spirit lectures, discourses, and voice-to-voice conversations selected by him for publication in his books. In addition to the material arising from his investigations with Mrs. French, are a few examples of collected seance memoranda from approved fellow researchers, which Mr. Randall had included in his books. These first-hand accounts are accompanied by Mr. Randall's moving commentary. All spirit words are featured in bold print in this section and throughout *The French Revelation*.

## Part III

The only documented work dealing with testing the powers of Emily French by an outside agency without the presence of Edward Randall is featured in this section. The tests were carried out by Dr. Isaac K. Funk[1] and a team of his associates. Although

---

1. Dr. Isaac Kauffman Funk (1839-1912) was a noted psychic researcher and author. He co-owned the prestigious publishing house, Funk & Wagnalls, New York/London, publishers of The *Psychic Riddle*, by Dr. Funk, 1906. The material found in Part III of *The French Revelation* is from this book.

psychic science as a whole owes a great debt to Dr. Funk for having published the results of the study which would allow readers of his work the opportunity to examine the evidence and decide for themselves what they believe, it is also blatantly obvious that the results presented by Dr. Funk are colored in some areas with predetermined assumptions. That Dr. Funk left so many "loopholes," as Mr. Randall referred to them, was an unquestionable act of cowardice, allowing him and his committee a way of avoiding the dreaded scorn of the scientific community by being safely suspicious. A prime example of one of these "loopholes" is evidenced by the "sly, tricky person" comment made at the end of this report. Even though the test findings were manipulated, certain facts add to the superior evidential nature of the case: the advanced age of Mrs. French (72 years), her weakened physical condition and her being placed in a location completely unfamiliar to her. Certainly the methods of the investigative team were at times too aggressive and disregarding of the fragile state of Mrs. French, so taken at its fundamental value, the outcome of these tests—remarkable, given the circumstances—only upholds the name of Emily French and substantiates even further the statements of Edward Randall.

## Part IV

This section contains the final perspectives and deductions by Mr. Randall; a moving tribute to his faithful friend and partner in whose presence the angels came, Mrs. French, and concluding words by an advanced spirit.

The appendices contain all additional biographical information that I have been able to collect, interesting excerpts and quotes, a reading list consisting of later works dealing with the phenomena of direct-voice, and lastly, "My Thanatopsis," the farewell funeral address penned by Mr. Randall for himself and sent to me by his granddaughter, Virginia. It was a great honor to speak with her and have this precious document included in *The French Revelation*.

## When the World Is Ready

Compiling the work of Randall and French over these many years will stand all the days of my life as one of the most rewarding things I could ever have done. It has been a spiritual and philosophical adventure, one which, I can say now, has run full gamut, after having experienced myself the extraordinary phenomena of the independent voice recently in England. The setting of this culminating experience was such that even the possibility of fraud was out of the question. Thus, I feel that I can share unequivocally with Edward Randall the deep conviction that indeed the dead are very much alive. The works of Randall have been instrumental in leading me to this point, but I would not have begun my journey were it not for the loss of a young woman who I once knew and deeply loved. Experiencing profound loss is the starting point for many individuals, who then go in search of spiritual answers, seeking the meaning of life, and consequently they may be led to the study of psychic phenomena and survival research. Such was the case with me. The remembrance of her vibrant energy and happiness, unlike any I had ever known, was the sole basis of my belief and hope that *she must be somewhere.* For me, the banal, repetitious humdrum of church teachings had nothing substantial to offer and I found its content often contrary to common sense. Where there was once only searching speculation, I have found answers; ones that appeal to Reason, the very criterion by which Mr. Randall insisted that his findings be judged. It is my hope that by having compiled the records of these events, others may perhaps gain a sense of understanding that will help them. Not everyone will have the opportunity to experience the voices first-hand, but neither did the majority at the turn of the century. Many of these, perhaps thousands, were guided from distress through the written words contained within this work, having no greater substantiation than the very presence and personality of Emily S. French in this case, and the integrity of Randall's interpretation of the spirit's message.

The Spirits have said:

**"We communicate with you not merely to prove survival but to attract attention to the important truths connected with it. We are anxious to show mankind that earth-life is not complete in itself, but contributes to a larger order, that it is an episode in a stupendously larger drama."**

God does seem to work in strange and wonderful ways, and psychic research can unfold many wonders along the way. After having finished compiling *The French Revelation*, I found in a musty-smelling little sequestered nook in his hometown library yet another faded obituary notice for Edward Caleb Randall, and in it was a statement from his memoirs which he completed before his death in 1935. He had written that the world would not be sufficiently advanced for the theories set forth in his work until another half-century had passed; at a time when, as he expressed it "the world is ready." It was precisely fifty years later, in 1985, when I came upon, quite unexpectedly, Randall's great classic, *The Dead Have Never Died*, and determined shortly after reading it, to try and locate what other research he may have done and compile it into one complete edition. My entire mission has now come to pass, and I bow in thanks to the Infinite Intelligence who, it seems, has allowed me to have played a part, however large or small, in fulfilling the futuristic prophecy of this great American researcher, Mr. Edward C. Randall, with the psychic wonder of the world, Mrs. Emily S. French.

May these glorious truths, given to the world by these two tireless explorers into man's greatest mystery, now infused with new life and set on its course once again, provide a more clear and rational understanding of life's progress, and by so doing, enrich the world; complimenting God, natural laws, and substantiate to a profound degree, man's rightful place in the unceasing march of evolution.

N. Riley Heagerty
24 February, 1995
Oswego, New York

# PART I

## The Meta-Psychic Philosophy of Edward C. Randall

Based on Observation and Experiment with the Phenomena
Known as The Direct-Independent Voice

# CHAPTER 1
## From Agnosticism to Belief

*The wise are instructed by reason; ordinary minds by experience; the stupid by necessity; the brutes by instinct.* —Cicero

To understand things as they are the world must have truth. While it has made gigantic strides in all the arts and sciences, hardly a step has been taken in the way that leads to a knowledge of man's ultimate end.

In the presence of dissolution, faith, belief and creeds wither and decay, and doubt goes hand and hand with grief. In such a presence we feel what speech cannot tell, and hope that what seems night here is somewhere else a dawn. In the majesty of this silence, how acts and deeds burst into perfect form. When loving hearts are breaking, and heads are bowed above an open grave, how dare any priest presume to tell what he does not know?

Belief will not change natural law; Faith will not save or condemn one; Ignorance will not excuse one; Traditions stay progression, while doubt is the dawn of reason. Why not find out now, if possible, some solution of this problem and what this life leads to? Little at best can be known of the afterlife, so boundless is its scope; yet enough can be learned while in the body, to dispel the awful fear and to lighten the sorrows that fill the human heart, as well as to make men lead better lives because they can live more intelligently, and so enrich the world. That I may increase this knowledge, I have investigated every natural law that I have had the opportunity and ability to study, and now, owing to present freedom of speech (circa 1906. —Ed), I publish the results of my investigations without fear. In many ways I have sought the

14

thought of men, both in and out of the body, ever drawing my own conclusions, and making my own deductions. I have felt the thrill of success in the discovery of new laws and in the proving of new facts.

The bridge of death no longer rests upon clouds of hope, but upon the great piers of knowledge. Every act is but the product of conditions, and the heart applauds the brain when one works to increase the force of universal good.

I know that matter is eternal and that only form is new, and that one who but yesterday in the flush of health faced the storms of life with splendid courage, and whose body lies tonight in the embrace of mother earth, is no exception to the rule. All that was matter, as we use the term, the outer garment, all that gave him physical expression, will mingle with the substance from which it was formed: but his spirit is eternal, his progression will be unbroken, and his horizon will widen, as he reaches the sphere of psychic discovery.

I know that to the limits of that plane in which he lives at first, the human voice will carry, the thought will reach. The so-called dead live here about us, know our sorrows and grieve with us. They share our happiness, they know our hopes and ambitions, and, by suggestion, through our subconscious brain, they influence our daily conduct. I know that there in the after life they have feature, form and expression, and, therefore, bodies composed of matter, for there cannot be form without substance. The substance that forms the bodies of spirit-people, vibrating more than five octaves higher than the violet ray, few in earth-life ever see, though spirit people see and talk with each other, and with mortals when necessary conditions are secured. I know that every hope, ambition, and desire of earth are continued beyond this life, as is also the burden of wrong. I know that we are as much spirit now as we ever shall be; that in death, so-called, we simply vacate and discard the gross material that gives us expression in this physical plane. All about this matter world of ours, there exists, in fact, the psychic or spiritual universe, more active and real than this, peopled with all the countless dead, who, no longer burdened with a physical body, move at will within the boundaries of their sphere, in what appears as space to mortal man.

Long ago I became satisfied that nothing ever dies, that those who in dissolution pass from this earth-plane still live, and that, if the conditions were made right, they could talk with us voice to voice. Now, after fifteen year's scientific research and experiment, I have made a condition so perfect that, with the aid of Mrs. Emily S. French (whose psychic powers have been developed), I am able to

15

carry on freely conversation with spirits out of the body. Thousands who have passed through the change called death, who live and labor in the world of thought around and about us, have told me something of the laws that govern all life beyond, what they find, how they live, have talked of their occupations and their progression. Their life is an active one. All the new conditions, all the great laws by which they are to be governed, must be learned, and only by individual effort can they live intelligently and well. I know that a wrong act in the earth-life must be lived over again in the next sphere, and lived right, before advancement is possible; that labor is often long, but that families and friends are, in time, reunited and take up the thread where it was broken. I have heard them talk amongst themselves, and to me, and many eminent men and women, upon my invitation, have heard the same that I have heard in the material conditions that we have made.

I do not seek to prove that soul-life follows dissolution–that is self evident to all intelligent men and women–but to give some information of the character and condition of that life among the spheres of progression. I would reach the thinkers, those who reason. Pearls of thought are for those who dive deep; in the shallows one finds only pebbles. These pages will not appeal to those who fear damnation as the penalty for searching for truth. But there are many who, working in the fields of knowledge, will welcome a co-laborer. Such would I join, bringing with me these teachings from planes beyond.

I know something of the democracy of death, and all that mankind is beginning to hear and march to the silent music of reason. I know, to, that the highest duty of everyone is to contribute what he can to the prosperity of the many, who though rich in material goods, are mentally poor in the land of opportunity, and that this individual life of ours, whether it has had birth within the palace or the hut, no matter how it turns and curves and falls among the hills as it courses from the mountain-tops, through valley-lands, or, lies at times in stagnant pools of ignorance and vice festering in the sun, must some day reach the great ocean of eternal life, from whence it came, clean and pure. I am told that:

**"Beyond the life that men call material, is another so much more real, so much more vital and interesting, that, when you enter into its fullest harmony, the little lives you led on earth will fade into the dim reality of a dream-like past."**

We cannot in the nature of things know much of the everyday life of spirits who people what to us is infinite space, because we are unable to grasp, to any great extent, the realities of their conditions. All can learn a little of matter and laws that control it beyond the physical plane, and to that extent can reason from cause to effect, without which there cannot be any rational conclusions.

I know that the tendency of all people is to do right, and that an invisible world, peopled by the so-called dead of all ages past, is interested in and is aiding our progression, that it speaks to our dull ears with silent voices; and I know that the great desire and hope of those beyond is to bring the world to an understanding of what dissolution means and of what follows so-called death, so that, knowing these two things, they may learn how to live the earth-life well.

It is time that men who know that those out of the body can and do talk to men, put away fear of the speech of people, and lend the weight of personality to this philosophy of truth. The age of faith is past. The teaching of the church no longer satisfies the hunger of heart and brain. This is an age of fact. The present calls upon men to think, not to believe; the torch of reason has been lighted, and its day is here.

I have no need of creeds nor use for faiths. Positive knowledge has displaced them both, and I have come to know there is no death; there are no dead.

I have written these pages with the hope that some heart, heavy with sorrow, may come to comprehend the truth about dissolution, and to know that those called dead are alive, and that all is well with them. We should ever look with eager eyes for gems of truth, and what we find, we should have the courage to express. I know better than anyone can tell me, how incomplete is this Metapsychic philosophy, but bear with me: I have gone, in my research, beyond physical laws and the books of men, out into the wilderness of fact; beyond the beaten path into another world, and what I have written, incomplete though it may be, 'are facts' and 'they are true.' Without arrogance, prejudice or preconceived notions, I have sat at the feet of learning, and, with eager and receptive brain, have listened to the teachings of splendid minds beyond the physical sphere and have weighed carefully each word in the light of reason and experience.

I know that origin and destiny are no longer beyond the grasp of the human mind: that spirit which is human life, when clothed with material, is visible to the physical eye; when separated is invisible; that dissolution is not annihilation, but liberation and opportunity.

I know that man has no Redeemer but himself; that God is universal good and dwells in the heart of all mankind. Now we sail the intellectual seas, making soundings and charts on the farther shore. We are coming to understand and master the blind forces of Nature, as we open the windows in the chamber of thought, and to comprehend the economy of Natural Law.

Some mortal lives are so lived that they stand out like trees aflame along the green and wooded shore where waters beat with endless wave; others, like undergrowth within the endless forest, remain unknown, but each must, according to the immutable laws of progression, at some time, obtain perfect development, which is the heritage of all; this is the law of life.

I have submitted this manuscript to a large number of advanced thinkers both in America and Europe, and the general criticism has been that it is so in advance of experience, so difference from the old teachings and beliefs, that few will grasp or understand the new propositions presented.

This is without a doubt true, but the facts as I have gathered them cannot be changed; truth is infinite. Volumes have been written by the world's foremost writers to prove the possibility of communication between this plane and the next, though few have been privileged to enjoy direct and independent speech to the extent that I have.

Those who read the pages that I have written must assume that speech is possible and that I have had the experiences narrated. I do not attempt to enter the elementary field; others have covered that branch. I have tried to transmit facts as they have been given me, and I expect many to accept them because they are in accordance with Nature's Law and appeal to reason.

It is a great privilege to be evolved out of the great mass of life, to obtain individuality with all its possibilities not by a miracle, but through positive law. But that privilege brings responsibilities, among them the necessity of living a clean life, of developing character to the utmost, of doing something to make others happy, and of making the world a little better because we have lived a day within its confines. These things are not difficult to accomplish if we are unselfish. To the new thought, to the progress of the world, each may give something. Great truths come from the obscure. The night brings forth the stars.

## The Great Question

Since mankind came up out of savagery, the great problem has been and ever shall be: What is the ultimate end of man? What, if anything, waits on the other side of death's mysterious door? What happens when the hour strikes that closes man's career, when, leaving all the gathered wealth of lands and goods, he goes out into the dark alone? Is death the end—annihilation and repose? Or, does he wake in some other sphere or condition, retaining individuality and identity?

Each must solve this great question, whether he likes it or not. Dissolution and change have to come to every form of life, and will come to all that live. With opportunity knocking at the door, mankind has but little more appreciation of it now than it had when Phallic-worship swayed the destinies of empires. It may be that, as a people, our development has been such that we could heretofore grasp and comprehend only length, breadth and thickness, the three accepted dimensions of matter; that in our progression we have *but now* become able to appreciate and understand life forces that find their only expression beyond the physical plane.

This was when all knowledge was handed down from one generation to another by story, song and tradition. When the Persian civilization was growing old and ambition towered above the lofty walls of Babylon; when Egypt was building her temples on the banks of the Nile; when Greece was the center of art and culture, and Rome with its wealth and luxuries held sway over the civilized world, they did not dream of type and printing press or applied electricity, and the many inventions in connection there with that were yet to come. Those people were not ready for such progression.

The world cannot stand still. The great law of the universe is progress. Two or three generations since, the idea that a cable would one day be laid under the sea and that messages would be transmitted under the waters from continent to continent, was laughed at as chimera. Only a little while ago, the world could not understand how words and sentences could be flashed across the trackless ocean from ship to ship, and from land to land, without wires, in space. And who shall now say that it is not possible to send thoughts, words, sentences, voices even, and messages, out into the ether of the spirit-world, there to be heard, recorded and answered? Has man reached the end of his possibilities; will all progression stop with Marconi's achievements?

This is the age of man; we have passed the age of the gods. If our development is such that we can comprehend the life and the conditions following dissolution, it must be within our grasp as surely as progression has been possible at all times and among all people since the world began.

Great changes are at hand. There are to-day, political, financial and religious revelations. Honest men are demanded for public office; the day of the corruptionist is passing. (As this statement was written by Mr. Randall in 1908, he would not be very pleased with the ethical state of modern politics today. —Ed.)

Captains of finance, who manipulate trust funds for personal gain in violation of the law, fear imprisonment. Priests are realizing that they are no longer regarded as infallible; congregations have ceased to accept their conclusions or interpretations of one great natural law; the pulpit is losing attraction, and attendance is slowly, but surely diminishing. People are doing their own thinking, and with thought comes doubt, the dawn of reason, the stepping stone to the temple of knowledge.

Assuming, then, that we have come to that period, when we can look upon all subjects and propositions impartially and intelligently, no longer bound by fear, past or present, and can open the book of life, we now appreciate that it is of the greatest importance to know what follows this life.

We are swinging away from the old moorings; new views come with changing times and conditions. Knowledge is the torch that fires our enthusiasm and makes advancement possible. It is not the past but the future that commands our attention. We may learn much of nature as she speaks, in all dialects, her various tongues. All truth is safe, nothing else will suffice, and he who holds back the truth, through expedience or fear, fails in his duty to mankind.

Our age is one of sudden and rapid changes; the people are in a state of transition. Most minds are sensitive and each must be alert and versatile. It is a period fraught with unrest and thirst for knowledge. What was true yesterday, assumes a different, one could almost say a diametrically opposite aspect, to-day. This is a period that will be fruitful in great wonders in scientific discoveries, and in the adaption of the universal law of vibratory action. Much that is said now could not have been explained a year ago.

Some have come to know what awaits over the great divide, have solved the great problem of dissolution, and with the confidence born of knowledge, based on facts proved and demonstrated, are ready to speak with authority. As one among the many, I again give the world the result of my continued research in the new science of Metapsychics.

The thought that there need be no more groping in the dark, makes the pulse quicken. The realization that fear can now be eliminated from the human brain, fills every heart with joy. The fact that we may come into touch with those in the spheres beyond and know that they live, will lift the burden of sorrow from every heart that mourns its dead.

The child learns readily for two reason, vis: (a) It has no preconceived notions or fixed ideas; (b) it has nothing to unlearn: its
mind is free and receptive. We, of older growth, are but children in
the wilderness of these new and subtle laws. Before we can grasp
and comprehend this Philosophy, we must free our minds and
eliminate false conceptions and erroneous ideas. That this is a
difficult task I well know, for minds filled with traditions and false
conceptions of the after-life, simply cannot comprehend the truth
when it is given to them. There can be no individual progression
until one becomes free, mentally poised, open to reason and willing to hear facts and to weigh them honestly. The blind are entitled
to our sympathy; we look upon those who cannot grasp a truth,
because it is not as they have been taught, with sorrow; but we
grasp the open hands of the free and walk with them in nature's
highway and reason with them.

Humanity is awakening. For two thousand years it has listened
to the song and drone of priest and preacher, and, lulled into a
sense of security, has lived indifferent to the end which each one
fast approaches. The mind has, at last, become active, and now
demands to know what fate awaits us beyond the grave. Man has
learned something about himself and the universe, and this knowledge has made him free. He is no longer in spiritual bondage. This
is an age of intellectual emancipation. Those who walk with open
eyes will find the truth, for it lights the way across the continent of
every human life.

## Spiritual Bondage

I do not desire to become identified with Spiritualism, Presby-
terianism, Episcopalianism, Catholiscism, Judaism, or any other of
the many "isms" that have grown up among men. I am working
among natural conditions, the same geologists, biologists, chemists, and other scientists. They do not ally their work with denomi-
national organizations; why should I mine, which differs only in
character? Bound a philosophy with an "ism" and you limit its
growth. No man preaching, teaching, or writing with proscribed
limits ever does his best. The great thinkers of all times have repu-
diated "isms." They have worked with open eyes and clear brains,
and climbing the hills, have left all superstitions, faiths, and creeds
far below.

Science has made some progress and declares: first, that there
exist in nature certain unknown forces capable of acting on matter;
second, that we possess other means of mastery than those of
reason or of the senses. In other words, science recognizes the

existence of an invisible world wherein unknown forces act intelligently.

One fact has been fixed and immutable since the dawn of time. Mankind has always known that the span of earth life is pitifully short at the most, that to each the hour will come when he must make the change called death, that he must journey alone in the dark, shutting behind him death's mysterious door, and that he must leave the mortal form. Space cannot stay this flight, sorrow cannot delay it, and mere man cannot go one step along the way into the unknown spheres.

We know that the physical body is material, or composed of matter, and that, through dissolution, it goes back, to mingle with the substances from which it was taken. We know likewise that it will be used again for other forms of animal and vegetable life. We know that the laws of dissolution have no exceptions, that the longest life is only a short journey, that the time will come when the brain will refuse its function, the mind will falter, the heart will cease to beat, and that man will leave the home built with infinite care, will leave all the gathered wealth of gold and, swifter than light, will speed beyond mortal vision. Is this oblivion? Is this the night that never finds the dawn?

Since the beginning of time, man has labored to solve the problems of the universe. He has searched the sky, named the stars and constellations, marked their course, timed their going and their coming, and even measured their distance in space. He has gone down into the earth itself and found in strata and rocks and stones, records of our planet's different evolutions. He has mastered the waves of the ocean and made the winds his servants. He has drawn from earth and air and sea and sky electric fluid to light the world and furnish motive power, to send the hitherto limited voice half across a continent, to speed messages through space at his command. With splendid courage he has tried to solve the workings of every natural law. He has faced fearlessly every question except one: *the problem of his own life.*

When man witnesses the magnificence of nature, the birth and development of visible life, he feels a reverential awe, and in his heart there exits the hope of a consciousness beyond the grave and of eternal life. Every people on the globe has this faith and expresses it in one way or another. All men feel that back of natural law is reason, that back of effect is cause, that back of cause is good. They believe that the infinite spirit who planned all things had some object in view when he set time limit to existence in a single sphere. Few have ever tried to work out the plan; have ever tried to learn what follows dissolution. The church that assumes to guide the thought and conduct of people, and to prepare them for an unknown hereafter, has never made an effort to prove that life actually does follow dissolution; has no real conception of the condition of a spirit when out of the body, has no idea where it will go, knows nothing of the future, and sets its stamp of disapproval on anyone who tries to find out. When a man discovers a new material law the world applauds the act; but should the same man try to prove that there is no death and that in another sphere spirit retains consciousness and individuality, and lives and labors on, what will happen? He will receive the censure of those who praised him but yesterday. The mastery and comprehension of this problem of life is less difficult than measuring the distance to the stars, the speed of light, the weight and course of the planets, the laws of gravitation, or of electric energy. Were only a fraction of the time and thought spent in modern discoveries and inventions devoted to this great problem the world would have some definite idea of the journey's end. That the great mass of people know practically nothing of this proposition is deplorable, and that they make little effort to find the truth is to many incomprehensible.

Below the heights lie the stagnant pools of ignorance and superstition. The time was when those who reasoned and had the courage of conviction were subjected to physical torture. When Copernicus demonstrated the movement of the earth and the stars according to fixed laws, which were in violation of Biblical teaching, he was forced to live in practical isolation and exile, the Christians were forbidden to read his writings. Bruno, one of the great thinkers of his time, laid aside the frock of Dominican monk, hoping to obtain freedom of thought and of speech. He wanted to know whether the sun revolved about the earth, as the priests taught, or the earth about the sun, as Copernicus claimed. For this research and for the expression of his opinion, he was branded as a heretic and burned alive in Rome. Cardinal Bellarmino said: "If the Copernican theory is true, it would be the absolute undoing of the Bible and the destruction of the church. If the earth is only one of many planets and not the center of the universe, and other planets are inhabited, the whole plan of salvation fails, since the inhabitants of the other spheres are without the Bible and Christ did not die for them."

Galileo discovered the isochronism of the pendulum and the hydrostatic balance, and invented the thermometer. With a telescope, or "magic tube," as it was called, he saw Jupiter's satellites, and the moon's libation. He was charged with witchcraft and was condemned not only for daring to deny the accepted shape of the earth, but also for suggesting that the Bible did not contain the final facts of science. For these things the greatest thinker of his time was put in a dungeon by priests and kept there until, broken in spirit, he was forced to retract his statements in his own scientific discoveries.

People shudder involuntarily when they recall the massacre of St. Bartholomew, the suffering of the Huguenots, and the other wars waged in the name of religion. When men now have the courage to think for themselves and question theological teachings, they remember the Inquisition, which was superior to all civil laws. They remember that its representatives, holding the power of life and death, went to all parts of the civilized world, hunting out thinkers, whom they called heretics, putting millions to torture and to death. They recall, too, that these practices were only entirely abolished seventy-one years ago, —that is, within the memory of men and women living today. (1906) While the loss of temporal power was a great blow to Catholicism, the Inquisition is to this day maintained as a branch of the Papal College. It holds supervision over the spiritual life of the church, with power to censure such writings and speech as it considers dangerous. The attitude of the Catholic Church has changed since the time of Bruno, Bellarmino, and Galileo. The determination to maintain its theories, whether true or false, is yet strong, but it cannot enforce them by the rack, the thumb-screw, the dungeon, or the wheel. The orthodox world remains a mighty power. Though it has failed in its contests against science, it still fights against modern investigation of the spheres beyond. There was physical punishment in the past for liberal thought; there is social persecution in the present for those who strive to understand the problem of dissolution. In France, during the eighteenth century, it was a crime punishable by imprisonment to have in one's possession a volume of the writings of Voltaire. Thomas Paine was exiled from England for publishing the "Rights of Man," and censured by the Christian world for writing the "Age of Reason." The churches, one and all, made common cause in fighting Robert Ingersoll, whose mission was to make men think. Unaided and alone, he waged relentless war on the whole orthodox world. His logic was unanswerable, his eloquence sublime, and he did more to free the world from spiritual bondage than any other man of modern times. He aroused the indifferent and, by his fearless example, encouraged independence. Alfred Russell Wallace, the foremost modern scientist of Europe, claims to have obtained positive evidence that life continues beyond the grave. His associates say he is fooled, cheated, duped. Sir William Crookes investigated natural conditions and

24

found an influence which he named "Psychic Force." He learned that there is an invisible world of spirit about us. His contemporaries accept his material discoveries and reject his spiritual ones. When any member of a community tries to solve a psychological question he is censured and condemned by the social world, as well as by the church; and no matter how well his propositions are demonstrated, few publishers will print his conclusions, since the fear of censure is still strong. Only such fields of research are legitimate as do not undermine old paths, traditions, and belief. Nevertheless, man has made progress of recent years, and he is making search for evidence of life beyond. Writings on the subject are also received in a more liberal spirit than they were a few years ago. The time is near when the public will receive knowledge of this field without prejudice and will even welcome it. Because men and women have long lived in spiritual bondage, because many generations have been taught that the church was infallible and have been denied the right of private interpretation, and because the punishment for independence of thought has been so terrible, two conditions have been imperceptibly brought about: I. Indifference on the subject. II. Secret investigation. The result is that men of character and standing who have obtained evidence of the continuity of life and the conditions of life in the next sphere hesitate to speak. Many who know something of what follows so-called death are silent because they fear the condemnation and disapproval that go close on the heels of public speech.

The church ought to welcome evidence that life, consciousness, and individuality continue after dissolution, and it would do so if the facts agreed with the teachings. It is only because the actual conditions do not harmonize with its theories that relentless persecution has for centuries followed the footsteps of individual effort. Such opposition has delayed the spiritual advance and development of many in the spheres of progression. What a mighty power for good the church might be if it would just solve the problem of death as individuals have done, if it would probe the conditions that one enters after dissolution, learn just how and where he lives, his occupation, his environment, and his evolution; trace the effect of conduct here on condition there, and then preach the simple, positive, forceful truth! Doubts, fears, dogmas, superstitions, theories, and beliefs would fade away, and truth, a new religion, would enrich the heart of all mankind.

The dream of the Pilgrim Fathers was to build a nation free from religious persecution, yet they hunted down those who had intercourse with spirits and burned them as witches. The Cambridge Synod found and spread on its early records eight-two opinions: "Some blasphemous, others erroneous, and all unsafe, besides nine unwholesome expressions, and dismissed them to the devil in hell, from whence they came."

The first amendment to our Constitution provided that "Congress shall make no law respecting an establishment of religion, or prohibit the free exercise 'thereof,' or abridge the freedom of 'speech.'" The theory was that the people should have perfect freedom of thought and of speech in all religious matters, without fear or favor. The practical result of this provision, however, was to make the church supreme. It has sought ever since to maintain its autocracy, holding itself independent of the Constitution and superior to it. The United States Government, with its Constitution, with its army and navy, with its courts and officers, cannot even now protect a citizen from religious censure when he experiments with psychic forces. (1909) For the thought of the people constitutes public opinion, one of the most potent factors in the world today. Officials fear it more than they do the law of the land. Governments are swept out of power by it and it holds kingdoms and monarchies in check. It is a force that one must contend with.

The churches do not want psychic investigation. They condemn all effort to understand the metapsychic laws. They fear that an understanding of natural laws will bring an explosion of many of their theories, will undermine faith, the cornerstone of their structure.

Why should the priesthood and the clergy, why should the church, ridicule and condemn a man for trying to prove there is an after-life? They themselves preach it. Why don't they join hands and say: "We will work with you. Let us help and, if your way can be proved, let us both serve as messengers to give the glad tidings to the doubting world?"

The psychic sphere is still unknown. Only the border lands have been explored. The field is a mine of wealth, rich in material that man can gather for his uses. The unknown is greater than the known. The material forces that we knew not yesterday we utilize today, and so it will be with these spiritual ones. When one natural force is discovered it does not follow that there are no others. The time will never come in this life when we can say we possess all knowledge, we have discovered all forces, we know all natural law. The scientific world, to which we owe so much, has devoted its energies to matter rather than to the life that is in all matter. In seeking the material it has failed to recognize the spirit. Science, likewise, has fixed and determined the limits and boundaries of research and looks with disfavor on any forces outside of its field. To such these writings will have little evidential value.

Men, dissatisfied with the old theories of life, are studying the psychic world in secret. They are working behind closed doors with spiritual laws. The silent thought looks for evidence that the so-called dead live again, but only a few ever try to prove it. Men dread ridicule as they do the pestilence. It is the weapon of ignorance, the whip of prejudice. Few of those who hold speech with individual spirits proclaim the fact unflinchingly. The weight of public opinion is against it. Millions of people, the bravest and the best in all nations, are seeking knowledge of the after life in a practical way. With crude and undeveloped mediums they are striving to master the laws of metapsychics and to receive words and messages from those in the life beyond. All that has been accomplished, as yet, simply demonstrates the possibilities within the grasp of everyone. Men are coming more and more to form their own conclusions and to think for themselves in all matters pertaining to this philosophy. The darkness of superstition is passing, the teachings of years are failing in results. Public thought has begun to change within the last decade. The time is near when, without fear of abuse, men will openly seek knowledge of life in the world of spirit around and about us and will proclaim this philosophy of Truth. The churches that shall teach these laws have already been built. Happiness will then multiply, sorrow lessen, and fear find no lodgement in the human heart. The world of spirit, this so-called psychic sphere, offers to science greater opportunities for discoveries than the material world ever gave. Let this research become popular and the results will startle mankind. So great is the unconscious desire and longing for the truth that only a match is needed to start a conflagration in which the great mass of erroneous writings will burn to ashes, and out of these ashes will rise truth, the new religion, to aid mankind to an understanding of universal good. The spirits have said:

**"There are those who know that there is truth in this philosophy and know that it reaches where all else fails. They feel its naturalness, its logic, its grandeur. They have grown beyond the old teachings and think about them with dissatisfaction and unrest. They would welcome the light of reason, but are afraid of the world's judgment of bold thinkers and pioneers. They are slaves bound with chains of fear and of tradition. Break the fetters, lift your faces to the light, and with strong, willing hands, help to tear the bonds from other burdened souls! Men! stand forth! fearless and powerful! A great, radiant happiness will be yours, and the censure of this little world will fail to sting."**

## Speech with Spirits

Thus far I have considered conditions and reasoned from material laws. Now, I want you to come with me, draw aside the curtain, and to contemplate the spirit-world toward which we speed with unconscious steps. Let me preface this subject by saying that I am not a medium, and that I possess no greater ability than another. What I have done all can do. What has been given me, will be given all, if they seek it with honest endeavor. We get nothing in this world without effort. The fish that swim the waters must search for food, the wild animals that roam the forest must hunt or perish; man must labor. No life can exist without action. Animal life, like human life, must learn wisdom by individual effort. Such is the natural law of being, and back of every natural law is reason.

For years I have traveled, following the blazed trail—Nature's paths—in the forest of knowledge. The criticism, opposition, and ridicule that follow any pioneer may come to me. If one walks with the crowd in the broad thoroughfare he goes unnoticed, but if one leaves the throng and takes a step into the unknown, he hears the comment, the sneer, and the jeer of ignorance and prejudice. Before me have gone Flammarion, the great astronomer; Ruskin, the critic; Tolstoi, the humanitarian; Savage and Newton, great preachers, and thousands of other thinkers and brave men, bearing torches that have made the pathway light. What has come to me through spirit teaching illustrates what is within the reach of any citizen of the state, without detriment to his business or profession. The dawn of knowledge and understanding has touched the night of doubt, and mankind is coming to feel and appreciate the possibilities of spiritual advancement here on this terrestrial sphere, without waiting for the next life.

I recall the quiet village where I was born, and the procession of men and women going solemnly to the old Methodist Church every Sunday. Dr. Hall, the pastor, was a grand man to look at, and each Sunday he told us what poor miserable sinners we were. "Repent, Repent," was his cry. "Remember the man in the horrible pit of miry clay, who intended to ackowledge Jesus, but didn't; remember that he went down in the quicksand, that he went alone, without hope, without God, to darkness and despair. "Confess your sins and acknowledge the Savior. Do it today, tomorrow may be too late," he shrieked again and again. "Remember the man in the quicksand." We listened in silence, and the locusts buzzed in the trees outside. Then we went out into the sunshine again, the flowers opened to the day, the robins, wooing and mating, sang merrily among the trees, and all the world seemed glad—all but I. I was thinking of the horrible pit of clay and going down to hell. When I entered business and professional life, I was forced to analyze propositions, to reach conclusions from facts. I attended different churches and heard many arguments. I read the Bible and the history of the time in which it was written. I went among the church people and found discord. I went into the wilderness and found harmony. I studied the books of many peoples and found that each had a Redeemer, that each had many "isms" and sects, that each claimed the road to Paradise ran through its creed. I was searching for truth, for an understanding of life, for the rights we possessed, for our duties to each other, and for the ultimate end. These questions troubled me. I was inclined to accept the Christian teaching, although the Vendantic philosophy appealed to me most; but both were unsatisfying. I read with satisfaction these words written by Omar Khayam in the eleventh century:

> I sent my soul out into the infinite,
>     Some letter of the after-life to spell,
> And bye and bye my soul returned to me and answered,
>     I myself am heaven and hell.

My search for light was long and earnest, the pathway often lonely, dreary, and unsatisfactory. Any man, witnessing the splendor of Nature, feels a reverential awe, and the hope of an after-life comes into his heart,—but where the evidence, where the door into the sanctuary of truth?

About the year 1890, a friend in whom I had confidence, said to me, "Will you go with me tonight to see Mrs. Emily S. French? She possesses a strange power, claims to get independent voices and messages from the spirit world." This was an unexplored world to me. I went, and found there two others, both men of national reputation. We sat in a dark room for two hours, and heard what purported to be voices, though they were only faint whispers. We were not at all satisfied, but could not condemn, because we did not understand. We found Mrs. French far along in years, of rare refinement, a beautiful character, and we were satisfied, a perfectly honest woman. We did not then believe that the whispers came from the great beyond, but, mystified, we determined to know what they were. To me there was a suggestion that offered great possibilities. Such was the prejudice, so unpopular the subject, and in awe of the speech of people did I start that I conducted my investigations, night after night, and year after year, in secret and in silence. Baffled in my analysis, failing to understand or to comprehend by what law the so-called dead could speak, my undertaking seemed at first an opportunity to demonstrate the falsity of this natural philosophy.

There is only *one* law governing *all* things spiritual and material. It is the law of Nature. I was told early in the work that there was no limit to progress if one would labor earnestly and honestly, and that it was possible, if I would aid in perfecting conditions, to get the independent metapsychic voices full and resonant; that, with such perfection, there would come teachings from the best minds that ever lived; that we could do a great work among those who, having crossed the borderland, now needed such aid as only those still in the body could give through material vibrations and conditions; that it was possible to work in harmony with natural law and with spirits who could and would labor with me, and to awake and bring to consciousness countless thousands. It was promised, too, that they would mingle mission work with information as to the state that follows dissolution, and that they would give me knowledge of the next world as fast as I was able to comprehend. The challenge was accepted. I promised, if convinced, satisfied and qualified, to give such spiritual enlightenment to mankind as I could.

Night after night Mrs. French and I sat and talked and listened in darkness. Why in darkness? do you ask. Because in light there is motion. In order that the spirit may talk with audible voice it must, for the moment, be clothed with *material*. Motion disintegrates *matter*. Everything that ever lives was born in the dark. In this condition, then, the whispers came more distinctly. Words were uttered, sentences formed, until in time, out of the darkness, in my own home, surrounded by conditions that I myself made, voices full and clear came, filling the room, reverberating through the whole house, —metapsychic voices which any could hear as well as I myself, and which many have heard. With these voices came splendid speech, great lectures, much knowledge. We were told that in space and from the beginning there have been "*two elements.*" One we call "spirit;" the other "matter." Spirit lives and feels and never dies. It struggles constantly after knowledge, and uses matter to aid its development. In our individual inception, according to natural law, an atom of life force from the great universe, which is all life, is clothed with material, and thus becomes an individual conscious spirit, ever growing, ever changing, ever developing, according to the unwritten laws of evolution and progression. Death is but one of the natural changes in the march.

It is no more radical than many others with which we are familiar, and no more to be feared. The body is but the temporary abiding place, the house of the spirit while here. Like the building of brick or wood, it wastes, decays, is repaired and renewed. When no longer fit for habitation, it is abandoned.

The spirit from day to day and from year to year gathers knowledge, learns to walk and to express itself in language, grows in stature, greets the mourning of manhood, knows the noon of labor, and, growing old, as we count time, rests in the evening of life. This, I say, the "spirit" does. The body utilizes the food, which, converted into blood, courses through the arteries and veins, carrying infinitesimal particles, to replace the waste matter on the framework of the spirit. The spirit form possesses and inhabits every material organ and limb of the so-called body, which is utilized as the outer garment. This changes constantly. The body that the spirit inhabited but a few years ago has already gone back to mingle with the elements. The important entity is the "spirit" the secondary matter is the body; yet mankind, mistaking the relation, develops the latter at the expense of the former, forgetful that the spirit can hunger and thirst, and that it, too, must have the active mental food we call understanding.

The room in which we hold communication with the spirits was constructed as directed by our spirit band. It is consecrated to this work, and naught but harmony enters. In the day, the sun, so essential to life, floods it, and in the evening, when our labor begins, the curtains are drawn and darkness fills the room. Cloud-like substances form and change, evidence of gathering spirits. Magnetic and electric lights float and fall, but give forth no illumination. Then they greet us, and we them, with words of welcome and fellowship, as do guests and host in any home. Usually, someone advanced in the other life is introduced, and he speaks on some special subject. In this manner, we are taught. We may ask for a lecture on any subject; and the same evening, or at a subsequent time, it will be given by a master mind. I have never heard such teachings and magnificent discourses in the material world. Our circle is known in that other life, and thousands are always waiting to come within the vibrations that have been formed. They seek to throw off material conditions that still impeded their progress. Our co-laborers bring those who are in a state of unconsciousness to awaken them beyond the grave through the material vibrations made. Hundreds in the same mental attitude are gathered at a time. One, two, or more, the best qualified, are selected who, taking on the proper condition, talk with us and with the band working with us; while the many wait, watch, listen, and so obtain the same lesson and the same help that the spirit speaking does.

In this branch of the work, a voice comes out of the darkness, in greeting, often bewildered. Many a spirit knows nothing of the flight of time. It grasps the thread where it was broken, and I have heard a sentence finished that was apparently started when dissolution came. The thought that was uppermost when the shadow fell is the dominating idea when the awakening comes. Then, with all the gentleness and patience, we guide the thoughts to the new surroundings. The spirits tell us that death nearly always comes before they are ready. It seems that those who belong to "*this class*" are so material, that we who are in like condition alone can penetrate the wall of darkness that they have unknowingly built about their mentalities, and so, reach them. When this is done, and they realize what and where they are, they look about and see those long mourned. Then come the joyful greetings. Hands clasp hands, and many voices speak words of welcome and courage. I have heard a man who, seeing the face of one whom he has wronged, cry out in agony and fear. I have heard words of happiness when a mother clasped a long-lost child; or husband, a wife. I have heard the trembling language of old age and the prattle of little children. All that I have said is but a suggestion of what has come and is coming.

In twenty years one sees that progress has come on lightning's wings. Then we could not see through solid matter, but Radio-Active substances have changed the theory of sight and revolutionized the practice of surgery. Then the voice was limited to hailing distance; now it spans the continent. Then the utilization of electricity was in its infancy. Marconi, in violation of all known principles of science, now conveys messages without wires. The discovery of Radium has shattered the foundation of which the scientific world has worked. Were it not for prejudice and for church teaching, would you regard these facts of which I treat as any more marvelous? But for these hindrances would they not be accepted and adopted? The telephone is the medium of communication between man and man, and it is now almost necessary in business for speech. I, too, use a medium in my intercourse, but it is human. She knows the wants and needs of those beyond; the thirst and hunger of mankind here, and gives her time and strength ungrudgingly for the elevation and happiness of both.

## Life Does Not End

My instruction has been splendid. Among the teachers have been such spirits as Channing, Beecher, Talmage, Ingersoll, Hough, Dr. Hossack, Segoyewatha, and hundreds of others. Lectures from such men, speaking in their own independent voices, materialized for the time, leaves no doubt as to what follows death. I have never heard such matchless oratory, such sermons, such thought expressed by the living as I have from the so-called dead. They tell me that we are as much spirit to-day as we will ever be. We are not all that we can become; but there will be no sudden acquisition. Death itself will add little to present knowledge; nor will it enlarge our opportunities to any marked degree. Opportunities are just as great with us here as they ever will be. Here and there all depends upon individual effort. Labor is endless. The goal recedes as we approach. There was no beginning, there is no end, and on through eternity there will be something for us to do. There will be greater heights to climb, greater knowledge to acquire, or work to do, we might then, in the interpretation of the Church, become gods.

According to my instruction, death is a moving out, a vacating of the earthly habitation, a separation of the spirit from the body. As it is, then, a natural incident, it is painless, sometimes conscious; but more often unconscious, and the awakening is like the coming from bewildered sleep. We were the same last night before sleep as we are this mourning, and we have the same surroundings. We shall be the same after dissolution as before, and probably we shall be in the same place. Where would you go, except to those you love, to those who, because they are ignorant of your presence, mourn your absence?

Death is like birth, with this exception: In death one takes with him the knowledge and development acquired in this "*material existence*" which we are told is a period of preparation for eternity, as we call it, the preface to the book of life. There is no break, there is only progression to greater possibilities. If, then, this stage was intended for preparation and development, what effort has been made to understand the laws of life? What spiritual understanding has come? One has labored here for the accumulation of money for old age, but what wealth has he accumulated for his support and maintenance down the pathway of eternity? How is he prepared to journey into the unknown? I blame the church for the ignorance of the world, and I pity those who accept its teachings without question.

Reasoning from material laws, it is hard to comprehend what spirit is. I am taught that it is conscious, visible thought-soul-life, freed from the confines of the body—that spirit appears to spirit as material, as does man to man. Assuming that he passes consciously, he may stand beside his body in the same room, see and feel himself as in life, move his arms, walk, think, and act, just as before. His old body is before him. He may see the falling tears of the loved ones, hear their cries, and feel the anguish that fills their hearts. He speaks, they do not hear. He cries aloud that he is not dead. His arms are about them; but they cannot feel. Then a great fear falls upon him. Why don't they hear? Why don't they answer? What has happened? This cannot be death. There is no Savior here, no God. He is still at home, though his body lies in its winding sheet, calm and still. Monstrous is the institution that assumes to prepare man for this change without any conception of what it really is! Terrible that men with splendid mentalities let the church think, act, and guide in a matter so important! Would you take a day's journey without preparation and thought of your needs and requirements? What, then, of this journey into the dark beyond? Would you accept the statements or opinions of the Church if a dollar was involved? Yet, viewed broadly, how insignificant is all the wealth of the world compared with the preparation for this time?

If this life has been lived in harmony with natural law, if one has done right, and, hearing the voice, followed the dictates of conscience (which is the spirit of God), if he has been just and considerate among men, and has done the best according to his understanding, then those who have gone before are able to reach and greet him with words of comfort and consolation. He sees and recognizes old friends, and they explain to him the laws and conditions that henceforth must govern him, under which he must live and work. They become his teachers. He comes to himself. He appreciates and sees that all solids here possess life and conscious individuality. He learns that all life, like man, has language, or means of communication. He learns that the rocks, the trees, the flowers and growing grain, all animal and vegetable matter, continue to live, and in the spirit-world there is the conscious spirit of everything that we have and much that we know not of, that dissolution is not the end. The spirit freed from material can climb the heights, like our thoughts, can speed over mountains of ice and snow, through the valleys, over oceans, through foreign lands, can circle the globe, and in time, in ethereal regions, go to the other planets, can soar through unfathomable heights to the stars; for in spirit, as in thought, there is no space or time. No limit can be placed on what is accomplished there. Here the spirit is confined to the body and, until such time as it is separated, it is limited in movement. The body forms the swaddling clothes of the soul, to be worn until it can live independent of material.

So, then, all is well with one who has lived in harmony and gone from among us rich in good deeds. Over the border, there is grat rejoicing. With the spirit the day of dissolution, like our day of birth, is one of gladness; for it means advancement, progress, greater advantages, greater development, and the love and companionship of friends. That is what all the world is seeking. This is Heaven, as I understand it, —a condition not a place; a state of being, not a locality.

## The Mental Grasp

Many will read the facts that are stated in this work and utterly fail to comprehend them or to grasp the laws that make such conditions possible. This I know from my own experience, for it took many years of research, study and deductive reasoning for me to comprehend, in a limited way, life in the physical apart from the gross matter. The trouble was in the imperfect mental grasp.

As stated earlier, when Copernicus said that the earth moved around the sun, and not the sun around the earth, as had been held since the end of Egyptian astronomy, the voice of all Europe was raised in protest against such a proposition; people could not comprehend such a fact, for it appeared to them that, if the earth moved from one side of a vast orbit to the other, the stars would be displaced. Tycho Brahe, the great mathematician, gave up the Copernican theory because he said, if true, his brain could not comprehend the magnitude of the universe. After Cassini upset the observation of Hooke and Flamsteed, Molyneaux, an amateur, constructed the "zenithsector," and measured the distances of the stars, but many years elapsed before this fact was accepted, for the human brain could not realize such tremendous distances. And Roemer, when he measured the speed of light, met the same reception and died before his discovery was accepted.

The age could not grasp the stupendous conception; such inconceivable velocities were too terrific, and the minds of able men were overwhelmed and confounded in the majestic and awful presence of nature.

We are told that on a clear night, 6,874 stars, from the brightest to the sixth magnitude, are visible without optical aid, half of them being above the horizon at the same time. Down to the present time, more than one million others have, with the aid of the telescope, been counted with more or less accuracy. (circa-1908.) Sirius, the brightest of all, is seven hundred times farther from our earth than the sun, and it would take ten thousand stars of the eleventh magnitude and one million of the sixteenth, to emit the quantity of light poured forth by the mighty Aldebaran. Every star is really a colossal sun at terrific heat, and the center of a solar system like our own. Who shall say how many more shall be found in the depth of infinite space? To the average mind these facts and figures mean nothing; such distances are incomprehensible; such numbers stagger us; we have heretofore had nothing with which to compare them. No *mortal* has journeyed to other planets or suns, or gone such distances; therefore, these facts are practically beyond the mental grasp, like many here presented. Any subject outside one's knowledge and experience is beyond his comprehension.

It is a law that knowledge, which precedes appreciation, must be acquired by individual effort, by study, by labor, deduction, reason; and, as the world has devoted its research almost entirely to matter, meaning thereby matter in its lowest form, it is, therefore, densely ignorant of anything beyond the physical plane.

When anyone fails to understand the simple facts here presented, it is because he has not carried his observation beyond the physical, for I have discovered only what anyone can by making well-directed and persistent effort. The situation as to these propositions is not very different now from what it was when Copernicus discovered the earth's movement, except that now they do not burn men for proclaiming a new discovery. It is as difficult for the mass of people to realize today that there is an invisible world about us, as it was when Bruno lived, to comprehend the movements of the earth.

When I say that there is life after so-called death, and that spirit people have form, feature, individuality, identity, and occupation; that this world invisible to our physical eye is here, on and about this earth, and in what we know as space; when I say that those thought to be dead walk our streets, enter our homes, and are with us as much as before, the great majority can no more comprehend such a condition of things that they can the number of stars in the sky or the distance of Sirius, the brightest of our constellations, or what the parallax of Canopus is. I know of the after-life by reason of having talked with thousands of persons now there, who have proved identity in a most emphatic manner; but, after many years of conversation with spirit-people, I frankly admit that I can comprehend only in a limited way their life and environment, so different is it from the physical. If I do fail to comprehend their daily life fully, what will one do who has never devoted an hour to the study of matter and life-forces in their higher vibratory conditions?

We should not expect to understand and appreciate individual progression beyond the physical, or where and how people live in the next sphere, from an abstract statement of the fact. To gain knowledge of this condition, we must approach this vast problem as we would any other great subject we desire to master. First, we must know something of the origin of physical life, how it is started, how it develops and grows; the object of material existence; how soul and body are nourished and held together; something of the theory of heart action, blood circulation and the vibratory conditions of matter; what dissolution really means; what life-force is and where it comes from; the effect of conduct here on conditions in the after-life, and how to live so as to enrich ourselves when we cast aside that physical substance that gives us expression. These propositions, stupendous as they seem, are in fact only elementary, and their mastery is a condition precedent to appreciation of life and environment in spirit-spheres. Knowledge on this subject, as in any other field of research, must be acquired by study. You would not expect to know the history of the earth's evolution and movements without studying geology and gravity, or the difference in the flora without knowing something of botany, or the chemical constituents of matter without the study of chemistry. The same law applies to psychic force and to life beyond the earth-plane, as on the earth-plane. It is a great science—a wholly new philosophy. Few intelligent minds have ever entered this great field of knowledge; little effort has been systematically expended on it, and the results are, at best, only commensurate with the effort. No one man, or class of men, can bring these laws comprehensively to the human mind. All who study the subject can help, but the knowledge and appreciation that will reach the inner chamber of thought must be acquired by individual effort born of the desire to know. Those who cannot comprehend new propositions, must remember there are problems in trigonometry that many do not understand; but if we commence with simple mathematics, and work along step by step, they will become as simple to us as the multiplication table. The same process must be used if we would grasp the principles and laws of Metapsychics. Abstract statements are of little value except to stimulate interest. Effort and well-directed study are of great importance. There are no schools or universities where this philosophy is taught, and few are qualified to teach it. Few books have been written that one can accept. But, for all that, one has nature all about him, at all times, calling in all tongues, and in all languages. The fact that life is everywhere, that nothing can die or be destroyed, speaks to our dull senses in a thousand ways; sings of joy and peace through the forest trees and woos us with bud, flower and growing grain. But so blind is the world that but few can read intelligently the book of nature, ever open to view. It is the great misfortune of the human race that these laws, more important than others that have been mastered, are practically unknown, though the peace and happiness of everyone depend upon an understanding of them.

Let me make a more simple statement. Before all form is mind. The desk I write on, the pen I use, the chair upon which I sit, the books on the shelves, the rugs on the floor, the lamp on the table, and the telephone on the wall, every machine that moves; each was conceived and fashioned in the mind before it was physically constructed. All matter, as we use that term, is the expression of thought; every planet in our solar system and all the countless suns that light the night, are but the expression of thought.

All the great discoveries of modern times are simple when understood; the difficulty is with the understanding. When once we know the why and the wherefore, all natural laws become so plain that "he who runs may read." What we cannot grasp, we regard as mysterious. When we discover one of nature's laws, we marvel at its simplicity. There is nothing in nature that is supernatural; there is no supernormal, these are but names given to conditions not understood.

The working and development of a human mind is intensely interesting. Mr. K., who spent one year with me in this research, was a man of much learning and a great thinker along material lines, and when I endeavored to explain life, apart from the physical, it was so different from his experience that he was at first utterly unable to grasp it. As we progressed, step by step, confining our discussion to cause and effect, he came to appreciate the force of simple facts, and when he heard and had talked, voice to voice, with spirit-people, his progress was wonderful, he could appreciate the fact and the reason for it. On the other hand, I tried for weeks, with as simple words as I could use, to explain this philosophy to another who was anxious to know, but who had an untrained mind, practically without making any impression. The one was a thinker and a worker; the other was indolent and undeveloped mentally, and consequently had a limited grasp of such facts.

From these experiences, and many others, I conclude that the vast majority of mankind, having but little knowledge of this subject, cannot appreciate much beyond the visible and tangible, though they may be learned in other ways. Individual life, beyond the physical and similar to it, will be hard for many to grasp, because they have not investigated the elementary laws that form the groundwork of Metapsychics.

If I can arouse human beings from their indifference to this great question, more vital to them than money, and get them interested in this new philosophy, they will find the truth in their own way. For a thousand years the individual has lived in fear, bound by creeds and dogmas, and has been told what he should and should not do, how he must think, —a slave to superstition and prejudice. But fear no longer sways the mind, superstitions have been outgrown, creeds have lost their meaning, and prejudice, the child of ignorance, no longer dominates the way on the crowded avenue of knowledge.

## How Do I Know?

How do I know that individuality, personality, identity, and life itself, continue beyond the grave, and that the psychic world is about this world in what we know as space? If it is a fact, what method have I used to demonstrate it? Whether man lives after death is to science of more importance than how or where he lives. If the facts are finally accepted as I shall state them, then "what fools we poor mortals be," not to understand such a simple proposition! Let me ask these questions: (a) Do you know whether death is, or is not, the end? (b) Have you ever made any personal effort to find out? and (c) Do seventeen years of careful, earnest, intelligent work qualify one to speak? (circa.1907)

I have only reached the noon of life; but, many years ago, not content that others should do my thinking, and unwilling to accept heresay evidence, tradition and blind belief, I determined to discover the facts about the future life, if they were obtainable, and from those facts, draw my own conclusions.

The progress of the world has been so great that even the masses are coming to demand facts, —and facts that appeal to reason; less will not do. Have the great truths of nature been placed in the keeping of any class or set of men who alone are competent to explain? Or is the task left to any who seek truth in any guise? I long ago determined, having no preconceived notions, faiths or prejudices, and having at least nothing to unlearn, to devote such time to study and research on this subject as was possible. Furthermore, let me say that over twenty years in the active practice of law, largely in the trial of cases, coming in contact with many great minds, has qualified me to do certain things: i.e., to estimate the weight and value of evidence fairly; to detect fraud in any guise; to know when a fact is proved.

In conducting my experiments, I have always insisted that they should be done in my own home under such conditions only as I should provide. I use a room 10 by 14 feet, with windows opening to the west so that the evening sun will enter it daily, with shutters to break the rays of light and make it dark, when experimenting and working with psychic forces. Again, why work in the dark, so you ask? Because spirit-people, when they speak, must take on gross matter, must clothe their organs of respiration, or the voice would not vibrate in the material atmosphere. Light is motion; and so sensitive are they to light waves that break down the material atoms with which they clothe themselves, that absolute darkness is a condition precedent, at least in my work, for them to speak. The room is remote from, and has no connection with any others; is so ventilated that the atmosphere is always pure; its only furnishings a carpet, chairs and a small table; its decorations are red—the warmest of colors—and here, with the aid of a psychic, I have year after year talked with those called dead.

Mrs. French, the finest psychic in the world today, has been a co-worker with me throughout the entire part of my investigations. This splendid woman of culture and refinement, now 76 years of age, has, without compensation, devoted the evening of her life to aid me in solving the great problem of dissolution.

She contributes to the experiments such psychic force as is required, while I give the physical force that makes speech possible. Space will not allow me to go into the process used by spirit-people in taking on the material so that they can speak in our atmosphere; it is sufficient that they do. Remember, they have bodies of the same size, shape and contour as before; and, if clothed with gross matter, they can formulate and utter words just as well as when in this life. The question now is, do they speak, not how do they speak.

Mrs. French and I simply go into this room, already described and sit in darkness, with the small table only between us. The occasion is not solemn; nor are the surroundings gruesome; rather it is a school-room and the lecture hour devoted to the unfolding of nature's simple laws. Since I possess no psychic sight or hearing; what I hear must be material. Any can hear as I do. If, in this dark room, I see or feel anything, it is because the spirits have so reduced their vibration, so retarded, for the time, their atomic and molecular action, that they are, in fact, physical.

One mourning, when Mrs. French and I were in this room talking to a physician who lived in the time of Alexander Hamilton and was one of his friends, a member of my family raised a window-shade in the attic, allowing sunlight to flash all over the room. The rays were reflected through the ventilator in the ceiling, partially lighting the room directly over where a spirit-being stood talking. I saw his form perfectly. Without a break in his discourse, he stepped to one side toward the corner where it was darker, continuing his discussion, simply saying as the place where he stood became partially lighted: **"We have promised the time should come when you should see us, but we scarcely expected it would be this mourning."** He stood there in full materialized form, else how could I have seen him? He was a spirit, for Mrs. French and I were in the room alone, and no other man could have come in without opening the door and letting in the full light of day. I not only saw him, but I heard his spirit-voice, as I have heard it many times since. This is a fact: I saw, I heard, I know.

Physical demonstrations have never interested me. I have always wanted knowledge; and moving matter without application of physical force, granting it to be possible, has never appealed to me. I have had but few physical demonstrations. When Mrs. French and I were in this room some years ago, conversing with those in the planes beyond, I was told by one of my co-workers in spirit that they wanted to give me a test of their reality and power.

Remember, Mrs. French and I were alone; the shutters were closed and the room was darkened; but outside the sun was shining. A spirit whose voice I recognized, said: **"When I say 'now,' let Mrs. French stand, reach both her arms across the table, and you take hold of them firmly, regardless of what happens."** The voice soon said, **"Now."** Mrs. French arose; I took both of her hands in mine, determined to hold them with great firmness, which I did, with senses keen in anticipation, but with no intimation of what was to happen. So firm was my hold on those hands that I knew, whatever happened, her hands could not aid in the demonstration. Soon the room was filled with the perfume of fresh flowers; one swished in the atmosphere and fell at my feet; my grip tightened on those frail hands. There was no movement of Mrs. French's body, but flowers came apparently from every direction, even from the ceiling, striking me on the head, face, chest, back and side, falling on the table and around us in great profusion. I immediately opened the door and hurriedly called others of my household to see the display. We found upon the table, chairs and carpet, upwards of one hundred pure white sweet peas, fresh, with dew sparkling in the petals. The stems had been twisted off. At a later time, I asked how such a demonstration, so at variance with physical laws, was possible. I also asked whence came the flowers? I was told that no law had been violated, but that physical laws which mankind has not yet discovered, had been used, that spirit people took sweet peas from a garden where they grew in too great abundance, changed their vibratory conditions, as we change water into steam, conveyed them in this state into the room, altered the vibration back again into its primary stage which restored the flowers to their original condition and color; then they threw them on and about me as I held Mrs. French's hands. They did this to show me their strength and to demonstrate a vibratory law. To this day I have kept some of those sweet-peas given by those spirit people.

At other times when alone with Mrs. French, I have been told to take both her hands and to hold them firmly, during which time spirit-people have come in full physical form, stood beside me, and put their hands on my head. Their hands are warm and firm, but the touch is strange because they are in a state of intense vibration; they do not tremble or shake, but they seem to pulsate with a rapidity that I have not words to describe.

I can sit in this room with no one present but Mrs. French, one hand upon the table, her mouth upon the back of that hand, my other hand on top of her head, holding it firmly so as to prevent the possibility of her speaking or moving her lips, and hear the spirit-people telling of life as they find it in the land of silence, as it is called.

At the demand of science, at one time, I permitted Mrs. French to go under test conditions. They wanted to apply what is known as the "water-test," that is, filling Mrs. French's mouth with water, to see if spirit-people could speak while she so held the liquid. At my request she consented. A man of science was chosen to make the experiment. He came and I gave him the key to the room in the afternoon, so that he might prepare his own conditions. In the evening, this learned professor, Mrs. French, and I, without lighting the room, and without any knowledge on our part of what condition it was in, entered. Mrs. French was given a certain quantity of liquid which this man put into her mouth. I could hear her breathe with difficulty. A moment's silence, and then a voice came in the darkness, unusually loud and strong, saying: **"You see we can speak under the conditions you have made."** I turned to the professor, asking: "Are you satisfied?" and he said, "I am." Then I said: "Remove the liquid; please measure it, and see if the amount expectorated is equal to the amount put in, and of the same color. I did not know the color or the amount. Upon examination, both were found intact. The test was evidential.

This man declined to publish this fact, saying it was in advance of the times. He was afraid that science, so-called, would not accept his statement. In view of such conditions I made arrangements some four years ago, for Mrs. French to go to New York at the request of Dr. Isaac Funk and his associates. She sat with him for eleven nights, the record of which is published in "The Psychic Riddle." Results similar to my own were obtained, and at a later time, Dr. Funk, at Rochester applied the water-test again, and spirit-voices spoke to him while Mrs. French's mouth was filled with liquid. Such conditions demonstrate: (a) that Mrs. French does not do the talking, for her organs of speech are not used; (b) that the voices are independent. By that I mean that spirits use their own vocal organs.

Such facts convince me that people I have known in the body continue to live when the physical has gone back to dust, that they have the same individuality, the same continuity of thought, and the same characteristic speech in the after-life as this.

By such experiments it is proved to be a fact that life continues after dissolution; that death is only a change of vibratory conditions; that the soul, mind, thought, by whatever name you choose to call this ego that thinks, reasons, and is, in no way changed, only its actions is governed by new laws controlling in the higher vibration of which they are a part. They are the same person as before; and, given the required conditions, can talk just as well as ever. The requires no deductive reasoning; it is a fact proved and by many accepted.

One in spirit-life said to me, in discussing this subject this day:

**"You know because you ask, and fact and reason answer. It is so even now, that few truths reach the intelligence of men which are not bought in wrappers of superstition, tied with baffling unreality. All creeds, founded on the little ambitions of a sect of men seeking their own renown, are being swept aside, and the truth, naked and unafraid, founded on nature's laws, is coming to be understood.**

**"Nature does not hide her laws, but holds them subject to the call of men, asking only that man shall qualify himself and know how to use and apply them intelligently, when they are unfolded to him. Nature is no wiser, but is ever ready to give of her abundance."**

## Spirit Identity

"How do I know," must be told on every page in different ways, but let us continue with the independent voice, for, in the history of the world as written, and as spirit-people tell me, never before has such freedom of speech been known; never before have spirit-people of a high order of intelligence found an avenue of communication with the physical world so effectual. How could it be more convincing than by voice to voice? My work has ever been conducted with great care and caution; every known safeguard has been adopted. I have never sought fraud, and have never found fraud; have ever sought truth, and have always found truth. A man's mind is like a magnet and the thought-waves emanating into the ether, attract waves of like character.

The key to the after-life is passivity, not concentration. By centering the mind on some particular thing much desired, the thought waves are contracted, brought to a slower vibration. Spirit-people in higher atomic activity, cannot come into a mental condition pulsating at a slow rate; but into the passive mind where the waves are more active, more nearly in harmony with a spirit's vibratory condition. So we talk for a few moments preceding spirit-speech on general matters, filling the room with vocal vibrations which are taken up and used by spirit-people, –our thoughts intent on no particular subject or person.

When we meet to continue our investigations, a period of ten to twenty minutes elapses before spirit-people speak, during which time I feel as though some great power was in some indefinite way drawing upon my physical strength, at times almost to the point of pain; then the hush of expectancy; then the greeting, as in any drawing room, and quite as natural, as they come in one by one.

Working on the spirit-side of life, aiding this work, was originally a group of seven persons, who built up conditions every time we conducted experiments, the most important of which is the chemist, for he must know at once what conditions will harmonize, and what elements can be used and applied to different spirits to enable them to use their organs of speech so that their voice will reach our ears. We contribute, as I have said, physical vibrations, while spirit-people bring spiritual, that is a higher vibratory state, which the group manipulates. The condition under which we get these voices, is a utilization of both.

Certain of the spirit-group arrange these requisite conditions, while others direct the work. In the beginning of my investigations, the voices came usually in whispers, the people speaking

44

were generally persons of less than average intellect, those in the lower walks of life; such characters predominated, and the most we could get from them was the conditions in which they found themselves, —interesting, but not particularly instructive, as they had little knowledge of life beyond the earth-plane. It was all, I see now, that we were able to comprehend; but our progression was to be commensurate with our capacity. Year by year, as we grew more accustomed to the work, and more able to understand these higher laws, there was improvement, until now the finest minds of modern times devote their time to our instruction. From the ungrammatical speech of ordinary men and women, step by step, it has changed to the finest diction, the most splendid English to which I have ever listened; and it is our privilege to enjoy, night after night, oratory finer than was ever delivered from any platform. Is it any wonder that I find such work intensely interesting, and have the courage born of knowledge to give the world what I have learned?

So mighty is the force of human thought, and so delicate are the conditions of a spirit's body when it has taken on material in preparation for speech, that, by word of command or even by thought-projections, I can break down its conditions and prevent speech. This is why those who oppose this philosophy so often get negative results when they seek demonstration; by their mental attitude or thought-conditions, they make impossible the very thing they seek; they so intensify their thought-substance that spirit-people are not able to break into the conditions they make for the occasion.

Here is another piece of evidence which proves that the voices are not those of mortals. Spirit-people in speech with me, while using their organs of respiration, do not breath as we do. I have often heard a lecture twenty minutes in length, without a break, the voice rising and falling in inflection, speaking with great force and clearness but not drawing one breath in all that time. This is a physical impossibility for any mortal man.

Each voice has individuality. When a new spirit comes for the first time and takes on the condition of vocalization, there is often a similarity in tone quality, but this soon passes away, as they grow accustomed to speak, never change, and are easily recognized. Of such we never ask their names, for we know. There is no similarity of thought or words; these differ in different people in that world as in this.

The strength of the voices varies greatly; one of our group speaks with sufficient volume to fill easily a great auditorium, and his lectures ring through the whole house. Another whom I have in mind, always comes with great dignity and courtesy, is careful in speech and considerate; but his voice, while very distinct, has not great volume. The voice of another, who was very near to me in earth-life, is as clear, strong, and natural as in the days when we discussed this philosophy, or walked in the forest trying to understand and come in touch with the law of life; and we have since his going talked as much, and with as great freedom, as in the latter years before his going. There has been no subject of knowledge common to us both, that he ever hesitated to discuss in all its minutest details. This friendship of many years is continued without a break, and I enjoy his presence and our talks as I never did before.

One night, a voice of great volume and strength came out of the darkness, clothing thoughts with such speech as only one man has ever used, telling of life as he, who was one of the world's great agnostics, found it after dissolution; of his life-work and duties there, and something of the environment of a spirit and the possibilities of progression, closing by saying, **"I am Mr. G.,"** as we will call him.

I said to Mr. G.: "It is one of the rules, long in practice in our work, that when one comes as you have, teaching philosophy, identity shall be proved. Can you do this?" He said: **"I think that can be done without difficulty."** I replied: "Did you ever meet me?" He said: **"Yes."** "Where?" I asked. **"At the Niagara Hotel in your city."** "When was that?" He said: **"I don't now recall the year, but it was when I gave a lecture on Progress at the request of the Real Estate Men's Association."** "What was the date of the lecture?" He replied: **"I don't recall, but it was in the early nineties."** "Where was the meeting?" **"At the Music Hall, as I now recall."** "Do you remember who sat in the box at your left that evening?" **"My recollection is,"** he replied, **"that my wife and daughter did, with others."** *This was proof; it was all true.* This is one of the ways adopted to prove identity; and this man stood the test to my entire satisfaction.

Another instance: In my early work, in fact one of the first times I attempted to have speech with spirits, Mr. K., we will call him, was with me. He was one of those men who are always looking for tests, it was his ruling passion. He wanted tests more than he did knowledge, and as we were not seeking the same thing, we soon went different ways; but, whenever he met me, not having the courage of his desire, he would whisper; "Have you had any tests lately?" Whenever I saw him coming I knew what his question would be. So he lived, and so he died; and within a week, out of the darkness came a voice in greeting. I said: "Who is it, please?

Can you tell us who you are? Give us something that will establish your identity. Can you?" **"Yes,"** he replied, **"I am through looking for tests."**

One evening one spoke who said he was a physician of Philadelphia, and was brought in that help might be given to complete the separation from his physical body. When he finally became fully conscious, he told his name, the number of his residence, and much about himself. The papers the next mourning had a full account of his death early the evening before.

Mr. N., we will call him, was one of the most prominent members of our bar. He was supposed to be in perfect health, but late one evening he was found dead. I had no knowledge of the circumstances. He told me his name and proved his identity without the slightest difficulty, for I had known him intimately. He asked me to send word to his brother, of New York, who, he said, was then in Europe—a fact I did not know—and told me where he himself was and what he was doing when dissolution came. The circumstances were verified by his son at a later time. Space forbids detail. I have mentioned only a few out of thousands of similar cases.

In the beginning, much time was wasted to prove the identity of strange spirits who were allowed to talk, to find if what they said concerning themselves, was true; and while I know that spirit-people, as a rule, are as prone to deceit as mortals, I recall no instance of it. At one time, a few men of my acquaintance passed on who did not come and speak with me; but now the strength is so limited, owing to the great age of our psychic, that personal interviews are not frequent, the time being used in giving information concerning this great problem and teaching this new philosophy, that the greatest good can come to the greatest number.

Hundreds, yea thousands, have come and talked with me, and to many whom I have invited to participate in the work, —thousands of different voices with different tones, different thoughts, different personalities, no two alike; and at times in different languages.

Spirit identity is a subject I have always considered important for many reasons: (a) It may be said, if a spirit can prove identity, that it is evidence that life continues; (b) by knowing who he is, his education, experience and opportunity for observation, one can tell what weight to give his teachings, for, as I have pointed out elsewhere, spirit-people differ concerning many great questions just as people do in this life, and we must ever exercise our reason and draw our own conclusions. That is the way character is developed. Every statement made and every alleged fact that comes to us from either world, must be tested in the crucible of reason and must appeal to our common sense, before it can be accepted; and unless it comes from the retort pure, we discard it.

No spirit ever feels at liberty to come into our sessions without the invitation of the spirit-group or of myself any more than a stranger would come into my house for social purposes without an invitation. The same laws of privilege and hospitality which operate in the earth-life, prevail in the spirit-world.

There is opposition to this work in spirit-spheres just as in this. The Catholic Church exists as an institution in the after-life, and is just as jealous of its domination as it is here. In our earliest work these opponents often tried to prevent speech by interrupting and disorganizing the conditions we sought to maintain, fearing that the truth might cause loss of temporal as well as spiritual power; and great efforts were made by the spirit-group, comprising our co-workers, to control and maintain the conditions, and to keep them out. I recall one evening when my stenographer was taking a lecture in shorthand, that a Catholic spirit gained admittance; and such was his material strength that he suddenly wrenched the stenographic book from the hands of the stenographer, and threw it with great violence against the wall of the room. Our group finally forced him out and, as he was leaving, I heard him say, **"What can one man do among so many millions?"**

## Of Many Minds

The greatest fallacy of the human race is the belief that people after dissolution, know everything, or that they agree, upon great propositions, any more than in this life. There is absolutely nothing in metapsychics to warrant such a foolish assumption. Nothing in the world is acquired without effort, and there is no evidence that the scheme of nature is changed by what is known as death. Those who hold that through the change from the physical to the spiritual men become gods, know very little about evolution, and wrongly assume that there is one law for the physical and another for spirit-life. The fact is, all nature's laws are universal, and apply alike to both planes, for, to some extent, both occupy the same space. This being so, we can appreciate the wisdom of creation and that is worthwhile, if one continues his life and work beyond the physical, to acquire all possible knowledge and development while living in the physical plane, to the end that he may be better equipped when going beyond it.

Dissolution is a step in evolution, and involves no mental change, adding nothing, subtracting nothing, but simply increasing the opportunities for observation and learning. As men regard this subject with so much indifference, it is easy to conceive how overpowering will be the situation presented when separated from the physical body: no going away; no flight to the sky; no sudden acquisition of knowledge; no personal God; but self in a new light, in a true light; many of the so-called dead rushing to meet the newcomer as he takes the little step out of this life, into spirit-existence, while, as his eyes open, and the truth flashes upon his dull senses, he discovers that God is Universal Good, which has been, and is, the dominant factor both in the physical and spirit-plane; that this force for good has held kingship since the world began; that man has been, and ever will be, a part of that force, increasing the sum total of that power of which he is a part, according to the measure of his progression! This he does by developing the atom of good that he became at the moment of his conception. It came from the great force of Universal Good; and, let him go to and fro as he will, yet, drawn by an irresistible force, he will return to the goal from which he came originally; and, inasmuch as there is some good in everyone, the sum-total of that force for good will be enriched to some extent by his return. But his will not come at the moment of dissolution, for that is only one step along the way, and no matter though he live in the body beyond his allotted time, his life is practically only just beginning.

When dissolution is passed, and one has paid all his obligations to the physical world, (no progression being possible until this is done, for nature's laws are terrible in their exactness), and realizes his condition, the necessary thing is to take an inventory of his equipment, and to determine how far he is qualified to assume the duties and responsibilities awaiting him. He may be a great lawyer, an eloquent divine, a great financier, a learned professor, a good merchant, or an honest farmer; but how will that help him when he is in spirit dealing with matter in so high a state of vibration that it no longer resists muscular effort, the existence of which he has never before known? How will such a man deal with conditions of which he is so densely ignorant and which control his every thought and movement? There is but one answer: he must form new conceptions based on known facts and necessities, and, aided by the limited knowledge that he has acquired, he must commence again, commence, at best, where dissolution overtook him; the better equipped here, the more advanced there. When I say equipped, I do not mean with material knowledge, but with a broad comprehension of natural laws; this alone will aid one in adapting himself to the environment in the new community of which he has become an inhabitant.

In this material world of ours there are many opinions on every great subject; each works to a conclusion from known facts, but the conclusions arrived at are not always correct. Spirit-people hold to their opinions until they are changed by the new facts presented. Thy do not agree on many great questions any more than we do. They fail to understand many of nature's laws as mortals do, and are continually laboring to come to a better knowledge of them just as we do here; and there, as here, are "many minds," but as to what immediately follows dissolution all agree.

The fact that spirit-people, though advanced and learned in many ways, greatly differ on many subjects, was impressed on my mind by one in the after-life while discussing the subject of "sound," when he said:

**"One of the facts that has been repeatedly proved by our experiment, is that stress-condition, which I have heretofore referred to, is an existing condition, that when a blow is struck upon various kinds of substance, a very widely differing sound is produced, and that the distinctive notes are, of course, the resulting vibration of the particular mass struck.**

**"It is not, to me, a satisfactory explanation that the sound that reaches our ear is only the result of the elasticity of the particles of the mass acting strictly among themselves, the vibration of the mass itself and, also, the vibrations of the particles of the mass; but, the true solution of the problem is, I think, and many agree with me, that the blow upon the mass may bring the particles of the mass momentarily to a state of rest, and so the mass itself may be temporarily reduced to a similar state, or both the particles and the mass composed of the particles may be, for and during the period of the concussion, rendered, so to speak, physically dead, —this phenomena being based on the fact that all matter is in constant vibratory motion. And now, granting my hypothesis that all matter produces in the surrounding ether a state of stress, the mirrored condition of its actual self, I think it necessarily follows that if the acting substances were brought to a momentary state of rest, the lines of existing stress reaching out from the object struck, would, on the instant, feel the effect, and that something called sound would be the result of their sudden interference, and the prolongation of the apparent sound would depend upon the length of the period of the suspension of the actual vibration of the object struck.**

**"This and many other facts lead others on this side of life to advocate the stress-theory. And again, there are many well-**

informed men on this side of life who argue against such a theory.

"When this matter was brought to the attention of such on this side of life as are interested along these lines, much discussion occurred, and it is, and has been, argued from two viewpoints: first, as simply impossible; and second, as reasonable, if the theory of existing stress, in the ether surrounding known substances, be logical, all of those trying to assist you, hold the latter."

Such discussions impress one with the reality and earnestness of the people beyond, and show how they labor to comprehend natural law.

# PART II

## The Voices

The Historic Voice-to-Voice Conversations and Spirit Discourses
Stenographically Recorded, Between Edward C. Randall and Spirits
of the Living Dead; Collected Materials and Seance Memoranda

# CHAPTER 2
## The Mind

*Read not to contradict and confute, nor to believe and take for granted, but to weigh and consider.* --Bacon

## Thought and Mind

There are certain expressions and sentences in our language which are, at present, substantially meaningless, because the mind is unable to grasp what it cannot analyze. That "thought is substance," and "mind is matter," mean but little to mortal man, notwithstanding his wonderful progress, because so little is known of matter outside of and beyond that which resists muscular effort, or which he cannot observe with his physical eyes.

Those that are educated along material lines see only in earth, water and air, certain atoms, molecules and chemical combinations. All must admit that matter is governed by force, and that the force that governs and directs matter in its association, composition and change, possesses intelligence; but, being unable to follow matter through its evolution and refinement, they deny what they cannot comprehend. Back of the atom, back of all substance, back of all people, is a mighty force, called mind, --the Master Mind we may term it, that directs and controls all substances visible and invisible by fixed and definite rules, which are termed "natural law."

To attempt to bring to the comprehension of mankind a definite conception of that mind, that force, is difficult beyond anything I have undertaken, because of my limited knowledge of the subject; for those in the sphere beyond the physical are able to give me but little information, for they have only limited knowledge. Simply because they are out of the body they do not know all, nor are they infallible; so they, acting as instructors, can give me only that which they know. Perhaps I can deal with this difficult proposition in no better way than to quote what spirit-people have told me concerning the question.

**"Back in the past centuries, when the world of spirit had not its present development, there was little original inventive thought. Man built a shelter, killed his food, and fought his enemies, as any animal does. As the spirit-world progressed, and became more intelligent; as it obtained greater understanding, and grasped, with greater power, the life forces, or, in other words, more power of thought, and more ability to help mortal development, then, by reason of spirit-suggestion, acting through man's sub-conscious mind, he began to feel an awakening for something better, and the process of civilization began."**

This statement emphasizes the fact that all life in every sphere ever has been, now is, and ever shall be, progressive; that there was a time in spirit-planes, as well as on this plane, when they did not possess the intelligence, comprehension and power that they do today, not nearly as much as they will in time to come.

Of what lies beyond the next, or first spirit-sphere, those who live there know but little. Knowledge is acquired only by effort, there, as here; and only as we comprehend the economy of natural law and mind power, do we progress. We know that those in the next spirit-sphere, like people in the earth-sphere, develop their mental powers through acquired knowledge, and therefore, increase the sum-total of the Master-Mind of which they and we are parts; so that not only is the individual spirit gaining advancement, but being Spirit, and a component part of the great Mind, this force increases in the ratio of individual development; each day they and we are contributing something to the great intelligent force which directs and controls the Universe; and its increase is measured by their and our progression.

What the Master-Mind is, beyond the fact that it includes the individual minds of all who have lived, and now live, in any plane or any planet in the universe, we cannot know; we could not grasp the infinite, if any spirit knew and tried to explain. That there is an intelligence controlling all matters and all people to some extent, we do know. Again this spirit said:

**"Beyond and before everything is mind; that is, understanding. Mind is matter, as you use that term, with this difference; it is carried beyond the physical into a higher vibration. Let me illustrate in this way: Good thoughts have a higher and**

more rapid vibration than bad thoughts, and bring us into closer harmony with spirit-intelligences. There is no barrier to thought; it carries us to the uttermost parts of the earth; to the heights of perfect joy and to the depths of woe. The people of earth are just beginning to gain some knowledge of this force for good within themselves. Once let that fact be understood, and mortals will come nearer to understanding their destiny."

Another said:

"Mind is the aggregate of all thoughts. Mind is the universal thought. As a drop of water signifies but one infinitesimal part of the great ocean, so a thought is but one infinitesimal part of the great ocean of mind. Thought is creative energy, the essence of all things, and expresses itself in form. The vibratory energy of thought waves produce form, sound and color, though they are never perfectly expressed in the physical plane. Not until men have arisen out of the physical condition can they come to an appreciation and comprehension of matter so refined as to be known as mind. Thought belongs to the universal man; mind to the race universal."

Words are but symbols used to express thoughts. There is nothing in a word except that it conveys an impression or ideas to the mind. They are coined as new conditions arise. When Newton discovered the law of gravitation, he had difficulty in finding words to describe the fact, so new was the proposition. So it is with metapsychics, that is the philosophy of life beyond the physical; this science is so new and so little is known on the subject, that words have not as yet been adopted that will allow of exact detail or comprehensive report.

There is no such thing as space; what seems so to us, in fact, contains all the elements that produce objects, but it is so fine in its particles and in so high a state of vibration as not ordinarily to be visible. All in the earth and sky is substance and holds within itself life force. The wind is matter, for we feel it in our faces, and it is a force for it drives great ships upon the seas. Water is slower in vibration than atmosphere, so we feel and see it, while ether, which is atmosphere higher in vibration, we neither see nor feel, yet it permeates all things and all space and is likewise a substance.

I said to a spirit who in earth-life, was the foremost scientist of his time, "What is ether, and what is mind?" and he answered:

"Ether is simply atmosphere in more intense vibration than which surrounds the earth. Ether surrounds spirits unless they go into the earth-plane. Mind, I mean the thought, not the habitation of thought, when the earth-life is over, becomes the entire being. It is the only part in man that is of such vibration that it can enter in and progress to spirit-life. The brain is so constructed that there is an opening for spirit-force or suggestion; consequently, it proves that the entire mind is of such vibration that the spirit-force can reach it; otherwise suggestion would be impossible.

"Mind is the essence of being, —the ego. It is material, but differing in vibration from the body. Spirit-force surrounds the flowers, teaching them how to grow and bloom, but they have no conscious original thought."

And so we find matter rising higher and higher in vibratory action. First the earth, then water, then atmosphere, then ether, and finally mind, which is matter as much as the earth is matter, yet it directs and controls all substance in a lower vibratory condition.

Let me illustrate: Over the land that a man owns, and the waters under the land, he has some control. He can dig into the earth; he can draw the water from it; he can use the air and, to some slight degree, deflect its currents, by the mind directing hands and other agencies that he can employ. He holds *limited* dominion over gross matter under certain conditions. Now, spirit-minds, that make up the Master-Mind, higher in vibration than ether itself, hold absolute dominion over all matter in the physical universe. But, to attempt to analyze that Master-Mind, or one's own mind even, to give the component parts of mind-matter or its chemical composition, is beyond my power.

One of my spirit co-workers said:

"Be tempted to one extravagance only in this book of ours. Use every argument and all the forcefulness you can, to show what a little thing, a tiny span, the earth-life is. Real life begins when the heavy, material body is left behind, and the soul springs upward into the unlimited regions of thought-life. There all grows, learns, expands into perfect fullness of being until one becomes a perfectly developed spirit, able to blend with other spirits similarly developed and perfected. There is no beginning and no end, then, to the heights he can ascend; no joy that is unknown or untasted; no wonder of the universe of which he does not become a part. It is being, then, that state which cannot be defined to unthinking and incomprehensive minds. But try to grasp this idea, for it gives such an interest and zest to every-day life. Some day each shall be a part of the great force that makes all things work in unity. Before the force was so strong, there was not so much good working among men. They were cruel, barbarous and uncontrolled. Much has that mind-force, working silently but constantly, achieved in the past ages, and much more will it achieve, now that mankind has become receptive to our suggestion.

"Thought is the expression of mind; it is partly caused by spirit-suggestions through the subconscious mind, and partly an expression of oneself. Deeds are thoughts grown to maturity, and yet a thought unspoken or unlived, will exist through all the ages, as though expressed."

Another spirit speaking on this general subject has said:

"You all give off an aura, and if you knew the conditions emanating from some people, you would very quickly eject them from your home. In those whose lives are not strictly upright we find the aura very bad, mixed, cloudy, confused. The emanations of people of good health vary in shade from white, pale pink, to rose color. When the auras approach the dark colors, browns, greys, and blacks, we know that the person is wrong in some way. Now this aura is influenced by passions such as hate, envy, malice, evil speaking, anger, and when one sets out to do an injury to another, let me assure you that he injures himself far more than the other person."

I have been told that a clean, highly developed thought goes out into the ether with the appearance of a search light, starting from a central point and radiating through space. Once again, mind is matter, and thoughts are things, and so wonderfully active is the operation, that we are continually forming our mental creations in such refined substance.

With all our development, and it has been great, we are able to hear only a few of the sounds that vibrate in our atmosphere. With all our achievements we are unable to see motion except it be slow in movement and in physical garment. On this subject one said:

"We can also read the thoughts of another—conditions being favourable—as readily as you can gain a knowledge of a language not your own. Thoughts being motions of the mind, assume specific and definite forms, and when distinct in the mind, can be clearly perceived and understood by any spirit who is in sympathy with the mind in which they are generated."

On turning once again to the lectures from the more advanced minds in the next expression of life, I find the following:

"Thought is a wonderful force and even we cannot grasp its magnitude, nor understand all its power. It is a living, vital thing. A thought born in your mind is for good or evil, a thing to be reckoned with again, when it will confront you face to face and claim you as its author. The best thoughts are those born of Nature in its beauty, rather than those that have had the touch of material hands. I would like to say something, too, about the beauty of pure thought, how it returns to one after earth-life, laden with sweetness and intensified tenfold. You cannot realize all each good, generous, noble thought will mean to you someday, even if it never grows into an act. Evil thoughts breed darkness and despair, cling to the soul, go with you into the after-life, and become your close familiar friends. You are never rid of them a moment until you have taken them up one by one and lived them over again. The power of suffering for evil is increased on this side of the vale, just as joy is intensified beyond anything you can feel. Such joy you have from your good thoughts and deeds. A thought can have many branches, but the parent stem is planted deep in your own soul, and only your hand can remove it in the future. If it be good it will bear richer fruit each year. When you have traveled and especially enjoyed any scene, you have a picture of it in your spirit-home, just as books you own are found on the shelves. Music will fill the home of the sensitive, and so on indefinitely. This is the home of which spirits speak. It practically becomes your house. Your thoughts do not look to us like anything in a material sense. They are felt. They create an atmosphere that is like a cloud around you, and this condition is easily discernible by us and felt by sensitive spirits in the body. All thoughts are not necessarily known until the spirit himself is confronted by them. Then they stand out prominently to him. But even then, others may be only conscious of his character by the conditions he is forced to undergo before he can overcome the evil ones. We may know the thought when it is formed, and then, again, we may know it by the condition made in spirit-life. Thoughts are around the persons who create them, but they are not confined there, for they go as well to build the home in the spirit-world. While it is true that they are stored in millions of brain cells, they are also all about one, forming an aura. This is the influence one feels when he comes into the near presence of strong mentalities. Sometimes it is pleasant, often, not. This is the spiritual part of the thought. What is in the brain is more material, —of a consistency that is easier for man to use, if he desires to retain knowledge of any kind. These ideas are hard to put into words. They are subtle. There is a color, a note of music, a perfume, a spirit all in each close harmonious thought. A chord of music will cause the color vibration that belongs to it; the perfume that belongs to that same vibration can cause the same color, and the perfume can cause the harmonious thought. You can truthfully say that thoughts are different notes of sound."

## Dual Minds

It is now known that we have two minds as well as two bodies. The subconscious mind functions in the etheric brain of the inner body; the conscious mind functions in the physical brain of the outer body. The subconscious is the mind that survives dissolution, carrying the imprints made on it by the conscious mind, which does not survive, but which perishes with the physical body. The subconscious mind, the real mind, suggests to the conscious mind, although often the prompting of that still small voice is unheeded. Now the conscious mind is mortal; the subconscious is immortal.

It has been my privilege for many years to hear great lectures from learned philosophers and psychologists, long inhabitants of the next state, of which I have the stenographic reports. I quote from one of these lectures of the spirit psychologist:

"It has always seemed to us that the subject of mind, or minds, is one which your people have been little interested in. It is difficult to conceive of a more essential subject. I dare say, speaking conservatively, there are in your world few who know that they have such a thing as a subconscious mind. We do not care particularly for the term 'subconscious.' It is a misnomer and we object to the nomenclature, because this mind is not really sub-conscious; it is super-conscious.

"If mankind had an understanding of the importance of the relationship between the conscious and the subconscious minds, it would make a great difference in the courses men would lay out for themselves in earth life, as well as in their lives after the transition.

"Perhaps it is well to speak first of the conscious mind, which, to most people, is the only mind they have, that mind which makes or creates a cause, of which actions are the effect, that mind which controls the voluntary actions and the muscular contractions of the individual.

"Now then, the conscious mind is something else besides being a center of nerve impulses controlling the actions and movements of the body. It has a far greater relationship to the universe, to our fellowmen and to God. The mind is the dynamo that is constantly generating thought forms. These thought forms have shape, size and color, and potentialities appalling to those who understand clearly the functions of the conscious mind.

"These thoughts that emanate from the minds of mankind are at a fixed rate of vibration, going forth into the universe at the same rate as that of the mind which gave them their impetus. They are constantly impinging against the receptive minds of earth-people and also of disembodied people who are in what is known as the spirit world. They may be uplifting; they may be charitable, sympathetic, kindly; on the other hand they may be destructive, causing injury, exciting conditions which often results in actions sad and distressing indeed.

"The sub-conscious, or super-sensitive, mind, which so many people know not, although they possess it, is a fourth dimensional mind, or the mind of the astral body, contained within your three-dimensional, physical body. The sub-conscious mind, being fourth-dimensional, is subject to that unerring law of accuracy which is dominant in the fourth-dimensional or etheric plane. Therefore, the sub-conscious mind, because it is accurate, should dominate the conscious mind, which is likely to be inaccurate because it operates only in the third dimension and is subject to the desires of mankind, limited by environment and by all sorts of conditions.

"When man is sleeping, when he is tired, it is the subconscious mind which builds up the will-forces in the body, sees that everything functions smoothly, supervises the beating of the heart, regulates the respiratory functions, and makes it possible for you to exist.

"The subconscious mind is very much higher in vibration than the conscious or objective mind, the three-dimensional mind of the physical body. Now, then, it develops upon mankind to accelerate the vibrations of the conscious mind so that it may be in unison, or nearly so, with the vibrations of the subconscious mind, which alone survives.

"The subconscious mind is always right. From the subconscious mind comes the 'still small voice,' that thing which people know as the conscience. The conscience is a definite

61

manifestation of the subconscious mind, trying to dictate to the conscious mind that it is in some way or other in error.

"The conscience is a manifestation of the subconscious mind, registering encouragement or protest on the conscious mind. The subconscious is always present. Sometimes—a great many times, I am sorry to say—it is dominated by the carnal, or conscious mind, but it is always there, ever active in its endeavor to lead mankind aright."

I had long known that we are here and now possess two bodies, but the suggestion that we also, here and now, have two minds was new. I did not accept it when made—it troubled me. I knew that spirit people were as prone to error as mortals, and I have ever rejected statements from that source, as from a physical source, that did not appeal to reason.

Troubled with the proposition, so new and original, I took the question up with Dr. David Hossack, whom I have already quoted. Dr. Hossack has been an inhabitant of the spirit world for more than a century, with him I have been in communication for thirty years and more, and whose statements I have ever found reliable. I asked him this question:

"Is it a fact that we possess two minds as well as two bodies, and that the conscious or material mind does not survive?"

This was his answer:

"As you have two bodies, the material and the spiritual, so you have two minds. The spirit mind is that which comes from the infinite, and is clothed with the material at conception. It is life-force, and cannot be destroyed. This etheric soul or mind is the force for good that is in each of us; it is in embryo during earth life, finding full development only in the spirit world.

"The material mind is the conscious mind. It functions through the direction of the spirit mind, unconsciously, of course, as the spirit mind, in the majority of men, enwrapped so closely with gross material folds that it is rarely discernible. However, the two are as separate and distinct as your two bodies.

"You do not take the material mind with you into this world, any more than you take the earth body. The conditions here are such that you could not bring either with you. Yet the soul is the mainspring and the compelling force of both bodies and both minds. The spirit mind is the only conscious mind. By that I mean that it is the only real, living, eternal Mind. As your earth progress goes on, this spirit mind is the life-force which you feel and know as the real part of your existence. Your conscious, earth mind is only the store room for the subconscious spirit mind to build on and grow within you.

"When you pass on, you take the wares from this store-room with you, but earth consciousness is transitory and not real; only the inner richness is carried on and becomes part of you when, in dissolution, the two are finally separated."

# CHAPTER 3
## The Spiritual, or Etheric Body

*It is sown a natural body; it is raised a spiritual body. There is a natural body and there is a spiritual body.*

—1 Corinthians 15: 44

## Man's Etheric Body

The ancients thought that Ether filled the sky, and was the home of the Gods. It was contended by Aristotle that it extended from the fixed stars down to the moon. Modern science has heretofore contended that all space is filled with a substance having rigidity and elasticity, with a density equal to our atmosphere at a height of about 210 miles—easily displaced by any moving mass—compared to an all-prevailing fluid or derivative of gases through which heat and light are constantly throbbing.

In "Modern View on Electricity," Sir Oliver Lodge[1], speaking the last word concerning Ether, says, "It is one continuous substance filling all space; which can vibrate as light, which, under certain unknown conditions, can be modified or analyzed into positive and negative electricity; which can constitute matter; and can transmit, by continuity and not by impact, every action and reaction which matter is capable. This is the modern view of Ether and its functions. The most solid substance in the world is not iron, is not lead, is not gold, is not any of the things that impress our sense as extremely dense. The most solid thing in existence is the very thing which for generations has been universally regarded

---

1. Sir Oliver Lodge (1851-1940): World famous mid 19th-century British physicist; author, lecturer, and fearless champion of survival of death.

as the lightest, the most imperceptible, the most utterly tenuous and evanescent beyond definition or computation; it is the Ether. The Ether is supposed to permeate everything, to be everywhere, to penetrate all objects, to extend throughout all space. The earth moves through it; the sun and all the stars have their being and their motion in and through the Ether; it carries light and electricity and all forms of radiation. Nobody has ever seen it, or rendered it evident to touch or to any other sense. It escapes all efforts to feel it, to weigh it, to subject it to any kind of scientific experiment. It plays no part in mechanics. It neither adds to nor takes away from the width or substance of any known substance. We are assured by some of the highest authorities that the Ether is millions of times more dense than platinum, one of the most solid metals known."

Surrounding us and filling what we know as space and permeating all things, is that substance termed Ether. It is a subtle essence hard to define that is in the atmosphere we breathe, highly sensitive, through which the light of the sun travels in undulating waves, but just as much a substance as the very rocks and stones. There is a gross Ether and there is also a refined Ether. Through the medium of the grosser Ether we send our ethergrams, but of the finer, more sensitive Ether, we know but little.

The suggestion that all life has *etheric form*, is entirely new. Whether we are advanced enough to appreciate a proposition so beyond our experience, is a question, but a moment's reflection, and we do comprehend that all life comes from the invisible, and ultimately goes back to the invisible. The unseen then is the real, and the seen, the result of the invisible causes. There is a world within a world, all contained in this wondrous universe. We see and touch only the outer garment of the etheric universe which, temporarily clothed with gross material, is working out its development. A directive intelligence has made all Nature's laws, through which each inhabited planet moves and has its being, has its domain in the invisible. The invisible then becomes a legitimate field of inquiry.

I am assured by those versed in the physics of the afterlife, with whom I have speech, that all life, down to the atom, and beyond, has etheric form; that every atom that makes up mass of rock; that every molecule of earth that covers the barren stone; that every grain of sand that forms the ocean shore; that every seed, and plant, and shrub, and tree; that every drop of water that flows in creeks, falls as rain, or constitutes the lakes and seas—all have etheric form. The etheric requires for growth a covering of matter lower in vibration than itself, the same as the seed planted in the earth, and in the outer garment it increases and reaches a higher development. No life force can exist in the physical unless it has a garment suitable to that purpose. Dissociate the etheric form from the outer garment, and the individual can no longer remain an inhabitant of this sphere, dissolution has taken place. Could we follow into the condition beyond, we would ultimately find that every star and constellation has etheric as well as physical form, and that they are visible only because they are clothed with gross material, the same as our own planet, for all laws hold continuity throughout the Universe.

It is the etheric body that sees, hears, feels, smells and tastes, evidenced by the fact that the physical body has none of the five senses when separated from the etheric. The ear, for instance, with its complicated chamber and auditory nerves, really hears through the etheric brain. Sever the nerves, destroy the tympanum, and you destroy the communication; put any of the very fine mechanism of the auditory chamber out of commission, and you either cannot hear at all, or at best, very imperfectly. Every concussion causes an ever widening circle in the atmosphere, that is, in the ether of the atmosphere, which at least reaches the auditory chamber, an ever widening circle in the atmosphere, that is, in the ether of the atmosphere, which at last reaches the auditory chamber, communicates with those fine nerves and with the brain. By that wonderful process we understand the difference between harmony and inharmony, between sweet sounds and discords. Similarly, through a disturbance set up in the ether we understand language.

Horses, cattle and sheep will exist and wax fat on grass and water. Put them all together in an enclosed field in a tropical country and keep them there indefinitely, what happens? They feed on identically the same food, and multiply; the flesh covering wastes and is from day to day replaced, a complete change being ultimately brought about. Why do they not inter-breed, why does each hold individual form? It is solely because each has an invisible form, that is a form composed of matter in a very high state of vibration which holds continuity, having reached the state termed etheric, at which point the life form neither disintegrates nor enters into new combination. Man differs from the animals only in development. At the moment of conception, he possesses an etheric body, minute and perfect beyond comprehension, and if permitted to inhabit the physical body for the usual period of time, attains a normal growth.

When by heat we break down the outer garment of a lump of coal, when the physical will no longer hold the energy, the life, or the etheric form, the two are dissociated; in other words, the energy or life-form escapes, to pass into some other state; the outer garment, the cinder or ash on the other hand returns from whence it came, ultimately to be taken up by another form of life, until in time it shall have been so refined that it will hold continuity because it has become etheric. And all this to demonstrate that man is a part of one stupendous whole, evolved from the etheric life in the mass, refined to the point where he holds individuality. Death, so-called, is the passing out of the individual spirit or etheric body from the flesh covering. Released from that outer garment it becomes an inhabitant of a plane where all is etheric, but to the etheric sense and touch all things are just as tangible, real, and natural as when in earth-life.

It is utterly impossible for a human being to understand the change in which death so-called occurs unless he realizes that every individual possesses a spirit form composed of etheric atoms, just as much matter as the flesh garment that is visible and tangible. Knowing that fact, he can then understand that dissolution is simply the separation of the physical from the etheric body when the former by accident, disease, or age can no longer obey the will of the occupant. When the physical body can no longer do its part, the spirit or etheric body, by a natural law, abandons the flesh garment, and by that act ceases to be an inhabitant of the earth-plane. This is all that occurs at the time of dissolution.

## The Inner Spirit Body

"There is a natural body, and there is a spiritual body." Those words have fallen from the lips of priests, over the bodies of the so-called dead, for thousands of years, yet not a single minister who uttered them, nor one among the millions of mourners, who for centuries past heard them, ever formed any rational conception of what they meant—and for ages the world has been filled with sorrow.

Had they understood nature's purpose, and known the advantages which the so-called dead gained through the process of dissolution, they would have been comforted. In the presence of such truth, all creeds whither and decay, and old teachings fail to satisfy. That this is a fact, every one who mourns must testify. There must be something wrong with a system of philosophy or a teaching that always fails when put to the test. When the earth clods fall upon the physical body of one held dear, hope sees a star; but hope is not knowledge, and tears fall on furrowed cheeks. If those who still remain but knew that death, as it is called, was only change—a progression—and that the departed still live, and if they knew about their present abiding place, the world of gloom would turn to one of joy.

There is a natural, and by that I mean a physical, body, and there is a spiritual body, but those bare propositions, standing alone, convey nothing to the human mind. They must be followed by facts explaining, if it be a fact, how there can possibly be two bodies in one, when only one is visible to sight and sensible to touch. Without knowing the law of nature involved, without proof that one survives, although the other goes back to mingle with the elements from whence it came, it is utterly impossible to comprehend what was intended by the words first quoted.

I have seen spirit bodies materialize, have touched them and found them as the natural. I have heard them speak and tell over and over again that they had bodies, the same bodies as when they lived the earth life. Still I was not satisfied, and sought to know the character of the two, how they blended, how they worked as one, what natural law was involved, what happened in the dissolution process, why two were necessary, to the end that I might comprehend the fact, for until such knowledge was acquired I had only a very hazy idea, if any, of the situation.

As fast as I was able to comprehend the facts, they were given me, and lo and behold, like all natural laws, I found all simple.

This planet is but one in the federation of the infinite. All the universe is filled with life, and on this earth, as on others, this force impregnates, finds lodging, and is clothed in physical garments, to the end that it may increase, multiply, develop, and in time go back to the infinite from whence it came. In that manner and through that process, it increases the sum total of what we call God or universal good, but it is only by change that the process designed by the Infinite can be carried forward, and death, so-called, is but one of the steps in life's progression.

When matter is receptive, an atom from the life mass is clothed, and from the moment of conception commences its journey back to its source. How fast it develops, what progress it makes, depends much on environment. Its form depends upon the substance which clothes it. Whether physical expression appears as man or animal, in earth, rocks, growing things, or the water of the sea, depends on how, and under what conditions, it obtains its start here. All is life, expressed in visible form, and where there is life there is thought, and neither life nor thought can be destroyed.

There is also physical evidence tending to prove the same proposition. One has his leg amputated, and still feels that he can move his foot; another loses his arm, but still can use his hand and move his fingers. Such is their impression and feeling. Many with whom I have talked are very serious in this matter, and they are right, —amputation can only remove the covering of an arm or leg; no part of the etheric body can be cut off. This remains intact, whatever occurs to the outer covering, for in dissolution it appears intact. A body in that advanced plane may be undeveloped, shrunken and deformed, but it will be all there, and it will appear just as one has made it.

Life is expressed in form; without form it could not function. We cannot see the mighty oak in the heart of the acorn, but it is there in all its splendid promise. We cannot see man, the wonder of creation, in the fluid that first clothes it in its conception, but man is there with form and feature, strength and character, which will ever have continuity.

With mankind the spirit body is clothed, in the beginning, with a flesh garment, a material vibrating more slowly than the ether of which it is composed, and the process of growth commences. The next change is the physical birth; then comes earth-life and the development, physical and spiritual; next is the separation of the spiritual from the outer covering in the change called death—no more wonderful and not half so mysterious as birth; then on, to climb the heights of everlasting life. Such are the teachings that have come to me, voice to voice, from spirit people—some whom I personally have known, and others whom I have come to know and respect in this work.

Volumes could be written on this subject from what is now known. Every man, woman and child living on this earth-plane, did possess in the beginning, and possesses now, *an inner or spirit body*, composed and made up of that material we call ether, a substance and material so fine and of such rapid vibration that the physical eye cannot see it. This inner or etheric body alone has sensation. It takes form and feature, stature and expression, while earth-life lasts, and retains these in the next life as well.

This inner-spirit body, during this stage of its development, is simply clothed, covered or housed in a visible, slowly vibrating garment that we call flesh, which has no sensation. This is evident from the fact that when the one is separated from the other, the outer body has no sensation or motion, so that it decays and loses form.

That experience called death is nature's process by which the two are separated. The habitation, for some cause, becomes unfit for further occupancy. The spirit, or the inner body, is released for further progression from the tenement which is no longer habitable. The earth-body goes back into its elements, to be used again to cloth other forms of life. The inner or spirit-body, holding its same form, invisible then as before, but functioning as before, labours and finds further opportunity for growth and spirituality. This it finds in the zones or belts that surround this globe, and when proper conditions are made, it answers to our call, and tells us of life in its new plane, invisible to mortal eye.

I asked this question of Dr. David Hossack, who has been in spirit life nearly a century:

"Is my understanding correct, that here and now we have, and possess, an inner etheric body, which, divested of its flesh garment, passes intact into the spirit world?"

In reply he said:

**"There is an inner, etheric body, composed of minute particles, of such substance that it can, and does, pass into spirit life. Your outer bodies are too gross and material to effect the change. The inner body is but the mind, the thought, the soul of the person. It is in the semblance of the material body, but whether beautiful or ugly, strong or weak, depends upon the inner life of the person to whom belongs that particular spark of the great radiance called life, or God. Some there be who build a fair body, and some there be who come into this life with a body so misshapen and sickly it takes much effort to effect an upright, clean one. They all come with bodies naturally, as all things have minds, after one fashion or another; but the conditions of these bodies are very different. Naturally, the mind, being the reality of man, is that which lives on, —beautiful or disfigured by good or evil thoughts, as the case may be. The only comfort is that everyone has opportunity here to work out the change in himself, and sometimes those changes are very rapid.**

Another said:

**"In earth life I gave all for wearing apparel; and when I reached the spirit world, I did not have rags enough to cover me, and the beauty of my form had vanished. I was misshapen and distorted. At first I could not understand that it was my spiritual body that was so deformed, for I had not given the spiritual part of me a thought while on earth. In fact, the earth was all in all for me, and I did not trouble myself to think of another life, deeming the time better spent in enjoying the things I knew I possessed. A spirit came and offered to clothe me, but no sooner did the garments touch my body than they were discolored. My progress has been slow, but after many**

**years of suffering I have developed my spirit and restored its beauty, but it is different from what it was in the life below."**

But evidence of all things spiritual must, of necessity, come from those who live there. Their condition is different, their laws are different, for they live in a world invisible to our eyes, and we cannot insist, if we could understand their life, on applying physical laws and methods. It is from spirit people that I have sought knowledge, and from them, and through years of investigation and research, I have come to know as a fact that "there is a natural body and there is a spiritual body."

# CHAPTER 4
## God, Creation and Force

*Poise the cause in justice' equal scales,*
*Whose beam stands sure, whose rightful cause prevails.*

—Shakespeare

## Spiritual Conception of God

In order that one may have some idea of the character of my work, I give in this chapter a report, word for word, of a discourse given me on God. The spirit who gave it has aided me much by his teaching of the higher life. He said:

"I have some ability and am given much thought. I was interested in metapsychic philosophy, and naturally I was in very bad repute among those who thought they knew life and its problems. I could and did receive inspired writings, but they were destroyed after my death by a sister. I knew something of spiritual law, and I practiced it to the best of my ability. I appreciated the need of helping others. This led me to establish a harbor for the sick. (Heriot Hospital, Edinburgh.) Someone sent me the thought that I was needed here, —I do not know who it was, but it was my desire to be with you. I am interested in your work, because my own life was so much given to this thought. I did not have much enlightenment save from phenomena, but it was enough to make me ready for the change. Yet I was dazed at first, it was all so beautiful. I found a dear younger sister waiting for me, and together we have climbed to great heights.

"Progression is unlimited. It stretches away into the vast future. One may climb and soar, but never reach the end of all

72

that can be done to make oneself a perfect being. I understand that there are seven spheres. I am in the Fourth, but the last is without limit. Each plane is more ideally beautiful than the preceding; each, harder to tell about to earth's ears. I cannot describe the wonderful sounds we call music; they are so rich, so harmonious; they find an echo in the deepest places of the heart; they create beautiful thoughts, and help one's development in every way.

"The fields are blazing with posies, and filled with songbirds of brilliant plumage. Everything the heart or eye can desire is there, only enhanced in beauty beyond our comprehension, and as we pass from plane to plane we are always astounded. It becomes sublime. When one is away from the earth-plane there is no more mixing with the lower classes, except as your work takes you among them when they need help; but you live among your own kind and often meet them as neighbors through many planes, if your progression is about the same.

"In coming back to you we pass through all the planes below us, taking on their different conditions as we come, taking on a little more material in each one. I can explain it only in this way, although, of course, it is not material, a little less spiritual would be a more correct expression. It is not difficult to come back, but it is a little strange. To go into the lower spheres seems like taking a plunge into muddy water. As a rule, each plane helps those directly below it, except in special cases like this. I think many of your friends have not progressed as far as I have, and I was sent for because it was thought that I could explain further. Those in the lower plane have only to come near, for that is the earth-plane. You are on the material plane, which is lower still, and does not count among the spirit ones. Our home may be said to be space and what thought makes it. We simply create the different conditions about us by thought. A spirit in the earth-condition, can, by his better thought, change the conditions that exist where he is, and be able to see different good spirits about him.

"I would give this message to the world: Be clean, faithful, and strong, and your progression here will be rapid. I would add to this: Be tender of the weak, and, even if you understand nothing of the future life, your progress will be good. You ask me who and what is God? I answer, God is universal good. I mean the spirit of good that is in every man's heart, tho' it is

sometimes covered with dust and dirt. I said universal, because I know it is there. Sometimes it will grow and blossom.
There will come a time when man will know he is a part of the
great scheme of the universe, and will realize that this scheme
is good. More of God will come into his heart, the dust will
scatter and the bud will grow. God is the life, the spirit entity
of each man, all the better part of him. God is the spirit that
permeates all the best in man and matter. The word 'God' is
used by us. It is the thought-term of good. The Christian Saviour was simply a type such as all religions have, —a symbol of
a perfect man. Each one should lead a good life, the best his
conception suggests; then he will know that good is a blessing,
more lasting than riches and renown. One cannot talk to the
Church, my friend, but to individuals, and through them hope
to reach the Church itself. Through the shepherd, you reach
the flock. The change is very disappointing to many. They
expect to find something very different, and cannot make up
their minds that they are not to throw all their burdens upon
someone else. As I have said, when people have been conscien-
tiously good, they are very easily taken into their right place.
Sometimes they are stubborn for a while, but it all comes right
in time.

"The best any can do is to try to make the world realize that
the best in everything is most desirable, and that everything
filled with good is best and lives on when evil is found despi-
cable. One is happy when good; fearful and miserable when
bad. Nature is God, is always good, always smiling even in her
storms. Nature is but fulfilling her promise of future plenty,
as a mother goes through the storm of childbirth, that she may
replenish the earth. Be not wiser than Nature. Follow her as
closely as you can. Nature is natural in all her changes. The
God-spirit is breathing through every fold of the rose, every
leaf and ear of corn. Let the sunshine pour into your heart,
and be generous, natural, and abundant with your goodwill
and cheerfulness. The rains will come when they are timed.
They will replenish the green of the harvest and make it richer. The storms of life may beat upon you, but you will find
they only break down the dead branches and you will be more
straight and fair for their passing. God is in all this, and if you
but open your heart and let into it all the good there is, you
will find peace and exaltation. I will come again. Good night."

This is what is now coming to me from a little beginning, and I give these words to you as I received them, unaltered and unchanged.

## Origin of Man

The subject next in importance to the future condition or state is the origin of the spirit or soul of man. Darwin, Huxley, and many other great naturalists, biologists, and scholars, have reasoned and speculated on this theme with great force and logic. They do not claim to be authoritative, and they offer to the expectant world no definite, tangible facts. All is theory. Their reasoning from a material standpoint is unanswerable, and if my authority is no better than theirs these words ought not to be written on this subject. Certainly, I would not assume to treat of a subject so vast without definite information from splendid minds in the higher spheres in the great beyond. I know of no source in this material world where any positive knowledge on the subject can be obtained. Anything definite must, therefore, come from the more advanced planes. If life continues and greater knowledge is acquired, life at some time in its progress will come to know something of the inception or origin of the spirit that is on the earth for a little time to develop character and individuality, and to fit it for the next plane. Some who have obtained such knowledge in their progression have talked to me on this subject.

I do not try to grasp and comprehend the infinite Mind or the spirit-force that holds the universe in place and guides the stars, planets and constellations in their courses, for I know that it takes ages and ages of development and work among the spheres of progression before minds become broad and receptive enough to grasp and to comprehend such teaching. So we in the lowest sphere can at best but touch the outer garment of spiritual knowledge and understanding. The Earth is yet young. When it came into being and was first peopled, millions of other stars and planets, teeming with life, were growing old. Those who had lived on them since the dawn of time had long before met the change and mounted upward, through the spheres of progression surrounding their planets, on the journey to the Sphere of Exaltation. When a spirit enters the Seventh Sphere he throws into the dominant life force all the knowledge and good that he has gathered in his journey toward perfection, and his perfect soul becomes a part and parcel of that power we call universal good. This spirit of good that radiates and permeates around, about, and through every terrestrial body, this life-force that is here and everywhere, is the combined souls of the exalted, and has power to speed embryo life. A spirit speaking from the higher state has said:

**"When matter, according to natural law, becomes receptive, it is impregnated with this life-force of the universe, and with the help of material nature develops a soul. This overpowering spirit-force, so strong and harmonious with Nature, is able to enter into the seed and give the power to live. It is like the touch of a hand that starts a machine into motion. The great spirit of life, called God, is the match to light the fire. Material must be laid ready, for spirit cannot create in earth planes. It is not reincarnation, because individual spirit does not enter. Only the touch that generates life in the material seed is given."**

Before occupation, this life-force was universal. The moment it is clothed, it becomes forever individual. The spirit of man comes from the Sphere of God, or Universal Good, and it returns sometime, enriched and glorified, through the spheres and planes of progression. So it completes the circle and adds its dominant force to the universal spirit that speeds embryo life and holds dominion over all worlds. Little understanding we have of the strength and power of mortal mind. No one here can have much appreciation of the power of one earth-mind after it has developed for ages.

Little will any man ever know in this material world of the power of all the minds that have ever lived in this and all the other worlds, working in perfect harmony as one in the Sphere of Exaltation. Yet to this mighty force in and about us and all the other worlds we give the indefinite name of God. This spirit-force, universal in character, this life that is not visible until clothed, enters, when material is receptive, and substance closes about it. What it becomes, whether vegetable or human, depends on the character of the matter that it inhabits, depends, also, on how much spirituality has entered. Gross matter will not receive as much of the spirit of God as refined material. What further becomes of it depends on the environment, teaching, and effort as it comes to maturity. Children of the base do not receive in the beginning as much of God as the children of those who have developed and who live spiritual lives. The more spirituality one takes on in embryo life the better life he will lead, the nearer to Nature he will come.

Spirit may enter matter and start it on the journey, but does not dominate it. This spirit that is clothed with a body becomes individual, is free to act and free to think. If filled with spirituality, the labor will be easier than for one on the lower planes. But all starting with what Nature was able to give and with what they were able to receive, must work with what was given them; for it is only by labor and trials that character is made and the germ of spirituality increased. Little can be given in the beginning to anyone. All can make much of it, and must, in this or some other sphere, bring it to perfection by gradual growth. Spirit is a seed planted by Nature in each material body. Let the soil be fertile and kept clean, and spirit will develop, adding to the beauty of this and all the worlds to come; but without care of effort, spirit will not radiate; the weeds of vice and wrong will choke and smother, and it will lie dormant within the confines of the unclean substance that does not nourish or aid its development. Without culture and help it will not grow; it will not die; its progress will be stayed by mankind and it will be held in darkness. The spirit within us must have the light shed by kindness, and be watered by tears of sympathy and sorrow for the suffering world. The hand that does good unconsciously cultivates the soil and the hungering soul is nourished. It grows with wonderful speed with such aid, and vibrates within the body it inhabits, drawn outward and upward by the dominant force of good from whence it came. This is the longing, the desire, the hope, the ambition of mankind for better things that speeds men to higher life.

This soul of ours was first a part, then, of the universal spirit of the exalted, which man calls God. It was an atom which in the instant of conception impregnated and entered receptive matter, which clothed with material became individual and commenced its journey on this earth of ours. It must go back through this and the other spheres of evolution and progression to God, whence it came. This is not done in the moment of dissolution, but must be reached by ages of labor in developing and perfecting the soul according to immutable laws. Not one step can be taken until it is earned. No wings will aid this progression to the higher spheres; only honest, earnest work will avail. This is the watchword of future life.

## Great Problems

Though we talk freely, when all conditions are at their best, with men and women after they have passed through the change called death, though we find that they retain consciousness and individuality, and are told much of their occupation and environment, many problems still remain. The spirits do not solve them, because they know little more of the solution than we do. They, like mortals, know what they have been taught only.

One who has worked with the American branch of the Society for Psychical Research and its great thinkers, who has himself made this thought the study of a life-time, read some of these chapters, and asked me pertinent questions, which I submitted to spirit-intelligences. In answering, I use the words given me by spirits as are included within marks of quotation.

What of Creation?

**"The beginning of things was brought about long before this world existed. The universe was in a chaotic state for many centuries, while this solar system was gradually forming and becoming perfected. The great forces were very slowly evolved. The original propelling force came from a mere atom of good, that permeated seething, massing material. This held the tiny element of upliftment. Very slowly light came where there was darkness. Worlds were gradually fashioned. Finally, life began to take on form, —first in vegetable; second, in the lower animal; third, in man. All these simply came from an element of progress, impossible to understand or resist."**

Many seem to think that one out of the body must know all about the universe. My own impression is that if he possessed the information a complete answer requires, he would have advanced so far that he would return only with difficulty.

What of the personality of God?

**"We have tried to explain the personality of God to you before. We have said that we do not know absolutely. Many spirits think that God has personality; others, that God is but the combined soul of men, risen to the sublime height that makes them one with the universe. Spirits, just as mind on earth, form ideas from experience. I, myself, do not think there is a God other than this great united force of good."**

I cannot conceive of a man-God, with personality. The universe is so vast, and this earth and all thereon so small in comparison, that I cannot understand how such a conception could be possible. But, comprehending in some little way the power of one man's mind over matter, I can appreciate the power and force of all minds in the universe working in perfect harmony. I can see God as a principle working universal good. I do not know what God is beyond what is told me. I cannot grasp the infinite; neither can spirits, until they become one with it.

What of the Christian Saviour?

**"Christ was a wonderfully spiritual being. His communion with spirits was unlimited and he lived His life in an exalted state, which made Him seem different from other men—that is,**

of course, believing his life was not a mere legend. If He did live, He could, since He was so spiritual, have risen rapidly to the highest sphere and mingled with those other souls—exalted through gradual purification, —and so fulfilled His inspired promises to mankind. From time to time you have such unusual spirits among men. Religions have been evolved from their lives, all tending to uplift men. Christ was the highest type that has come to us, and the influence for good in the story of His life is still unlimited. I have never seen the so-called Redeemer, nor anyone who had; nor have any whom I know ever found any evidence here that He lived among men."

Why, then, is there conflict between spirit revelations?

Why ask a spirit to tell us now that which he, himself may not learn for a thousand years? Spirits do not know what is beyond them any more than we know what is beyond us. If life is endless progression, how can they? From actually living in the next spheres, they form opinions, based on such information as they have obtained, just as we do on economic questions. Those ideas may be honest, but may differ in conclusions.

I have positive knowledge that there is no death; that it is instead a continuation of earth-life. My neighbor has positive evidence of his present life, but no information as to any beyond, and he denies that life continues beyond the grave. He and I are honest and each maintains his own opinions. So it is with spirit-people. All there, know that life goes on. They know that they live, and think, and act. They see and feel their environment and learn something of the new laws. But it is absurd to expect them to tell us all about the universe, or to what progression leads. They know positively only the conditions that immediately follow earth-life. In this belief all spirits agree. They can only form an opinion based on their knowledge as to life in the further spheres of progression. Therefore, many spirits differ about the creation, about the personality of God, whom they have not seen, about the divinity of the Redeemer they have not found. A conclusion based on an unknown hypothesis is pure conjecture.

It is not necessary or possible at this time for mankind to have positive information concerning the creation or the personality of God. It takes ages of labor and development to reach the sphere where dwells Universal Good. We ask too much of spirits. They know but little more of the creation of God, and of the Redeemer than we do, and one should not expect their opinions to agree regarding life and its conditions in spheres unknown to them.

Those in the same sphere may disagree as to future progression, and still be honest. One may believe that individuality is lost in the Seventh Sphere, while another may believe it continues. These questions are too vast for human comprehension, and are not necessary for human welfare. What we want to know is, does life continue? If so, in what form? Truth is always in harmony with truth, but this does not mean either spirit's or man's understanding or expression of it. I condemn the teachings of no honest spirit concerning life beyond his progression, for he can only express his opinion, as those spirit-intelligences working with me express theirs. They do not differ regarding the lower spirit-conditions, about matters they know as facts. Many mortals, not content to wait until individual development shall enable them to comprehend the answer, ask to know the Infinite, to find God, to see His face, to find a personality, to call Him, Father.

I see good in every act of kindness, in all the words of tenderness that fall from human lips, and to me the universal sum of all the good in all this world is God.

A short time ago I saw a strong man die. Throwing aside the dust that once it wore, a human soul went forth into the night, swift as an arrow sent from the bowstring, leaving no footprint on the trail. His own people were gathered about him, and with aching hearts and tear-dimmed eyes they saw the shadow fall. They did not know how or in what unfamiliar guise the soul left the world of men, —only knew that love and their restraining hands could not cause one hour's delay. Time lost its power and even space could not hold the spirit back. The spirit sped out from the sight of those once held dear. Only thought could follow. Looking upon the mystery of death, we did not see the spirit rise above the clay and mount to a higher sphere, but how can we say that it did not? If so, where and in what plane is this splendid mind that held dominion over the body, now lying inert, senseless, and useless? Is death the end? Is that sleep so deep it never finds its day? This has been a problem of life ever since men came out of savagery, of greater importance than all the aims, ambitions, and desires combined. We fear the mysterious, but fear is lost when understanding comes. All that is natural is good, and all that is good is for mankind.

A great wave of thought is sweeping over the civilized world. Men are not content to remain in ignorance. They are seeking to solve this mystery. They are working in secret. They are hungering for knowledge. They want to know where and in what sphere those they love and hold most dear live and labor. And to those who yearn for definite information regarding the condition of the so-called dead they have lost and mourn, I send this greeting: There is no death, there are no dead. Those who have lived their time and passed from sight, still live and love and labor in the fields of everlasting life. Make the condition that Nature requires, and their voices will speak to you and greet you as of old. Make the condition, and they will write with the old legibility. Make the condition, and the hand of the spirit, clothed for the moment with material, will clasp your hand. Make the condition, and you will see their faces. All these possibilities have been realized by me, as year by year I have made our conditions more perfect.

I want to emphasize this fact, that each one possesses latent psychic qualities which are subject to development in some degree; that in almost every family ordinary investigation will demonstrate that some member will be found who, in harmony with these laws, can get intelligent movement of solids, do automatic writing, see the form, and hear psychically the voice of spirit; and, in rare instances, contribute those qualities and conditions in which spirit-people may clothe their vocal organs and speak with independent voice, vibrating in our mental atmosphere, so that any one can hear as I do. When such research is carried on in the home and results are obtained, they will aid understanding of these laws, because the source cannot be questioned. I have made the experiment in five well-known families and succeeded in four of them. While many others working quietly communicate with their friends out of the body with great freedom, and some I know who, having developed their psychic sight, see members of their family who have gone on, and other spirits, as distinctly as we see mortal.

These laws are all simple and natural. Those things that to mortal minds are mysterious in this philosophy, are called phenomena. But Nature never made anything phenomenal. Things seem so to the undeveloped mentally. Mastery of these laws does not require the labors of the scientist, who is a materialist and only dealing with material, has no comprehension of the laws that govern life. This understanding is within the grasp of the family in any household, and it is from this source that knowledge of these laws must come.

Many great problems cannot be solved by mortal, but the primary question of continuity of life beyond this physical condition and the environment is the first spheres of progression may be learned by almost any household in the world today, by developing those psychic forces there possessed.

## Force is Life! A Mystery Difficult to Comprehend

**"Force, wherever found or however expressed, is life."** These words fell from the lips of a profound spirit psychologist who was talking with me many years ago. I have ever since been trying to comprehend them, but so tremendous is their import that I have not made great headway. I can appreciate that there is force in all matter, and that life is in all substances. What would keep the atoms in touch with each other unless it were the force of attraction? Can we imagine force without matter, or matter without force? Force must be attached to something. We cannot conceive of life in any form except expressed in matter, for we understand that life in every form is governed by law.

Again, there can be no destruction of force. If it disappears in one form, it appears in another form. This law is established in the so-called physical world. It is only in man, the highest expression of life force, that question is raised as to whether or not, when he disappears from the physical, he continues in the spiritual. If there be any who concede this last hypothesis, why not give to the subject a little constructive thought? Reason by analogy with me for a moment. If you reason well, you must concede the following:

There is no limit to space. Time is nothing in the universe. All creation is united, but erected by multitudes of individual atoms, the physical builders of the universe.

There are three physical laws in matter: repulsion, which tears down; attraction, which builds up; and arrangement, which produces form. All life, within a prescribed limit, is destined to be torn down, but all life that passes through the tearing-down limit is destined to continue forever.

By analogy we come to another idea quite as startling—that force, wherever found or however expressed, has intelligence. I do not mean that the force or life in the tree has intelligence equal to man's, but that it must have some intelligence, for it reaches into the soil and draws from it that substance which will clothe it with material suitable to its kind. The same may be said of all vegetable growth. All life in ocean depths exercises intelligence in its search for food and reproduction of its kind. Animals that roam the forests reason; many domesticated animals understand language. The fact that they exhibit love and fear shows that they must reason to some degree, for all will give their lives to protect their young, quite as quickly as humankind.

Life is expressed in force. Force is the evidence of life, and force functions in everything in Nature. No spirit that I have been in communication with knows the exact nature of the creative entity from which force emanates, but it is their understanding that there is a central vibratory source in the highest sphere, outside earth, from which rays radiate, lessening in vibration as they extend outward.

Each planet of necessity functions in that particular position where it is placed; therefore some are in higher and some in lower vibration than our plane, and the inhabitants of some planets, we may assume, are more advanced than we are, although some are lower than we are on this planet. Spirit teachers assert that only those in the highest spiritual development can approach this apex of the universe, that some of the other planets are so intense in vibration that if one in earth conditions should go there he could not see life, any more than we, under normal conditions, can see spirit people, for we can see and come into touch only with those within our own vibration.

Force, being life itself wherever found, is also sexed, and has language or means of communication with forces of its kind. This applies to the mineral, vegetable, and animal, as well as to mankind. Life that finds expression here, in whatever manner, comes from that one central source which we term the Kingdom of God, in which infinite domain is the Master Intelligence which has made the perfect laws which we know as the laws of Nature, governing and controlling the expression, the development, the functioning, of all force in the universe. You and I, and all Nature, have within us an atom of that force, emanating from the Great Intelligence, which, according to His great plan and purpose must at some time develop and return whence it came. So the Life-force, the God-force, is increasing in power from day to day and from age to age. This is necessary in the great plan, that the cycle may constantly expand, one within the other, an endless chain of progression.

Is there one God, in the semblance of a man, who created and personally directs all things in the Universe, who rewards or punishes each soul on a judgment day, to whom we can talk, and on whose shoulders we can cast our burdens? I don't know, and none with whom I am in touch know. Such contention does not accord with known facts, nor does it appeal to reason. One's first reaction is that force can have no personality; but a more careful analysis shows that force not only has intelligence, but must have personality. You and I have within us force, and of necessity, personality; so in a lesser degree all life in Nature has force, although not all life force in nature has developed to the stage where its personality will survive.

"Where is the line of demarcation in individual survival and non-survival?" I asked a learned Etherian. He answered:

**"Every atom that makes up your globe has life-force and personality, but it is only when that life-force has progressed according to Nature's laws, until the individual atom is clothed with material finer than earth substance, that it will have continuity. All life-force below that vibration will re-form, to produce, clothe and protect man, the highest expression of life on your earth. All Nature is working to this end. All life-force which functions on your earth in a flesh garment survives."**

I then asked:

"If you have within our cosmos a part of that living God-force, so that ultimately we shall become a part of that directive force, are we here and now in reality mortal Gods?"

He replied:

**"Embryo Gods! But in the end all will work as one, creating new worlds and peopling them, so that the infinite creative life-force may be increased. Such is our understanding. Nature can no more stand still than the individual. If it did stand still it would begin to decay, for stagnation means dissolution. New stars and constellations are being formed from time to time, as your astronomers know, which ultimately will become peopled, for progress extends throughout the universe.**

**"The minds of all who in ages past have inhabited your earth are even now journeying back to the source from which they came, and will function ultimately in and with that infinite creative force. Destiny is really beyond our comprehension as yet, but the privilege that is ours and yours we should ever have in mind, so that we may make ourselves able to develop to the utmost, wherever we are.**

**"Force, then, as you use that term, is the evidence of life as it functions physically. In fact, force and life are one and the same. All life-force is intelligence and dominating good. The elements are made up of all the right influences, motives, and deeds of all the spirits of eternity. This force grows as the spirit-force is increased, and that force is increased continually by atoms of this force being brought into earth-life through natural conceptions. This is necessary that the cycle may constantly expand, one within another, an endless chain, the greater cycle being that outside an enveloping lesser cycle."**

# CHAPTER 5
## The Drama of Death

*And he showed me a pure river of water of life clear as crystal.*

—Revelation. XXII.I

## The First Condition

The first step in progression is so earth-like it is at first difficult of comprehension. We have been so long taught that the death change is so marvelous, a spirit is reluctant to accept the simple situation. It has been compared to the going from one room into another. While surroundings are changed they are similar; like, yet unlike; but the thought and individuality are in no-wise altered. These are identical; the mode of expression and the touch only are different. This is not what is ordinarily expected, therefore it is oftentimes reluctantly accepted.

I speak now of those who have lived a fairly good life. The inability to touch the bodies of those in earth-life, or to speak so they can hear, together with the meeting with those who have gone before, bring them to appreciate the natural change that has come to them. Then comes the thought of what and where they are. The vision is enlarged, and while they see all that was visible to their material eyes, a mental curtain is parted, and there comes a conception of sights and sounds not possessed before. They find, not a walled city with guarded gates and streets of gold; not a judgement-throne before which they must appear like criminals at the bar of justice; but a simple, natural world; this world spiritualized. They are helpless then, but they soon learn the first principles, and are able, in a measure, to act for themselves. They must learn to seek the truth and know self. These cannot be found in searching

85

for falsehood. Where one has all this life been taught error, he clings tenaciously to old beliefs, —more in fear of punishment than anything else. In time, when he does not find the condition he was told he would meet, and when he finds instead that friends who braved damnation and accepted truth are not burned, courage comes, and old doctrines, faiths, and dogmas are abandoned. Then grows the desire to know the law as it is. There is no real awakening until the earnest crystallizes. Then the spiritual vision broadens, and, first of all, he sees himself. The thoughts of earth-life crowd for recognition. Every act awaits reenactment. The only throne he finds is of his own building; the only judge, himself. He is told that God is universal good, and that only through good shall he find advancement or changed environment, and that good must be of his own gathering. He is taken to the home that his life-work has builded. He is left among those surroundings for reflection, left to think over again the thoughts and deeds of his former daily life. One by one they come, more real than his imagination ever pictured, each claiming his authorship. Little acts of kindness, words of sympathy or encouragement, possibly performed or spoken half unconsciously, return in peace. The vibrations set in motion by some deed of charity are gathered, and in them the spirit is uplifted. He hears again words of thanks for some good done, like distant music. On the walls of this new home, more real than artist can paint, are pictured in many colors, every kind act, deed, and thought, and in retrospections, the heart is filled with unknown joy. The happiness that one gives to others in every-day life is only loaned, and in the hour of awakening it comes back to him who gave it, laden with the joy it carried. One may sow happiness broadcast, like wheat, and, like wheat, it will find fertile soil. The great harvest comes in this hour of need, returning good for good many fold. The doorway will be open, and those who have gone before, who have been helped and aided by the new spirit, come with eager words of thanks and welcome, and in this joy and greeting the material world is for a moment forgotten. This is the home of a good man, a true man, a natural man, one who lived close to the heart of Nature, and did good because he loved it. In this new life his heart is full, his joy unspeakable. The good he did lives and Heaven is about him. But no man's life was all good. This is not possible in the material existence.

If good multiplies and brings much happiness, why should wrong not follow and be intensified, laden with despair? Bad thoughts help to build the same as good. They enter into and become a part of the structure, and are visible to the awakening soul, side by side. Both are to be met; both to be dealt with. The good at some time, in some place, will overcome evil and predominate; but this will be in the spheres beyond. Here, among the beautiful mental pictures that adorn the walls and enter into the substance of the structure, are evil thoughts which show with equal distinctness the record of a man's life. Here, in startling detail, the spirit sees the wrecks he has made, feels the sorrow and hears the words of anguish wrung from lips of suffering because of his cruelty or oppression. Those in spirit whom he has injured appear before his vision, and the evil he has done returns to claim him as its own. He finds he cannot put this burden on another's shoulders, that he must face it and have it always before him, and his soul cries out in agony, "This is Hell." This is the first plane. The home of the spirit, —in part beautiful and in part horrible, in part good and in part bad, —he soon learns it is just as his thoughts builded; that if he would take one unsightly picture from memory's wall he must live the act over, must undo the wrong, and, in living again, must live it right; when he makes compensation for the injury, he finds the act no longer visible to him. And so, one by one, he must live each evil thought or act over, and make it this time in harmony with all that is good. The way will be shown, but the labor is his, and the journey is ofttimes long.

Out of these trials, that which was weakness becomes strength; hard natures become softened, and the spirit, through remorse and suffering, finds greater development. When every harsh word has been recalled, every evil eradicated, each wrong undone, each vile thought made clean, new conditions will surround the spirit. The unsightly pictures and memories will pass away, and this first home of the spirit will become filled with happiness, a fair place to look upon, and one he may proudly call home. This first condition is the lowest plane of the spirit-spheres, and the saddest one. In it the conscience is awakened, and all the wrong, all the evil, ever wrought in knowledge, or wrought in ignorance, must be lived again ere the soul can take one step on the road of eternal progression.

## The Transition

I have had many descriptions of life and conditions from those in the next world, among them the following:

**"I have no recollection of my transition. I awoke and saw the smiling face of Grandmother. It seemed natural, and was intensely real. I had in my illness no thought of dying, so that it did not occur to me at first that she had long before made**

the change known as death. I had been very fond of her. She met me with words of tenderness and love, and gradually explained just what had happened.

"I will not speak of the shock it was to me to witness the grief of my parents. I wished to get up from my bed; with the desire, I was out of it and felt loving arms about me, heard joyous words of welcome, and behold, I was clothed with soft white raiment—this without volition of my own. I was taken to her home, a cottage surrounded with wall and garden where flowers grew in abundance. There I found, in his young manhood, a brother who had passed on in infancy.

"I had much to learn, but there were many to help. I marveled at what could be done by thought. The home and its environment were thought creations, and in a little time, by concentrating my thought and visualizing things desired, they took form and appeared, seemingly out of the invisible, but to me tangible and real. Thus I furnished my room, and hung on the walls thought pictures of those I love.

"But do not imagine we have any magic wand that will enable us to fashion everything desired. We have our limitations, the same as you do. I have now just such a home as is suitable to my condition, but by work I can change, improve, and beautify it. Some people who, in earth life, lived in palaces, now live in hovels, under conditions most deplorable.

"Until now I never knew what it was to be absolutely well. A vitality is within me I had never before known. I feel no weariness with the work I am doing. Another condition that impressed me was that all time is now, and all distance annihilated. We live in the present always, and if we desire to enter another condition within our zone, or go to a place on your plane, we concentrate our thoughts, and we are there. This is to me, even yet, most marvelous.

"You ask of my friends here. The most wonderful thing about this life is the way harmonious spirits get together. The communion of souls spoken of in the Bible is a literal phase of life here. It is the finest and most satisfactory companionship I have known, and so enduring. You just seem a part of them and they of you, for the law of harmony holds you together and makes a perfect union. There is nothing physical about it, of course; it is finer than any physical thrill you have ever known. One feels so contented with this perfect understanding and mingling together. I do not seem to get lonely anymore. I am busy and interested; life on your plane seems like a dream, and now the only time I have really lived."

"What of your occupation and work?" I asked this spirit, who left this world in the dawn of young womanhood, and whom it was my privilege to know. She replied:

"There seems no end of things to do. There are many crippled children here who have never walked, and I have been impressing them with the thought that they are no longer crippled. We have no bodily imperfections, you know, and I am teaching them little dance-steps, and observing their joy as they realize that they can use their legs. I am also going to classes in higher ethics, to understand the way motives and thoughts are power for good or evil. The mind is so powerful, and one's thought react through eternity. The minds of many people are really deplorable. The days fly, and I am very active. The forces are such that one has to work and do something all the time, and comes the satisfaction of accomplishing things. I find more and more congenial people. Life is free and lively, with no restriction in space, time, or energy. If we want to do some particular thing, we seem to have all the energy imaginable to put it through, and we get so much out of it.

"There are those who are constantly influencing people in earth life. I am intensely interested in their work, although I never believed much in it when I was with you. But now I can see the results of wrong thought and I find I can at times prevent a little, and it is interesting to do that. I am going to make a big change in my life here very soon. I mean that I am going to progress a little further; so I am doing more to express myself. That is the great joy of being here. When you get to the stage of self expression, you feel the great thrill of creation, because you are creating yourself and becoming one with the great Power, instead of being moved by higher laws. I do not mean that we are not governed by higher laws. We all are so governed, but progress is an expression of the force of creation, so that when you advance, you feel that you belong to the higher forces and working with them."

## A Soul's Awakening

Experiences and Surroundings Described.

"First of all—I awakened free from pain, care, and toil; no grief, no cold or heat, no thirst or hunger; and above all, the pleasure of being reunited with those I love. Tender arms enfolded me, and I heard the tones of well-remembered friends, long lost, almost forgotten, whispering words of welcome. I gazed around and saw a brilliant, happy circle of loved and loving friends, companions and kindred, beckoning. No more parting, no more death, no more sadness.

"I saw white, spirit cities, long bright roads, embowered in groves and waving trees, and outstretched flowery plains, all full of lovely, happy, busy people, radiant with joy and life. Such was my awakening; such the rest my tired spirit encountered.

"It is only when I return to the earth-plane, and come in contact with grief and sorrow, that I take on earth conditions. I feel no sense of weight. I sped like the lightning's flash through space, on the buoyant waves of ether; I see the dull round globe, at times, far, far below, with its canopy of clouds, and mankind, insect-like, swarming upon the surface. I look up through happy tears to the heavens, so dim to earth, but so gorgeously bright to me.

"Vain would be the effort to speak of things and scenes, modes of life, for which earth has no language or parallel. Some few conditions of this better land of ours I may describe in human speech; more we are not allowed to give, lest it tempt many to end earth life, with work undone.

"Our home is the place where our loved ones cluster, to which our divergent wanderings tend back again. Home is the place where all our tastes find expression, where one may rest, grow, and exchange glad greetings with all he seeks or loves—a place to think in, until we grow ready for another advance. Every spirit has a home, a center of love, rest, and in-gathering of new powers and forces—a place where all one has desired, most wished or longed for, takes shape and becomes embodied in the soul's surroundings.

"Sometimes a spirit gravitates as mine did, to some lonely, church-like hall, a quiet place of inner rest and contemplation, where the past resolves itself into shadowy pictures which come and go, mapping out the minutest event, thought, or word of past earthly life. I saw that ineffaceable record, which every soul must read again and again, as the past returned with its appropriate judgement.

"Many events for which, at the time of their occurrence, I felt regret, I found as inevitable results of previous acts, without which my life would have been incomplete. Deeds and actions on which I had prided myself now showed the littleness from which they sprang; sorrows, which had wrung my spirit, appeared as blessings; and thoughts which I had once lamented, I find to have been inevitable effects. I saw myself to be, as it were, a chemical compound, made up of what I have been, or what I had done, said or thought.

"All things appeared in judgement, and, stranger yet, all that I had and all that I possessed, enjoyed, or saw, the very air I breathed, was tinctured by myself; so that I saw, felt, heard, and enjoyed only as my inner nature colored my surroundings. All things are real around me, but my capacity to know and use them has sprung from my inner self.

"In our land, ideas are all incarnate realities and living things. Nothing is lost in the universe. All that ever has been, can be, or shall be, is garnered up in the ever-present laboratory of being. It is a glorious privilege to roam throughout the endless corridors of time, and still to find an eternity in which to progress."

## The Death Change

What happens at death? What are one's sensations, and what meets the vision on awakening? This has been described thousands of times, and I quote from my records something of what I have been told on the important subject:

"It is a privilege to tell you of my transition. The last physical sensation that I recall was one of falling, but I had no fear—it seemed so natural. At the same time I heard voices speaking words of encouragement, voices that I recognized as those of loved ones that I thought dead. For a time I had no recollection. Then I awoke in this spirit sphere, and never will I forget the joy that was mine. I found myself, saw my body, which appeared as usual, except lighter and more ethereal. I was resting on a couch in a beautiful room filled with flowers. I looked through a window and saw the landscape, bathed in rose-colored light. There was a quiet that was impressive, then music, the harmonious vibration of which seemed to rise and fall softly. Then one appeared, and, though she spoke no words, I seemed to understand and answered. In this thought language she told me that she had been my guardian while in the old body, and now that I had been released she would take me over the home that I had in my life been building.

"She said: 'This room so beautiful is the result of your self-denial and the happiness you brought to others, but there are others not so pleasing;' and we passed into another that was dark and filled with rubbish; the air was heavy. 'This,' my guide said, 'was builded through my selfishness.' Then to another, a little better lighted. I was told that every effort to do better created something brighter. Then into the garden where, among beautiful flowers, grew obnoxious weeds, the result of spiritual idleness. 'The house must all be made beautiful,' she said, 'the weeds of idleness uprooted; and this can be done by yourself, through work in the lower planes, by helping others.'"

My father's experience he described to me as follows:

"You will recall the day of my dissolution. I had been in poor health for some months. That mourning the air was so soft and warm, and the sun so bright, I wanted to be out in it, so I took my horse and buggy and started for a village about seven miles distant. As I drove along, a weakness seemed to come upon me and I partially reclined upon the seat. Even then, though seventy-six years of age, I had no thought that my passing was near. As I arrived at the house where I was going, the sensation of weakness increased, but I was able to walk in unaided and sat in a chair. The faintness increased, and, raising my eyes, I saw your mother standing in the room, smiling. Startled, I arose to my feet, and my last earthly sensation was falling—and, as I now know, I did pitch forward on my face. I do not recall striking the floor, or pain in my death change. When the separation came, I was like one in sleep. The next I recall was awakening in the same room, with the leader of your spirit group holding my hand, helping me up. I had heard his wonderful voice many times when I was privileged to come into your work, but it took me some little time to realize what happened to me. I saw my body on the floor. This startled me, for the body I then had was to my sight and touch identical with the one lying so quiet. I saw people hurrying, and heard the anxious talk, not yet comprehending my separation from the physical body. I turned to your old friend, and mine, and asked him what had happened. He answered:

"'Have you not been told when you talked with us in your son's home, that death was the separation of the inner from the outward body?'

"'I recall that statement,' I replied, 'but I never comprehended it.'

"'You have just made that change,' he said; 'you are now an inhabitant of the spirit world and one of us.'

"I was deeply impressed with what he said, but dazed. I could not realize that the something called death was behind me and that in me there had been no change, for I was the same in appearance and thought as before. Then memory quickened, and I commenced to think of what it meant. I could not think clearly, and my guide said, 'Come with me for a little time and rest, and all will be well with you.' I went with him, and those I saw and what I was I will tell you another time."

This is another's description.

"I remember seeing about me those that had been dead for a long time. This impressed me greatly, but I did not realize it fully. Then I felt a peculiar sensation all through my body. Then I seemed to rise up out of my body and come down quietly on the floor.

"I was in the same room, but there seemed to be two of me, one on the bed and one beside the bed. All about were my family in deep grief, why I could not tell, for my great pain was gone and I felt much better. Some of those whom I recognized as persons who had died, asked me to go, and with that thought I was outside and could apparently walk on air. My next thought was that it was a dream and that I would awake and feel again the terrible pain. I was gently told what had happened, and I felt that God had been unjust to take me when I had so much to do, and when I was so needed by my family. I was not satisfied with the place I was in. About me there was a fog, and I started to walk out of it, but the farther I walked the more dense it got, and I became discouraged and sat down by the wayside in deep grief. I had ever tried the very best for those dependent on me. Where was my reward? Then some one approached, came as it were out of the fog, and I told him of my life work and complained of the condition I was in, and questioned the justice of it. He replied, 'Yours was a selfish love; you worked for self. You should have made others happy as well as your own.'

"He promised to help me in my great trouble, if I would help myself. Together we have worked, and now all is well; it is light and glorious. But that first awakening was not all that could be desired. My greatest disappointment after my awakening was when I returned to my old home, for I discovered that none could see or feel me and all grieved for me as one dead, and their sorrow held me. I wept with them, and could not get away, until time healed their sorrow."

How terrible it is that the world that has made so much progress in many things knows little of this greatest change, and the little it does know has almost been forced upon it by a few that know this truth and have the courage to stand for it.

These descriptions, as I review what I have written, do not give a fair idea of an average death change, and looking through my records I find another more normal:

"I left the physical world rich. I had little money, but day by day, during a fairly long life, by some act I made others happier, and so spiritualized and uplifted my spirit. Such was my only religion.

"When the separation approached, though I had no actual knowledge of what was to come, I had no fear. I had been very sick, felt greatly exhausted, and longed for rest. I realized the presence of my family and their grief. There came to my senses harmonious vibrations that sounded afar off, like string and reed instruments played by master hands. It seemed to approach and then recede, and was lost. It soothed and comforted me. Then I realized that others were in the room. I could not see their faces distinctly, and wondered at strangers coming in at such a time. Some one spoke, and, rousing up, I saw more clearly and recognized many of my friends whom I had thought dead.

"I was not startled or frightened—it was all so natural. They greeted me cordially and asked me to go with them. Without effort, other than desire, I arose and joined them and went with them, for the moment forgetting the grief of my family. I seemed to travel without effort. Then I met a great company of men and women with radiant faces, clothed in white and blending colors. Their greeting was one of joyous welcome, and happiness was in everything. It was like meeting old friends that had been gone for a time; it was simply glorious and so intense that for a time I gave no thought to the tremendous import of it all. Then I looked about. There was harmony in everything. I was in a new country. About me I saw great variety of landscape, most picturesque mountain ranges, valleys, rivers, lakes, forests, and the corresponding vegetable life of all that I had known. It was suggested that I go to a rest house, where my strength would be restored. I did and seemed to fall into a deep sleep almost immediately. After a time I awoke, when some one whom I knew and loved said, 'Come with me now and view your inheritance.' I went, and the glory of it was, and is, beyond my power of description.

"I should like the privilege some time to tell the world of the beauty in which I live, and the pleasure I find in the work allotted to me. This plane, and all planes, I am told, is governed by law—Nature's law, the same as yours—and it is the privilege and duty of every one to develop the spirit by study and helping others. There is so much I should like to say of my return to my family, but, as I am asked only to describe my spirit passage, I will leave that and tell you more concerning the joy of the spirit at some more opportune time."

There are those in the next life who have qualified for, and are assigned to, the reception department, whose duty it is to solace and comfort such as are grief-stricken because of the sudden severing of social ties, as it seems to those taken suddenly out of the mortal. This is a description:

"I am here to describe as well as I can the actual scenes over here, as the new born spirits, divested of their physical bodies, come over. They come to us, not one or two or three, but in crowds, by thousands and more, some not awakened to consciousness, some just waking, some fully conscious. Few realize for some time that they have passed the portal you call death, but a realization comes and they understand, their thoughts are of their strongest ties.

"What a commotion of feeling one hears! The same intense feelings exist when out of the old body as when in the physical, and those feelings are just as discernible to spirit sensation as before, only the mode of expression and reception is changed.

"As I was feeling my soul leaving the physical sheath, I heard mysterious chords of rhythmic melody rising and falling like distant waves of the sea. A voice said in thrilling gentleness:

'My child, pass from vision into luminous light, from night to day, from death to life.'

"Then a light beating slowly passed away from about me and to my utter amazement I found myself resting at a place quite free and transcendent with divine light. A deep and gentle sound vibrating through the etheria firmament filled me with joy and happiness, and nothing was perceptible to me except this vibration of the sound. I felt that I must wait till a divine messenger came to guide me into the regions yet unseen. The atmosphere of awe and reverence that swept over me for the moment gradually paled away and, rising as I thought, I walked through the darkness which then encompassed me. As I did this, my other hand was suddenly caught by some one in a warm and eager clasp and I was guided along with an infinitely gentle but commanding touch, which I had no hesitation in obeying. Step by step I walked with a strange sense of happy reliance on my companion and guide. Darkness and distance had no misgivings for me. And as I went onward with my hand yet held in that masterful but tender grasp, my thoughts became, as it were, suddenly cleared into a light of full understanding of the celestial world and its joy. And so I went on and on, caring little how long the journey might be and even eagerly wishing that it might continue, when presently a faint light began to peer through darkness, first blue and grey, then white, and then rose. The light, so sublimely luminous, gradually condensed into matter, and in a moment a celestial being of beauty, richly wrapped up in pure white and silken robes, stood before me. After the thrilling sensation, caused by this sudden manifestation, had given a little way for courage and hope, I beheld the same figure transforming into an almost manly and commanding attitude, with radiant face and brilliant eyes now turned towards me. It asked, in a gentle but firm tone, whether I would like to remain there in the ethereal world and enjoy the pleasure stored up for me as a requital for my past life on the earth plane. Overwhelmed with awe and respect, I could give no answer. Seeing me thus puzzled, my guide placed his right hand upon my forehead and a gentle massage filled me with strength and fresh energy.

"I became bold and courageous, looked my visitor in the eyes, and knelt before him. He lifted me up gently and said I could for a time remain in those ethereal regions where all was pleasure and happiness. He said the place I was then in was the destination of those who spend their lives and energy on earth for the sake of their fellow-creatures, people who do great deeds for the uplift of the oppressed and harassed, —the abode of people who showed equal compassion to both men and beasts. This was my welcome, such my second birth. This was my greeting when I crossed the frontiers of the After Life."

## Spirit Passage

Every particle of matter that goes to make up this visible body of ours came from the ground, and it must go back to the ground. Nature in her wisdom has provided on some part of the earth's surface all that mankind requires to make his natural growth, to maintain the waste that is going on day to day. Consider for a moment the construction of the body, consider what it uses, and the widely different parts of the world from which its needs are supplied. The water that runs in streams, flows in brooks, and falls as rain comes to us in every form of vegetable life we use. Wheat, born in the dark, like all life, shoots upward to the light, clothed in garments of green, reaches maturity, and, waving in yellow fields, awaits the reaper's scythe in many lands. Tea comes from China, coffee from Java, spices from the island Ceylon, meats from the grazing lands of the West and the blood is purified and made red by the winds that sweep through great forests and over the bosom of the waters. The whole world contributes to this earthly habitation of ours, which wastes and is repaired day by day, changing completely once in seven years. We do not wear the clothing now that we did seven years ago; neither do we inhabit nor wear the same body. Why, then, is the last moving out any more to be feared than any previous change?

We are only tenants in this house of the body for a limited time, and when it becomes unfit for habitation, through disease or accident, we move out, we separate from it, and the material body, that cannot hold its force without nourishment, decays and mingles with the earth from which it was borrowed. So far as I know, no man has ever attempted to describe the final separation of the spirit from the body, in the change called Death. Indeed, such a description from this material plane is impossible. With the ability to talk with those beyond, I have been able to obtain descriptions of the separation of the spirit from this temporary home. Not long ago an eminent judge, about six o'clock one evening, while at work, passed away. At nine o'clock the same night he was brought to me in his spirit body and I talked with him with the same freedom and satisfaction as I had only a few days before. I asked the one who brought him, how he was able to come so soon. He replied, **"I met a friend this afternoon and he told me that the judge was coming, and suggested that we go down and witness the separation. We did so, and brought him here that he might the more quickly appreciate his condition."**

Among the stenographic notes taken eight years ago, I find the following description of a spirit-passage, given by a spirit who with his company of spirit-workers aids the great change to the after-life:

"But a few hours ago we were called to help in the separation of the spirit from the body. Lying before us was a young woman. When we say 'young,' we mean in maturity. Bodily pain and sickness had been hers, and now dissolution was taking place. The one who should have given her words of encouragement and help was on his knees praying to the God of mercy to give her strength to pass through the terrors of death. About her on every side were weeping friends. She knew they were grieving because she was leaving the body and it made the passage darker and harder. The first bodily chill touched the feet. Slowly, little by little, it was creeping upward until it reached the knees. A light began to rise, a clouded substance, gradually increasing in size. Closer approached the loved ones who had gone before. They were waiting and watching and giving her strength, that she should not feel herself alone and that she should not think all was darkness and terror. We saw her face brighten, her lips part in a smile. She saw us close about her. Her hand raised slowly and she whispered, 'They are coming. I see them all. They are waiting for me.' The light from the body rose higher, slowly creeping up, just as a white fleecy cloud settles before a storm over the earth. She did not appreciate that a change was coming over her, she only realized that friends were standing near. She did see the weeping ones as it grew brighter. She heard a faint echo, as of music, a song of gladness coming to her in this cloud of change. It took definite form just above her. The brain weakened, the eyes drooped, she slept with the loving voices speaking. The music was not heard by mortal.

"The spirit was taken out, was held just above the body, with gentle hands, and then she met the loving friends. Her eyelids were lifted, she saw one who had waited for her, whose every thought was in unison with her own. How was it that she, just released from the body, could see all this? Because she had lived a life according to her light and understanding. She will not have to go back to earth and take up a consciousness that would have been compulsory had her life been one of lying and deceit. When she touched the hand of the mother who had gone ahead, she realized that there was a condition between them, but that little by little it would be removed and that she would enter into the home that awaits her.

"She wept, not as you weep, but through happiness, through joy in the fact that she had met the mother-love, that they had come together again where all the conditions of earth are swept aside. She saw herself as she is and as she was. She realized that at times in the earth-life she was human. She regretted and asked her soul to forgive. As she advances farther into this realm of thought, into this new condition, into this perfect life, she will see no darkness, and all shall be well."

By the destruction of matter, life multiplies. Through decay of material, the life force increases. Through separation the spirit is liberated. Released from the confines of an earthly body, it finds greater scope, more opportunities, better advantages, continual progression. This spirit passage is natural. It comes to all living things. Every step on growing grasses crushes life into life, separates it and forces it from its temporary abode, from the material covering it has gathered. Through some seeming destruction vegetable life, like human life, is liberated. The journey of evolution is hastened, and the perfect life is more quickly.

## The Awakening

When the journey is done and the night is passed, all must awake and open eyes in another world. What happens and what thoughts speed with them through the brain? I asked a spirit, well known in this life, to describe the awakening. This was his answer:

"It is usually hard for a spirit to get its breath in the different atmosphere; the earth conditions cling to it; this it must shake off and it must then adjust itself to the new surroundings. So the first condition is purely physical, or rather, mental. A spirit feels this change, yet does not understand why it is different. It gasps and struggles. This is soon over and forgotten. Then it is taken to a home it has built—on its own—and left to realize things a little. Some spirits are in a condition that admit of immediate help and counsel, but others are dazed and must have quiet and time in which to be alone. When a spirit is able to comprehend, its past life comes before it like a panorama. The good thoughts and their results are arranged on the one side; the evil thoughts and their results, on the other. Then begins heaven and hell. The poor soul realizes, perhaps for the first time, how much evil he has wrought, and his spirit is in torment, for he thinks there is no reparation. When this phase of his punishment is over, he is shown how, by influencing thought in earth-life, he may wipe out the consequences of each sin. Then comes peace from the torture of remorse. I am speaking of the average man, with the average conscience. Some there are who have led lives that need very little of this punishment. Others must wallow for a long time in the mire of their own sad sins, —too vile or too timid to find a way out.

"There is another phase. One who has strong earth ties will be held by them, so that spirit-friends cannot get it away at first. The ties may be of different kinds, —family, business, or simply selfish, animal ones; in any such case progression is slower. One who is thoroughly bad, who is surrounded by his own sin, sees nothing else.

"These, as I understand, are earthbound; that is, they cannot sunder the material conditions which made up their lives. In the earth-life, they never lived on the higher planes; they had little, if any, spiritual development, and so across the frontier they practically live on this material plane although in another way. It will take a long time, and some unusual incident, to awaken these to their true condition. Some men are blind to all but material interests, and the spirits of these are blind to all interests except those embraced within their limited plane. One can no more see beyond this condition than we can see beyond ours. There is no advancement for such men, or for any man, until the desire comes from within. We can catch a glimpse of the next plane and hear voices. So can they, but progression will not be given fully until they are prepared to receive it. It may be said that many, many in this life are today more progressed than some who have gone to the lowest plane of spirituality; for in the change they unconsciously pass directly to the next condition beyond. Those who pass the lower sphere of the earth condition may at first only reach the second plane of the same sphere. They cannot reach the higher planes, because they are not fitted. They must go among those of like character to themselves, in a like condition with themselves. The unclean spirit cannot go into a pure atmosphere, because they would contaminate it. These will find themselves surrounded with the thought matter they have taken with them, to the home they have made, and all the other homes and all the other people they see will have similar conditions and like homes. This may be called the first conscious sphere, the plane of restitution.

"When the soul awakens here and sees about him the wrongs he has committed and those that others have committed, the effect of those wrongs and the condition produced by them, great remorse will come."

This condition of awakening has been described, perhaps unconsciously, by Theodosia Garrison in stronger words than I can use.

> The three ghosts on the lonesome road
>    Spake each to one another,
> "Whence came that stain about your mouth
>    No lifted hand may cover?"
> "From eating forbidden fruit,
>    Brother, my brother."
> The three ghosts on the sunless road
>    Spake each to one another,
> "Whence came that red burn on your feet
>    No dust or ash may cover?"
> "I stamped a neighbors hearth-flame out,
>    Brother, my brother."
> The three ghosts on the windless road
>    Spake each to one another,
> "Whence came that blood upon your hand
>    No other hand may cover?"
> "From breaking a woman's heart,
>    Brother, my brother."
> "Yet on the earth clean men we walked,
>    Glutton and Thief and lover;
> "White flesh and fair it hid our stains
>    That no man might discover,
> "Naked the soul goes up to God,
>    Brother, my brother."

These stains must be washed away; these unsightly burns healed before the pathway shall cease to be lonely, before peace and happiness shall come to the suffering, wandering soul. Such wrongs, such crimes, are the burdens one carries. The sunless way is long and the journey is weary; joy is not a companion; but there is a way that leads to spiritual health, a way, called reparation.

There are those who lived so close to Nature, who were so true to neighbors and to themselves, who developed the spirit and clothed it in garments of harmony, that in dissolution they awake in the sphere of understanding, beyond these earth conditions. Nature takes them to the most advanced condition they are qualified to enter. It works on the same principle as a school here below. A child ignorant of the multiplication table does not go into higher mathematics. It is graded according to qualification. This next life is Nature's University and in it she teaches morality and spirituality. It, too, has many grades, and one is classified according to progress and development. No one possesses perfect character; but those who have done their best, who have listened to the voice of conscience, feel the touch of loving hands and hear the words of welcome as they unconsciously speed through the planes of darkness and despair. They had builded on the high land where the sunlight always touches and the shadows never fall. These, too, in their quiet hours of contemplation see conduct in its true light, and will not be content to go on, even if they could, until acts that were harsh are softened, words that were unkind, recalled. The way will be shown to these, and they will be anxious to cheer mortal and spirit whose burden they have increased. The weary will know who is helping, and will bless the hands that help. What joy will fill the hearts of those who have lived honest lives, when they awaken as peacefully as dawn touches the mourning, and find death behind them and its terror gone; when they see those whom they mourned coming with radiant faces, in eager greeting; mother, wife, children, all there to show the love that has been waiting. Words are meaningless in any attempt to describe such joy! If the world only understood this law, men would strive so to live that they might reach this condition at once. Knowledge is always a ray of light. The sun touches the mountaintops before it reaches the valleys. It never penetrates the caves, where ignorance and prejudice dwell.

If these writings awake and call only one man from the cavern of doubt, and show him the path that leads to the heights of understanding, I shall be paid for all my labors.

## Told in the Afterlife

If there is one thing this world ought to know, does not know, and wants to know, it is the process in which and by which an inhabitant of this plane of consciousness leaves the physical body to become an inhabitant of the next or etheric plane. I speak of the earth and the etheric plane, of a here, and a hereafter that I may be understood, but technically this, the next, and all planes of existence are one, differing only in vibratory activity, or modes of motion. The universe is all a part of the stupendous whole.

Only one who has made the great change, can adequately describe conditions under which people live in the sphere beyond. For many years I have been exchanging with other psychic scientists reports of conditions and lectures from this source. T.W. Stanford of Australia sent me a communication from the after-life received by him, which my group says is a statement of fact, and, therefore, with his permission I quote it as follows:

"**In my weakness I became unconscious of all around; but soon I became conscious of several things. I realized that something that had held me down and fatally gripped me was gone. I was free, and in the place of weakness and pain and sickness, I had a virility and a vigor which I had never known upon the earth plane. I was also aware that I was in new surroundings, most beautiful. Then I became conscious that I was in the midst of a company of fellow souls, whose voices were filled with happiness, all welcoming me, and others whom I had temporarily lost while upon the earth plane. I then knew that some great change had occurred which had taken from me everything that I had desired to get rid of, or some power, had given to me a delightful experience, which I had often in a measure imagined, but dared scarcely believe that it could be possible.**

"**Surrounded by an innumerable company, I was quite dazzled with the appearance of some who, it was explained to me, were exalted personages. Then there approached one who seemed to be the chief speaker. He said, before me was the universe, that time was for me no more, that I was henceforth an inhabitant of a new country. You will ask me, —was it all pleasant? Extremely so. How can I illustrate it so that you will understand? Have you ever, after taking a long journey, become extremely tired and weary, and, at last, at the end of much striving and travelling, come to a house of rest? How you sank down upon the downy couch. Oh, the delight of it! With no dreams to disturb your rest, you awoke like a giant refreshed! To me it was something like that; although even that is a weak illustration. But that which brought me greatest happiness was the knowledge that I had gained what I had once believed I had lost. I had health, strength, vitality, friends, and relatives restored to me forevermore.**

"**I have always been fond of the beautiful. I have spent days, weeks, and months in the picture galleries of Europe, looking at the work of the old masters. Many of them lived hundreds** of years before I came upon the earth plane, and yet I seemed to have known them all the days of my life. I have dreamed about them. Da Vinci has always been my companion; Murillo, a choice comrade; for Giotto I had a deep, lasting friendship. I loved the beautiful in all its forms. I loved Nature, —the beautiful lakes of Italy and Switzerland, the glorious mountains, the everlasting hills. My friends in spirit life said to me, 'Come and see the House Beautiful.' Try and understand, if you can, that not only are the landscapes spiritual, but so is the beauty of all that there is on the other side of life. The physical is only the gross imitation of the spiritual. There is no tongue which can describe the beauty of the spiritual realms, wherein are the souls of those who have just entered on their progressive existence, —souls who have striven to do their best according to their light. I say that there is no tongue that can describe the beauties of that land. Take the best that you have, and it is poor in comparison. Then I came next to the spiritual houses, and there I met with more friends, more relatives, and, greater, grander still, with those royal souls who have been my affinities on earth, —been companions, comrades of the brush and palette, and others whom I had deeply reverenced in my soul.

"But I found them much greater, grander, nobler than they ever were in their earth life, and I was privileged to be one of their companions. Still I pressed onward. I came to a Rest House. That will sound peculiar. You will say, how can you have rest houses, if you don't know what it is to be weary? No, there is no weariness like that you have experienced on earth; but there are rest houses, where in the spiritual life we may rest and have delightful intercourse with our friends. In the spiritual rest house, therefore, we entered, and found there relatives and friends. Somewhere not upon the same plane of existence as I was, but they had been permitted to come down to my sphere to meet me, so that in effect I could say, 'He that was dead is alive again, he that was lost for a time is found.' And then memory, think of the joy of memory! I had carried personality and memory into the spirit world, and I compared the existence in Rome with that which I was then enjoying. I tell you that it was the expectance of what was still to be which gave me the greatest pleasure and the greatest joy. There is no joy on earth like that which is in Heaven, for it is unalloyed.

"I became conscious that I had to do something, and that I should have to work, and it was a joy. Could I be a messenger? I thought of some on the earth plane I had loved so dearly, and remembered that they were in spiritual darkness. I inquired, 'Where is the Heaven of orthodoxy?' 'It does not exist,' was the answer. But my friends were in darkness, and a yearning came that I might go to them and tell them what I knew. I wanted to say, 'Do not be mistaken; there is some-thing better, brighter, grander, nobler for human souls than has been taught you.' I was told that I could return, and became conscious that I could communicate with those still on earth if I found a certain channel, an avenue, an instrument. How could I find it? 'All things are yours,' is the promise. Therefore I must find the way and the instrument. This I did, and you have helped me. That is the work which I am doing, and it gives me increased happiness.

"I was told that there were greater beauties of the spiritual landscape which I had not yet seen, and which I could not yet understand, because the universe is illimitable. There is something overpoweringly grand in the thought that you are not cramped or shut up in a small space of a few millions of miles. No, this universe is vast, and the field is mine to explore. It became mine by right. I had worked for it. Take special note of that. I was to work and earn the right to explore God's dominions, and get happiness from every place, state and condition of my spiritual existence.

"Do you like grand architecture? From what source do you think that the old Greeks got their first designs? Phidias and Praxiteles were, no doubt, the greatest Greek sculptors. There were wonderful architects in those days. When I was upon the earth plane, I made a nine months' tour of Greece, Rome, and Sicily to make a study of the architecture and the ancients. I visited every temple, whether in ruins or in perfect order, and I tell you they are heaps of stones, they are utterly beneath contempt compared with the spiritual architecture of the homes and houses in the spirit world. If you have a spiritual body, there is no reason why you should not have a spiritual house. Get rid of the idea that you are a puff of wind in the life hereafter. Even wind may be solidified, for wind is atmosphere in motion, and it is possible to solidify the atmosphere. Then I came to the inhabitants of that spirit world. I had never previously believed or dreamed that these could exist in such beautiful forms. To most people, beauty of form is a source of joy and comfort. The Greeks and the Romans loved beauty of form, and I know that you do likewise. I saw the most exquisite forms as I progressed, and every day, to use language which you will understand, I met with some that I had previously known upon the earth-plane, and what words can tell you the joy of it? To some of them I had done little acts of kindness. And let me impress upon you that of all the pleasure I have received on the spirit side of life, the most came from those to whom I had previously done some act of kindness. If I had my earth life again, I would spend every hour in doing good, —I would spend my life in doing acts of kindness.

"In our spiritual rest houses we frequently meet, not only with loved ones, but with those whom we reverenced and adore. We make also new acquaintances. We get a knowledge of great and grand souls, and come in contact with them. After a time, I was appointed by an Intelligence to do a certain work. I was to help others to see the light, and I had permission to come back to the earth again. Then my instructor said, 'That which will give you the greatest pleasure, do.' Then I came back.

"I have met with many great and noble characters, who lived upon the earth plane. I am frequently in the companionship of those whom I loved, and I have never yet found cause for offense, and never will. No one has entered into my surroundings who has caused me a moment of sadness. On the earth-plane even your best moments are clouded because someone in your midst was objectionable to you; but each one on the spirit side has gravitated to a certain spiritual level. If he be good, then his spiritual status is good, his affinities will be good, and those who come in immediate contact with him will be good also. There will be no one to offend.

"So vast are the realms or dominions of Nature that in the few years that I have been on the spirit side of life, I have been able to explore but little. When I have been upon the etheric plane for some billions of years I shall perhaps have seen a little of it. But throughout the countless ages of eternity I shall be evolving, developing, getting knowledge and light and wisdom. I shall become in tune with the infinite.

"What there is beyond, I do not yet know. Even on our side of life we are not given more knowledge than we can make use of for the time being. It is all a matter of progression. I have told you that we all have to work. There are no drones. But it is work that is congenial and satisfactory; it is a labour of love. It is appointed by a Higher Intelligence; it is given to you to do; and if you do it, your progress and happiness are assured. Realize that there is no coercion on the spirit side of life, but the spiritual eyes are opened to their responsibility. They see everything at a glance. In the spirit side of life you are not left in any doubt. You have full knowledge that to obey is better than to sacrifice, and to do the will of God is to bring happiness in your progressive existence, throughout eternity. Mothers have had their children taken away by death, and the bereaved ones say, 'We have lost our children.' You have not lost them. They may have been lost from vision for a while. Perhaps there are some here tonight who laid to rest in cold earth a little form, a sweet child. I do not seek to stir up your feelings, but you remember how the burning tears came to your eyes; you rebelled in your soul when a child was taken away. There was an aching void in your heart and you murmured. That life was only taken and planted in another garden, and when you get on the other side, you will know your child. But not as a babe, for all grow to full spiritual stature, radiant, glorious in immortality, with souls filled with love for you, nevermore to part.

"Is it not worth striving for? There is no condemnation to those who are good, those who are living the life, those who are seeking to do that which is right. Let me tell you, that the time is coming when all earth problems, religions, and theology, will pass away. Men are tired of such discussions. They are sick in their soul of being told to trust in another; they cannot fathom the scheme or plan of salvation, but they do know that around them is a world of misery, of unhappiness and shortcomings. It is only the true spiritual philosophy which teaches man to rely upon himself and become his own saviour by being true to himself. There is no religion higher than truth. To serve God he must serve man. That pleases the Father, and continues eternally. We must become servants of each other."

## A Conscious Dissolution

"Yes, I know that I am no longer an inhabitant of the earth sphere, that I am numbered among the dead; so because I thoroughly understand the great change through which I have passed, the group of spirit people working with you, and controlling conditions on this side, have asked me to speak to you, and through you to all those in sorrow for their dead. You know, of course, that in speaking I am now using my own voice."

Out of the silence, out of the darkness, in a room devoted solely to psychic investigation came those words; one whom the world calls dead was speaking. I have never ceased to be startled when a voice first speaks from the invisible world—so unusual, so marvelous, so wonderful, and yet to me, so natural. I know of but two psychics who are able to contribute to conditions that make the direct or independent voice possible. Emily S. French, who devoted to my work the best years of her life, was one of them, and on this occasion she was alone with me in the room in my own home devoted solely to such work. At this time the conditions were such that it was possible for those out of the earth body to so talk that their voices were audible.

The public wants to know, and I always wanted to know, the sensation involved in the death change, in the awakening; what it is that the eyes behold, or the ears hear when first consciousness continues or returns. So when this man spoke so clearly and strongly, I determined from one who had made the change a comprehensive statement of the mental state, not only before but after the transition.

"So much," I said, "of the information that we get from the plane where you now live is general in character, won't you be specially specific and tell us, first, something of your occupation and of the conditions immediately preceding your dissolution?"

**"I came,"** he replied, **"from a long line of soldiers. My ancestors fought in the American Revolution, and were among those who aided in establishing your Republic; possibly I inherited a martial spirit. When the first shot was fired by the Confederates, and Lincoln issued his call for volunteers, I was possessed with a desire to enter the army. I had a wife and two children, to whom as I now know, I owed a far greater duty than to my country, but the speech of people, the danger of the nation, the condition of slavery prevailing in the Southern States, and the preparation for war, incited me. With forced words of good cheer, I left brave wife and little children, enlisted, and became a soldier in the Union.**

**"I will not take the time to tell you of my life in the army, except to speak of the nights in camp when my thoughts went out to those at home, knowing as I did that funds were slowly diminishing. Ever the idea was dominant that the war would**

be soon over, then there would be the home coming, and the plans I formed to make compensation for my long absence would come to fruition. But the war did not end as battle after battle was fought with success first on one side, then on the other. I participated in many, seeming to bear a charmed life, for while thousands about me fell, I passed unharmed, and so grew fearless."

"Under what circumstances did you meet your end?" I asked.

"It was at Gettysburg," he replied. "I can see and feel it all over again as my mind concentrates on that tragic event. It was the second day of that great fight. I was then a colonel and commanded a regiment in reserve; in front of us the battle roared. Shot and shell filled the air and fell near us, muskets belched forth their fire, the earth seemed to tremble; wounded in great numbers were carried to the rear, and we knew that countless dead lay where they had fallen. We waited, knowing it was only a matter of hours, possibly minutes before the order would come to advance. I looked down the line at blanched faces, we all knew that many would not answer the roll call at night. Still we waited. Suddenly out of the smoke galloped an officer from the general's staff. 'Forward,' came the command.

"There was no faltering now that the hour had come. The column moved. Soon shot and shell fell among us, on we went. All was excitement, fear was gone; we had but one desire, and that was to kill; such is the lust of battle. I recall but little more. We reached the front and saw the grey line charging up the hill toward us; then, oblivion. I now know that I was shot."

"Tell me of returning consciousness and what you saw," I said.

"You must remember," the spirit answered, "that these tragic events occurred nearly half a century ago, and that at that time it had not been discovered that there is another life, a plane as material as the one you now inhabit, where life continues. I had no conception of a hereafter, for with all my religious teaching I had no idea of what or where the future life might be; nor was I at all sure there was one; so you can imagine how startled I was to awake as from a deep sleep; bewildered I got to my feet, and looked down and saw my body among many others on the ground. This was startling. I made a great effort to collect my thoughts and recall events. Then I remembered the awful battle; still I did not then realize I had been shot. I was apart from, still I seemed in some way, held to the body and yet separate and apart from the covering I had thought constituted the body.

"I tried to think and realize my situation. I looked about; others of the seeming dead moved, seemed to stir. Then many of us stood up, and like me seemed to emerge from their physical bodies, for their old forms still lay upon the field. I looked at other prostrate bodies, examining many; from each something was gone. Going among them again, I found other bodies inhabited, still living as you would say, though wounded and unconscious.

"Soon I found myself among thousands in a similar mental state. Not one among them knew just what had happened. I did not know then as I do now, that I always possessed a spirit body composed of material called Ether, and that the physical body was only the garment it wore while in the earth life."

"What brought you to the full realization of what had happened?" I asked.

"I am coming to that," he said; "While the passing out of the old body was without pain, it is a terrible thing to drive a strong spirit from a healthy body, tear it from its coverings. It is unnatural, and the sensation following readjustment is awful. In a short time I became easier, but I was still bewildered. It was neither night nor day; about us all was gloom, not a ray of light, nor a star. Something like an atmosphere dark and red enveloped us all, and we waited in fear and silence; we seemed to feel one another's thoughts, or to be more correct, hear one another think. No words were spoken. How long we remained in this state I cannot now tell, for we do not measure time as you do. Soon there was a ray of light that grew brighter each moment, and then a great concourse of men and women with kindly faces came, and with comforting words told us not to fear; that we had made the great change; that death, so-called, only advanced our sphere of life; that we were still living beings, inhabitants now of the first plane beyond the earth; that we would live on forever, and by labor reach a higher mental development; that for us the war was over, we had passed through the valley of death.

"I will not attempt to tell you of the sorrow that came with such a realization, not for myself, for I soon learned that only through death could we progress, and that the personal advantages beyond the physical were greater than those in the physical; it was sorrow for the wife and the babies; their great grief when they learned what had happened, bound me to their condition, and we sorrowed together. I could not progress or find happiness until time had healed their sorrow. If only those in earth life knew that their sadness binds and holds us, stays our progress and development! After coming with the aid of many friends to full consciousness, and being made to move at will, I followed at first the movements of both armies. I saw the route of Lee's army, the final surrender at Appomattox, and I want to tell you of the great effort of this land in which I live put forth, not only to prevent war, but to bring peace when nations or people are at war, for war has never been right. No taking of human life is ever justifiable.

"This is the first time it has been my personal privilege to get a message through to the world I once inhabited. It has been a great pleasure to tell you something of the sensations during and after the change. There is one experience that I want to relate, for it made a profound impression. One day I saw many people passing into a building having the appearance of a great Temple of Music. I was told I could go in if I desired, —I did. There were assembled, I should judge, five thousand people. They sat with bowed heads in a silence, so absolute that I marvelled; turning, I asked one beside me the object of the meeting, and I was told they were concentrating their thoughts, sending out peace vibrations to nations at war. I did not comprehend, but, curious, I waited. Soon above that great company arose a golden cloud that formed and moved as if directed. Having learned that I could go at will, I followed and found the cloudy substance enveloping another battle field. Again a dark condition with flashes of red, immediately surrounding and above two great armies, for the thoughts of those in battle give out emanations producing such effect. It had substantially the same appearance that prevailed on my awakening. As I watched, the dark condition seemed to change, to dissolve before the peaceful conditions of the light that I had followed, just as mist dissolves before the sun. With the change a better thought filled the minds of those engaged, an inclination to treat more humanly the wounded and the prisoners. This is one of the ways those experienced among us help the mental, as those among you aid the physical; both are equally real.

"Among us are the great who counsel together and work to influence those in authority against war, while others among us, by thought suggestions, help to sustain those poor soldiers forced into battle, either to satisfy the greed, selfishness, and ambition of those in authority, or to defend a nation or the integrity of their country. We know neither the one side nor the other. We see only the suffering of humanity, a mother's mourning, a wife's breaking heart, a child's sobbing. They are all human, and without distinction or class we labor to comfort and help them by mental suggestion. In such work we enter their homes, a great invisible host, and many a heart has been cheered through our ministrations. Other wars will come, unless the thought of those now in authority changes; then a great work will be required of us, for which we are ready."

"This is exceedingly interesting, but just one more word. How does your earth-life appear, after so many years?" I asked.

"How much do you remember of those first years, when as an infant you gazed upon your world?" the man replied. "So it is with me. I have but an indistinct recollection of the events that made up my earth-life, only a memory remains, still enough to make me regret many lost opportunities. I was not then a thinker, only a drifter; I accepted what was told me without question; the result was that I did not develop my mental faculties. This life offers such splendid advantages, my joy of living in the present is so intense, that I seldom think of the earth-life at all. All the trials, sorrows, and sufferings incident to birth and the few years in your physical world, were necessary, and from my present vantage ground the matter of living a few years more or less, the manner of my going were unimportant; it is all forgotten now in the wonderful reality about me. As soon as I came to understand what death was and to what it led, I immediately commenced to complete my education, and build a home for the wife and children, and I am happy to tell you that again we dwell together, for they are all here in this land of happiness and opportunity."

In the presence of such an experience, listening to an individual speaking from the world beyond, telling of another, an unknown land, where all the so-called dead live, think, move, develop, and progress, the learned should understand and comprehend that three dimensions and five senses do not explain the conditions beyond,

"The Spring blew trumpets of color;
  Her green sang in my brain.
I saw a blind man groping
  'Tap-tap' with his cane;
I pitied him his blindness;
  But can I boast 'I see?'
Perhaps there walks a spirit
  Close by who pities me,-
A spirit who hears me tapping
  The five-sensed cane of the mind
Amid such unknown glories
  I may be worse than blind."

## After Dissolution

When the end comes at the end of Life's short day, we with loving hands dress the vacant tenement and tenderly and reverently consign it to the earth, from whence it came, again to mingle with the elements. But what of the invisible inner body, the living, thinking individual that has left the physical housing? What is its vision, sensation, thought, experience?

This is best described by one who passed through the change, —one who had lived a good life and had necessarily entered into a fine environment. This spirit, describing where she went and what she saw immediately following dissolution, said:

**"You wish to know where I went on leaving the earth. Well, there seemed to be a period of unconsciousness; then I awoke and found myself in an entirely different place from any I had known on earth. I was somewhat confused at first; most people are, and find it difficult to realize where they are and what has happened to them. I was not afraid, however, because I had believed I would be taken care of, and would go on living somewhere. My ideas about the after life, however, were very vague, as are those of the majority of people. Psychic work will change all that, however, and people will know better what to expect; instead of fearing and dreading the dissolution of the body, as so many millions do now, it will appear to them as it really is, —just a sleep and an awakening!**

**"You are wondering, and often have wondered, why I was taken when I seemed to be, and was, so much needed on earth. You have blamed God, and thought it cruel and hard and not**

by any means as an act of love. This is the result of your limited vision.

"I will give you a description of the place in which I found myself when I awoke after what you call 'death.' It took me some time to realize the beauty of my surroundings, as my eyes were blinded by the sorrow which my going had caused on earth. The grief of my people kept me so sad at first that I was not able to see or think of anything but earthly sorrow. That is why grief for departed friends and relatives is so wrong, and is so harmful, both to those on earth and to those who come over. The longer the grief continues and the more hopeless it is, the more those mourned for are kept to earth. Instead of being able to go straight on when they come over, seeing and realizing the beauty and wonders of their surroundings, and helping others to see them also, they are kept in a state of helpless grief, which renders them incapable of either helping themselves or others. Fortunately, the grief of my people on earth was not of this desperately hopeless variety, and I was enabled in time to rise above it and get on with my work of helping others.

"This is a life of service. Self must be eliminated. That is why folk who have lived unselfish lives on earth get on so well here. They do not need the preliminary training which more selfish spirits need. It is a very long time before some spirits who come over are of any use at all in helping others. This is caused partly by their own selfishness and partly by the selfish grief of their friends and relatives on earth. That is why so many of the messages sent through are a plea to those relatives for a more hopeful outlook.

"All that I have said is necessary that you may better understand what I am about to tell you. When I had been enabled to throw off somewhat the effects of the grief which others felt for my passing, I began to see how beautiful the place I had been brought to was. It was where most spirits go on leaving the earth. They are taken there by other spirits and every effort is made to help them to forget the earth and its cares and worries. This lovely palace is called the 'Palace of Light,' because that is what is most needed by the spirits of human beings when they come over, —more light, to enable them to see and understand many things which have not been clear to them while on earth. Human vision—the earthly kind—is very narrow in most cases. People fail to grasp the wonder and beauty even of the earth, so it is no wonder that they need more light and a considerable amount of training before they can see and realize all the beauty and grandeur to be found over here.

"Everything is so surprisingly beautiful that, once their eyes are opened and the full majesty and splendour of it all begins to dawn on them, they are transformed and become beautiful likewise. Once this transformation is accomplished their training is at an end and they can go on their way rejoicing in all the beauty of their surroundings, helping others to see and realize it, too.

"It is almost impossible for us to help some spirits, as they have no desire to be different or better than they have always been. Prayer by those still on the earth is the only thing which can help them. It will give them a desire for better things. Until there is that desire in their hearts, thy will remain much as they were when they were in the flesh. Their spirits still inhabit the earth and they are the evil, or sometimes mischievous, spirits I have told you about before. Prayer is not only a protection against them, but is also their only hope of salvation. Indifference is the greatest sin there is. As long as folk desire to be better, there is some foundation to build on, but if that desire is lacking it is very difficult to do anything with them.

"I really cannot give you an adequate description of the beautiful Palace of Light. It is so marvelous and so stupendous that it would not be possible for any one still on the earth to grasp its significance. It is not just a building, as the word 'Palace' might suggest to your mind. It is a wondrous land of light, where the beauties of Nature, as seen on the earth, are brought to perfection. There we have sea, sky, hills, mountains, valleys, and grassy plains, in all their beauty of form and coloring, but without blemish. There are no barren or desolate places and there is none of man's handiwork to mar all of this loveliness.

"There are forests of noble trees, great rivers, waterfalls, lakes, streams of all sizes, all crystal clear, and lovely meadows carpeted with the most beautiful flowers, over which hover myriads of gorgeous butterflies. There are countless numbers of the most beautiful birds everywhere. Animals of all kinds abound too. Some of them are dainty and graceful, and others are stately and dignified. It is one vast panorama of loveliness, for those who have eyes to see.

"The great pity is that it is so long before some spirits even begin to see it as it really is. Some of these spirits, who have not progressed far enough to see and realize the beauty about them, when communicating with their friends on earth, give them quite wrong and dissimilar impressions of conditions over here.

"You are wondering just what we mean by the term 'progression.' It is the spiritual condition entirely, and has nothing to do with the place the spirits happen to be in. It is the developing and the unfolding of the spiritual nature which is necessary before the spirits concerned can fully appreciate and enjoy the wonderful home prepared for them. Spirits are not obliged to stay in some particular place until they have completed their development. They are all free to go about and see these wonders of which I have been telling you, except that they are not allowed to go and worry the children in their carefree land. Until they develop spiritually, they can not appreciate all the wonders about them.

"I have not told you anything about the music we get here, except that which the birds make, have I? There is always plenty of beautiful music to listen to. All kinds of instruments are played, and those who desire to do so can play in this great orchestra. Then there is the singing. It is wonderful. Everyone is free to join in this great paean of praise. Those who have not been able to sing as they like on earth, and have always desired to do better, are able to realize their longing here. It is good to witness their joy over this, when they have progressed sufficiently to hear the singing, and when they are able to join in it, their happiness is complete."

Let it not be inferred that all who have experienced this change have such a delightful experience. The plane one reaches and the character of one's surroundings depend on the refinement of spirituality of the individual. Each will find the condition he has fitted himself for, and they are such as money can not buy.

Another has this to say:

"I appreciate your kindness in receiving me so kindly. I speak to you tonight about my experiences in the 'spirit world,' as you call it, —I call it the 'higher existence.'

"In describing my passing to the higher, progressive life, I am pleased to say to you that I am giving my own observation, and I do not expect you to accept it as being the testimony of other friends who may have passed over. With what they met, I have nothing to do; I have only to state what I have experienced.

"I may state, concerning my experience on the earth, that I lived for a long period of time, a little over ninety years, and I led, shall I say, a fairly good life. I should like to say concerning the latter days that, though old in years, I was not at all feeble in body or in mind; but as I advanced I felt my powers were failing, and that soon I should be called to leave the scenes of earth for something greater and grander. And so it happened.

"I remember well, on one summer's day, arising in the mourning and feeling weak in my body but without pain. It was a weakness, the result of natural decay of the system. And I remember on this occasion that, as the day advanced, I felt more weary. I laid me down upon a couch and fell into a kind of sleep—not a perfect sleep, because I was partially unconscious of persons around about me.

"I awoke somewhere about four o'clock in the afternoon, looked around, and spoke to one or two near me. One was my attendant, who came and asked if I should like something to drink. I said I should. I lay back and waited, and as I did so I felt a strange but not unpleasant feeling come over me. I can only describe it as a sensuous drowsiness, which seemed to be gaining upon my faculties. The scenes round about me were fading, almost imperceptibly at first, but passing away from me. I was conscious only of that which was just around about me, and then that also seemed to fade away, and my sleep or weakness was merged into sleep which became profound.

"How long that could have continued I do not know, but after a time I again returned to consciousness—these are the only terms I can use to convey to your minds my experiences. Then I realized that I, the Ego, was there just as really as before. I realized that I, the personality, was there, though some change had taken place. I felt as one feels who had dropped something which had burdened him; as a man who had carried a load for a considerable distance, a load that had not been extremely heavy or painful, but still a burden, and I had left it behind somewhere.

"And then, dawning on my spiritual senses, I was conscious that I was in some other state of existence, wherein I was not subject to physical forces as I had experienced them on the earth plane. For instance, the wind did not blow upon me, the sun did not shine, nor did the cold affect me. This I found and experienced with great joy. In place of it I found what you would call, on your mundane sphere, an even temperature, a calm and placid state. I felt that if peace and contentment could be reached, I had reached it. And then I was conscious that round about me there was an innumerable company of people,—they were fellow countrymen.

"As I gained a little more experience, or perhaps, as you would say, as my consciousness deepened, I knew that I was attended by spiritual messengers or attendants. Looking to the one upon my right, I said—if not openly, I said it within myself, because the Ego speaks within itself, because it is the Mind—'This being is perfection.' Diving my thoughts, the guide said to me, 'No, you are being perfected. There is only perfection in the infinite. Him thou shalt know; with Him thou shalt come into contact.' This helped me considerably. If my guide, my messenger, who was to conduct me through this higher existence, was so perfect in mind, so perfect in every way, what then would be the Author of his perfection? I was satisfied."

# CHAPTER 6
## The Spirit World

*I am fully convinced that the soul is indestructible, and that its activity will continue through eternity. It is like the sun, which to our eyes, seems to set in night; but it has in reality only gone to diffuse its light elsewhere.* –J. von Goethe

## Etheric Environment

Desiring a clear comprehension of the etheric spheres outside the physical, and having opportunity to speak with one very learned and advanced in the after-life, I said: "Describe, if you please, the spheres in which you live, with special reference to the tangibility and materiality." The gentleman answered:

**"There are seven concentric rings called spheres. The region nearest the earth is known as the first or rudimental sphere. It is just one step higher in vibration. It really blends with your earth sphere. Growing more intense and increasing in action are six more, distinguished as the spiritual spheres. These are all concentric zones or circles of exceedingly fine matter encompassing the earth like belts or girdles, each separated from the other and regulated by fixed laws. They are not shapeless chimeras or mental projections, but absolute entities, just as tangible as the planets of the solar system or the earth upon which you reside. They have latitude and longitude, and an atmosphere of peculiarly vitalized air. The undulating currents, soft and balmy, are invigorating and pleasurable."**

"How does the landscape appear to you?" I asked.

He answered:

"**The surface of the zone is diversified. There is a great variety of landscape, some of it most picturesque. We, like you, have lofty mountain ranges, valleys, rivers, lakes, forests, and the internal correspondence of all the vegetable life that exists upon your earth. Trees and shrubbery covered with most beautiful foliage, and flowers of every color and character known to you, and many that you know not, give forth their perfume. The physical economy of each zone differs from every other. New and striking scenes of grandeur are presented to us, increasing in beauty sublimity as we progress.**"

"Do the seven conencentric rings, or spheres, move with the earth as the earth moves?" I asked.

"**Although the spheres revolve,**" he said, "**with the earth on a common axis, forming the same angle with the plane of the ecliptic, and move with it about your sun, they are not dependent upon that sun for either light or heat; they receive not a perceptible ray from that ponderable source.**"

"From what source do you receive your light?" I then asked.

**We receive our light emanations,**" he said, "**wholly from an etheric sun, from which central luminary there comes uninterrupted splendour, baffling description. We have, therefore, no division of time into days, weeks, months, or years, nor alterations of season caused by the earth's annual revolution, for the reason that we have no changing season as you have, caused by the action of the sun on your solar system. We, like you, are constantly progressing from day to day, but our ideas of time and seasons differ widely from yours. With you, it is time. With us, it is eternity. In your sphere your thoughts, necessarily bounded by time and space, are limited, but with us thoughts are extended in proportion as we get rid of those restrictions, and our perception of truth becomes more accurate.**"

"How do you use matter, change its form and condition?" I asked.

"**Matter,**" he said, "**with us is only tangible as the mind concentrates upon the subject. Then the force of the mind or thought sends its vibrations around the object, holding it in a measurable tangible. Of course, this is something very different from what you call tangibility. Without this mental concentration the vibration pulses indifferently. That is the natural condition of matter in our zone. It requires the thought to** change its form and condition. The vibrating action of matter is measured by the space necessary for the volume."

"How can this material condition in which you live be demonstrated?" I asked.

"**One cannot prove,**" he said, "**to a child that steam, that pretty fascinating substance, is harmful until the finger is burned; neither can one instill the truth into an older mind until it is not only opened but has the capacity to comprehend. That all is material in different states of vibration is easily grasped by the thinker. It is impossible to prove by your laws, to actually demonstrate the existence of matter in the higher vibrations in which we live so that men may comprehend. When you deal with matter in the physical, you apply physical laws. When you deal in matter spiritual, you apply spiritual laws, practically unknown among men. The best possible evidence is the vision of the clairvoyant together with deductive reasoning, which, as we have said, is really the highest order of proof.**

"**Have you ever thought,**" he said, "**that the result of every physical demonstration reaches the consciousness through the avenue of reason? The mentality in a higher state of development comprehends a fact in Nature without physical proof.**"

"Tell us something of your social life, your scientific research, and religious teaching in the plane in which you reside," I asked.

"**With regard to the social constitution of the 'spheres,' each is divided into six circles, or societies, in which kindred and congenial spirits are united and subsist together under the law of affinity. Although the members of each society unite as near as may be on the same plane, agreeing in the most prominent moral and intellectual features; yet it will be found on careful analysis, that the varieties of character in each society are almost infinite, being as numerous as the persons who compose the circle. Each society has teachers from those above, and not infrequently from the higher spheres, whose province is to impart to us the knowledge acquired from their experience in the different departments of science; this, we in turn transmit to those below. Thus by receiving and giving knowledge, our moral and intellectual faculties are expanded to higher conceptions and more exalted views of Nature, the power of which is no less displayed in the constitution of spirit worlds than in the countless resplendent orbs of space. Our scientific researches and investigations are extended to** all that pertains to the phenomena of universal truth; to all the wonders of the heavens and of the earth, and to whatever the mind of man is capable of conceiving. All of these researches exercise our faculties and form a considerable part of our enjoyments. The noble and sublime sciences of astronomy, chemistry, and mathematics engage a considerable portion of our attention, and afford us an inexhaustible subject for study and reflection.

"Nevertheless, there are millions of spirits who are not yet sufficiently advanced to take any interest in such pursuits. The mind being untrammeled by the gross material body, and having its mental and intellectual energies and perceptions improved, can by intuition, as it were, more correctly and rapidly perceive and understand the principles and truths on which the sciences are based. In addition to our studies, we have many other sources of intellectual, moral, and heartfelt enjoyment from which we derive the most ineffable pleasures, some of which are social reunions among children and parents where the liveliest emotion and tenderest affections of our nature are excited, and the fondest and most endearing reminiscences are awakened; where spirits meet in union with spirit, and heart beats responsive to heart.

"We have no sectarian or ecclesiastical feuds, no metaphysical dogmas; our religious teachers belong to that class of persons who were noted during their probation on earth for their philanthropy and deeds of moral bravery; who, regardless of the scoffs and sneers of time-serving multitude, dared to promulgate and defend the doctrines of civil and religious liberty. They urge upon us, too, the necessity of cooperation in the reformation and advancement of our more degraded brethren by instructing them in the divine principles of love, wisdom, and benevolence. They instruct them in the soul-inspiring and elevating doctrines of universal and eternal progression, and in the sublime truth that evil is not an indestructible and positive principle, but a negative condition, a mere temporary circumstance of existence; and furthermore, that suffering for sin is not a revengeful and malevolent infliction of God, but a necessary and invariable sequence of violated law.

"They teach also that, according to the divine moral economy, there is no such thing as pardon for sins committed—no immediate mercy—no possible escape from the natural results of crime, no matter where or by whom committed; no healing of a diseased moral constitution by any outward appliances, or ceremonial absurdities; and finally, that the only way to escape sin and its consequences, is by progressing above and beyond it."

"What is spirit, as that term is used?" I asked.

**"Spirit,"** he said, **"is the one great power in the Universe. The combination of spirit forces is the great power for good, and through the absence of that force many undesirable conditions develop in your world, —all in the Universe is but an expression of this great force, and if this spirit force were not material, were not a substance, how could it take form and have growth in the physical plane? Those still in your world make a great mistake when they for one moment imagine that our world is not a material one; it is foolish to think of an existence without substance. How can there be a world beyond the physical unless it is material? Without it there could be no after-life. Strong invisible bands of force hold the great system of spheres in proper place. It is all mind-force, and all force is life, mighty, unchanging, unyielding, and this mind power is increased by every individual life that is developed in your creative sphere. It has become a part of the individual life force of the Universe, and each day it adds something to that force called Good. This addition is made, not at dissolution, but from hour to hour, as the mentality increases."**

"Such teachings appeal to reason, and I accept them. Our earth is still very young; before it took form and shape and a definite place in the procession of the world, other planets and solar systems were growing old. It was but yesterday in the calendar of time that the convulsions and eruptions of this earth in its effort to make definite form threw up the mountains, made valleys for the seas, and destroyed in its labour the peopled continent of Atlantis. It was but a little time ago that the pyramids were built and temples were erected upon the banks of the Nile, that Balshazzar in the temple of Babylon saw invisible hands write upon the wall. Grecian and Roman splendour, Mohammedan culture and refinement, Napoleon's conquest, and religious freedom are all things of today. Time is no more measured by the calendar than a grain of sand measures the extent of the desert.

There are so many things which we as a people do not know! We have gone into the depths of the earth and learned just a little of geology; we have done something in botany; we have searched the skies, discovered planets, measured distances, and learned just a little about astronomy. We have succeeded in putting a single harness on electricity without knowing what it is, and have developed our individual senses in about the same proportion. But we have really no conception of space or of the thousands of suns and solar systems connected with ours, or of the medium between them. Science has no conception of the nature and origin of the magnetic force, the part that it plays in Nature, or the influence it has in this world of ours. The world has little conception of matter except in its grossest expression. It knows nothing of solar space. It has not developed sufficiently to comprehend that the Universe is material, and that the different planes are similar, except in density. The race has not yet developed sufficiently to understand what life is, or the source from whence this atom that develops self has come. Nor do we yet appreciate or understand the duties and responsibilities that rest upon the individual and his relation to society and to himself. Certain elementary propositions have been enunciated and demonstrated, and many so-called great minds say that beyond them we cannot go. Life force is as much of a mystery to science to-day (1917) as it was before the Christian era.

The primary propositions which must be understood are these: the earth is one of many creative planets; progress has only commenced; nothing in this physical world has or will reach perfection; all present knowledge is elementary; there are no limitations; life is eternal and will continue to develop, expand, and increase through the untold ages yet to come beyond man's comprehension of time. Our beginning we cannot know with our present development; knowledge of our end is equally impossible, but the present is ours.

## Life Among the Spheres

One from the higher life said:

**"There is so much to be considered in putting this knowledge of the future life before earth minds. The incredulous and ignorant will only jeer."**

**"Remember,"** said one who has been in spirit-life nearly four hundred years, **"the world in which you live is in a very low order of development. In many of the other planets this philosophy of life is universally taught, but you have comparatively only a few minds high enough out of the slough of materialism to comprehend it. In the Fourth Sphere, where I am, that of trial, we are fitted for a higher order of life. Here, any weakness a spirit may still hold becomes doubly alluring and seemingly irresistible. We finally overcome this by throwing it out**

124

of our spirit. Sometimes it is a long, hard task. We are made to do anything we do not like to do, or, rather, we must learn to like to do it. Often when we help others, the task is irksome and we long to keep ourselves free for spiritual development, forgetting that each deed for others helps our own growth. In the Sphere of Truth the spirits learn all about the other planets and become wise and uplifted, so that they can enter into perfect harmony with the universe. Of course, this needs special preparation and a high degree of development. There, they are not taught by contact with teachers from the higher spheres—in fact, in my sphere we see no teachers, everything comes through suggestion. Our minds are receptive enough to be taught and guided in that way. Each sphere makes suggestion just a little clearer and easier to grasp than the one before, and so we are fitted for the last, where we are able to throw our individuality into the dominating forces of the universe.

"The Sphere of Harmony is a preparation for the last great sphere, that of Exaltation, where all the universe becomes one. There, they mingle with all in the universe, and are helped and encouraged by them until they are ready to enter into a glorious communion of spirit. This means becoming an inseparable part of all the great forces of the universe. I have never heard of any spirits coming back to the lower planes from the Seventh, except through suggestion and influence. But through these, they are very near all spiritual natures. They really constitute the dominating force for good that is in and around everyone. The spirit of good in the universe is not individual, but universal. In the last sphere each spirit keeps his individuality, but each has by then become so great and magnificent that it can mingle with other spirits in harmony, making one grand, wonderful whole. If the spirits in the Plane of Exaltation could by any possible chance become out of harmony, the universe would be obliterated and cease to exist. But this cannot be. I simply say this to show how they govern and dominate everything. You ask if any from your earth have ever reached the Seventh Sphere. I am not sure. Your world is young compared with almost all the others and so there could be comparatively but few.

"Some of the planets do not have as many as seven spheres to perfection. They begin with a higher order. There is not much more that you can grasp, my friend. You have learned the essentials of each sphere, and the minor details are so vast and varied that you would have to write a book on each one. Besides, as I have said, it would be hard to convey the knowledge to material minds. Yet it is simple, and on the same lines as the rest that I have told you."

No voice from the Seventh Sphere ever spoke to human ears. Spirits from this sphere do not return and speak to those on the lower planes. Their work is done through suggestions. In this way they come close to us all, but only the conscience hears.

One from the Fifth Sphere told me a little of the life there and the conditions prevailing. He said:

"I am told that you have never had anyone before from this sphere. Here, we are taught all knowledge and how to use it for our individual good. We are brought face to face with the great problems of life, the reason for all things, and the ultimate result. These are vast questions and are not yet fully comprehended by us, but they must be understood before we can enter into Harmony, where we are taught how to attune ourselves to the universe. There, we will be taken into the life of the worlds, but not until the last sphere are we able to merge our individualities into the creative dominant force. In the Fifth we are taught all there is to know, but in the Sixth we learn by actual contact, and how to adapt ourselves to all conditions of the universe. We are all working toward perfection, and labor to gain the last great Sphere of Exaltation. My friend, I cannot explain our life to you, because you would not comprehend it at all. We are all tending toward one great harmonious whole, and each day brings us nearer that state of harmony we desire. In these last spheres our home life is almost lost sight of. We are bands of congenial people, of course, but we are separate, individual beings. Man no longer, like the animals, chooses a mate and carries her off to his lair. Here, there is something much higher and better a universal brotherhood and companionship, always growing closer and higher until complete blending is formed. It is hard to put this into words, because it is so vast and wonderful and I doubt if you could grasp the whole beauty and force of it.

"There is life on many planets. Some are more advanced than yours; a few are even newer. Each is striving toward the same end and must reach it through many spheres of spiritual development, just as you will, until all are one. Life on the different planes varies, of course. On some, the people are stronger, both physically and spiritually. Some have a first sphere that corresponds to yours. Others combine into one sphere what we do in three. When a planet is prepared, the life-force of the universe is clothed and individualized. When the soil is ready, the seed is planted. Other planets than the earth teem with life. I have not been to them, but have been taught of them by suggestion and know something of each and what degree of development each has attained. I will not be able to visit them until I gain the Sixth Sphere. I lived in England during the reign of Queen Elizabeth, so you see my progress has been rapid. Fortunately, I was a good man and had no prejudices to start with."

From this I conclude that in the last sphere the soul of man reaches perfection and becomes a part of the great spirit that rules the world. Some idea of what this is may be obtained by considering the power of man's mind over matter, in the material sense. By the power of his intellect on this earth-plane man makes matter, in a limited way, subject to his will. This mind through ages of development and change grows in strength and power, becomes pure in thought and uses itself for good. When one possesses all that is to be gained in the lower spiritual spheres he will enter into the last sphere of strength, beauty, power, and splendor. His mind, which has gathered much power in its journey, mingles with all others that have ever lived, and that have reached perfection. This spirit-thought from all the worlds, blending as one, makes the force that is called God—or universal Good.

### The Spheres—Their Infinite Variety and Conditions

Here is a description of the spheres received from the beyond:

"The Spheres! No tongue can describe them. There are thousands, all rounded into complete worlds, and all the habitations of those who cherish the special idea which rules the sphere. These spheres are not permanent, but the temporary homes of those who pass through them. They are the garners into which are gathered the sheaves of earth, there to rest and gain experience until they become distributed and amalgamated into eternal life. There are spheres of love, where tender natures cling to one another until they are drawn by higher, broader aspirations to broader planes of thought.

"There are spheres of every shade of mental light, thought, and knowledge; spheres of special grades of intellect and wisdom. In all and each is a special need of happiness; but, also, in all and each are prevailing impulses to branch out further, to press on, to grow, so that every soul, partaking of the special characteristics of every plane in turn, may glean and gather in at last the good of all, and thus become a perfect spirit.

"Worlds in space! Thousands, millions of them; worlds within worlds, the finer permeating the grosser filling up the space of the still more dense until at last you see no finite lines, no end to the infinitely dense. I see the concentrated scheme of the whole solar system with earth, and its zones and belts of spirit spheres, countless in number, various in attribute. Myriads of rare and splendid beings speed through the spaces, piercing the grosser spheres, invisible to all but their own grade of beings.

"Myriads of duller, grosser beings live in these spheres, unconscious that they are permeated by radiant worlds, all thronged with glorious life, too fine for the gross to view. Each living creature is surrounded and enclosed by the atmosphere to which it has belonged, which restrains his vision to the special sphere in which he dwells, just as you cannot see us in our sphere of life, through your atmosphere. Yet the finer realms of being can view, at will, the grosser, just as I found I could do; I am putting this knowledge into practice in coming to you. In fact, I found the secret of will, which is power.

"In these spheres that so lock and interlace, I saw that the lowerest and nearest the earth were dull, coarse, barren spheres, dreary and unlovely, where dark and uninvited beings wander to and from, seeking rest and satisfaction which earth alone could give them. No homes were there, I mean no real homes, where loved ones were reunited. No flowers, no friendly gatherings, no songs of music; the hard cold natures of the wretched dwellers gave out no light, no beauty, no harmony or love, yet all felt impelled and obliged to toil. Toil was the genius of this place; yet whatever labors were performed became instrumental in breaking the clods of hard and wicked natures. Every occupation seemed to come perforce as something that must be done; yet all seemed destined to open up new ideas and new sources of thought, and to impel the helpless laborers to aspire after better things and higher states.

"I saw the flitting lamps of spirit workers, who fill your leaden spheres with their gracious influence; and yet, though often felt, these were unseen by the dull-eyed inhabitants. I do not care to linger on the awful, grand, and wise economy of being; the seal of mortal life is on my lips. The spheres are not all of earth, though countless in number; myriads there are where vicious spirits linger, bound and captive as it were, the ignorant, dull, idle, and criminal, who had not done with earth and who must learn, perhaps for ages, all that belonged to their human duties, before they can pass the threshold and enter upon the life of the upper spheres.

"You cannot look through the radiant realms of upper air and see us; but you can feel the streams of pitying love poured out in tender sympathy, as you stretch your weary arms toward us. Spirit life, glory, peace, and happiness left me for the time, for I felt that it was my duty henceforth to help these unfortunates. This is my present work."

## Spirit Occupations

Again we come to a practical question: the occupation of the countless so-called dead, their daily life, and the method adopted to reach a higher development. If there be occupation, what is the average citizen qualified to do, and in this connection, we must here consider qualifications.

It is a fact to be noted from experience that it requires years of study and close application to do anything, except hard labour, well. One who aspires to the law must now have a fairly good education, if not that of a college graduate. Then he must enter upon four years of study, followed by years of practice, before he is qualified to do good work. It is the same with the physician, and all other professions. High position is gained by years of labour. Only when fitted is one entrusted with responsibilities, and the ambitious work long and hard to qualify themselves for the positions they would occupy. This is just and proper.

Childhood is taught, youth studies, and manhood labours to qualify for the highest place which in life they may be called upon to occupy. It is a fact to be regretted that in most instances high positions are sought for the purposes of acquiring money, and the largest amount of money possible. Worldly ambitions and desires relate almost wholly to physical things. It may be said that the development of mankind, and it has been splendid, has been along physical lines, and the question may be asked, "How are men qualified to take up work, and what is the character of work in the after life, if there is work?"

Before taking up that question, let us remember that nothing physical passes into the spirit world. All the money and property acquired is, as we know, divided among earth people entitled thereto, and usually is spent with all convenient speed. Litigation pertains to property, and, there being no physical property in the after-life, the lawyer will have no practice. The physician and surgeon will have no occupation, for the reason that the physical bodies on which they practice are not there. The only ills are mental. Scientists who recognize only matter having three dimensions will not at first be qualified intelligently to work with spirit material that is so high in vibration that they know little of it.

Nature's great purpose contemplates that mankind in this life should first of all develop the spirit, refine the inner body in which the individual functions, and qualify by years of effort to meet the conditions of all mankind, for this life is but a prepatory school in Nature's great plan.

How can we acquire spiritual riches? What must one do to become so developed that he many intelligently meet the new conditions and take up the work that will be required of him?

These are questions that can be answered. The answer is, *play fair*. In every transaction do to others as you would have others do to you. Help those who are less fortunate. Scatter words of kindness lavishly; lend a helping hand to those in need; let the thought be clean and pure; do not teach what you do not know; do not mislead; and labour to understand all natural law. These things and such thoughts will refine and develop self and qualify one to enter into the new conditions in the life to come, without shame and without regret. Such has been my teaching from those in spirit life. If everyone knew that here and now every act and thought was photographed in his psychic ether, and that in dissolution all became visible, some at least would hesitate. The thought that wrong can be hidden gives many courage. Thought makes character, and in the end character is visible.

What have I learned of the daily life and occupation of the living dead? One long an inhabitant of the higher plane has said:

**"We have schools here for the development of the soul of man, and to teach him his relation to mankind; to instruct him in the wonders of creation, impart to him knowledge of the inhabitants of the numerous worlds in space, to aid man, also, in experimenting in chemistry and all other branches of science, for in this life we can explore the uttermost extent of the universe. We also instruct in political economy and laws governing humanity. We also point out conditions and means**

whereby to help the unprogressive and helpless portion of mankind."

Another states:

"In the spirit world, as in your world, are numerous libraries. There men and women grow intellectually. Many books are composed and written in spirit spheres, and the authors endeavor sometimes to impress their words and wisdom upon the brain of some sensitive ones upon the earth sphere. Again, a book written by one in your plane is by mental activity first created in spirit substance. It had to be before it could be clothed in physical substance by you, and we have all those books, as well as those wholly written by spirits, but none are permitted in our libraries that are not founded upon truth. It is interesting to see the vast number of spirit people thronging our libraries, studying the works of the more advanced spirits, similar to what is done in the libraries of earth."

Another said:

"We have hospitals, many of them—mental hospitals, where the insane, weak and mentally deficient are treated and developed, and those who understand that work labour to restore normal conditions, for dissolution does not restore disordered minds or develop mentality.

"There are homes to build, and homes commenced on earth to finish; and they are as different as the homes of your earth. Yours are first fashioned in our ether, then constructed out of earth material by the hand of man. Ours are made out of etheric material and fashioned and erected by and through mental or, to be more correct, spirit thought. All this, as with you, requires effort. You may hire others to build earth homes, but here each builds his own, and many are very busy doing it.

"You ask me to speak particularly as to the occupation of our people. It is a subject vast in extent, for our labours transcend yours, though our methods are different. While our labour is largely in the mental or spirit field of action, yet you must remember we have fields and vegetation where those versed in such work find occupation. But it is in the more advanced fields of chemistry and philosophy that spirit people seek to enter, and here millions labour to understand and comprehend the laws of Nature, and how to apply them. It is a busy world and no drones are found, except in the earthbound or lowest of the spirit spheres."

Concerning different avocations, this one said:

"I am here in this way to tell you of some of the conditions of our world. Here we have different avocations assigned to us, according to our needs and desires.

"Some engage in teaching and training the intellect of those who need and desire such training.

"Some with great love of children find ample opportunity for the use and enjoyment of this attribute of their natures in the kindergartens for the many thousands of children continually arriving on these shores.

"Some are most happy in endeavoring to assist the friends of earth into higher and better conditions and in counteracting the abnormal influences of undeveloped and misdirected spirits over the minds of mortals.

"So it is that there is work of benevolence and philanthropy for all who are prepared for such work.

"The exercise of active philoprogenitiveness furnishes the same delightful enjoyments to the soul over here as with you, and greater; for here we more clearly discern the far-reaching consequences of our endeavors to do good to whomsoever is in need of assistance."

Another said:

"Let me speak of the music here, of those harmonious vibrations that touch the soul, that universal appeal that is understood by all races, regardless of the language they speak. The music of your world is crude, indeed, compared to celestial compositions and songs. Here we have harmonious vibrations, expressed in what is called music. It elevates the soul, and we devote much time to its cultivation and to instruments for its expression. It is all vibration. Many are occupied in this work. It is only now and then that our songs and our music are impressed in on earth's sensations.

"We do not devote so much time to spirit matter as you do to physical matter. With you it dominates your thought. With us, matter is secondary, and spirit development dominates. It is so much more vital.

"The coming of infants unborn, babies and children, requires the attention of many. Those women who never in earth life knew the joys of motherhood, find it here and do that work. While some care for these little ones, others teach them."

Again, one said:

"In the lower spheres, when those who are held there realize that the only way to improve their condition is by helping others, and have a genuine desire to help, the way is shown.

"This question of spirit occupation is too great for special treatment. Occupation varies and is as diversified as the thoughts of men. But this you should know: there is work and a place for each new spirit. The pity of their poverty! Few have made any effort to find out what nature requires of them here; few ever gave the subject a single thought. And so they come, one by one, but withal a great crowd every hour, and only now and then we find a spirit that can take up and do good work; the others have to be taught, even as little children are taught the simplest things."

Another said:

"Those who have led clean, fine lives, and have enriched the world, come here and, without a break, take up their work and go on."

I could write a volume on the occupations of those who have preceded us, but enough has been said to impress mankind that the after life is real, and that there we work to develop and adorn the physical, while the spirit hungers and development is stayed.

What position will the average individual occupy when he enters the new life? What position has he qualified himself to fill intelligently? Stripped of all earthly possessions, money, goods and chattels gone, he has nothing left but the spirit clothed with kindly acts that have enriched his soul. If he has made the world happier and better, he goes radiant and glorious.

Ideals are like stars. We shall not succeed in touching them with our hands, but, like the traveler in the desert, we take them as our guides. Should not the young be impressed with the fact that the ideal life is one that has enriched itself spiritually, and that material wealth is in all cases a secondary consideration?

Again, one describing conditions in the great beyond says:

"The realities of the spirit world are beyond description. I might spend hours telling you of it and not reach your minds with any conception of its glory, its greatness, its grandeur. It is so vast in extent, so marvellous, that any attempt to give you more than a faint idea would be futile. Not until you get here and see for yourself can you have any conception of the home of the soul. We have our mission—to try to get knowledge through to the shore line of your earth. We are working our best to enlighten the world and prepare its people for the death change. It is our business to instruct those who need

**help, the same here as with you. Many thousands of your people cannot even read, and reach us with so limited mental development as to need all our energies in their advancement out of ignorance, wrong education and false religious teachings. Few on your earth have any idea of the changes that take place along the lifeline. As they come, we gather and instruct them as you do in your schools—especially in your night schools, where the ignorant seek enlightenment."**

I am impressed with the fact that very many of those called learned, will realize at the end that they are among those that need teachers, and will find it necessary to attend night school in the spirit world.

## What is the Next Life?

Neither the old nor the New Testament makes any suggestion that in the after life there is further advancement to be made or any work to be done. On the contrary, according to its promises, we find rest through death, an eternity without labor. We find that as we are, so shall we ever be, that there is no further opportunity to do, undo, add to, subtract from, or improve; that death ends all growth or progression; that we are weighed and our account is balanced. For argument only, assume this to be correct, and consider the result. The infant prematurely born must remain in ignorance and in helplessness. The child that had only commenced to form its words would never learn to convey its wants, necessities, or desires in language, or reach the splendor of manhood or womanhood; those suffering mental disease, must remain idiots or lunatics; cripples must always be cripples; old age must totter through all time. Those who were ignorant at the time of dissolution must always be ignorant; the vicious, always vicious; the selfish always selfish; the good always good. Education and improvement have an ending with this life. As we go out, so shall we remain for time and eternity. As the tree falls, so shall it lie.

I cannot subscribe to this doctrine. Around and about us Nature is always progressing, always developing, always becoming more beautiful. There is no time, according to natural law, when Nature ceases to progress. If this is conceded, should man, a part of Nature, be denied what is allowed vegetable life? If life is endless, the time spent in the body, even though the years pass the Scriptural three score and ten, is infinitesimal compared to eternity, and opportunity for progression and preparation, according to orthodox teaching, is far from fair. "We are just as much spirit now as we ever shall be." These words have been often spoken, and I repeat them, that we may fully comprehend their import. If we are spirit in the life to come, we are spirit now, always have been, and ever will be. In the change of death, nothing is lost but the outer shell, termed the body. The spirit was no more visible to the human eye before death than it is after, yet it exists the same in each instance. The physical eye cannot see thought, yet it is seated in the brain. The soul is invisible to mortals, yet it is within us. This being accepted, is it wonderful that we do not see spirit out of the body when we did not see it in the body? In each instance we have evidence of spirit without seeing the thing itself. We do not see the magnetic forces, but the effect is visible. We do not see electric fluid, but evidence of its existence is found in the lightning's bolt, and in instruments which utilize its energy. In converting water into steam, or even separating it into gases, we do not change its component parts. By utilizing magnetic forces we do not annihilate them. Harnessing the electrical current, and thereby turning the wheels of industry, does not destroy it.

So the individual spirit of man at the moment of separation from the body is identically the same, has the same thoughts, the same ideas, the same knowledge, the same ties, and possesses the same spirit that he had a moment before. The infant is an infant; manhood is still manhood; old age, still old age; the vicious, still vicious, selfish, still selfish, virtuous, still virtuous; the good, still good. But they do not remain so forever and ever, any more than they would have done on earth. There is no more stagnation in the spirit-world than here. Neither does that simple step in Nature give spirit wings or make angels. If angelic, the spirit became so before going. Death does not immediately add to character nor detract from it. In death, the spiritual body steps out of the old garment which loving hands take to its resting-place, and cover with earth from which it was made, that it may mingle with material and be used again to clothe other life. The spirit did not come from material and does not go back to the material, but in splendor and in spiritual strength, faces the new conditions into which it has entered. We are taught that progress and evolution have never stopped, and never will stop. They are a part of this and all other worlds, and a part of the spirit-world. This is a fundamental principle, has always existed and always will exist. All the so-called dead that in the ages past have lived on this and other planets still live and labor. Education, like time, is without limit; opportunity, without boundaries. Spirits come to know and appreciate the new laws under which they live and work one and one; they feel the companionship of friends, the joy of more intensified life, and feel the inspiration that comes with knowledge.

In the spirit condition the spirits have, first, all that we have here; or perhaps I should say that we have here the counterpart of same phases of the spirit-world. Then they must have homes. Not having material, these homes cannot be builded of brick and wood, but are made of thoughts, which, in spirit become things. This home is being builded by every one of us from day to day, thought after thought, act after act, is building in spirit a structure that will await our coming. These homes can be made, I am told, beautiful beyond our comprehension. Indeed, all material building here is fashioned in imitation of those homes in the world to come, for suggestion comes from spirit that aids our designs. Aided by spirit-thought, we are unconsciously imitating that higher world both in building and in living. It differs only in beauty and in substance. That home may be large and have many rooms, richly furnished, peopled with love and happiness; or it may be a hovel, cold, cheerless and lonely. Every one is his own architect and builder. Every act of charity, kindness tenderness, and love adds to its beauty and comfort; while every act of selfishness cruelty, and oppression casts a shadow; so that when one opens the door of his spirit-house, he faces the deeds of the earth-life. The walls are hung with mental pictures depicting the record made from day to day. A little act of kindness, a word of sympathy, a tender touch, are reproduced, framed in harmony. Selfishness, unkindness, immorality, wickedness, and dishonor are also pictured and hung on the walls of that home, there to remain until individual restitution shall cover or remove them. We are building a home of some character, and furnishing it with the thoughts and deeds of daily life. It is the only place to which we can go, when the material existence is ended. If this thought could be brought home to all mankind, how it would fill the world with joy! How it would lessen the ages of suffering and unhappiness caused by wrongs done in ignorance, an ignorance fostered by orthodox teaching! Natural law is immutable, and ignorance is no more excusable than violation of the civil law. Both are established, and it becomes our duty to know and understand both.

We are told that in the spirit-world there are colleges and universities of learning, teachers and students, all working and striving to comprehend the philosophy of Nature. Chemists are experimenting with the action of chemicals and making discoveries; naturalists labor to know more of Nature; astronomers are studying the planetary systems; scientists are aiming to utilize forces, and a great army is working to bring all spirit-kind to understanding what life is. Mental hospitals are maintained, where the idiot and lunatic may be taken, where the darkness overshadowing their lives is dispelled, and their spirits quickened, that they may take up life where it was suspended. Women who never knew motherhood gather unborn babies that have been murdered, infants who pass in tender years, indeed, all children, they still their cries, nourish, comfort, teach and rear them, taking the mother's place and doing the mother's part. Art studies abound in the spirit-world. Those who stood foremost in the art ranks on earth are taught by others more advanced, to paint though will-power alone; they, in turn, are teaching those not so far advanced as themselves. When a picture is perfect, art spirits endeavor to impress it upon the mind of some artists on this–a lower–plane. Ideal pictures are the result of such impressions. All inventions are perfected in the next sphere by spirits interested in that work before they are impressed on some sensitive mind still living on this earth-plane. If those impressions are received as they are transmitted, we have a perfect invention; if the impression is faulty, the invention is imperfect. Those who are gifted musicians and composers do not change occupation or pursuits, but, like the artists, are taught greater harmony, are perfected in execution, and then coming close to a sensitive brain interested in the same thought, aid in the composition of a masterpiece. Does it seem natural or right that composers, men of letters, scientists, musicians, and all those who have spent a lifetime here in developing themselves, should have no use for such learning after dissolution? If this were so, is it worthwhile to make an effort?

Here, the ear is limited to a few vibrations. We hear only a small number of the many sounds that fill the air. There, the sense is developed, and there seemed silence are really many voices. Here, the eye focuses on only few objects that fill space. There, the lenses are clearer and they comprehend that all space is filled with intelligent and comprehensive life. Harmony predominates in the higher spheres, and permeates every condition. The melodies and songs that we produce appear to spirit as the rolling ocean wave to us. All occupations which have to do with the mind are continued. Physicians study that they may learn what remedies are required to assist Nature in its effort to restore natural conditions, and as they are able to see clearly and to diagnose disease, impress upon the doctors of the earth diagnoses and treatments. Thus the inhabitants of spirit-land work, on and on, acquiring understanding and perfection in those fields of labor for which they are best fitted. They know the joy that comes from time well spent.

How do spirits subsist? Do they require food? We answer, yes. In the lower sphere they absorb the essence, just as mortals take the substance. We inhale the invisible perfume of flowers; they the essence. So close are they about us that ofttimes their thought and suggestions are our desires. As we take food and drink, they find their substance in the essence. But as they progress, they absorb spiritual foods and spiritual fruits. In time, they can live on these alone.

With many people the earthly life is one great masquerade. They live behind the mask of material, and are never really known. In the spirit-world, we appear as we really are. On earth, all are free to choose place of habitation, surroundings, associates, and to wander where desire leads. Suppose that here and now the secret thoughts, motives, selfishness, greed, and desires of men could be photographed, suppose a camera would make character visible, how startled the world would be! How many would hide! In dissolution this mask falls from the face. Men are seen, and for the first time, in the mirror of Nature, they see themselves as they really are. Thoughts and desires, the record of every act done in the body, are visible to all the spirit-world, even as it was before, for they have always known the deeds and understood the thoughts and desires of our daily life. Even now we hide nothing from spirits. The spirit, then, comes to fully appreciate that his life has always been an open book. Here, there is hypocrisy and doubt; there, hypocrisy is unknown and deceit is impossible. The language of spirit is thought, and thought is visible. The spirit freed from material shows what it is, and all that great beautiful world knows how opportunities have been improved, how character has been developed. How many around and about us would be willing that the spirit-world should know every thought and witness every act, with the motive actuating it? This is a fact, whether we would have it so or not. In that life, each one will be drawn into that condition and into that society for which he is fitted. Harmony is Natures first law—universal, fixed, determined, inimitable—and it draws one into the condition for which he has qualified himself. It may be among beautiful characters, in happy homes surrounded by the loved ones who have gone before. It may be among the selfish and ignorant, with strangers, in darkness and sorrow. The freedom to select society or residence is no longer possessed. Nature's irresistible power, that can no more be changed than the path of a constellation, draws individual spirits to its own.

No good ever came or can come from teaching falsehood, but bad comes and must always come. It is the duty of everyone to teach and speak what he knows to be true. Having this knowledge, if mine were the only voice in the land, I would raise it. Into the dull face of superstition I would throw the shining lance of reason; into the darkened room of prejudice, I would light a single torch.

But I am not working alone. Men are no longer satisfied with Christian teaching. They are thinking, and orthodox teaching and thinking along those lines do not harmonize with each other. When one begins to think he begins to doubt, and doubt is the dawn of reason. Around and about us are great forces of occult power. Vast influences are continually at play upon the well-being of man. Research is making this field classic. It is no feverish excitement or vain ambition that leads men to this thought. It is a higher feeling, a holier motive, a desire to understand and to comprehend the economy of Nature, and to grow wiser and better through that knowledge.

## Spheres in the Afterlife

Early in my research I understood that life continued beyond the grave; that personality was not lost; that when one had compensated for all wrongs and made them right, he would progress; but it has taken many, many years to reach these advanced spirits, and from them learn just what was beyond the first sphere, where our work had hitherto largely been confined. We have often asked what was beyond, or to what progression led, and have as often been told to have patience, that when we were prepared to receive and to understand, the knowledge would be given.

At last the knowledge that has long been desired has been revealed, and we find that the future has seven spheres, each containing many planes; they are as follows:

1. Restitution.
2. Preparation.
3. Instruction.
4. Trial and Temptation.
5. Truth.
6. Harmony.
7. Exaltation.

I have written of the conditions in the first sphere as I know them from work done there and general information given me by spirit people; but in taking up the spheres beyond the first, I am now able to give the language of those who live in them and who describe them.

One said:

**"I know what we all know, —that there are seven spheres. I have just reached the third. Sometimes a spirit can speak from his sphere to the next higher, as you do while in the body, but only in the same way. I mean that there is no mingling togeth-**

er. When a spirit goes from one sphere to another, it is quite unlike dissolution in earth-life.

He is warned that the change is near and has time to put his mind into a higher plane of thought so that he will be prepared to meet the new life. He says farewell to all his friends. They join in a general thanksgiving and celebration, all congratulating and helping him on his way by strong uplifting thoughts. When the time comes, he is put quietly to sleep, with the thought dominant in his mind that he is to make the change. When he awakes, he is in his new home in the next higher sphere. He has disappeared from the old. There is no old body to bury and decay. Each change is for a higher and better life, and the home awaiting is more beautiful, as he builds with a surer, wiser hand, or rather, spirit. His home ceases to be among his former friends when this change comes. Thought has fitted him to progress, and when that thought which held him to the lower plane has ceased, the embodiment of the spirit, which is held together by his thought, is visible no longer.

"Each new change is more difficult to explain to you than the one preceding. It is simply a higher life and a busy one in which to develop ourselves along all lines, especially the ones suitable to the individual's taste. In this way, each spirit becomes better fitted to be a teacher and helper. It is a very active, pleasant life, and sometimes seems like a big university town or country, with busy students hurrying from lecture to lecture and class to class. All are congenial and lighthearted there.

"In the lower sphere one sees much suffering among those still earth-bound. They, too, are busy working out past faults and they are often heavy-hearted. Generally speaking, the first sphere is the one where restitution must be made, and where the final wrenching away from earth conditions takes place. The second is one of instruction, a period of study, during which the spirit gains knowledge of self and natural law. The third is one of teaching those in the lower spheres, as I have said. The fourth sphere is one of trial and temptation. The fifth is truth, where error and falsehood are unknown. In the sixth, all is harmony. In the seventh, the spirits reach the plane of exaltation and become one with the great spirit that rules the universe.

"There are others, more advanced than I, who can better tell you of the spheres beyond. I have not been to the fourth, and only know of it as you do, by the teaching of those who are there. We are told that the spirits in the sphere of exaltation do not even there lose individuality. They are embodied in all the beauty and good of the universe. I do not know that I can make my meaning clear. Although they keep individuality, they permeate the universe. They have become so great and universal, we sometimes think they go beyond and must lose their personality; but we have no definite knowledge, and it is generally accepted they do not. It is difficult to understand or appreciate what this last sphere is, the development is so beyond our comprehension. Those in the second sphere do little, except to fit themselves for a broader and better work. Before reaching this condition they have freed their spirit from the burden of wrong done in the body, repaid every debt due mankind, dispelled the darkness of the first sphere. They work with open eyes and clear spiritual vision, and are at peace with all. This must precede the sphere of study and development. I have classes on purity, beauty, and patience, and there are classes on every conceivable subject, —music, chemistry, everything. They are different from those in earth-life, and one has to adopt different ideas. One of our engineers magnetizes your room each time you hear our voices. It is easier for those who have advanced to higher life to reach us than for us to reach you; there are not so many barriers. Yes, we always have places that resemble homes. Thought is not indefinite, and that makes our homes, and while we keep that thought, our homes are permanent. You ask where is that home located? I would say to you that all that is space is peopled with spirits."

This lecture gave to us the sphere of progression. As you see, we were told not only their names, but something of the occupations that are pursued in the higher life. Not much can be told, I assume, but possibly all that a finite mind can grasp. I believe what I have written, not only because I know the one who talked, but because it appeals to reason, and is in harmony with natural law, as I understand it.

True, it is hard to understand where these spheres are, but there are many things quite as difficult of comprehension. Astronomical instruments have shown that it is ninety-three millions of miles to the sun, but this really conveys nothing to the mind, because one cannot comprehend such a distance. We know that light travels at a rate of one hundred and eighty-six thousand miles a second, but what that rate of speed is we cannot understand, for there is nothing tangible with which to compare it. Our actual knowledge of electricity, or magnetism, or even of gravitation is limited, as are all of Nature's laws. Then, is it strange that one finds difficulty in appreciating what space is and how it is peopled? This thought of ours is even now free and can pass through space, but it goes with closed eyes, hears no sounds, and feels no touch. At dissolution, each sense is quickened, and all life that fills space is visible to the spiritual sense and tangible to spiritual touch and brain. Space must then take form, substance, and reality, —in a world of thought, boundless and endless.

One in the after-life gave me a description of the spirit-home of a great, splendid mother, built by the labour of ceaseless love and ceaseless charity, —in the physical as well as in the spirit plane in which she now resides, —one who worked long and earnestly to make women understand the truth so that they might live nearer to the best in nature.

Here is the description as it was given me:

**"Before me is the interior of a splendid home, the home made by a spirit, created and builded by the thoughts, acts, and works of one who, thirty-two years ago, lived on the material plane. The room opening before me seems like pure white marble with lofty ceilings; around the four sides runs a broad balcony supported by columns gracefully turned; from a point beyond the center is a broad stairway curving outward; at its foot, on each side, are niches filled with beautiful statuary. Going up the stairs now, I find each step a different color, yet all blending into one; on all sides of this upper gallery are windows through which come soft rays of light. Opening off the sides are rooms; and, as I look, a door opens and a beautiful spirit comes out, taking on, as she enters, the old material condition that she may be recognized. She has reached maturity in years, and has a face of rare gentleness—the beauty of purity—she smiles as we describe her and her home to you. With her is a daughter just reaching womanhood; one that never lived the earth-life but was prematurely born. These two, drawn by the invisible bond of affection, have builded this home and made it rich with love.**

**"Passing down the corridor now, the mother's arm about the daughter, they approach the other end of the building and descend a stairway similar to the first, and go out upon a broad terrace, along walks bordered with flowers, into the**

garden of happiness. **Turning now and looking toward a valley, I see many trees heavy with foliage, and through them I behold the waters of a lake, rich as an emerald in color.**

**"About the vaulted room which I have described are many others of like material, filled with all that this mother loves. Books that she uses in her work are seen; pictures, created by acts of tenderness, adorn the walls. Musical instruments unlike those of earth await spirit-touch. This is a home where girls, just budding into womanhood, are taught purity—this is a mother's home, and suggests to you the possibility of spiritual surroundings. It was not builded in a day, but is the result of labour in the earth and in spheres of progression, where the surroundings are in harmony with spiritual development; the home of a good woman, builded by helping others."**

I said to one of my friends in the after-life, at another time: "Tell me of the homes of spirit people," and, in reply, he said:

**"That is a most difficult thing to do, because earth people expect to find everything so different, while, in reality, the homes here are practically the same as in earth-life, except that there is in the advanced spheres no discord, no lack of harmony, nothing but light, beauty, music, laughter, blended with earnest, thoughtful study. I am describing the home of a spirit who has grown to know the life principle. There are many poor, struggling, souls willfully, or ignorantly, looking down instead of upwards into the great possibility of the future, who are living in squalid huts which their deeds and thoughts in earth-life have made for them. Very few have beautiful homes ready for them when they enter spirit-life, for most people live in such ignorance of natural laws that they find insufficient shelter awaiting them, but the wise ones start to build by perfecting their way of thinking and by undoing wrongs on earth, and also, by helping others. No actual physical touch is given these homes, but, as the soul grows in beauty of thought and deed, the home grows to perfection."**

"Are these homes as real to you as ours are to us?" I asked.

**"They are the abiding places of spirits who gather into them the objects of beauty they love, and their harmonious spirits come and go, as in earth-life. They are as real to them as yours are to you. But we look at things differently; we think them, and the thought is expressed in waves that are visible and real as long as we hold the thought."**

143

## Where is the After Life?

Where is the after life? Just where do they live? Where are its boundaries? These are questions that I have some difficulty in understanding, and much more in explaining, and I am frank to admit that I have not had all the information sought on this subject. However, I have some knowledge, gained both from my friends in the spirit-world and from my ability to deduce from common facts.

Let it be remembered that those in the after life have frequently said that every physical thing of this earth was but a poor imitation of what they have there—that all things exist first in the invisible, and that all that we have is a reproduction in form of some of the things that exist there.

Here is what one said on this subject:

**"We have often told you, and tell you now, that your earth and all things of your earth have their exact counterparts in the spirit world, just as real, just as tangible, just as substantial, to the inhabitants of this world, as material things and forms are to the inhabitants in mortal form upon your earth."**

If this be true, if we have earth and rocks, so do they; if we have shrubs and trees and growing grains and flowers, so do they; if we have houses, schools, great buildings, so do they, if we have oceans, lakes, rivers and flowing streams, so do they; if this earth is peopled, why not theirs? I am told they have also many things that we have not, as they cannot be clothed in earth garments nor function on our planet.

The density of that plane differs from ours, as the density of our atmosphere differs from that of water, in which marine life functions. We move more rapidly and with greater freedom than the life that exists in the deep; so those in the higher etheric plane move more rapidly and with greater freedom than we do—all because the material conditions become higher in vibration as we ascend the scale of motion, and there is more resistance the lower we descend.

Striving for more detailed description, I asked a spirit in our work one evening:

"Where is the spirit world? What of its substance, and where are its boundaries?"

The spirit answered:

**"It is difficult to explain to you who know little of matter, the location and boundaries of the various planes where we live. First let me impress upon you the fact that energy, that is, life, cannot express itself except in substance. The idea that**

spirit people function without substance and that they and the plane in which they live are unsubstantial, is preposterous and illogical. The gases that compose water, taken separately, are as substantial as when united. Why should it be thought impossible, since matter was created, for Nature to create other material than physical, to create spirit material? There are millions of worlds inhabited by human beings in that space you call the sky. Don't for a moment think that yours is the only world, and that God made the universe for you alone.

"This spirit world is in reality just as much a part of your planet as the earth and the rocks you tread upon. Around and about your globe, and forming a part of it, are separate material, concentric belts or zones, varying in width and vibratory action, and therefore in density, into which all mankind and all planetary life passes, on the happening of that event you call death.

"I only know the boundaries of these planes in which I live and labour. I do not know any more about the boundaries of the planes beyond me than you know of the planes beyond you."

Others have reported of these localities as follows:

"Your earth has belts, but they exist in a cruder condition than those of Jupiter and Saturn. The belts or zones that lie around your earth are designed for the habitation of spirits out of the body; and as they outgrow the passions of earth and become more refined, they pass to another or higher zone.

"I have discovered, while living here, that there are several magnetic belts encircling your earth, similar in general appearance to the belts the surround the planet Jupiter, and beyond those zones there exists, outside earth's spirit sphere, a vast spirit world traversing the innermost heart of space."

Another said:

"I, too, am permitted to gaze back at earthly scenes; and, for a time, to dwell on earthly memories while bringing to you for your world some experiences and observations of my own, both in mortal existence and the spheres.

"I have observed that there are innumerable states and conditions and diversified experiences in spirit as on earth. We may illustrate by different highways, thus:

"Let one condition be represented by a certain highway, and another condition by another and differing highway, leading through a different country.

"As no two highways of your world lead over the same country and present the same scenery to the traveller, so of the children of earth; no two travel over the same highway or have the same experiences; to each are presented different scenes from those presented to any other.

"One person travelling one road is landed into the spirit world at one point, and one on another road enters spirit life at another point; and a third, on yet another road, enters at a different point from either of the others. And so on the endless procession moves, landing its infinitude of differentiated individualities; and each one has a different idea to relate. Therefore no two relates the same story of the earthly journey.

"But the varied highways of earth continue into eternity, and the traveller on each goes eternally on his own road from the earth life. And thus all travel on in the spirit world, having different experiences here, as with you; and, on returning to you, we have different experiences and differing descriptions of the spirit world to relate to you, according as each has realized for himself."

I can readily appreciate that spirit people along the Frontier and among the rudimentary spheres cannot tell how many there are beyond, and may not all agree, but here is what another says on the subject:

"There are innumerable spheres in the spirit world. If it were not so, progression would be a myth. Some tell you that there are only seven. That is because they have no knowledge beyond that sphere. I do not mean a place fixed by boundaries, for the spheres or degrees in spirit life are only conditions and are not confined to a limited space; as a soul develops, it naturally arises above its surroundings and consequently experiences a change in its spheres or conditions."

Impressed with the suggestion concerning Jupiter and Saturn, I examined the works of the foremost astronomers, and this is, in substance, what they say:

Jupiter is marked with bands, more or less wide, more or less intense, which show perfectly near its equatorial region. Saturn has a number of what appear to be broad, flat rings surround it, but separated from it on all sides, which lie all in the same plane of inclination to the ecliptic. The inner and broader of the two belts or zones is the brightest near the outer part, and shades off toward the planet, —gradually at first, more rapidly afterward. Its inner portion is so dark that at one time it was regarded separate and called "Crape" or "dusty" ring. Modern telescopes show the inner part of this ring transparent.

The physical constitution of the rings is unlike that of any other known objects in our solar system. They are not formed of a continuous mass of solid or liquid matter, but of discreet particles of unknown minuteness, probably widely separated in proportion to their individual volume, yet so close as to appear continuous.

To know the location of the next plane helps one to appreciate conditions that exist there. Our finite minds can comprehend little that we have not actually experienced, and so we mentally grope in our efforts to comprehend what is told us of those more advanced spheres, and must in a measure rely on deductive reasoning. I have also found that spirit people do not agree in many respects, any more than we do. Each reports according to his knowledge and understanding; therefore, each must form his own conclusions, based on reason.

In order to get another impression, I read what I have written to Dr. Hossack, one of the leaders of the spirit group with whom I worked so many years, and for whose statements I have great respect, and in reply he said:

**"What appears as space about your earth is composed of ether. There are three distinct circles, the outer filled with more radiant vibrations than those within. Beyond these, the spheres, or circles blend with those of other planets. Each circle is very, very many miles in depth, according to your standard of measurement."**

I am much impressed with such statements, as they seem natural and appeal to reason. So far as I know, no one has heretofore attempted actually to locate and fix the boundaries of the after life. Two thousand years of Christian teaching have not enabled a reasoning mind to form any definite conclusions as to where that place called heaven is, or concerning the conditions prevailing where the so-called dead reside, and it seems quite time that we have a scientific explanation, or at least a start along the road.

When Columbus discovered the continent of North America, the whole world at once accepted the fact, changed their ideas about the earth's shape, and still celebrate his achievement. The psychic investigators within the last seventy-five years have discovered not a continent but millions of inhabited worlds, and now actually locate the planets, begin to understand the substance that composes them, and know something of the light that fills those zones, —achievements that transcend all discoveries of modern times. Our descriptions, so concise and brief, but serve as texts,

147

however, and from them we must make deductions and bring understanding to ourselves.

It will be noted that there is a similarity between the circles or rings about our earth, and those of Jupiter and Saturn. Our astronomers contend that these circles or rings are not formed of a continuous mass of solid or liquid substance, but of discreet particles of unknown minuteness, unlike any other visible objects in our solar system. These statements demonstrate that matter has phases or conditions not generally understood by earth dwellers.

Those who have spoken—Faraday, Denton and Hossack, and others above quoted—are in a position to know something of the substance that fills that plane, and they all say it is ether. And what is ether? Our encyclopedias explain it as the upper, purer air; the abode of the gods. Our astronomers say that it is a hypothetical medium of extreme tenuity and elasticity, supposed to be diffused throughout all space. Spirit people say that ether is matter similar to earth substance, but in a very high state of vibration. According to them, the universe is all material, substance or matter in different and varying states of vibration, and those rings, circles or envelopes that surround this earth of ours are just as substantial, visible, real and tangible as anything we have. Those zones vibrate in substantially direct proportion to our thoughts, and may well be called the mental plane.

No thoughtful person can read these statements from distinguished and scientific spirits without being impressed, and without drawing from them rational deductions. Beyond the visible is the true field of discovery. Here secrets are veiled from physical sight, and the mental powers, based on the statements of spirit people, are the only means available to push discovery to its ultimate.

I know that these gentlemen made the statements quoted. The world counted them not only honest but great scientists, when they resided here. Their statements appear in accordance with nature's tendency. They are rational and I accept them, and, basing my opinion thereon and on other knowledge obtained from persons in the after life, I state without qualification that about his earth there are material concentric belts or zones, composed of ether, which become more radiant and higher in vibrations as they extend outward. In these zones all the so-called dead reside and have their homes, where the family relation is ultimately restored. For the first time the local habitations of spirit people have been discovered, and the spheres or zones can now be named.

## Actualities of the After life

After birth, death is the greatest privilege that comes to mankind. If death did not occur, there would be old age, feebleness, poverty, pain, and suffering forever; with it, splendid life on through the ages, progress, perpetual youth and vigour. Such is the heritage of all who have lived, or who shall live in the ages to come as inhabitants of this plane; such are the benefits coming through dissolution.

"**Physically considered, in the final separation of the soul or spirit body from the flesh garment there are no discomforts. As the etheric form goes out through the process called death, pain ceases, and then for a short period comes what is usually called unconsciousness. During the passing of the soul, when the individual leaves the tenement of flesh, when the spirit of man hurried forth from the old housing, there is no sensation. That period of time may be characterized as a sleep; then comes the awakening, the return of sensation, consciousness. Such is the true resurrection, and the possibility of that perfect life, unattainable to an inhabitant of earth. After leaving the earth-plane the immortal has been divested of the physical, and progress is unlimited.**"

Again, it was my privilege to have speech with those living beyond my vision. The room in my house in which I carried on my experimental work was intensely dark; as usual, only Mrs. French and I were present. The thought, before so intense, had for a moment become passive; then out from the silence came the deep-toned voice of him who spoke the above quoted words.

Ever alert to obtain the personal observations of those who have gone on, I said:

"I have been told that the after-life is intensely real and that with you everything is just as tangible as it was when you lived among us. Tell me something of matter surrounding and composing the plane in which you live."

"**The most learned scientist,**" he replied, "**among the inhabitants of earth has practically no conception of the properties of matter, the substance that makes up the Universe—visible and invisible. I did not when I lived among you, though I made a special study of the subject. That which you see and touch, making up the physical or tangible, having three dimensions, is the lowest or crudest expression of life force, and notwithstanding my long study of the subject, the idea that the physical had permanent etheric or life-form, that which you call**

149

space was composed of matter filled with intelligent and comprehensive life in higher vibration never occurred to me; so when I became an inhabitant of the plane where I now reside, I was wholly unprepared to grasp or comprehend the material conditions of the environment in which I found myself."

"Tell me," I asked, "of your awakening, and how things appeared to you as consciousness was restored."

**"Of course,"** he replied, **"there was the meeting and greeting of my own who came to welcome me, as naturally as one returning after along journey in the earth-life would be welcomed. Their bodies were not so dense as when they were inhabitants of earth, but they were like my own. Then I was told that my body and the bodies of all those in that life were actually the identical bodies we had in earth life, divested of the flesh covering. I was also told that that condition was a necessary precedent to entering the higher life, and that such bodies in earth life had continuity and, further, that in leaving the old, I had come into a plane where all was etheric, that is matter vibrating in perfect accord with my spirit, technically speaking, the etheric self. To me everything seemed perfectly natural to sense, sight, and touch.**

**"Again, let me tell you,"** he said, **"that the outer flesh garment is not sufficiently sensitive to feel, the etheric body alone has sensation. This I have said as leading up to a clear understanding of what I experienced in meeting the new conditions here. I found little body-change, —I had sensations and vision—and my personal appearance was in no way changed except that my body was less dense, more transparent as it were, but the outline of my form was definite, my mind clear, the appearance of age gone, and I stood a man in the fullness of my mentality—nothing gained or lost mentally.**

**"What impressed me most after the meeting with my own was the reality and tangibility of everything and everyone. All those with whom I came in contact had bodies like my own, and I recognized friends and acquaintances readily. Now I will tell you of the one thing that impressed me most on coming here, —that was that matter in its intense refinement, in its higher vibration, was capable of intelligent thinking and direction. Shape and grasp this proposition if you can; I could not in the beginning—nor could I comprehend at once that all**

in the Universe was life and nothing else. This fact, which we now know, will overturn all the propositions of science.

"In all the orthodox teaching of nearly two thousand years, not one law has been given tending to show how it was possible for individual life to hold continuity. Theology has claimed it without explaining how or where. This no longer satisfies the human heart or mind, a fact which accounts for the great unrest among your people in every land. For this reason it has been our aim to explain the law through which life is continued, and so simply to state the facts and explain the conditions that all may understand. The key to comprehension is first to realize that your Earth does not contain all the matter of the Universe, that all that you see and touch is but the substance used by life in growth. When one leaves the earth-condition, divests himself of the physical housing, he, through such change, ceases to be mortal. By becoming a resident of the new sphere he is said to take on immortality, but in reality, he has always been immortal.

"You regard the telephone as wonderful," he said, "wireless telegraphy more wonderful still—but we communicate with each other by simple thought projection. You regard the phonograph as a marvellous instrument, but it is crude beside the instruments in use among us. When you appreciate the truth that we live in a state no less material than your own, you will understand that with our greater age and experience we are much in advance of you, and make and use appliances and instruments that could hardly be explained to mortal mind. At some other time I may be permitted to discuss the subject more fully."

## Poverty in the After Life

One who attempts to modify the thoughts, ambitions and desires of mankind, is undertaking a great task. The American people, more than any other, are taught from infancy that the desired goal is wealth—and, such is the prodigality of the times, money is necessary for the pace that is set. Money—the ring and shine of gold—becomes alluring, and the ambition of each is for its accumulation. The length to which some go, and the things that some do to possess themselves of it, stagger the mind, at least of those who have a clearer vision.

It is right and very proper to provide for those dependent, in a suitable manner; but, we owe it to ourselves to provide for and enrich ourselves, both here and hereafter. Some few gather spiritual wealth that enriches beyond this life, but the many go out into the great beyond—paupers.

I am impressed to urge the importance of so living and doing that when we leave this world and also leave the material wealth that we have gathered with such great effort, we may possess a spiritual wealth of vastly more importance than stock and bonds and physical properties. This involves an awakening, a change of ideals, modified ambitions, new thoughts, new hopes, and new desires.

This spiritual wealth that becomes ours for all time, and enriches us in the great beyond, is accumulated without great effort. It is gathered simply by being fair in all our dealings, just to all men, and by helping those less fortunate than ourselves. This does not necessarily contemplate the expenditure of money, for a kind thought, a generous act, a little sympathy, an encouraging word, sets in motion vibrations in and about us that become a very part of us, refine our natures, spiritualize our souls, and better our conditions both here and hereafter.

We enrich ourselves by helping others, not by cheating or taking advantage of those with whom we have dealings. When we are unfair in a transaction, get the best of another and obtain his property, while we may do so without violating any civil law, we gain no profit, for in the end the wrong must be undone and the property retuned. There is a law, taught in the dawn of civilization, that transcends the rules of modern times. It is, "Do unto others what we would have them do unto us." And eternal justice requires compensation for violation of this great law. If we build about us crude conditions, we must expect to enter into the environment which our acts and thoughts have created. This is fair, this is justice.

I do not speak from a religious standpoint. This work has nothing to do with religion of any kind. I am writing about facts and conditions, here and beyond, as I have come to know them; they are interwoven now and always have been and ever will be. Every act that we do is known here, and is visible and lives there, for we take them with us.

Take an inventory, look the situation over squarely and fairly. What have you done that will provide food, raiment and home in the After Life? How have you developed? The idea that here and now we can and should do and provide all those things has not been well impressed on the human mind. Would it not be the part of wisdom to give this subject a little thought, give half as much to the accumulation of spiritual as you do material wealth, and so make happier and richer those who are now in the hereafter and ourselves and others here?

Let me quote directly from one in the next life, who has given this subject thought and who speaks from experience. This statement should create a profound impression on all thinking men and women; it is from one who actually lives and labours in that place we call the After Life:

"The majority of people are so intent on things material that those of a spiritual nature are either thrust into the background or forgotten altogether. This is a deplorable state of things and one which we earnestly desire to remedy.

"The mere struggle to live and provide themselves and their dependents with what they consider the necessities of life, engage many folks' attention to the exclusion of everything else. They just battle on from day to day because they must, or else become a burden to others. Such endeavor in their case is right and necessary and, if it is carried on in a brave and hopeful spirit, it is greatly to be admired.

"At the same time they would be greatly helped, and their burdens lightened considerably, if they would take time from their incessant struggle after material things to store up for themselves treasures of a spiritual nature.

"Wealth of this kind is of inestimable value and well worth a little trouble to procure. Unlike earthly riches it makes life on the earth easier and pleasanter for its possessor and his associates, and ensures for him a happy and useful time when his earthly life ends and his spiritual existence begins.

"One who has given all or nearly all of his time and thought to material things has so much to learn on arriving here, that it is a comparatively long time before he begins to 'find' himself sufficiently to understand and enjoy the spiritual life. Such a one, if he had given more time and thought to spiritual things during his earth life, could have immediately have claimed his spiritual treasures—which would have been carefully stored up for him until such time as he had need of them—and he would have been helped and his new life made much easier and pleasanter by the possession of these riches. As it is, he has to make his way as a penniless wayfarer, on arriving in a new locality, must set about earning his daily bread in the material world.

"Everyone knows what a handicap the lack of capital is in your world. Well, exactly the same thing applies here. Folks arriving here in the spiritually destitute condition before mentioned have just as hard, if not a harder, struggle to make their way in the spiritual life as anyone who is left without means on earth. People placed in the latter condition may and very often do receive financial help from friends and relatives, or societies which deal with that sort of thing, but their are no charitable institutions here. That is to say, no spirit ever gets something for nothing, or without effort on his part. Though we old spirits can and do help newcomers, we cannot give them spiritual riches—we can only show them how they may acquire them for themselves."

Another spirit says:

"If newly-arrived spirits have a desire to learn how to make a spiritual living, so to speak, we can instruct them, so that in time they will become independent and will know how to set about the task of amassing wealth of a spiritual nature for themselves.

"Such wealth is not easily acquired, even here, but it is possible for any and every spirit to become possessed of it in time, if he only desires it sufficiently and is willing to work hard to get it. This may sound as if selfishness is encouraged here, but that is not so. Spirits can become possessed of the wealth here spoken of only by loving and unselfish conduct toward others. They must learn to work gladly and without thought of reward before they can hope to enjoy the fruits of their labours.

"There must be literally a 'labour of love,' and when self is utterly forgotten in a desire to help others, great and satisfying will be their reward. No goal on earth is, or even can be, so well worth striving after. For, after all, though it is difficult to make humanity realize it fully, the things of the soul are so much more worthwhile, and infinitely more lasting, than any earthly joys and pleasures can possibly be."

So little thought has been given to the necessity of gathering spiritual wealth to enrich us beyond this physical life, so little thought has also been given to means and method, that the question may fairly be asked: How is it done?

To answer so important a question requires little thought and some reasoning, for it is only through the avenue of reason we comprehend the intangible.

Every physical act has a physical result, every cause its legitimate effect. Advancing the spark to meet the gas, we have combustion, and the energy released is expressed in motion visible and tangible. We lay one brick upon another, embedded in plaster or cement, and we build a wall. Everyone endeavours to have a home of his own, —all the result of effort, every fine spiritual act and thought changes the etheric condition about the individual. Every thought has color and is expressed in shade. Nature abhors stagnation; every hour we are improving or impoverishing our very selves; one cannot stand still.

But how can individual acts enrich us in the after life, you ask again? There is not one law for the spiritual world and another for the physical. There is one law for both, for both blend and are really one. Simply the one to our present eyes is invisible, and the other visible, because of the different vibrations or modes of motion. Dissolution simply changes the plane of action.

We illustrate. To help another with kindly words and suggestion, to give where hunger stalks, brings joy and happiness to giver and beneficiary. Giving of material wealth is no more important than words of encouragement and tender sympathy. The peace and comfort produced by such acts are reflected, and enrich us not only here but hereafter; charity enriches the donor more than those to whom it is given. It has been well said that the only wealth one carries into the great beyond is that he gives away here, and it will be remembered that in the next life, where money is no more, the only way one can enrich himself is by helping others. It is well to have a good start by commencing here, for the only genuine happiness we gain now is by helping others to better their condition.

We are building character every day, and, on the threshold of the After Life, stripped of all material wealth, we face the endless future, either rich in generous acts or paupers in a world of plenty. If mankind understood these conditions, there would be more fair dealing, less selfishness, —a happier world, a richer world, a better world, and as we go one by one, we should meet the new life with the wealth of generous acts and thoughts and deeds.

Thoughts are things, and every act and thought functions around and about us in that substance called ether, sometimes called the aura. That substance, woven of the warp and woof of an act and thought, envelops us now and ever will, invisible to us now but ever visible to all in the life that follows. With this in mind, let us pause for a moment and seriously consider what kind of an etheric garment we are weaving day by day, and how our spirits will appear as we approach the Frontiers of the After Life. Will we go with a consciousness of a life well spent, rich with generous acts and kindly deeds, and, radiant with the soul's emanations, meet the outstretched hands and proudly reply to the words and songs of welcome? Or shall we approach this goal with soul shri-veled by selfishness, lust and greed, from which no light of gen-erous acts pierces the gloom?

I have talked with many who have gone out into darkness of their own creation, poor and alone, and long have they sought for the light that ultimately comes to all that live.

## Their Daily Life

In my investigation I was always anxious to obtain a descrip-tion of the occupation and daily life of those who live in the plane beyond, and asked many practical questions.

"What is the death change that seems so horrible to the average mind?" I inquired.

**"Death change,"** one answered, **"is simply the liberation of the spirit from from the physical body, composing the outer flesh garment, perfectly natural and painless. Every change in Nature is beautiful, and dissolution is no exception to the rule. One simply ceases to be an inhabitant of your world, and in an instant one becomes an inhabitant of the world in which we now live. The second world or plane is just as natural to us as the first, but, of course, we live under different conditions. We pass our daily life as before. Our spirit is just as perfect a human form as it ever was. For your clear understanding of the modus operandi of the death change to this plane we may say that one parts with the physical body only. We lose none of our intelligence; neither is anything added to our under-standing."**

"What of your daily life?" I asked.

**"Our days are very busy,"** he said. **"There is no stagnation, but on the contrary, intense activity among everyone, that is, when we have emerged from the earth conditions. There are countless millions of children unborn physically who are plunged into this world of ours, and there are millions of women here who have never known motherhood in earth life, who take and care for them, watch and aid their growth, men-tally and physically, and in that manner satisfy the craving of motherhood.**

**"The insane pass from the earth-life insane still, and count-less numbers of our people are required to care for them and give them proper treatment so that their mentality may be restored to normal. Murderers at war with humanity, hanged or electrocuted on the earth-plane, are liberated in this com-**

munity, and we are obliged to do what the world of men failed to do—control and educate them. Then, again, we have the ignorant and vicious. The atom of Good that has found expression in them must be developed and directed. Few people come into this life with any conception of what or where it is, or of the controlling laws. The ignorance of the masses is pitiful. They enter our portals as helpless as the babe enters yours. So you see dissolution making no mental change, and life being material and continuous, there is just as great need for schools, colleges, and universities as exists with you. In fact, it may be said that everything you have in your earth life is but a poor imitation of what exists here and is largely the result of spirit influence and power."

"What of your homes?" I asked.

"We have houses in which the family relation is continued, where every member-spirit is seeking enlightenment. The law of attraction is the dominant force here. We have a great number of thoughtful men seeking to discover and develop the hidden forces of Nature; we have great lecture halls where those who are learned, discourse upon hidden forces; we have teachers who develop the spirituality, and discourse upon the great force called Good and its function in the universe. It is a busy world where everyone is doing his or her part. We do not have any strife for money or need for money; so you see the occupation of the great majority of your people is gone. It is only by helping others in this life—that one betters his conditions and enriches himself. This is the law. The only happiness that the inhabitants of earth really get is through being charitable, doing good, and making the world happier. The only wealth that any man carries beyond the grave is what he gives away before he reaches the grave."

"Tell us something of your foods. Do your require nourishment?" I asked.

"Yes," he answered, "but not in the manner or in the way that you do. Our digestive organs continue their functions, and we require food, but we take the essence while you take the substance. You take food day by day in earth life. The substance is absorbed in the physical garment, but it is the essence of the food that nourishes the spirit body from day to day. The substance is no longer necessary, but the essence is necessary just as it was before. So you see there is very little change in physical necessities."

"Tell me of your political economy," I asked.

"**There is,**" Dr. Hossack answered, "**no aristocracy in this land of ours, but mind and merit. The law of Nature which is the Supreme force, called Universal Law, has to be obeyed, in order that each sphere may be reached. Every individual remains on the plane for which he is fitted, until he subjects his will to the Universal Law. As he progresses, he learns new laws, but they are fundamentally the same, only they grow more intense and vital, until he becomes a part of that law himself.**

"**The political economy of the spheres has reference only to wealth, which being unbounded and free as air and light, can, of course, be appropriated by each and every member of society, according to his or her capacity of reception, the supply being equal to the demand. Hence it will be seen that we have no occasion for gold and silver which perish with the using; but the currency of moral and intellectual worth, coined in the mint of divine Love, and assayed by the standards of purity and truth, is necessary for each one.**"

"Tell me something of your social life," I said.

"**With regard to the social constitution of the spheres,**" he answered, "**each is divided into six circles or societies in which congenial people live together agreeably according to the law of attraction. Although the individuals composing such society unite as near as may be in thought, agreeing in the most important moral and intellectual features, yet upon careful analysis we find that the varieties of character in each society are almost without number. They are perfectly analogous to the numerous members of the different societies on the earth-plane. Each group has teachers more advanced than the members of the group, and teachers often come from higher spheres. They impart to us the knowledge they have acquired in their progression in the different departments of science, which we, in turn, transmit to those below us, just in the same manner as we are transmitting knowledge to you now. Thus, by receiving and teaching, our intellectual faculties are expanded to higher conceptions and more exalted views of Nature's laws. Our scientific researches are extended to all that pertains to Nature, to the wonders of the heavens and of the earth and to whatever the mentality is capable of conceiving and comprehending. In this manner we get our progression and enjoyment. The sciences of mathematics and astronomy** engage our attention. These subjects are inexhaustible. Chemistry is the most interesting of any of our studies, as it would be to you if you only appreciated the fact that all change in Nature is the result of chemical action."

"You do not mean to say that all of your inhabitants are sufficiently advance to do that work?"

"No," he answered, "there are millions of inhabitants of this life who are not sufficiently advanced to take any interest in such studies. As we have passed beyond the rudimentary sphere, our intellectual energy is increased, our perception improved, and we can by intuition, as it were, more correctly and rapidly conceive and understand those principles and truths which are the basis of all scientific work.

"In addition to our research we have our diversions from which we obtain great pleasure. We come together in social intercourse, just as you do. Families meet and have reunions, just as you do. Not one particle of love is lost, but rather it is intensified. Everything is intensified to a degree that you cannot imagine. Your pleasure and amusements can in no way compare to those which we are privileged to enjoy."

"What of the religious movement among your people?" I asked.

"In the lowest of the spheres, that is, in the earth-bound spheres sectarian strife and religious movement are just as strenuous among the people as they were before these persons left the physical body. That state of transition is but little removed from the physical, for, while the majority there know they have left the body, others have such an imperfect appreciation of the change, or have led such immoral lives that they are not conscious of the fact. Here the dogmas of orthodoxy are dominant, and the old religious teachings are promulgated, and the priesthood still holds power. One would think that an individual having passed through the portal called death and finding nothing as he had been taught, or as he had believed, would give up the old notions and try to comprehend the economy of the natural law under which he continued to live; but, strange as it may seem, many even then cling to the old beliefs as if in fear, as if to doubt were sacrilege, and in many ways excuse their failure to find what they expected. They go into your churches and mingle with other people, a great invisible host, hear the same old teachings, say the same creeds and continue in the same mental attitude until some condition is brought about them that guides them into the avenue of knowledge, and as time goes on, one by one they break the shackles about their mentalities, and by progression, through individual effort, become inhabitants of the first spirit spheres.

"Everyday matters are no different in our sphere than in your sphere. You do not progress and obtain knowledge and advancement until you break away from the old beliefs and creeds. Neither do those out of the body in that earth-bound condition. You see there is but one law for you and one law for us. All of nature's laws are universal.

"Our laws are meted out on a scale of exact justice. All Nature's laws are exact laws, and from their reward there is no appeal. Punishments are but the natural consequence of violated laws, and are invariably commensurate with the offense, and have reference to the reformation of the offender as well as to the prevention of future crimes."

"What are the results that will come to mankind through communication with your people?" I asked an inhabitant of the afterlife. He answered:

"I will briefly call your attention to a few of the most prominent of the beneficial results which will flow from spiritual intercommunion. It will settle the important question, 'If a man dies, shall he live again?' It will reduce the doctrine of the immortality of the human spirit to certainty, so that the world's knowledge of the fact will not be the result of a blind faith, but a positive philosophy. It will show the relation existing between mind and matter; it will make men thinking and rational beings. It will establish a holy and most delightful intercourse between the inhabitants of the terrestrial world and the departed spirit friends. It will expand and liberalize the mind far beyond your present conceptions. It will fraternize and unite all the members of the human family in an everlasting bond of spiritual union and harmonious brotherhood. It will establish the principle of love to God and your fellows. It will do away with sectarian bigotry. It will show that many of the so-called religious teachings are but impositions on the credulity of mankind."

"I am anxious for a further description of yourselves, your pleasures, your intercourse with each other, and it is difficult for us who have only had experience with matter in its physical state in any way to comprehend life in another state," I said.

"We derive much pleasure," was the reply, "from the exercise of our talents in vocal and instrumental music, which far excels the noblest efforts of musical genius on earth. When we convene to worship God in our temples, whose halls and columns beam with inherent light, our voices are blended together in songs of praise and adoration to the Almighty author of our existence.

"We are moral, intellectual, and sensitive creatures. Instead of being, as you may imagine, more shadowy and unsubstantial entities, we are possessed of definite, tangible, and exquisitely symmetrical forms, with well-rounded and graceful limbs, and yet so light and elastic that we can glide through the atmosphere with almost electrical speed. The forked lightnings may flash, and the thunders roll in awful reverberation along the vault of heaven, and the rain descend in gushing torrents, but we can stand unharmed by your side.

"We are, moreover, endowed with all the beauty, loveliness, and vivacity of youth, and are clothed in flowing vestments of effulgent nature suited to the peculiar degree of refinement of our bodies. Our raiment being composed of phosphorescent principles, we have the power of attracting and absorbing or reflecting the rays evolved, according as our condition is more or less developed. This accounts for our being seen by clairvoyants in different degrees of brightness, from a dusky hue to an intensity of brilliant light."

## Light in the Spirit World

There were few nights in all the years of my research that Dr. David Hossack did not address us on some subject. He always came with charming courtesy and great cordiality. His voice was low, but he spoke clearly and to the point. No more distinguished or delightful guest ever entered my house. It will be noted that I make no distinction in speaking of those who enter my home. It matters not whether for the moment they function in the spirit or in the physical plane; they are all people and can discuss questions, when proper conditions are provided, with equal freedom. During the period when I obtained these discourses from the beyond, I formed or provided the conditions requisite and necessary, as I have explained elsewhere.

The question of light in the next world has always interested me, and it is one of the subjects upon which I have sought information. I speak of Dr. Hossack, for the reason that he has given me the most satisfactory explanation of any. This was my question to him:

"What is the character of your light, and how does it differ from sunlight?"

The answer:

**"The light we have is obtained from the action of our minds on the atmosphere. We think light, and there is light. That is why people who come over in evil condition are in the dark; their minds are not competent to produce light enough for them to see.**

**"There is great intensity of light as we go up through the spheres, which comes from the blending of the more spiritual minds.**

**"Our life is merely the condition of mind which each one has. We create images in thought, and have the reality before us, just as tangible as your houses and buildings are to you. You do not have any conception of the great power and force there is, or may be, in thought. It dominates all conditions and makes us what we are. One who realizes this may control his destiny.**

**"Thought is a fluid, which becomes substance to us when once it is formed into an expression. It is a vibrating, living thing, and should be recognized as such and controlled accordingly."**

Another spirit speaks of light as follows:

**"When you speak of the sun in the spirit world, you mistake, for there is no such thing. There is light here, radiated from the atoms. Our light is very different from your sun. Your light is grosser than ours; it is unnatural to us, and therefore, painful to the spirit. Our light is soft, radiant and very brilliant. Your physical eye can never behold it; it is so ethereal, so beautiful, that it blends with sensation."**

But why? What natural law produces spirit light? If this were explained in detail, nothing would be left for deductive reasoning. These descriptions but serve to spur one on to greater effort, and must, of necessity, make deductions and partly by that process understand spirit conditions. I have ever noticed that in seeking knowledge of after-life conditions, something is left for one to do if he would attain the desired result. This is in accordance with the oft-repeated statement that the spirits only help others to help themselves. Another's understanding follows:

**"There is a great central force, the rays from which gradually lessen in their vibratory action. This force comes from the**

outside of your world, as you call it, and reaches the lowest ebb in the center of your earth. This central vibratory action is in the highest sphere, and is so intense and vivid that the souls that are in the finest state of development are the only ones who come near its circle. It is the apex of the universe, and that is why there are lesser degrees as it is rayed out through infinite space. These vibrations of light reach the earth and all the other spheres, and the vibratory action of light on each plant depends on its distance from the seat of this creative or central force.

"Some of the planets are much higher in vibratory action than in your earth, and if you were to go to them, and could still retain the earth conditions surrounding you, as usual you could not see any life because your vibration would be so much lower. The need of this condition is so apparent when once one grasps the immensity of the universe and the harmony of its laws.

"If you were able to see all the conditions and people beyond you, life would be chaos and confusion—each sphere mixing with another—with no regulations or harmony anywhere. As it is, each has its own place in the scheme of progression, and this visible wall of vibratory force is the safety guard to continued rational living.

"This force is life, intense, vibrating, dominant. In conception there is the merest touch to this elemental force; consequently, life is forwarded and the continuation of the species insured. It is something discernible as a part of nature and nature is but an expression of this great force.

"Those souls that progress through each step are slowly, but surely, becoming a part of that great force which is life; life itself is light, and ultimately individuality will be lost in the immensity of that great, harmonious life force and will become, in turn, a tiny part of the new conception in the earth form again. I do not mean that this is reincarnation. An atom only is needed to create life in the lower earth forms, and that is taken from the immense whole. This is the law of the universe. There seem no words to tell you, or to make you understand clearly, the plan and purpose of creation; one must accept it and try to realize that one's own life, seemingly so important to one's self, is in reality such a little thing in the immensity of the universe, and yet just as essential to the whole as one petal of a flower is to the perfect rose. It is a part of the perfect whole, and necessary.

"Make that part that is developed by you clean and wholesome, and the going on will be filled with beauty; it will be but the going into a new country, among good friends and great advantages, along spiritual and harmonious lines. But to those who live in the dark and do evil and selfish things, the going will be along rough and stormy places and the helping hand hard to find."

We know so little of light. We have always had the sun, but even now know little about it. Man first devised the torch, which not so long ago was all we had; then came the candle; then whale oil and the lamp; next petroleum assisted man; and, within our own time, he has invented the electric light, —evolution of the primitive torch. The ether is light, as is evidenced by the fact that the dynamo draws from the atmosphere this substance and condenses it. We may behold electricity, which is a physical expression of the ether that fills all space in the whole universe. The more a man knows, the more he is willing to learn. The less a man knows, the more positive he is that he knows everything. The question of light is a legitimate field of inquiry, in which any man may make researches, as little has been told concerning it. The suggestion that there is light of another character and that life itself is the light which lights the spirit world, is no more startling than that made concerning the electric lamp a few years ago. There are still many things in nature that we do not know, with all our boasted knowledge.

Our sun is physical. All that is visible is physical, but nothing physical enters the planes that surround this globe. As I understand, nothing physical is visible to spirit people unless they descend into the earth or to lower spirit planes; then they visualize as when in the body. There are countless numbers of spirits also, that for ages never rise above earth conditions nor see the radiance of the higher spheres.

A great law governs spirit, as well as physical, sight. A beautiful, tender, loving thought radiates and goes out from the mentality in long, undulating waves. The longer the thought wave, the finer the thought, the higher its vibrations and the lighter in substance, but a selfish thought sends out a short wave, and, because of its deficient length, it is dark. The mind is a shuttle and is ever weaving about us a condition that will surround us completely on the day of our dissolution. If we develop our minds along fine lines, the thought that goes forth from the soul in the next life will illuminate the path of our progression, but if we fail to observe that law, we pay the penalty, for each soul furnishes all the light discernible along its own pathway in the spheres beyond.

The source of life—that is, the source of energy—does not seem to be known by spirits. Only the infinite can comprehend the infinite. They simply know, as I gather, that there is a great, central source of power from which emanates the life force that finds expression in the various places of consciousness. They know something of conditions that exist in the plane on which, for the time, they live, and, just as we of the earth, they labour for a better understanding of nature's wonderful laws. Our progression to this next sphere will not change our ambitions or desires, or our comprehension and vision—what we see will depend on the light that our souls will radiate. We cannot touch a button or turn a switch and light our way, nor can we borrow a lamp. Self-effort and a clean life along right lines will light the way where the great law places us when the night comes after earth's fitful struggles are over.

## The Record of a Night

"Tell me more of the actualities of your daily life," I asked.

**"You think,"** she answered, **"That you have vision, but your eyes have never looked upon life itself. You think you have hearing, but your dull ears have never heard one strain of our divine music. You have taste, but your tongues have never touched the essence. You have smell, and the aroma of roses carried by etheric atoms fills the nostrils, but you cannot appreciate the perfumes of this land of ours. You feel the touch of the coarse covering of living form without having any conception of the delight of touching life itself. In this sphere we have opportunities for education, joys, and happiness unthought of by you in the earth-land, but these are only for those who have come out of the gross material condition in which they were born. We live in homes largely in groups where harmony of thought and action is perfect, but we too have as many grades of people as you do, and in our earth-condition is found degradation as great as that which you know. Here are found the ignorant, the wicked, the immoral, and the vile. Dissolution does not improve or uplift character; that must come from the germ of good in the heart of every living creature.**

"**Tell those who fear the end,**" the voice said, "**that what they call death is very wonderful and beautiful; that with us, as with you, though you know it not, love is the one great force in the universe; it is the motor that drives the world and causes action. All things are done in and through it, and because of it. Affinity so-called, is the process through which the love-force finds expression. But in this connection let me suggest that love is good, and of God, and walks in the path of honor, never into dishonor. It never brought unhappiness; it is never 'born of lust.'**

"**It has been a joy and a privilege to speak to you tonight, for if any words of mine can help or make happier a single soul, that joy is reflected about me, and I am happier for having made others happy. Such is the law of God, and the secret of the world. Good night.**"

## How Spirits Build Homes in the Afterlife

There is no flight of imagination. Let me bring home the truth by an illustration. Yesterday I purchased a country place, which must be modernized and adapted to our requirements. I have been thinking what changes are possible and what I should like. It was a mental effort to take into consideration the situation and work out a plan. It was all done in thought. I can, by a mental process, see the changed approach, the graded lawns, the enlarged veranda, the great fire-place and the towering chimneys. In thought vibrations these changes have already been made. They exist in mind, which is matter, and all that remains is to have the mental plans put upon paper and sent to the builder, who will give them physical expression, by constructing in gross matter what now exists in refined matter.

So it is in the after life. The home and environment are designed in thought, created in spirit matter, which is also mind, and its beauty and grandeur are only limited by the purity and progression of our earth life. They do not give their thought physical expression; they have nothing physical. Those in the other life have limitations, as we have. We differ in our creations only in the manner of expression. The one must be suitable to physical requirements, the other to spirit requirements; both are mental processes. One is expressed in gross matter, while the other consists of spirit matter and spirit expression.

The next life, in its inception is the sum-total of this life, nothing more. And the structure fashioned by our acts and deeds here, is that which we must inhabit when we enter the spirit world.

The idea that all space is peopled and that in the universe there are no wasted places, is startling, but it must appeal to our reason. The Master Mind, in creating, so planned that all space should be of use and occupied, for some purpose. The spirit world does not need our land, our waters, nor our physical atmosphere; they have their corresponding elements. Who shall say they cannot live and move in the invisible sphere about us, and surround themselves with thought creations? They live beyond and outside physical bodies, beyond our vision, yet with us. While their presence is felt by the many, it is known only by the few. This is the great misfortune of our so-called civilized world.

Whatever of the spirit sphere we are prepared for when we leave the earth plane, that spiritual sphere we shall inhabit. Our homes will be such as we have made ourselves. Kindred souls mingle together there as they do upon earth, sympathizing with and enjoying the society of one another. The homes there are as varied as upon earth, but each one is his own architect.

I have never been told, and I do not comprehend, just how in this life we are actually building the homes we shall occupy in the next. Probably it is because we can not grasp the action or product of thought, which never for one moment is inactive. Comprehension of this process will come some time.

I have never been able to make clear in my mind just the process in and by which our thoughts and acts create in the after life the environment that they do. Take the following description:

**"One passing from the earth plane finds a home which, to his perception, is substantial, objective, familiar and real. It embodies and represents his thoughts, purposes and attainments, the outward expression of his mental, moral and spiritual self. That home is healthful, attractive, artistic and beautiful, if he has provided the requisite conditions. Whatever it is, it is home."**

In this regard, it may be noted that our thoughts must, and do, find expression. A thing I thought out before it is carried out, and if those relating to the physical are builded, why not others that relate to spiritual conditions? This subject is but one of many I do not as yet understand. Then, again, I wonder if I *fully* comprehend any matter relating to the next life.

There are many spheres in the spirit world. To some the highest spiritual life is full of activity. No such heaven will appeal to the tired earth soul. He will long for some friendly haven of rest, and he will find it. To those in bondage, the after life is freedom. To the sick, it is health. To the cripple, it is strength and unlimited space in which to wander. To the tired laborer, it is eternity, a place without time and where there is no thought nor care of time. He will find that there is no more wear and tear nor fatigue for him. No matter how many journeys he may make, he will not feel tired and worn as upon earth.

Duties there must be, where many are gathered together, but they are such duties as will be one's greatest happiness to perform.

The more noble the soul, the more it feels the encumbrance of the earthly body; it is at times an uneven partnership—that of an immortal spirit and an earthly body. How often the willing spirit is unable to keep the tired body at its many tasks, and what a release when dissolution takes place and the spirit is able to descend higher.

What one has gained and needs will be his in the spirit spheres. There is the closest love and quickest sympathy between the earth plane and the spirit world. We shall each find a different home, suited to our work. Our work now lies upon the earth plane, and it is for us to perform the duties allotted to us. We may not be able to give to the ignorant—learning, nor to the hungry—food, but we can inspire their spirits to nobler, better deeds, while someone else, who is able, provides food and learning. Let them feel our love and sympathy, and let them see that, even if the clouds of adversity hang low over their heads, the soul is able to ascend to higher, better spheres. It is well to know that we do not travel the stony path of life alone, to feel that, no matter how rough or dark the way may grow, we can, if we will, stretch forth the hand and feel an answering clasp—a clasp that makes the heart grow braver. The Creator seems so far away to most of us that, unless we can have the love and help of one another, we feel lonely. It will ever be impossible for the finite to grasp the infinite, but it is possible to help one another, and find, in so doing, something that gives us courage.

# CHAPTER 7
## Mission Work

*God is not the God of the Dead, but of the Living.* –Matthew 22: 32

There is a part of our work equal, if not greater, in importance than any heretofore mentioned. This we term mission work, and we conduct it among earth-bound spirits who are unable in the next sphere to go beyond the first conditions, or who lie dormant in the darkness of their own gathering. Each night, when we are thus engaged, the time is divided by those in charge—a portion is given to our instruction, and at least an equal part is given to helping those who need aid, suggestion, and direction. Remember, that in the spirit-world the principle occupation is that of giving help, through which means spirits aid their own progression. In earth-life the ambition of the great majority is to help themselves regardless of others. Here, each one is for himself. There, each is for all and all are for each other.

It is my experience that nearly all, whether they are educated or uneducated, have little, if any, conception of the condition and state which immediately follows dissolution. Education, as that term is used, does not necessarily aid the primal condition, though it may further one's progress, by enabling him to grasp more quickly the principles which govern progression. One may have learning without spiritual development; one uneducated in the sciences, may have so developed his spirit that he is more advanced than the other when the new day dawns.

There are many who in that new life are helpless, who are like new-born infants in this world of ours, except that they possess all the knowledge gained on the earth-plane, and know the joy that comes of good and the burden that comes of wrong. Though they are like children, and enter consciously, they must be taught to walk, to take sustenance, to labor, to work, and to know the laws that control spirit. For where on this earth can such instruction be obtained? Assuming that one has led a good life and is conscious of his surroundings, he must learn all these lessons from those who have gone before, and there are many eager and ready to help. We labor largely among those who have not awakened, or who fail to understand their condition. Those who lie dormant, who are surrounded by darkness ofttimes cannot be aroused by other spirits any more than human beings can touch the mentality of an idiot within asylum walls. They stay in this condition until Nature restores and strengthens the mind, or until they are brought into the material vibrations made by mortal and spirit working together. When we work, we throw out material vibrations, into which the group brings many, sometimes hundreds, at a time, all in practically the same mental attitude. One spirit is clothed with material, is awakened, is selected to talk. The others there assembled listen to the speech and appreciate all benefits. This chosen one made be heard to gasp as he takes the first breath of our atmosphere. Since voice is produced by the organs of respiration, they must be clothed with material. I do not know all the laws that control this production of sound among spirits; but the production itself is a fact that permits no argument.

Those spirits that greet us on such evenings usually know nothing of the flight of time, or even know that they have separated from the old body. They awaken from a dreamless sleep, as it were, with the old thought dominant, with individuality the same, but with strange surroundings. Imagine, if you can, the varied thoughts that flash through the mind as consciousness comes. Never are two alike, any more than any two persons. When I say that I have talked with a few that have not had one intelligent thought or seen a ray of light for seventy-five or one hundred years, and that they speak of the world as it was when they left it, you may at least gain an impression of what it is possible to make for ourselves in the sphere beyond. True, these are unusual cases, but one can create such a condition, and some people have created it. Few have no clouds in the horizon of thought.

The speaker is clothed for a time like us; but the condition that holds the material on the spirit-form is sensitive, and any sudden fright or mental shock will disintegrate the atoms and cause them to fall. Then the spirit loses the power for speech. The first question is often one of inquiry. The spirits are astonished at the strange faces and the new surroundings, and are anxious to know where they are. Few of them even know what has happened. Our first effort is to calm them, and when they are most quiet and reasonable, the thought that was strongest in mind when the change came is expressed and retold. Often that thought was of approaching death, and they tell of the awful fear that filled their hearts and of their seemingly fortunate escape. We then bring them to a discussion of what death is, and make them realize fully that they are alive and in possession of every natural faculty; we teach them by degrees that there is no death, and that the change they so feared is passed. No matter how cautiously this information is imparted it is always followed by a great shock, and often the material clothing then disintegrates. Then, with a cry of fear and alarm, they lose their power of speech. If possible they are restored to a vocal condition, and our efforts are continued. Our work is not finished when they are brought to a conscious state. They must next be taught what spirit is and how it may learn the new laws that will thenceforth govern and control all their thoughts and actions. When one finds that he is out of the body, the thought of those left behind crystallizes, —anxious the inquiry, great the sorrow! Why should not the separation be as hard for him as for those left behind? Then, again, the change may have come before he was ready, when he was needed by friends or family, and many a cry has gone out: "What will they do; how will they live; who will care for them now?"

Those religiously inclined at once want to find the Saviour. Many who had been taught that they could be saved only with His help, say they must find Him, and when we tell them that he was only the symbol of a perfect man, and that one has no redeemer but himself, they hesitate to accept our statements. Often only the words of personal friends who have gone before bring conviction. Many give up the idea of a Saviour very reluctantly. We next try to bring these spirits to an understanding of what life in the spirit-world is. Those controlling the conditions usually take up the discussion, and spirit talks to spirit. All of us take part in trying to demonstrate and convey to the new-comer ideas of the life he has entered. The spirit-company are able, by laws that have not been explained, to make him see every act and deed that made up the sum total of his former life. As the scenes passed one by one, like a flowing stream, I have heard them shout with joy and shriek with fear. Little can be done except to bring the spirit to a sense of realization, and to point out the avenue called restitution. When the desire to live again the deeds of earth life comes from the heart, others in spirit there show how the acts of selfishness and wrong which created the darkness and which surrounds them may be relieved. But each spirit must carry his own burden; he must go his own way; he must perform his own labor, and no hand may lift the weight from his soul. Each act lived over and lived aright will dispel the darkness that it caused, and so the home and the surroundings will grow lighter and more beautiful. How long the way is, and how unnecessary! If only mankind were taught the truth here! We may sin in ignorance, but this brings sorrow—not so much for the condition it makes for us, as for the misery it causes others. When we appreciate what our wrong-doing has brought to others, and what is denied us for that reason, our grief is great. Remorse is ours, and misery and unhappiness become our close companions. With the knowledge that men have no Saviour but themselves, spirits usually assume the responsibility of their own acts readily, and are eager to commence the undoing, through which they shall reach higher planes. Sometimes many spirits in practically the same mental attitude are brought in, and I am asked to take up the discussion of some subject in which all are interested and in which all need knowledge. It seems that my thought and voice vibrate so keenly that their attention is attracted. They become interested and gather close about. I am told that sometimes thousands in a single evening come and listen. When I have interested them and one is, perhaps, talking with me, and many are talking with each other, teachers from other spheres take up the work and carry it on.

This, then, is a suggestion of what our mission work is, and how with the help of an intelligent and powerful group of spirits we labor to aid progression and to dispel the darkness that holds a soul prisoner in the dungeon of despair. But our work is not confined to those in trouble. Others come who have never known that condition. They live among those they love, and work with songs of joy and gladness in their hearts, radiant and happy, climbing the hills of knowledge. These tell me that when the first sphere is passed they know the intensity of life; they are free and understand the joys of freedom. Then they find that popes, bishops, priests, and kings are dead; that the aristocracy of this world has perished; that the personal god whom mankind worshiped, never existed; that truth is a religion that sheds joy on all the spirit spheres. Beyond the plane of restitution they find a world at peace, where honest effort meets its true reward. They find spheres, bright and clear, the married harmony of form and function, where there is no disease of flesh or brain. Then their conception of Nature broadens, happiness unknown before fills every heart, fear is dead, and ignorance and prejudice are left far below.

## Mission Work
### Part II

Among the thousand cases that came into our mission work, some teaching great lessons stand out prominently. There lived in my home city a few years ago a man of great wealth. He had reached the age of four-score and ten, was of unimpeachable character and at the head of some of our largest financial institutions, but he was close in money matters, very close, and saved the pennies as well as the dollars. I knew him intimately, for I had an office for some years in the same building and saw him frequently. He was counted a good citizen, but not much given to relieving distress, —such was the public estimation of his character.

The day came when he passed from the world of men, and was soon forgotten. Five years elapsed, during which period I went on with my work, helping those whom my co-workers brought, regardless of who or what they were, for in the democracy of death, wealth and worldly distinction are lost, and only character survives.

I recall vividly the evening I shall describe, for it taught one of the greatest lessons I have ever had from this source. This night I was not alone with Mrs. French; I had as a guest Louis P. Kirchmeyer, who had psychic sight and could actually see spirit people before they spoke, as could Mrs. French. If a spirit was personally known, either could call him by name, and if I knew him well, I could usually recognize his voice. This condition made identity in such cases beyond question.

Again, this chapel in my home where my work was carried on, with the non-luminous ribbon of light above our heads, indicated that conditions were favourable. There was never a night when we knew who would come or what we should be called upon to do, as much depended on our mental and physical condition, and then atmospheric conditions had to be considered. I seldom asked for any particular individual, —ours was a scientific work, and those who needed help were brought in after the lecture, usually.

**"It is so cold and dark,"** a voice came out of the darkness. Mr. Kirchmeyer and Mrs. French both psychically saw and recognized the gentleman mentioned above, and told me his name. After he spoke, I recognized his voice, which was somewhat peculiar. I had a high regard for this man, and, considering the lapse of five years since his passing on, was startled by what he said.

"Mr. W——," I said, "I am surprised after this lapse of years to hear you make such a statement. Tell me more of your condition."

173

"There is around and about me a wall of money, nothing but money; it shuts out the light. It is so dark, and wherever I go I cannot get away from it, around it or over it," he replied.

"This man," said one of the spirit group who was helping in the work, "spent his whole life in accumulating money. It dominated his whole thought, it was all he builded, and in coming into this life he found only the condition he had created, and, never having developed his spirit, he sheds no light on his pathway."

Having learned how to help in such cases by suggestion, I said, "Mr. W——, I think you will see light if you will look. What do you see?"

"It is coming," he said, "just a ray, but wait, I see a highway leading away in the distance."

"And what do you see on that highway?" I asked.

"Nothing," he answered, "not a living thing."

"Look again," I replied.

"Yes," he said, "I now see sign boards along the sides as far as the eye will reach."

"And what, if anything, is printed on those sign boards?" I asked.

"I can only read on the first one the word 'charity.' What does it mean?" he asked.

"I will tell him what it means," the same spirit who had spoken before answered. "This man never thought of charity, which is the helping of others, either by kindly words or by material aid, so with all his millions of money, he came into this world a spiritual pauper. He has now found the light, will realize his mis-spent life, and must learn what charity is. When he has practiced it, he can read the second sign. That highway is his to travel; it is long, but it will ultimately lead him to happiness and to a wealth he has never known."

This experience teaches us that we owe something to our fellow men, and that the more we have the more we owe to those less fortunate.

The following incident occurred on another night, and illustrates that all who pass on are not earthbound, —in fact, the great majority pass at once to a higher spiritual plane and more comprehensive life. All find just what they make for themselves, be it good or bad, and enter into the particular condition for which they are fitted. The power of money is no more; the only wealth carried beyond is that given away here.

"My years have gone swiftly," another said, "since my earth friends said farewell, and I journeyed on. I was glad to make

174

the change for myself, but regretted I could not make those left behind understand that I was not dead and that it was for my good that I stepped out of the tenement of clay and put on the garb of the immortals. I realized at once that I was out of the body, but I stayed about the home for some days before I was taken away, when I took up the work of helping those in the lower spheres. I have been familiar with your work for a long time, and am permitted to bring a soul that you can help. When his vocal organs are clothed, he will speak."

"I understand fully," another spirit said, "that I have left my physical body, and I was relieved when I knew it was not to be done. This is a beautiful world, in which I live, with opportunities beyond your conception. When earth conditions do not bind me, I can attend great lectures, and in temples of music hear celestial song. But I am bound to earth by the sorrow of my father and mother. They brood and weep, and sorrow for me as one dead, and that holds me like bands of steel, so that I can only at times do what other boys do. They don't understand that I am more alive than ever before, but until they give me happier thoughts my progression is stayed and I am as unhappy as they are. And I could be so happy and accomplish so much, if they would let me go. Won't you go and tell them what I have said, and change their thoughts? Tell them that death is life boundless and endless, and our sphere is filled with happiness. Please promise."

I did promise, and I did go and do what I could, but human nature loves to sorrow for the so-called dead.

How miraculous, how marvellous, you say, is this work. Not at all, it is no more marvellous than what you observe from day to day, and to which you give little thought. You plant a tiny seed in the dark ground, and in a little time you see a plant full of beautiful blossoms. You plant a kernel of corn and see grain reproduced. You note the reproduction of man himself. Do you suppose that the laws which do all these most mysterious things are notable to clothe temporarily a spirit body so that he can speak and be heard by mortal man?

I remember how stubborn I was in the beginning of my psychic investigation. For a long time I would not admit to myself, much less to the public, the conviction that was growing within me. I had not the capacity to comprehend these simple truths. Every one who walks in the woodland, stands by the sea, reads a book, looks at a picture, or hears a lecture, gets all the intellectual wealth he is capable of receiving, and no more.

## Speech With the Dead

It was in the year 1892 that I met Emily S. French. She was a woman then over 60 years of age, in delicate health, and very deaf. While she was conscious that she possessed powers out of the ordinary, she had little more comprehension than I of that into which the force would develop. At the suggestion of a number of prominent citizens, I was asked to meet Mrs. French and explain, if I could, the unusual phenomena obtainable.

In one of our early investigations we sat in a dark room, three of us forming a half circle, she facing us. After a time, seeming whispers were faintly heard, and the gentleman sitting with me insisted that he recognized his wife's voice. It was unsatisfactory to me, but I was interested and immediately made an investigation of the character of the psychic. Finding her of good family and more than ordinary education, I determined to know how the phenomena was produced. Of course, at that time I could not comprehend the direct-voice, nor the possibility of speech with the so-called dead. I was then agnostic. As I look over the situation now, I see that I had neither the experience nor the ability to appreciate the facts, any more than the average reader of this book can comprehend some of the statements made in it. I had to learn, first, that the after-life is etheric, and that people take into the after-life the same spirit body which they had in this life divested of the outer flesh garment. In those days I did not know that we have etheric bodies.

I found in the beginning that Mrs. French stood very much in awe of the play of this psychic force. One always fears things which he does not understand, and not understanding the unusual phenomena present, she was often very much afraid. I investigated far enough to find that she was possessed of a vital force unknown to me. She was just as much in the dark regarding it as I, and just as much interested. Accordingly she undertook to joining me in an investigation, to devote her time without money and without price to the mastery of that force in the hope that good might come. Out of that compact came over twenty years of continued work, and experiences which to me seem worthy of record.

It has been said that we have but five senses. That is to say, the average individual has but five senses developed; some persons, however, have seven. To the five accepted senses I add "psychic sight" and "psychic hearing." Mrs. French possessed both of those. At times she could see people moving in the after-life, not with her physical eye, of course, but by means of psychic sight. She could perceive them so acutely that they were just as real to her as if an impression came upon the retina. This is true, because she could see and describe these people in the dark just as well as in the light. Again, she had psychic hearing, for I have been able on many occasions in the broad daylight to carry on conversations with persons out of the body (she repeating their words) as satisfactorily as if they were still in their physical bodies, and in such talks I have gone frequently beyond the knowledge of the psychic.

In the beginning, spirit speech was faint from the sphere beyond. I was able to get in touch with only a very ordinary class of spirit people, and I often became impatient that those I most desired did not come. I did not then understand as I now do my own limitations, for now I know that instruction was being given me as fast as I could grasp it. When a new fact was stated, the law and the conditions making such facts possible were explained. The first propositions were very simple, but as the years rolled by, we made great progress. We learned how to form the required environment; there was a whisper and then a voice; then the voice took form and individuality. In course of time, those of the group of whom I was accustomed to have speech were easily recognized.

There was one person in particular with whom, from the very first time I worked with Mrs. French, I was desirous of talking. This was my mother who left this life in 1873. Time went on, and she did not come. Finally she requested me to meet with Mrs. French under the necessary conditions on May 26, 1896, saying that she would come and go over many things in which we were mutually interested.

About ten o'clock on the appointed mourning the Brown Building in Buffalo, then being repaired, collapsed. The street was full of rumors that many people had been killed. The number was put, I think, at six or seven. Of course, there was no way of ascertaining the truth until the debris could be removed and this would require many days.

Mrs. French and I were scarcely seated that evening when my mother greeted me in her own direct voice, and said with great regret that owing to the accident that mourning she must forego the pleasure of our visit until a later time, we would be of great help to those whose lives had been crushed out; they needed assistance. Of course, I readily acquiesced in the suggestion. There was perhaps ten minute of silence; then a voice, choking and coughing, broke the stillness and cried:

**"My God! the building is falling, the building is falling. This way, this way!"** The situation was tense and startling. I half rose to my feet. Another voice answered in a strange tongue. The words were not distinguishable, but it seemed to me as if someone was responding to the first call, which was followed in a moment by a woman's voice crying out in great fear, **"We will all be killed! Help me, help me!"**

This was the beginning of what we term our mission work, that is, helping to restore consciousness to those in leaving the old body are not readily able to regain that condition. There was then, aiding in this work, as I have since learned, a group of seven spirit co-workers who had brought to us these unfortunate people whose spirit-bodies had been crushed out in the fall of this building. We were to restore them to a normal mental condition, and acting upon the suggestion of the spirit co-workers I quietly talked with them. After a time I told them what had occurred and brought them to a realization of their situation. Eventually they came to understand that in the fall of that building their spirits had been forced from their physical bodies, and when they came to realize that in the catastrophe they had gone out of earth life, their sorrow was beyond words. One told me on that evening that four people, namely; William P. Straub, George Metz, Michael Schurzke, a Pole, and Jennie M. Griffin, a woman, had lost their lives in the fall of the building. This was verified some days later.

After talking with me, voice to voice, they realized that they had gone through the change called death. Then their friends in the after-life came, were recognized, and took them and gave them such consolation as was possible under the unfortunate circumstances.

I asked the leader of the spirit group how it was that the voices when first heard seemed so strained, and speech so broken, why there was so much choking. He replied that a person, crushed out of the physical body suddenly finishes, as soon as consciousness and the mental condition are restored, sentences left unuttered when dissolution came; that in the awakening he takes on the identical state in which he passed out.

After they had gone, Mrs. French said:

"I see behind you a man probably fifty-five or more years old, strong character I should judge, who has been listening to this conversation. He is looking at you with amazement. He does not seem to understand."

I said to her, "Does he know me?"

She replied, "He answers, **'Yes.'**"

"Does he give his name?"

"No, not yet."

Of course, being in absolute darkness and not possessing psychic sight or psychic hearing, I could neither see nor hear him, but I asked,

"Did he reside in Buffalo?"

She answered, "No."

I then inquired concerning other localities, and named residents of a city where I had lived for some years, asking, "Was he a resident of that city?"

And Mrs. French replied saying, "He says that he lived there."

Then I repeated the names of many of my acquaintances, trying to identify the individual who was then present, with an idea that I might have speech with him. Finally Mrs. French said, "I see the letters H.G.B."

I quickly recalled the individual described and spoke his name. He had been a leading citizen of a neighboring city, a large manufacturer. I recalled many evenings spent at his house with his family, and particularly did I recall his voice. On Sunday evenings he enjoyed the gathering of young people, and at such times there was often singing of popular songs, and many of the old hymns. His voice was unusual, deep resonant, and he sang very well. It was a voice which, having once been heard, could never be mistaken. He had been out of the body then about five years. After a little time he moved around apparently to the side of Mrs. French, and greeted me. That deep masculine voice would have been recognized if he had not given his name; there was no mistake. He spoke my name as familiarly as he ever did in earth life, and I greeted him as cordially as I ever had in his home.

I had believed that this man had led an exemplary life, for this was the general impression which prevailed in the community were he resided, and I thought he, of all men, would find the best conditions after dissolution. However, he did not yet realize that he had separated from his physical body. He knew that some great change had taken place, but he had absolutely no conception of what it was, although five years had elapsed since it occurred. He told me that his wife and children no longer recognized him in his own home, that he spoke to them, that he called to them, that he got on his knees and shrieked their names, but he could not apparently touch them, he could not make them realize his presence; they passed him apathetically. His inability to make himself known in the home where he had always been the dominant personality, the indifference with which he was treated not only by his own family, but by others with whom he came in contact, had driven him nearly to desperation. He could not understand the situation at all, and he was fearful that he was verging on insanity,

179

if not completely insane. All was darkness about him, all things were unnatural, and he had become frantic. It was a delicate task to bring this man to a realization of the great change that had taken place, because his present condition was so intensely real. He was the same man, he had the same intellect, the same personality, apparently the same body. Why should he be ignored and overlooked by all whom he had known?

It was only after many explanations that he came to the realizing sense that he had left the physical world of men. Having in mind the exemplary life which he had led, I told him that I could not understand why he should find himself in such a mental state, and he replied that he had not lived the life for which he had been given credit.

A member of the spirit group said:

**"The wrong done in earth-life binds him to the earth condition. While he has left his physical body, he has not left the earth and its environment, and having no knowledge of the great beyond to which he has journeyed, he has never progressed beyond the earth plane where he formerly lived, and he cannot comprehend while in that mental state the change that has come to him."**

It appeared that he had never left his home, and the narrow environment about it, but in a half-awakened, half-conscious state had wandered from one to another until by good fortune he had been told that if he would attend upon our work, he would understand the change that had come into his life. With this unusual experience we said "Good Night" to our group of co-workers, and I walked homeward in deep thought.

What shall be said of our civilization that teaches nothing of the conditions prevailing in the after life?

## Helping the Dead

In my early work I was told much that baffled understanding. Things which now appear simple, then seemed impossible. The statement that there were many in the after life who did not know that they had made the great change and were out of their physical bodies, was beyond my comprehension, though many whom I identified so stated.

At this period of my work I had the usual indefinite, hazy notion that Heaven, so-called, was far away, that something survived dissolution, but what it was I had never been able even to define, any more than the average Christian can define it today. I did not then know that this inner body at dissolution advanced to material spirit zones that encircle this earth, and that those whose spirituality did not carry them into the higher spheres did not for a long time get beyond the earthbound plane, and that many were able to go in and out of our homes and offices as before, though they could not make us answer them or realize their presence.

Some are in such a state that the helpers in the higher life cannot reach them, and it is only by uniting our forces and working together that they see poor souls are brought to consciousness and shown how they can develop and progress. Those earthbound ones are the spirit people who need our help.

When I state that one-half of each of the evenings during all the years of my work was devoted, with the help of the spirit group working with me, to helping this class of spirits, one may get an idea of the great necessity of it.

Bear in mind that Mrs. French, the psychist in whose presence this work was done, did not do the talking. She was not in a trance, but contributed psychic force necessary in our work. Bear in mind, again, that when out of the physical housing, spirit people have vocal and respiratory organs as in earth life, and can speak as before, being heard by mortal ear when conditions are as I learned to make them.

Usually some learned spirit spoke on some phase or condition of the next life, which discourse, at such times as I was able to procure the services of a stenographer who could write in the dark, was taken in shorthand. Then came what we called our "Mission Work."

Thousands upon thousands of spirit people spoke in this work and never any two in the same condition or with similar ideas or experiences, for they were different as in this life. Many were awakened apparently after long periods of time; others were in darkness, and could not find the light; others did not realize that they had left the old earth body; others knew they had, but found nothing as they expected. Some had a craving for liquor and a desire to satisfy old appetites; while others came for suggestions and advancement. The procession was endless and the need beyond description.

Those who are advanced in the after life are ever ready and anxious to help any below them, and they do a wonderful work. But there are many whom they can not reach, and it is only by blending their forces with ours that a condition was created where these poor souls could be brought to a realization of their condition and started toward a higher development. Spirit people are not infinite; they are limited in their sphere, as we are in ours, and so, for twenty-two years, we worked together to help earthbound spirits. It was the most important work I ever did, beside which all my professional achievements sink into obscurity and are as nothing. This was a real pleasure and a great privilege. Let me illustrate the character of this work.

I was in my home one evening, alone with Mrs. French. A storm had passed and there could be heard the low moaning wind in the great trees outside. It was absolutely dark in the room where we sat facing each other with only a small table between us. The discourse on the scientific aspect of the next state was finished; then came silence and expectancy.

**"I have wandered for years, searching, searching,"** a voice distressed and low, came out of the darkness; **"and travelled, travelled, travelled; I have found nothing but vegetation, and I am so weary."** Then this benighted spirit apparently realized that I was visible, and he seemed to turn towards me, and said; **"I don't understand. I am seeking my Saviour; I was told He would meet me, but I can't find Him, and I am lost."**

I replied: "No man is ever lost."

He replied: **"I will be lost, if I don't find my Saviour. I have searched so long!"**

"Did it ever occur to you that you have no Saviour but yourself?" I asked.

**"That cannot be,"** he said. **"All my earth life I relied on Him to save me, and I must find Him."**

"Would it not be better to try to save yourself?" I asked..

**"No man can be saved except he believe in Christ,"** he answered.

"We have no Saviour but ourselves, and until we understand that fact and help ourselves and others, we don't find a very desirable after life. How do you account for the fact that you have travelled so far, met no people, and seen nothing but vegetation?" I asked.

**"I don't know; I don't understand,"** he answered.

**"I know that I understand,"** another spirit voice answered. **"This man lived a narrow, selfish Christian life, simply relying on the Bible teachings, believing that the Saviour would carry his burden and lead him to the great white throne, and when he realized he had passed the portal of death his first thought was to find that Saviour that he had been taught to depend upon. This idea became an obsession and he started travelling with only one thought in mind. So intent was he, so centered was his thought, he saw nothing of the people or the wonders of the sphere in which he had advanced. He could not find**

what he sought, and he could not see or sense what he was not seeking. His journey will not end until he realizes that he is his own Saviour."

"**That is a new idea. Who is that man?**" he asked.

"A spirit like yourself," I answered.

"**Is what he said true?**" he asked.

"Has it not occurred to you in all this time, that, if your teaching were true, your Saviour would have met you; and has not the fact that you were not so met, caused you to question your belief?" I said in reply.

"**It has not before, but let me think. Have I been wrong in my belief? When I came over and failed to find Him, I should have questioned; but I did not. I thought I must search and I have searched so long,**" he said.

I had learned that when a spirit was really awakened in the condition we had created where the earth and spirit spheres blended together, friends could come and help. I asked: "Don't you want to stop travelling, and see some of your family and friends?"

"**I certainly do. If I am wrong and have been wasting my life, I should like to know it,**" he replied.

"Look," I said.

"**It is a growing light. How beautiful! I see great throngs of people,**" he said. "**They are coming toward me, men and women, dead men and women, but they don't look dead. They appear just as they did before, and so do I. There comes a friend who beckons me. May I go?**"

"Yes," I answered. "The thought that dominated you is broken and now you are free. Go with those who have come to help you, and they will show you how to help yourself."

He was gone, then silence again, the night wind and the darkness; while in the room tiny non-luminous points of light appeared, and substance like faint clouds in a summer sky floated and visibly formed into indefinite shapes, as the spirit chemist restored conditions to the psychic normal. Again the stress and the expectant speech. We could always feel the effort that was apparently necessary to clothe with ectoplasm a spirit's vocal organs, so that its voice would sound in our atmosphere.

"**What are you trying to do?**" another voice spoke. "**I have been watching these manipulations with great interest; a gentleman told me to ask and I am curious.**"

"This lady and myself," I replied, "come together each week and with spirit aid create a condition where we can talk, voice to voice, with dead people."

"That is positively a most absurd statement. The dead can't talk," he said.

"Do you know that to be a fact?" I asked.

"No," he answered, "I don't know it to be a fact, but if it were possible, I should have heard of it."

"Have you ever heard of obtaining messages from departed spirit people?" I asked.

"Yes," he said, "I have heard such claims, but never for a moment did I consider it worthy of the slightest consideration."

"Did you ever really consider what would happen to you in the death change?" I asked.

"No, that was a subject I did not care to think about. I have the cares of my business, which are enough," he replied.

"Stop and think for a moment; where are you now?" I said.

"I don't know; this is not my office and the surroundings are strange. I don't quite comprehend this most unusual situation. Nor do I recognize you or this lady," he answered.

"Do you recall your name and recent events?" I asked.

"Certainly," he replied, "my name is ——, my office——, and, as I recall, I had just concluded an important conference; but this is neither my office nor my home. Where am I and how did I get here, and who are you? I have no recollection of meeting you or leaving my place of business."

"I am Mr. Randall, and you are in my home in Buffalo, and this lady and myself, with the aid of a spirit group, talk at times with those who have left the physical body, just as we are now talking to you," I replied.

"I don't know why you speak to me in that manner. I am not dead," he said.

"Look at your body," I said.

"I am looking at it. I see no change," he answered.

"Look again. Hold your hand to the light," I said.

"My God! What has happened? My whole body is natural but it is transparent. I can see through it. What does this mean?" he asked.

"Does it not dawn on you what we are trying to convey? Recall your last sensation," I said.

"I am," he replied.

"I was in my office—a feeling of great weakness came over me. I had a sensation of falling, and I don't recall anything more, until I found myself here. Do you intend to convey the suggestion that I am dead? Is that what this talk leads to?"

184

"There is no death, there are no dead," I answered. "There is only change. In dissolution the inner body, released from the flesh housing, passes to the next or spirit plane, which is as material and natural as the earth life, and so similar that in the beginning many don't realize it any more than you do, and I am inclined to believe from this talk that you never developed your better self to any degree, for which reason you don't understand what is actually being done now, nor the condition in which you find yourself."

**"Can it be,"** he replied, **"that death comes without knowing it, and that we continue to live in a world similar to that of the earth? It is a most astounding proposition. Have I really ceased to live the earth life?"**

I should infer from your statements," I answered, "that you passed out of the body suddenly, possibly with a stroke of apoplexy. What is the date?"

**"This is January 20th,"** he replied.

"No," I answered. "It is April, and for three months you have been unconscious."

**"The suggestion stirs me beyond expression,"** he said. **"Let me think. I was in good bodily health, as I thought, engrossed in business affairs, and the idea that death would come to me never was seriously considered, and now you tell me it has overtaken me, and that I am no more of earth, and that as a spirit I can actually talk to you still in the old life. I want to think it over—I am not fully satisfied. It would seem to me if I was a spirit I would meet other spirit people. Why don't I?"**

"Look about you again," I said. "While we have been talking, possibly you have not noticed what has taken place."

**"Why it is growing more light, and I can see about me many I thought dead and gone,"** he said; **"and they tell me they have come to help me out of darkness, teach me the laws that control in this sphere of life, and point out the method by which I can develop my spirit, which I have so long neglected. This thought and their presence overwhelms me, and I must have time to realize it all."**

"You have been awakened," I said, "and put in touch with those who will help you. Go with them and all will be well with you."

**"Good night,"** he said. **"I thank you."**

These cases illustrate the condition in which some spirit people find themselves, the method employed in bringing them to a realization of the change that has taken place, and something of the results obtained in this mission work. Volumes could be written from the records obtained, which would further show the urgent need of work of this character.

## The Earthbound

There were few nights during the years of scientific investigation that I did not talk with earthbound spirit people, usually with several, and I have learned much of their condition.

"What creates the earthbound condition?" is the first question properly asked. I answer, as I have been answered thousands of times:

"The lives they led, and the conditions they created for themselves, for as a man sows so shall he reap."

The laws of nature, the laws under which we live, are not only fixed and definite, but eternally just. Thoughts are things, and every moment as they emanate from each individual something is added to his character. It is enriched or impoverished, and if no light emanates from it, one is held at his dissolution within the lower planes that circle this globe. The selfish character, like the miser in the "Chimes of Normandy," the cruel, the immoral, and the wanton, the thief, the murderer, –is it not just that they be herded together until they have lived over each wrong act, lived it aright and made compensation, thus qualifying themselves for association with a finer group? The justice that meets human souls at the frontier is complete. They enter into a condition which is of their own creation. They find such light as they radiate, and no more. There is no escape in the after life from the consequences of things done and that in reality it is a part of it, the wicked, the malicious and base, and all those who have acquired no spiritual development, are held. This plane has various stages. Some are in total darkness, some in half light; all in all, it is at most a twilight zone between the spiritual and physical worlds. Here old appetites, thoughts and desires hold sway as before. In this zone a mass of undeveloped people of the same general character, with a desire for spirituality no greater than when living in the physical body, remain. Their condition is much worse than in this world, for there is not the opportunity for reformation that there was before. There the great law of attraction hold together those of a similar character, so that these live in mental poverty until they have a desire for better things. Then the way is shown and they work slowly out by their own efforts, but the labor is long and the path dim that leads to the zones of happiness and peace. Bruno said:

"Whatever good a man has to his credit, whether it be of much or little, it is the seed from which he grows eternally."

In my talks with earthbound spirit people I never found two exactly alike, any more than they can be found alike here. That change did not alter or improve them. This is evidently Hell, so much talked of and feared.

I recall so many earthbound that have told of the horror of their condition, that it is with difficulty I choose specific individuals, for I had speech with a great number. It is like seeing the paintings in the principle galleries of Europe. There are many, but some stand out prominently.

This is the story told by one:

"I was not a good man among men. I was selfish, cruel, took human life, and was, as I now know, killed while committing a crime. When I awoke it was very dark, and, not knowing what had happened, I called in anger, but my companions did not come. My voice echoes back to me again and again, and I began to think I was in a cave. I arose and groped about in the darkness, but I could not find the walls, though I walked for hours. I did not feel hunger or thirst, and days and months passed, while I was ever searching for the walls that threw back the echo of my call. Can you imagine the sensation you would have, to be lost in an open forest with the sun in the sky, to say nothing of being lost in darkness? My sensations and suffering beggar description.

"After a very long time I saw a light, and as it approached I saw that it shone or radiated from the form of a man. 'My brother,' the man said, 'you are in spiritual darkness; how can I help you?' He came and, putting forth his hands, would have touched me, but I was speechless and rushed away in fear. Thereafter when I saw a light I would hide, fearing I would be arrested, for at that time I did not know I had left my physical body. I became desperate, and the next time a light approached I waited. Coming to me, a man from whose body radiated, as before, said, 'What do you wish?' I replied, 'I want to get out of this prison.' 'You are not in prison; you are dead.' I cursed him for making such fool statements and he was gone.

"Again I was alone in darkness. How long this continued I know not, for, there being no day, I could not count time. Again there came one to me and again I demanded that I be released from my prison. He calmly and kindly replied, 'you are not in prison; you are a spirit.' That seemed to me the height of absurdity, for I was very much alive; but I listened and he told me that I had made the change and brought another, an artist, who drew pictures of my youth and the faces of my boyhood friends, and, one by one, sketched those acts and deeds and wrongs that I had done. Then the light faded and they were gone and I was left alone to think.

"When I had fully come to appreciate my condition and to regret the wrong done and the suffering caused by me, there came a desire to do what I could to make reparation. Then came other spirit people to encourage me and suggest what I must do to obtain spiritual growth and, with it, the light. Not one offered to take my burden, or to undo the wrong that I had done; that was for me; they only pointed out the way. I was told there were none to forgive me, except the injured; no Saviour but myself.

"Step by step I went forward; hour by hour I made reparation and lived again each wrong and lived it right; and day by day, as you count time, I undid my wrong and added to the right. The way was long, the labor intense, but in it I had found a happiness I had never known before. For I was building my character; the atom of good was striving for its spirituality. Now that is all behind me, and I live in the glorious and effulgent light of the spirit world, laboring among congenial souls. I was seared by the fire of selfishness and wrong. I paid, and paid to the last farthing, the penalty. Now I am at peace with all the spirit world, as it is with me.

"I send this message back to the world of men: 'There is not in the Universe a method by which any one can escape the penalty of wrong.' Had I known this fact, I would have lived among you honestly and been fair with my fellow men. I did not know it, and I have paid in full, as all will pay in full, for ignorance will not excuse.

"It has been a privilege to tell through you of my experience in the earthbound zone of the spirit world. If one man will hesitate when contemplating a single selfish or wrong act, and turn from it because of better understanding, it will reflect upon me and better my condition."

The following statement as to earthbound conditions is from another spirit:

"The belts or zones that lie close around your earth are designed for the habitation of undeveloped spirits when out of the body; as they outgrow the passions of earth and become more refined, they pass to another or higher zone. Many remain in the first or earth zone for years.

"We of the higher zones try to reach them that they must forgive and forget the wrongs of earth and in that work advance out of the earthbound condition, but many turn a deaf ear to our suggestions and try to revenge the wrong done to them when on earth; all this is intensely human, and this zone, so like the physical, is very real. Those who have progressed, those who in the beginning passed directly through this belt, because of their spirituality, would never come back into that atmosphere, were it not for their love for and desire to help humanity."

In explanation of this condition another spirit said:

"Many on leaving the mortal body are still in earthly conditions, found on the grosser spiritual side you call the lower sphere, where the spiritual senses are not yet awakened to susceptibility or spiritual discernment."

Again, one said:

"I find a great many come from earth life in a very darkened condition; and, of course, they gravitate or are drawn to localities or corresponding conditions. They don't know just where they ought to go or what to do. In fact, many are ignorant of any other than the condition in which they find themselves. Many, too many, are in a condition of slumbering, some in a deep sleep which lasts a long time, and great effort is put forth to awake such spirit people."

This is the experience of another spirit:

"I had been in the after life a number of years when I was taken into the lowest sphere, and what I saw has lingered in my memory ever since. I was taken by a guide accustomed to work in the earthbound plane. We move, as you know, with the rapidity of thought. My first impression was of a descent in the dark, all about me gloom, and to add to the horror, I could hear voices though I could not see any one. After a time, when as it seemed, I grew accustomed to the darkness, I could see people about me, poor men and women who did not realize they had left the physical body—some shrieking because they could not escape their victims; those they had wronged were not there, —it was their awakening consciousness that brought such vision. The guide spoke gently to them. Some answered with course jests, others with mirthless laughter; but a few came close and listened while he told them of their condition and what must be done to work out of this darkness, which was of their own creation. We have as much trou-

**ble in making these poor spirit people understand conditions beyond their sight and touch, as you have with earth people."**

In the beginning when I talked with spirits who did not know they were dead, as that word is commonly used, it staggered my thought. I could not then conceive that one could be in that condition and not know it. I did not then know that the next life was so material, so tangible, and, in the lower spheres, so like our own; neither did I know that here and now we possess an inner body, which, when separated from the outer flesh garment, is identically the same as before, with the same feature, expression and thoughts. With the first or lower sphere actually blending with our world as it does, how can those who have just gone understand their condition, if they possess no knowledge concerning this change?

In the presence of such known facts, the question of the continuity of life no longer remains, and we advance to the more important proposition of what are the conditions the so-called dead meet when they cross the border. Where is the border? Where is the after life and what is the new environment? These questions are vital and are being answered from day to day, though few ask the question, and of those who do ask, a less number understand. The world is too busy getting money to give this subject serious thought.

Let it not be understood that all the living dead are earthbound and held in such a zone of darkness; of all that go, only a few of the many are there held. But let it be remembered that conditions in spirit planes vary as the varying characters of men, and that each reaches that environment for which his earth life has fitted him. There he will live until by growth he has earned a more advanced zone.

The experience of these spirits were unusual, terrible in severity, and possibly extreme, but they are necessary to illustrate what the degenerate and wicked must expect. Others have told of the wonders and delights of the next conditions, as they were enabled to feel and visualize them in the beginning. Where spirit people are, what they see and enjoy, depends on just what their earth life earned. How many know this fact?

The fortunate should help the unfortunate; the strong should defend the weak; the intellectual should lead with gentle hands the mental poor. This is the highest conception of religion in both worlds, and a necessary process if we would enrich ourselves in either.

A spirit has said:

**"You have no idea of the nature and extent of punishment which some spirits have to undergo. There is no hell, nor is torture inflicted in the spirit world. Every one that comes brings the punishment with him in his own nature. When a spirit passes from the earth to this world, every trait of his natural habits, principles and passions is delineated on his spirit features. There can be no deception with us.**

**"You will be placed with those of similar character, whose natures correspond with yours.**

**"There is no night here, and consequently no day, at least not as I once measured, and as you still measure, time. Time here is measured only by emotions, events and deeds. There are dark places and darker souls, as there are on earth."**

## So Little Change

How can people be dead and not know it? This was the most difficult proposition ever presented to me. All orthodox teaching has been such that it is difficult for any one to comprehend the natural conditions about them. In my first years of this most interesting research, I talked with many who did not know that they had left the earth-life at all. Why did they not know that they had left the physical body?

Let me give a stenographic account of our work on the evening of May 10, 1897, illustrative of the point referred to and reported by Miss Gertrude Spaulding, now secretary to one of the United States senators from Minnesota.

The spirit controlling our work said:

**"Tonight, we must bring into your presence a necessity, bring one who needs help more than you need words of instruction. In this regular work, do not change conditions; if you want to invite strangers, take another night."**

A strange voice said:

Q. **I am interested to know what you are doing here. I don't want that woman sitting there to take down what I say.**

A. She is not here to take down your confession, if you make one. The work we are doing is of sufficient importance to be taken stenographically; that is what the stenographer is here for. Well, sir, how can we serve you?

Q. **I don't want you to call me "friend," but as I am here I will present a business proposition. You like money,** don't you? I suppose the rest of you like money too. It does a lot of things.

Q. Have you a speculation that you want us to join in?

**A. I have a certain block of stock I want to sell.**

Q. What kind of stock?

**A. Mining stock. It is mining stock.**

Q. Is that the most important thing in your mind?

**A. That's the most important.**

Q. Why do you wish to sell it?

**A. I have good reasons, but I don't say very much about it to strangers.**

Q. How did you get it?

**A. Never mind that. I have it and want to sell it.**

Q. How long have you had that stock for sale?

**A. I have had it for about five years. Have not sold it because everybody seems afraid of it.**

Q. Now, hasn't it occurred to you that if you have not sold it, there is something about that stock that isn't right?

**A. I know all about that stock. Are you afraid of it?**

Q. No, I am not afraid of it. You have offered it very cheap, I suppose?

**A. Not so very. I don't believe in cheap stocks.**

Q. You have travelled?

**A. Travelled? Travelled from one end of the earth to the other. I have been to Europe.**

Q. Now, does it not seem strange to you that you have travelled so far and not sold your stock?

**A. I'll tell you. It is strange to me because everybody that I have offered it to, has turned away after looking at it. People think I am a little "off."**

Q. Now, where is your family?

**A. You want my wife to sign the papers?**

Q. Will she sign?

**A. It is not necessary.**

Q. Where is she?

**A. Home.**

Q. Where is home?

**A. I will tell you if you want to know. She is in San Jose, California.**

Q. You have travelled a good way. Did you ever hear of the city of Buffalo?

**A. Yes, who hasn't?**

Q. It is a good city, isn't it?

**A. Very good, very good.**

Q. Now I live in Buffalo. I am in my own home now.

**A. You don't mean to say that I am in Buffalo?**

Q. Yes. You have been brought here for some purpose other than selling mining stock. You have travelled a long way. Now, my friend, where did you get those papers? Be honest with me. Have they not been a burden to you for years?

**A. That will do, gentlemen.**

Q. Did you get that stock honestly?

**The voice of the control interrupted, speaking with great force: "The man you stole the papers from, shot you."**

**Q. Who is that? How does he know? How does he know?**

The control speaking to us said:

**"He was shot while stealing those papers. When we cannot reach spirits of his kind, we find it necessary to bring them into the conditions prevailing here now; we want your help. In this condition their mental activities are quickened, and they are brought out of mental darkness."**

I said to the spirit: "If you will come and touch me, possibly you will gather more strength."

**A. You will put handcuffs on me.**

Q. You are among friends.

**A. I don't trust in friends or strangers.**

Q. I want you to listen to what I have to say. You are nearly three thousand miles from San Jose, California. When you were stealing that stock from that other man, you heard the click of a revolver, didn't you?

**A. Yes.**

Q. Did you hear the explosion?

**A. No.**

Q. There was one.

**A. I should have heard it if there had been.**

Q. There was a revolver fired at that time, I am told, and that ball penetrated your body. When that occurred, you passed out of the physical body. You live right on; that life is so like the life here, that you and thousands of others go right on without being conscious of the change; they find conditions so similar, and whatever was in the mind when the change occurred is held sometimes indefinitely. You have been wandering over the face of the earth holding the thought that the stock was in your hands. You are not as you were before you took that stock; a great alteration has taken place, but you are not dead.

**A. Am I a ghost?**

Q. Let me explain. Every week we sit in a dark room as we are now doing, and understanding the laws that govern speech between the spiritual and physical planes, we are able to talk with people who have passed on, just as we are talking to you tonight. Now, you are in a situation which you fail to comprehend. You must work out of your present condition and undo the wrong that you have done. You will be able in time, much time probably, to progress, and those who have progressed farther and understand your condition, have brought you tonight into this condition for the purpose of having us demonstrate to you the change that has come, and teach you how to compensate for the wrong that you did. If you will listen, you will be told.

**A. I believe none of that.**

Q. Do you understand that there is actually no death?

**A. No, I do not.**

Q. The majority of people in the physical world do not understand that change at all. One leaves the old, physical body as one leaves an old coat. But the etheric body, the individual self, with its tendencies and desires, goes on and on. Now, don't you think there has been a change with you in some way? Do you want me to demonstrate that to you?

**A. I am just like you.**

Q. That cannot be, for your body is composed of ether only. I lift my hand to my face. Can you see my face through my hand?

**A. No.**

Q. Now, lift up your hand. Don't you see there is a difference?

**A. Yes, I can see through my hand.**

Q. What do you think of that?

**A. If you think I am crazy, I had better go.**

Q. We are not trying to do you harm.

**A. Talk then in reason.**

194

The control interrupted again, saying: "We will bring a spirit that shall teach you what is reasonable, and he shall prove to you that you too are a spirit."

Q. Do you know that the man talking to you now, is S——, once a citizen of much prominence?

**A. He is dead.**

Q. He is talking to you. Is he dead if he can talk?

**A. You are a queer lot of people.**

Q. Possibly, but if you will listen to what he says, if you will earnestly seek the truth, you will find it. Things are not satisfactory with you, are they?

**A. Not very.**

Q. Now, you would like to get out of your present condition, would you not?

**A. I don't like to be called dead.**

Q. We will help you all we can. We want you to listen. I tell you again, there is no death.

**A. But you said I was a spirit.**

Q. Yes, I say that you are now in the after-life, and that you have an etheric body, almost identical with the old physical.

**A. Where are your ministers? Why don't they so teach if it is a fact?**

Q. Because the great majority don't know; and the few who do know have not the courage.

**A. I will go and ask Father Spencer if this be true?**

Q. Do you want to see Father Spencer right here? Is it possible at this time to bring Father Spencer here to-night? I asked the control.

**A. I am sending messengers for Father Spencer, who has also passed on since his going, he replied.**

Q. Either to-night, or at some other time, you shall talk with Father Spencer, as you are talking now with us.

**A. I will wait.**

Some years elapsed before this strange spirit came again, and then only to say that he found Father Spencer, and had come to understand the terrible condition which, by a life ill spent, he had made for himself. He then appreciated that he must meet again every wrong act of his earth-life, live it again and live it right, and by labour make retribution for all the wrong he had done. He further said that no man, if he understood the result of evil or its effects in the after-life, would do wrong.

At the time this work was being carried on, I did not fully appreciate the fact that one could be dead, so-called, and not know it. I had first to learn that there is individual life beyond the grave.

Then I was taught:

(a) That here and now we have spirit bodies composed of etheric material, as much matter as the flesh garment that covers them.

(b) That dissolution is simply the passing of the etheric out of the physical cover.

(c) That the after-life is just as tangible and material as this, intense and real beyond comprehension, differing from this life in vibration only.

(d) That the so-called dead have bodies as real and tangible to them as ours are to us.

(e) That many of the dead, so-called, move about even among us, little realizing that any change has been made, unless developed spiritually.

When I had learned these things, the teachers of the etheric world took up with me the character and conditions surrounding and governing life in the next sphere of development. Then I understood.

## From Death's Sleep

**"By what right do you presume to compel my presence in this house?"** The room was in absolute darkness; the voice of one called by the world, "dead," trembling with anger broke upon the stillness of the night.

"Do you understand the situation in which you find yourself?" I asked.

**"I do not, and will not allow any man to dictate to me,"** he replied.

"You are not afraid?" I asked.

**"Afraid! I am not afraid of God or man, and I will not remain here."**

"It might be to your advantage if you would," I answered. "I did not force you to come. You are as much a stranger to me as I am to you."

**"Who did force me to come?"** he asked.

"I do not know; tell me about it."

**"As it comes to me now,"** he answered, **"an irresistible force seemed to urge me from a dream-like condition. Suddenly I**

**was awake, in your presence, and immediately concluded that in some manner you controlled my conduct. That I cannot permit."**

"You are mistaken there, but does it not occur to you that some great good may come of this meeting?" I inquired.

**"I cannot in any way understand your suggestion,"** the stranger said, **"or see how any good can come of an enforced conference. If you did not bring me, who did? I had no desire to come, nor do I wish to remain. This house and its surroundings are unfamiliar to me. With your permission, I will retire."**

"Before you go," I said, "I should like to have you know something of the work we are doing, which may account for your coming."

**"Well, sir, finding myself in this unfamiliar situation I will not be lacking in courtesy,"** he said.

"For many years," I replied, "I have been engaged in psychical research, with this psychic who sits opposite me, trying to obtain a practical solution of that great physical change called death."

**"What has that to do with me? I am not dead nor am I interested in the subject,"** he answered.

"Wait a moment, please. You will be interested when I tell you that I have discovered something of the daily life and environment of the individual after he has ceased to be an inhabitant of the earth-plane."

**"You are entirely mistaken in your statements; there is no survival—no continuity of life. Death is the end."**

"Are you sure?"

**"Absolutely,"** he replied.

"Suppose," I asked, "I could prove to you here and now, that death, so-called, is but a physical change, the separation of the life-force from the flesh garment, that substance with which it is clothed during its journey on this plane—suppose I could demonstrate here and now that the individual has a spirit body composed of matter with form, features, and expression during his entire earth-life, and at dissolution simply becomes an inhabitant of the next plane of consciousness with the same spirit body, is in short, the same identical man?"

**"There is no such thing as life after death,"** he said.

"I am going to try to explain what life is, before I give you the absolute proof of what I state. Now follow me. At the moment of conception, an Atom of the Universal Force called 'Good' is clothed with substance vibrating more slowly than the life force clothed. The individual is as perfect at that moment as the giant oak in the heart of the acorn. We cannot see the individual or the oak tree before or after birth and growth. Life-force vibrates so fast that it is not visible to the physical eye, but ultimately we see the outer covering, the substance which makes both possible. This outer garment of the individual is composed largely of water. The physical body of ours changes once in seven years at least, but with such change we retain individuality, form, and feature. How is this done?" I asked.

**"I don't know, and I don't care,"** he answered.

"Follow me a little farther, please. This entity, this life-force, this soul, this 'us,' if you like, is composed of matter, differing only from the flesh substance in its vibratory condition. This accounts for its permanency of form, but no physical eye ever saw or ever will see this self, this spirit form, this soul, so-called, unless possessed of the psychic sight from which, speaking generally, few are endowed. Without it one individual can never see the spirit form of another while an inhabitant of this earth. We are conscious only of physical expression, and sound. Now in dissolution from accident or physical weakness, the body covering that is visible to us is no longer fit for habitation; then the separation, dissolution—death, so-called—occurs; the individual through, a natural process, releases itself from the flesh garment, and stands forth the same man or woman as before, though invisible to the inhabitants of earth. They see but the old flesh body that housed the spirit. They could not, as I have said, see the true self before, nor can they see it after dissolution, because of the intensity, because of the rapidity of the vibration of the etheric body, for our eyes are limited as to motion, as well as to distance."

**"That is all very well, but what has it to do with me? I am not dead,"** he answered.

"If you will be patient I will lead up to the personal application. When one has gone through this death change, one of two conditions may follow; we may never for a moment lose consciousness—it is then just good night to the old and good mourning to the new environment. This usually follows a respectable life. The man is the same still, nothing subtracted from or added to his personality, and in the mirror of Nature he sees himself with the same outlines, the same expression, the same thoughts, the same attachments, still a material body dissociated from the flesh covering, the same spirit form that had been his during his journey in the world. But he then appreciates that his body is lighter and more transparent than the flesh substance he has been accustomed to look upon, and he does not resist muscular effort as he did in the old covering; then but for the assurance of friends and relatives who assist in the change, as at earth-birth, and explain to the quickening consciousness, many would be afraid. There is this great difference in the two births. When this atom of life-force first becomes individual, an inhabitant of the earth plane, it possesses instinct but no intelligence; it continues to develop, with no knowledge of its previous existence. It could have none, for it came from the mass of universal life forces. The next great change is similar except that the individual retains all previous development; he knows little more of the laws governing, and the means available to aid his progression than an infant.

On the other hand, those who have led unclean earth-lives, who have been selfish, immoral, and have committed crimes against man and Nature, may not soon awake; if they do, they find themselves in mental darkness, in a prison of their own building, and there they remain until a desire comes from within for better things. Then the way will be shown by spirit people engaged in such charitable work. At the beginning, each awakening spirit is told that each wrong act done in earth-life must be lived over, that as he works he will encounter like conditions under which the wrong was done, and in the new life he must correct the error in the old in order to advance. I recall that an inhabitant of the next plane once said: **'The justice that meets a naked soul on the threshold of the after-life is terrible in its completeness.'''**

**"I cannot accept a word you say about a life after death. There is no other life—there can be none—a man dies like a dog,"** said the visitor.

"That is true in a sense," I said, "for the life force and individuality both go on. You cannot destroy an atom of matter, you will admit; so if life-force is matter, that cannot be destroyed."

**"This is all very strange talk, but why speak on such a strange subject to me? I am not dead; if I were and there is life beyond the grave, I should not be here talking to you."**

"I have talked just as I am talking to you with many who have made that change," I said.

**"Do you mean to tell me you have talked to dead people?"**

"I did not say that; I said that I have talked to those who have made the change called death. There is, in reality, no death; there are no dead."

**"Talk sense,"** he retorted, **"we have all seen dead people, have seen their bodies buried, and you tell me there are no dead."**

Again I said, "You fail to understand what I have been telling you. We bury the physical bodies but not the spirit bodies; one is just as material as the other."

**"I don't comprehend you, and I don't care to continue the discussion. I think I will say goodnight."**

"Just a moment and I will demonstrate the fact. Did I not tell you a moment ago that I had talked with many so-called dead?"

**"Yes,"** he answered, **"but I did not take what you said seriously; I made up my mind on that subject long ago."**

"Now to begin the proof—do you know where you are at this moment? Tell me if you know."

**"I don't seem to know. This is not my home; the room is strange to me; you are strange too. It is all unreal. Can you explain the situation in which I find myself?**

"Listen to me. This frail little woman, over eighty years old, who sits opposite me, is the most gifted psychic in the world. More than twenty years ago it was discovered that under favourable psychic conditions such as prevail tonight we could have speech with spirit people."

**"It can't be possible,"** he said.

"The suggestion," I replied, "is so far beyond the experience of man, that I am not surprised at your inability to comprehend the fact. Wait! Having such means of communication, we have not only learned much of the future state, but, acting in conjunction with a group of people in the next life, we have been able to bring many to a state of consciousness after the death change, in quasi-material, quasi-spiritual conditions, such as prevail here to-night; and when we are doing work of this character, many out of the body are brought for help by their friends, as you have been, that they may comprehend their situation."

**"But I am not one of these; the suggestion is absurd, I tell you. I am as much alive as you, and my body is quite as substantial as yours,"** he said.

"Hold up your hand as I do mine, and see if there is any difference between the two."

**"Yes,"** he answered, **"there is a difference, I now discover. Yours is opaque, but mine is transparent. I can see right through my hand. Is this hypnotic suggestion?"**

"No," I said, "you are facing new conditions to-night. Do you know that we sit in intense darkness—and cannot see you, although we hear your voice distinctly?"

**"I know,"** he answered, **"that it is not dark, for I can see you, and if I can see you, you can see me; but never mind that; what**

is the matter with my body? I think now I have been very ill, and one always looks as I do after long sickness," he replied.

"Speaking of illness, what do you recall about your last illness?"

**"My memory seems hazy, but it is coming back to me. I recall lying on a bed, the physician waiting, my wife and children sobbing. The doctor said, 'He is passing now.' That did give me a start; there were some who would like to see me dead—but I fooled them—for I did not die. If I had died, how could I be here?"**

"What do you know about death?" I said.

**"I don't know anything about it, and I don't want to."**

"But when that time comes to you, you will be obliged to know, whether you desire to or not," I replied.

**"Well, I am willing to wait, and I don't want to talk about it. I never did."**

"Suppose I tell you that you have already made that change?"

**"It would be foolish to tell me such a thing when I am here talking to you."**

"Suppose I now prove it to you? Those in spirit-life cooperate with me in this work and are often able to bring to the stranger those whom he has known in earth-life, and face to face and voice to voice, the proposition proves itself."

**"I tell you,"** he said, **"there are no dead people, and if there were, I don't want to see them. I have enough trouble with the living without bothering with the dead."**

"Is there no one in the next life with whom you would like to talk to if you could? Remember that your sickness may have ended in dissolution; your body is different, and you know you find yourself in a strange city."

**"Things have changed, but I don't want to see or talk to dead people."**

"You find life so material, so like the earth life, that I believe no method but actual experience will convince you that you have left the mortal state, and that lesson must be learned. You have been so intent on your conversation, I think that you have not looked around—look, what do you see?"

**"My God! People, people, people! All strangers, and all looking at me, all with bodies like my own; what strange hallucination is this? Where am I? What am I?"**

"You are no longer an inhabitant of this world but are actually living in the after-life. Are there no one you know among those you see, who, to your knowledge, are counted among the dead, so-called?" I asked.

"Not one, but wait, there comes—John—my old partner. Why does he, of all men, come? He is dead. I helped bury him. I was his executor. Take him and that woman and the boy away. I won't see them, I tell you. They are dead, all dead. They are coming to arrest me. How can they, when they are all dead? Tell me, tell me, tell me quick."

"What wrong did you do?" I asked

"Wrong? Who said I did them any wrong. I was faithful to the trust."

In answer another spirit spoke.

"No, you were not faithful. You stole the money entrusted to you for my wife and child, and left them to suffer. There never was, and never can be a secret in the world. When you kept from my loved ones that which I left for their support, and let them die in want, I saw, and all your friends in spirit life saw your act and working of your mind."

"No secret in the world? My crime known! The dead alive! Have I, too, left my physical body to find life when I thought to find oblivion? Am I to meet all those I have wronged? I cannot face the future! Darkness is gathering! I am falling! God help me!"

The voice faltered, struggled for further speech, and was lost. The gross material that clothed his organs of respiration disintegrated, and he spoke no more.

We had participated in one of the most remarkable experiences that it has been the privilege of man to have. We had talked with one who had left the physical body, and witnessed his awakening.

## The Record of a Night

"Good evening, Mr. Randall"; a deep masculine voice broke the stillness.

"We have," the voice of one of the directors of our group continued, "a great work to do tonight, and as atmospheric conditions are unusual, we have gathered a great throng in substantially the same mental attitude, and have brought them here for help. You have done this work so long that you, of course, understand that these people do not as yet know that they have separated from their old physical bodies and are no longer inhabitants of Earth. Won't you talk to them? They are living so much in your plane as yet that you can secure and hold their attention more closely than we can."

This was not a new experience. My records show upwards of 700 nights when this particular character of work had been done. As requested, I commenced to talk easily and naturally. I could not see, but Mrs. French could always see spirit people gather about listening, and some would come close watching me intently, while others would discuss among themselves softly so as not to interrupt my talk; they were evidently trying to comprehend the situation. I had long ago learned that those whom we were endeavoring to help must not be startled or frightened, as such shock would break the conditions that enabled them to speak; and therefore on this night, I discussed generally the unusual situations presented at this particular meeting, leading slowly up to the great change that had taken place. Had I bluntly told those assembled that they were all dead, the shock would probably have ended the work for the night. I have often known this to occur.

It had been my observation that some man among those assembled could take on material that would enable him to talk, and in that manner rivet the attention of all those who listened, and this night was no exception to the rule.

"I have," a strong voice remarked, **"been deeply impressed with what you have said, but I do not comprehend its import. Death is a subject that I did not like to think about; people generally give the subject little if any attention, and of course enter the next life ignorantly. I am afraid I am no exception to the rule. If I am to infer that such a change has come into my life, I am wholly unprepared."**

"Tell me," I answered, "what you now observe, for I assume your vision is clear."

**"For some time I have been watching the preparations being made. Substance appearing like bars of light about you and the lady opposite, was being worked and woven into place. Then I looked about and saw a great company gathered. One of those who seemed directing affairs asked me to permit material to be precipitated upon me so that I might talk to you. This was done without my understanding the process or import. Tell me the meaning of this procedure, if you please."**

"I am deeply interested," I said, "in the progress of man, after death so-called, and with the aid of this lady and the group you saw working with us I am able, when conditions are favourable, to have speech with those beyond the earth-plane."

**"I gathered that from your first talk,"** he answered, **"but all is so natural with me that it is hard to believe we are not in the old body, for we are like, yet unlike. Those who seem to con-**

203

trol the situation have bodies from which radiates light, while my own and those of all who are gathered listening, seem enveloped in something like a mantle of darkness; not that exactly, for we are surrounded by what I should describe as a dark, intangible substance carried by the individual as he moves. If, as you say, all these whom I see, except this lady and yourself, are living in the world of spirit, why do we differ so much?"

"The appearance," I replied, "is the result of a process of refinement. I don't mean in manner of speech, but in soul or spirit development. In the life you now live, the law of attraction holds full dominion, and all those who enter are irresistibly drawn in that mental state or condition that will accord with their own. That is what I am told. You will find, the intellectual, the high minded, the spiritual, the selfish, the wicked and immoral, all of them in different groups and in conditions as varying as character. There is no progress from one to another except by a purifying process through labour and suffering until the individual is qualified for advancement. This is a very natural and a very just process, is it not?"

**"The suggestion is very new,"** he remarked. **"I cannot say that it is not just, but I do say it is novel. I never thought of things in that way. If what you say is true, why has it never been taught before?"**

"I could answer your question in many ways," I said. "Knowledge is the one thing in the world we have to work for. You can't steal, buy, inherit, or bet it; it must be acquired by effort. Now, as the world generally speaking has never made any genuine effort to obtain knowledge of the conditions prevailing beyond, it is not surprising that men and women don't know.

"Again," I added, "the average mentality would not, could not, and will not understand, even if I should relate what is being done and accomplished this minute; but there are some thinkers, and their number is fast increasing, who can and will accept a plain statement of fact when it appeals to their reason."

**"I am thinking,"** he said, **"as I never did before, and I don't believe I could have comprehended that the death-change could be so natural, and so simple. What is beyond I don't, of course, know. I seem to be just waking; I realize that I am a living entity in no way changed. I now see I am no longer like you. While you have been talking, those whom I knew in earth-life have come and told me I have made a great change. That is about all I know now."**

204

At this moment another spirit speaking said:

**"You, my friend, have much to learn. Come with me for a little time for reflection; I want you to appreciate that with all your wealth you were a selfish man. The world was not enriched by your journey through it, and this accounts for the gloom that envelops you and all those who come with you. The first task that you must learn to do is to live for and help others, a process which humanizes and broadens the soul, and develops the man."**

## Lessons From Experience

One evening, we of the earth, who had gathered in my working room, were greeted by a minister who had been one of the leading preachers of his time. His voice was strong, his manner, imperious, his speech autocratic. He had no conscious appreciation of the change that had come to him. He was still, in his imagination, in his old body, still controlling his church, still the thought-leader and guide of his congregation. It took the combined efforts of our group and many of his old parishioners, in spirit, to bring him to understand that he was out of the material body. They came—those spirits—some with imprecations, because, while they had looked to him for guidance, he had deceived them, and they were suffering because they had accepted his word. Others, with more kindness, talked with him in a pacific strain and excused him, because he, too, had accepted blindly the word claimed to be of God, and had as blindly given it to them. Remorse and disappointment were his, when he found that his life-teaching had been a mistake. He wanted to find truths as he said they were, and eagerly questioned those in spirit to know if the Redeemer liveth. It was hard for him to believe that each must help himself. He would not accept this statement at first. He excused his false teaching by saying his father had taught him so, that he had been educated for the ministry; that he had learned to believe what the alleged inspired Book said, and that he only gave what he had received. When pressed by one who had accepted his teaching without question, he at last acknowledged that he had not fully believed all that he had taught; that what he taught was popular and what his people wanted; that to have questioned the Scripture openly would have lost him his position. Thus he showed that the love for gold was greater than the love of truth, and that without considering the wrong he might do to others he had guided them among old traditions, while he himself half doubted, only half believed. So the wrong he did came back, and he was told that his

205

progression would be stayed, until, standing in the portals of that new life, he should meet each one that came after him, call back those who had gone before, and bring each and every one he had deceived into the fields of true understanding before he would be able to advance.

In times of great disaster, when strong souls are torn from healthy bodies, there is much for us to do. They come trooping in with cries of fear and anguish, and I have heard better descriptions of great accidents from those who went out of the body in that way than were ever published in the daily press. When returning consciousness they feel at first that they have escaped from a terrible danger, and words of thanks fall from spirit lips. Then our task grows hard as we undertake to tell and to prove that they have passed the border line. The screams of terror and words of sorrow expressed in those first moments fill some of the sad pages of memory; but these are brightened sometimes by the joy of a father or mother, long mourned as dead, greeting them with words of tenderness and welcome.

**One of the most beautiful experiences that I recall was the awakening of a young girl who left this world just at the dawn of womanhood. (This experience was initially covered in Chapter 5–*The Drama and Experience of Death Itself*–entitled *Spirit Passage*. –Ed.)

She was the joy and sunshine of a splendid home, loved by a devoted father, and idolized by a great circle of friends. Life seemed to promise all that she could hope. She was one of the finest characters I have ever known, but almost in a day she sank into that dreamless sleep the world calls death. When we were at work that evening I heard the voice of one of our spirit-band speaking with great gentleness, words of encouragement. I was told that this young girl was coming and I was asked to add my welcome. Others seemed to be with her, upon whom she leaned. She was much excited and bewildered, and greeted me anxiously. She said she had been sick and had suffered great pain in her head; that she had heard her father's words of anguish and had heard others say she was dying; that at the same time there had come to her sweet music and she thought she saw angels with radiant faces; that she was so glad she had not died. My task was hard, –to tell this beautiful spirit that was in love with life and enraptured with the world, that she was no more in earth-life; that the music that came to her with such sweetness was from the spheres beyond, and that the faces she saw were just those of other pure girls like herself who came to welcome her into the new life.

With gentleness and with such words as I could command, I told her what was necessary, and as the realizing thought came home to her, a cry went out to the stricken father from that young girl's heart. It was with difficulty that she was calmed. Then, beautiful souls, in harmony with her own, crowded about her, speaking tender words of consolation, and she was comforted. She saw with clearer vision; and there came again the music, the same melody she had heard as her spirit was leaving the body, —sweeter, she said, than anything she had ever known. Then she was taken away. She had been brought fully to understand the change. When she left she was surrounded by beautiful characters who would teach her the way of that life and help her to find that joy and understanding which await the pure in spirit. After she was gone I asked of my teachers who remained, why I could not hear the music she described, as well as the spoken words. The answer was that the spoken words were of matter and vibrated on material ears; that the music was of spirit, and could be heard only by those already in spirit.

Much of our understanding of the next life and the conditions existing there have come from such experiences, and so we appreciate, although in a limited way, what life is in the spheres beyond.

Is there life beyond the grave? Can any ask when such things as I have described are possible? But this is not the question I seek to solve. It is, rather, what is that life and whither does it lead?

# CHAPTER 8
## *Children*

*I, Thy child forever, play about Thy knees this close of day. Within Thy arms I now shall creep, and learn Thy wisdom while I sleep. Amen.* – "Child's Prayer" by Patience Worth

## Child Life Beyond

During my many years of scientific investigation I invited many men and women to witness my work, and among them found a few possessing the psychic force that could be utilized by spirit people in sending messages. I recall that Mrs. S. was told one night that her young daughter, 12 years of age, could do automatic writing[1] if properly instructed. The trial was made. The child sat in an upholstered chair, with pencil and paper, which she magnetized by passing her hand over it for a moment, and then apparently she slept. It was a complete trance condition. After a few trials, her hand would write with great rapidity, and in that manner a conversation could be carried on with spirit people with great satisfaction. In this manner many evidential facts were obtained. There never was the slightest doubt that spirit people controlled her hand.

I have had similar experiences with several others, and there is not a particle of doubt in my mind, and in the minds of others who

---

1. Automatic Writing: In the hands of a man or woman spiritually or psychically developed, there are two phases of this method: the first where a person goes into a complete trance, in which case spirit people manipulate the hand and actually write; the second, where the psychic is fully conscious; in this case the messages and answers to questions are suggested to, and heard through, the psychics subconscious brain; dictated as one would dictate to a stenographer.

have witnessed such work, of the genuineness of automatic writing.

I wish to mention Mrs. H., a lady of rare refinement and great spirituality. I aided her development in automatic writing. She is today the most wonderful writer that I know—absolutely reliable. I make this statement after receiving hundreds of messages through her hand. With her, it is spirit suggestion. She gets the messages by dictation, knowing at the moment the word she is writing, but not the communication as a whole until it is read afterwards. This is a most satisfactory method, second only to the direct or independent voice such as I have obtained with the aid of Mrs. Emily S. French.

I mention Mrs. H. and her marvellous powers, for the reason that I am going to append a series of letters from a young boy in the spirit world, written automatically to his sorrowing mother still in earth life. (Not the medium. —Ed.)

## First Letter:

"Oh, Mummie, Mummie, don't cry so. It makes me so unhappy, and I can't make you feel my arms around you. If you would only smile and be glad, I'd be quite happy, because, dear little Mummie, I see ever so many lovely people who seem to be waiting to take me some place. They are all smiling, and talking together as they wait for me to be ready to go to them. One just came to me, a darling little girl; she says she is my baby sister, you told me went to heaven; she has the lovliest face—it looks all shiny, as though there was a lamp inside her eyes. Mummie, she wants to take me home with her, but I just can't leave you."

## Second letter:

"Darling, I held you so tight last night, and it seemed you must have felt me, for you smiled in your sleep and said my name. When I kissed you, because you seemed happier, I went with Marian to see our home. It is a darling cottage, and every room is so interesting. Grandma takes care of us and says the house is one she built when she lived with us; she says she did not know it at the time, but she was just as happy and good and did kind things for people, and each kind thing helped build the cottage. Some people do so much good, they have quite big houses, but they can't be any nicer than Grandma's. Hers is just filled with interesting things. She says she has lived in it and improved her mind. She said at first it was just warm and cozy, because she did not have an intellectual mind; but she has studied, and the rooms are filled with pretty things and books, and all sorts of things. When you are happier, I think I'll have a lovely time and learn a lot. Sister Marian's room is beautiful. She has lived there all her life, since a baby, and everything in the room is so beautiful and sweet."

Third Letter:

"Oh, Mummie dear, why do you grieve so? I am well and could be happy, only your sad face keeps me wanting to be near you and comfort you. I saw Marian do such an interesting thing today. She took me to a tumble-down hut, and let me look in while she went in. There was a man in there, moaning and crying. He kept saying, 'It's so cold and dark, I can't see a thing.' Over and over he said it.

"Marian just went to him and laid her hand on his eyes, which were closed. I could see what she was was thinking, without saying a word. It was very strange, yet seemed quite all right. Marian was thinking: 'Dear man, you are just cold and alone, because when you were on earth you never thought of any one but yourself, and were so selfish and cross and horrid; but you were not happy. Don't you want to be happy?'

"And the man said: 'Yes, I want to be happy, but I can't do anything.'

"Then Marian said: 'Oh dear, yes you can. Just think of some one very miserable you'd like to help.'

"And the man said: 'Why there was my foster brother. I was so mean to him; I'm sorry, —can I help him?'

"Because he said, 'I'm sorry, I want to help,' she took her hand from his eyes, and he looked around and could see. The hut that was so dark was beginning to get lighter. He began to look relieved and happier, and begged her to show him what to do and Marian said:

"'I'll take you where you can do a great deal for people. That is my business, to help people that way.'

"Her face was wonderful when she said it. I think I have a splendid sister."

Fourth Letter:

"Mummie dear, you have made me so happy, by being cheerful. I know it will be easier all the time for you, because you will come to know that I am not miserable and only unhappy when you grieve. Some way, here in this life, things seem so much more real, and it is so easy to learn things. Grandma says we have to go on learning until we are very wise indeed, because we must try to be perfect, and we can't be that unless our minds are full of good things. I love the music, —the air seems to throb with it some times, and it seems to go so deep inside of you it becomes a part of you, and afterwards you feel as if you had been having a drink of water when very thirsty, so refreshed and washed clean of everything but the nicest thoughts and feelings. There seems to be a good deal for people to do, besides learn things—chiefly, helping others. The very good girls, like Marian, just show people how to begin, and then they themselves have to work and help, and, more than all, have nice thoughts. So many people do not know about it here, and I am sure if they did they would not do lots of mean things they do, because it all counts against you and you have just that much longer to work before you can do all the beautiful things there are. We sing and dance and romp, in our recreation times, and then we listen to very wise people who teach us things. I always wanted to make things up—new machines and inventions—and that is what I am going to study for. When I know how, and have worked out something new and wonderful, I am to find an inventor and be with him a lot. In time I can make him think what I am thinking; then he will make my plans. Won't that be fun?" (This little spirit's plan is to mentally inspire a scientific inventor on earth, the invention betters the quality of life, and in turn the little spirit achieves constant progression in the spirit realms because of it. —Ed.)

Fifth Letter:

"Darling little Mummie, I have not talked to you for quite a long time, because I have been busy; but now that you know so much about me, and are feeling more contented, I can go on living here without worrying over you and trying to comfort you. You see, it's really just as though I was away at school, and at first one is always homesick; but now we can look forward to a vacation time when you will come to me and we shall be together always, and I shall have such heaps of things to tell you and show you. There is no wasted time here; waste means ignorance, and ignorance is almost wicked, because we should progress a little each day—that is one of our laws. We have to study these laws. I will try and tell you as well as I can some of them. In the first place, we must know what is good, and by knowing that, we know that right follows, and then love and harmony and knowledge and power, and then progress follows as naturally as a flower grows in the sun. You will think this sounds queer from your little boy, that I have changed a lot; but I haven't so much, Mummie, —I have just grown to understand the real things in life, —what we all have felt inside of us always."

Sixth Letter:

"Dear Mummie, I am learning many things that are necessary in this life, now you are so much happier about me and feel so sure that everything is all right with me. It used to scare me, when I saw any one who had died; or, when I thought of being put in the cemetery, it seemed awful, —so lonely and strange; but now I know how different it is and wish that every boy knew that dying is just like getting a new suit and discarding the old. The real you inside the new suit feels just the same, only we have to learn to think differently about most things. I mean, we must change some of our ideas, but the new ones are much nicer and make living here easier. I wish every one knew this before he came here and then no one would fear, and everything would be so nice and comfy.

"Marian and I came to you on Christmas morning and kissed your dear face; you must have felt all our love and happiness. We will come to you like that often, and some day you will come and live with us; then you will learn so many lovely things we cannot some way seem to tell you. There are such nice people always with us, and you will love it just as we do. Grandma says she is happy to have me with her, and to tell you that she, with the help of friends and teachers, will bring me up to manhood and that you will be proud of me when you come.

"Your own little boy."

Another spirit described child life as follows:
"I will tell you about the home for little children first of all.

212

No mother who loses a wee one need grieve, because she thinks the dear mite will have no one to love it and soothe its small fears and worries. You would love to see all the happy wee things we have here, some of whom had a very sad time during their brief sojourn on earth. Not one single baby, out of all the millions which come here, ever lacks mothering. They are surrounded by an atmosphere of love and just grow and blossom, as a result of these happy conditions, like so many rare and beautiful flowers. The place where they are rings with the sound of their happy laughter; there is no pain or sorrow for them here and they have no cause for tears. They romp and play and do all manner of things which delight the heart of a child.

"They are free to enjoy every moment, and they do. There are no quarrels or sulks to mar their happy times together. Their bright faces and sweet presences are a constant delight, especially to those folks who have always loved children. The men and women who were denied children on earth, and had always longed for them, are in their element when they come over and are free to lavish all their love for children on these darlings. The children grow up in time, as they would on earth, but they are free from sin. They can, therefore, go right on helping the spirits of those who spent many years on earth and are not free from the effects of sin. These spirits need help and guidance.

"I will now tell you about the place where the children come to grow up. It is a wonderful place and there are all sorts of lovely things they can do. The very tiny ones cannot play with the older ones any more than they can on earth. They just need loving arms around them and soft voices to soothe them. They get these always. There are always plenty of 'mother spirits' to look after the wee ones. It is the work they love and are best fitted for. We are all given the work we like best and are most capable of doing.

"As we progress, some of us are able to undertake more and more difficult tasks, and that phrase about 'the joy of being in the doing, not the task that is done,' is very true here. Most of us find a great joy in our work. I will tell you something about the doings of the older children. The toddlers are such darlings and would rejoice any mother's heart. Their faces are so bright and happy and they are so full of life, and bubble over with fun. There are no sad, wistful little faces here—as you often see on earth—caused by lack of love, the sins of their parents, and other things. These fortunate little ones have a delightful time. They run and dance and sing and jump for sheer joy. They paddle in crystal streams and build castles on lovely beaches, where the sand is like pure gold and the water is like myriads of gems.

"There are beautiful grassy places for them to play on, where they can run races and play all the games which children love. There are also exquisite fern groves, where every kind of beautiful fern flourishes, and dainty little streams tinkle gaily along, joining, it seems, in the children's merriment. There are so many beautiful and wonderful and delightful things in this enormous 'children's playground' that you will not have time to write down descriptions of half its beauties."

## Rights of Children

A celebrated French writer died in Paris in 1817. She was the daughter of a Minister of Finance under Louis XVI., enjoyed the friendship of Rousseau, Buffon, Gibbon, and other men of letters, and was exiled by Napoleon in 1812. One evening she gave the following talk to a company, which I had invited, on the subject of the early mental training of children and our duties to them:

"There are many things I want to say to you. I was the woman Napoleon feared and hated. I tried many things when on earth and made my brain a brilliant, polished receptacle. I was without a particle of affection or gentleness. I was proud of my wit and cleverness. I have to spend much time here trying to make a few bright flowers bloom in the hard soil, and to tar up the flaming, flaunting ones that had taken deep route there. It will help women very much to understand this philosophy. They are, as a rule, helpless and undeveloped souls. It is pathetic to see the way they follow blindly where they are taught to go, without once considering the wisdom of the teaching. I think this philosophy will teach them self-reliance, and will help them to understand themselves. Their children will profit largely from it and will make splendid new types. I am in earnest on this subject. It is my especial work now to bring understanding to women. I am above all things a worker, and so I find intense joy in thus making my weak sex understand what really great spirits they are. Sometimes I believe it is a mistake to think they are more spiritual than men.

They have not such large vices, as a rule, but their souls are small and petty, and few rise above sordid, every day duties, and see the great, beautiful, wonderful world waiting for them to enjoy.

"Many mothers are selfish and lazy. They either leave their children with servants, or let them grow up self-indulgent, uncontrolled men and women, simply because it is too much trouble to govern and correct. The poor children suffer for this all their earth-lives, and then progress is much harder. If women could be made to understand the great responsibility that rests with every human being, just within herself, they certainly would teach the little faltering feet the way to walk the path of life. Children must learn early to govern themselves, must learn to be generous, and, above all, must learn to think. Stop thinking for your children, you mothers, you stunt them! Teach them they must think in every little thing. Let them decide for themselves when it can possibly be done, and do not make little machines of the poor little souls. If you do, they will grow into larger machines. The brain can be trained from babyhood, and must be so trained to have the best results. Teach the children to see the beautiful in life and to appreciate their souls. Pour into them all the great thoughts of wise men, simplified for their understanding. Remember that you are responsible for their lives. Indeed, early training can develop a small virtue and kill a vice which might in after years grow large enough to make a man miserable. Never think it too much trouble to work for your child and with it. Your reward will be great and your joy unbounded when you see the splendid spirits of your children. You will remember that you developed them and watched them through childhood with intelligent eyes. Thy will be unblinded by the dead superstitions of ignorant men. They will be made keen and self-reliant through this new and enlightened philosophy. It sheds a light on all the dark places, and can easily be likened to that modern invention—the searchlight—which clears and brightens all it touches."

Another said:

"Children coming here in infancy are given experiences as nearly those of earth-life as possible, given those experiences that are needed, as it were, to form the soil for the plant to grow. Then they are taken to the Second Sphere, where they remain a long time. They make our best teachers, having nothing to unlearn, and they progress rapidly through all the Spheres. They need some earth-life, but naturally they are more nearly spirit when young, and easily take up the life and conditions here. I do not think early dissolution is unfortunate, unless the parents grieve very much. If they do, they act as a weight on the little spirit and chain it to them. The sweetest sound a good woman knows is the first appealing cry of her helpless child. Each day it grows more dear, and when the little lips respond and the tiny arms are raised, in confident love, the mother's heart grows rich with joy. Can you imagine the anguish of that heart when the child looks coldly into her eager eyes and turns from her aching arms without a sign of love or recognition? This is the anguish of the mother who deliberately destroys her unborn babe. That little embryo life must live, and it is cared for by tender spirits. When that mother enters into the new life, she feels the hungry, unsatisfied love of years beating in her heart, and every year the pain is deeper. She knows her child, but it sees only a stranger at whose door when helpless it had knocked in vain, and it turns away. The awakened mother's heart must endure intense agony before she can win the love she cast away. It is one of the saddest lessons in spirit life."

## Picture of a Child

The orthodox teachings make no attempt to tell us what becomes of children who go out of the earth-plane in infancy. How many millions of mothers have had too young for speech, boys and girls just able to talk and walk, sink into a dreamless sleep, and having kissed for the last time the lips of love, have seen the little bodies lowered with tender hands into the grave, and as the earth fell upon the casket have heard from the lips of ignorance "ashes to ashes, dust to dust." With hearts without hope, they have gone back to the house of sorrow, the toys, the little bed, the vacant chair, the ache in the heart, the tears that fall in countless thousands of homes, and the cries that go out in the night to know where in the vast universe the baby is, if it lives at all.

"What becomes of those who go out in infancy?" you ask. "Do they develop in mind and body? Shall we know them and meet them again? Will they know us? Is there any one to comfort and care for them, and teach them? Do they miss and seek the mother love?" These and a thousand more questions have been asked in

216

the countless ages that have gone, and are being asked in every desolate home in the world to-day.

Let me tell what I have learned of those conditions through many years of speech with those in the after-life.

I repeat what I have said before and shall say again, for it is the key to comprehension, and that the infant at conception possesses an etheric form, at that moment clothed in a physical garment or flesh body. This etheric form is material, composed of matter, and as matter cannot be destroyed; it follows that the etheric child-body cannot by any possibility be annihilated.

The infant etheric form by the process of dissolution passes out of the physical garment which it took on at the moment of conception, the same garment that it wore at birth, and becomes an inhabitant of the next plane of consciousness, where all is etheric, where nothing physical can enter. This change may be likened to an earth-birth. There are thousands of childless women, who never in earth-life found expression from the mother-love. These, with countless others who find their greatest happiness in doing good together with those of blood relation, attend at such a time and care for the little stranger in the new environment.

Let me give an instance that came under my personal investigation. It is a well known fact that children up to about three years of age are able to, and do see spirit people; some have spirit playmates. The instance I am about to relate was the passing of a little boy, only one week old, who had a sister a little under three years of age, with whom I was privileged to make an experiment. The little girl night after night saw the baby boy, and described him; he was in the same room with two spirit nurses in attendance, while another woman was from time to time described as being present. Again, this three-year-old sister often saw the spirit baby when she was away from home. On various occasions I verified these statements by inquiry from those in the after-life during our investigation, and found that what the little sister related had actually taken place. The woman who appeared from time to time was the grandmother; she, assisted by two nurses, cared for the little stranger, and on several occasions, before he could articulate plainly, prior to his fourth birthday, I heard him speak to me. This was a most valuable experience.

Children in the after-life are cared for very much as they are here. There are those who find their greatest delight in mothering the motherless, and teaching them words of speech and wisdom; so under such unselfish care the children reach mental and bodily maturity just the same as they would if they had remained in this world.

The etheric process of development is interesting; children need mother-love no less in spirit than in earth life, and as the mother sleeps, those in charge place the etheric baby-form close to her heart, where it rests absorbing the love so necessary to its existence. We little know how close the after-life is, how close its inhabitants come to us, the influence they exert on us, or the result of our thought vibrations upon them. Then again, as the children grow, they keep in touch with us from day to day, and when we go out into the after-life, they know and greet us as we enter the life that has no night.

There are in the next life kindergartens, schools, colleges and universities of learning just as we have here, and what is more, the inhabitants do not cease to study and increase their store of knowledge when they reach a certain age, but there are great lecture halls where the advanced ones teach the supreme laws of Nature, where all are welcome and all go, and so the secrets of the Universe are understood. There is but one aristocracy in the life to come, and that is founded on the refinement and development of character. Measured by this standard, how very poor are our very rich! I have often written that the aristocrats of the after-life have gained their position by helping others less fortunate. They rise by raising others. Those alone stand erect who stoop above the lowly.

Here is what a sojourner in the next plane has said of the little ones:

**"Many people have puzzled as to the state and condition of young children in the spirit world, and it is on that subject that I desire to speak, more particularly, to-night. There are millions of young children of all ages passing into the spirit world every year. Some of them are of very tender age, while others know right from wrong. It is an interesting subject to inquire as to what they do in the spirit life. At the outset, I must tell you that there is a divine law in the spirit world, that whosoever passes into that kingdom before he has reached to man's estate upon the earth-plane, shall grow mentally to the stature of a man. You can gather from that, that the youngest child, even the infant that has been taken from you, will grow mentally and spiritually on the other side of life. Clairvoyants and others have often described young children in the spirit-life, who have been recognized by mothers and fathers; they, perhaps years after, have been somewhat astonished to hear of the child looking much older, and they have not been able to account for it. You will understand that the presentation of the spiritual form is in order that those in the flesh may be**

**able to see them through the physical senses, and to note that they appear to be growing toward manhood and womanhood. I am afraid that many people upon your earth-plane today are neglectful of their responsibilities to their children. If God has given you such a flower as a child, it is incumbent upon you by example and precept to train that child in spiritual things, so that ultimately he will be with you in the kingdom of Heaven and will rejoice in the knowledge that you guided him spiritually when an infant. But how careless are many people with their children! They forget that the child is all the time taking grave note, not of what they are saying, but of what they are doing. I assure you that if you are unmindful of your responsibilities toward your children, you will undoubtedly have to pay the penalty when you reach the spirit side of life."**

Too little attention has been paid to the going out of children; the world has little knowledge on that subject. No greater blessing can come to the fathers and mothers of every nation and tribe than to know that children with bodies too frail to carry them through the earth-life are not lost in going from among us, but in the other life go right on with their growth and development under the care and guidance of good men and women who for love of humanity do the necessary work, and so enrich themselves.

I am impressed not to leave this subject without a word of warning to do no murder. Know that at the moment of conception out of the mass of the universal good, out of the life mass, an etheric atom, a body infinitesimal in size and perfect in form is clothed, and no matter whether the physical birth is natural or premature, that life-force so individualized has commenced its journey back to God, and all the power in all the Universe cannot change its ultimate destiny.

I am told that into the after-life countless millions of children have come and are coming who have never had the advantage of a natural physical birth and earth experience so necessary to their development, but that heartless mothers by abortive acts and with the aid of dastard physicians have done and are doing countless murders, more terrible in result than the taking of the life of a man, because the unborn infant is so weak and helpless. If this knowledge shall cause any mother to spare the life of her unborn child, blood of her blood, and bone of her bone, or the physician to pause in his criminal act, sorrow untold will pass both by.

Ella Wheeler Wilcox described perhaps better than she knew in her "Ballade of the Unborn Dead" the natural and logical result of the child murder . . .

219

"They walked the valley of the dead,
   lit by a weird half light,
"No sound they made, no word they said,
   And they were pale with fright.
"Then suddenly from unseen places came,
   loud laughter, that was like a whip of flame,
"They looked, and saw, beyond, above,
   A land where wronged souls wait.
Those spirits called to earth by love,
   And driven back by hate.
"And each one stood in anguish, dumb and wild,
   As she beheld the phantom of her child.
"Yea, saw the soul her wish had hurled,
   Out into night and death,
"Before it reached the Mother world
   Or drew its natal breath.
"And terrified, each hid her face and fled
   Beyond the presence of her unborn dead,
"And God's Great Angel, who provides
   Souls for our mortal land,
"Laughed, with the laughter that derides,
   At that fast-fleeting band
"Of self-made barren women of the earth.
   Hell has no curse that withers like such mirth.
"'Oh, Angel, tell us who were they, That down below us
fared;
   Those shapes with faces strained and grey,
"'And eyes that stared and stared;
   Something there was about them, gave us fear;
"'Yet we are lonely, now they are not here.'
   Thus spake the spectral children; thus
"The Angel made reply:
'They have no part or share with us,
   they were but passers by.'
"'But may we plead for them?' the phantoms plead;
"'Yea, for they need your prayers,' the Angel said."

"I want to tell you," a teacher in the after-life said, "of a little waif that came to us in infancy. We taught and carefully guarded, and schooled her in the pure conditions of our sphere until she approached womanhood, but she had no contrasts, therefore she could not judge of the relative purity and delights of her environment. In order that she should be able to enjoy her home and the glories of the world, it was necessary for her to have a knowledge of earthly conditions. And so I was instructed to conduct this child back to earth from time to time. When this child first returned to earth and was among your people, she could hardly endure even to examine the gross conditions, and could not understand how people could exist in such dark, crude elements. But, as I led her along from one condition to another, over the road she would have gone had she remained on earth for the ordinary allotted period, I said to her: 'Had you lived your time in the body, you would have been in the condition in which you see these people.' I also told her that this one had received a higher training. And we passed along to another place in the earth-life where there were children of the poor and ignorant, as well as the rich and learned. And we tarried until my little charge thoroughly learned the different environments of children on earth, and the great contrast between their homes, daily life, and schooling and those in spirit-life. This child had never known anything but innocence and purity, and she was far removed from the ordinary conditions of the childhood of earth. It was long before she could, in any degree, recognize it as a reality.

"And, having learned of the methods of training in the institutions of earth, we pursued our investigations farther along; and, finally we came to where there was a great ortho-dox church; and there, unseen, we mingled with the congregation. She said: 'This churchhouse is not like ours at all. What is taught here?' Presently the services began. I told her to listen attentively to the minister, for here she would get the average experience of the church methods and be able to see wherein a great work, in brave hands, is greatly needed on the spirit side. Then the minister proceeded with his discourse in his regular methodical manner, telling the people all he thought essential to prepare them to enter higher realms of the spirit. But the girl, now grown to nearly womanhood, could not accept the dicta of the minister, for she had up to now been raised in the spirit world and had learned nothing that was in harmony with methods attempted by the church to enlighten the people and prepare them for future realities. Therefore the teachings of the minister seemed to her so gross, so false, so out of line with all she had ever seen, heard, or read of in the land which had always been her home that she hesitated to remain, but I told her that her future work and welfare required that she learned as much as possible of the earth conditions in which your people live, and the kind of preparation such earth conditions make for their inheritance in our life. But the more the young lady heard of the sermon the more she disbelieved it. In fact, it was so much opposed to what she knew of the conditions of this side, and so different from what preparation while on earth for entrance to and enjoyment of spirit life should consist that at my suggestion she resolved to visit those who had just left the earth-plane, schooled under its teaching, and witness the effect of it; we, therefore, journeyed on."

**Mr. Edward C. Randall, circa 1934**
(see list of illustrations for details)

Emily Sophia McCoy French, 1871
(see list of illustrations for details)

Former home of Edward C. Randall (see list of illustrations for details)

EMILY S. FRENCH
1831 · 1912
MOTHER

**Mt. Hope Cemetery, Rochester, New York**
(see list of illustrations for details)

# CHAPTER 9
## Various Subjects

*To believe that any past generation held the monopoly of truth, or was able to give it final expression, is not only inconsistent with the teachings of history, but is a flat denial of the Holy Spirit, which was promised to guide us progressively into all truth. –Dr. Cyril Alington*

### Evolution

Little is known of that constant force known as evolution, or of the great laws that govern the process of advancement. I have eagerly sought information on this subject, have discussed it with many men in the next sphere beyond and have been told among other things:

"**A most encouraging indication of the progress of the present age is the fact that a few great thinkers and demonstrators of nature's laws have been able to grasp conditions beyond the physical, and are giving such information to mortals, who, because of their environment and duties, have not been able to solve for themselves these great problems.**

"**You ask me to say something concerning evolution, making that gradual, and yet positive, change in the world's condition that has finally resulted in thinking mankind. So be it. Then is not what I have just said a most wonderful and beautiful illustration of the progressive realization of the Master's great purpose—the gradual, yet positive, improvement of matter until an observant and grateful mortal is the final result?**

"**God, as you use the word, is the ALL. That is apparent to every thinking brain. Being, then, that ALL, God cannot be a** personality: every bit of matter is a part and parcel of that ALL; every force in nature is an expression of the presence of that ALL; and every thinking brain is a more or less perfect functional part of that ALL.

"To a sane and appreciative, active brain, free alike from arrogance and illusion, the proposition that mortal man is made in the perfect image of his Master, God, is the extreme of egotistical blasphemy. Far better is the expression of your countryman, Robert G. Ingersoll, that 'Man has made God in his image.' That part of mortal man that is in any degree like his Master is his thinking brain; otherwise, man is but an expression, in his form and physical functions, of that process of evolution spoken of as environment. All that is great in man is mind, and this greatness increases as he rises to the level of the ideal, the Master Mind.

"In a previous discussion, I mentioned the fact that we spirit-people do not always agree on many subjects of which we have no actual proof or convincing evidence, and so as regards the early stages of earth and the subsequent changes up to the existence of man, many among us differ; but I am safe in saying that the best informed hold that there has been a constant refining process of earth-matter since the cooling of the evidently original vaporous particles that gradually, by loss of heat, become solidified into rock and water; and that as the chaotic condition gradually assumed a proper separation upon cooling and solidifying, the process of refining gross matter began, and by the action of element upon element, of substance upon substance, the erosion of the primitive rock occurred, with the result of eliminating the fine from the gross; and, by the action of water in causing sedimentary deposits and the raising or lowering of the sedimentary or refined rock, and the consequent re-refining process, chemical action was allowed to come into play, resulting in a continuation of the process whereby gross matter is refined. Necessarily, as the cooling mass must have constantly given off heat, and also absorbed a certain amount of heat by chemical action, there came a period when the earth's crust could support the first life, vegetation. This vegetable life itself is but the chemical product of certain parts of refined matter, resulting from the gradual solidifying of the gaseous vapors fixed in space by the action of some of the planets undergoing a change.

"As regards the earth's actual beginning, there is no authentic knowledge among spirit-people. A theory based upon sound premises may be regarded as a general statement of the truth. From a knowledge of existing conditions, comparative reasoning can, and does, draw correct deductions, and so men of scientific attainments have, by study and investigations, demonstrated much that is not only evidence, but that may be said to be actually demonstrated.

"Among the best informed of the spirit-people the growth of a new planet results from the fixing in space, by the existing stellar system, —owing to that great principle of nature known as the law of gravitation, of some mass of matter revolving wildly through the universe, and the placing of it in a position of harmony with other masses of matter or planets. So must the earth have been caught when in its state of motion and vaporous matter, conditioned by its flight through space, not by any friction of the particles of its mass against the so-called ether, but because of the unusual disturbance of the particles of the mass among themselves; and also, because of the latent heat imparted to the runaway mass of matter that may be considered the nucleus of your planet. When finally caught and held in its place of career, it came into the lines of force existing from other planetary bodies, by gradual degrees its speed was steadied and, slowly but surely, it fell into the correct and dignified motion that is consistent with the laws governing planets, and it became one of the necessary keystones in the constellations of which it must have been elected a member. And so a new planet is born. Man has since called it earth. All the essentials of the present conditions existed at the very beginning of the earth's creation, have ever been, and are now, stored away in the mass of fugitive matter.

"Evolution is but the action of that great power called by mortal man, God, but which really is the process of refinement and purification of gross matter until the resultant product is living thinking moral man, and then the intellectual man. The next step in that ever-changing ever-progressing evolution, is the endowment of that physical, intellectual man, with what we call spirit.

"As each and every particle of matter depends upon some other particle of matter to allow of that progressive refinement spoken of, so it is throughout the entire chain, the spirit-people are as necessary to physical people as the gas exhaled

**from the lungs of living animalism is for the growth of vegetation, or as the refined chemical vegetable combinations are to animal life."**

The origin of life has been, and ever will be, a great mystery, until such time as we shall, by progression out of the body, come to a greater understanding of life force. We all know something of the process by which all planetary life, both animal and vegetable, is started; but the principle process of inoculation of matter with life-forces, is practically unknown, though we do know that it is governed by law. In the discussion of this great problem of the origin of life, we must take matter into consideration in its different vibratory conditions, from the generic rock to the Universal Mind.

As I have said before, when life, in its evolution, progresses so that it has *power of thought* and constructive reasoning, it has reached a stage of individualism that can never be lost. The power of thought and constructive reasoning, then, is the line of demarcation which determines whether the particular life force is to continue and hold individuality beyond the physical, or pass into some other form of gross matter. There is no matter in the universe which does not possess atomic energy, and, therefore, life force. When matter is brought to the proper state of vibration by physical action, and sufficiently refined; when, in other words, according to a natural law, temperature is increased and matter is rendered receptive because of its activity, an atom of Universal Good, of life-force, inoculates, enters into it, and it becomes clothed, and after the required period of gestation and growth, there is a physical birth.

It is, in reality, matter acting on matter; refined matter, or spirit, clothing itself with grosser material, thus obtaining physical expression and individuality. The atom of Good that finds individual expression in every birth is from the great ocean of Infinite Mind or Universal Good. Prior to conception, it was not individual; but from that moment it commences its journey back to the sphere of Exaltation, the highest mental state of which we can have any knowledge.

This life-force that finds expression in mankind, or in the animal or vegetable kingdom, is all from the same source; but just what it develops into depends upon the character of the matter with which it is clothed, and its evolution, to a large extent, depends upon subsequent environment.

Species have always been, and will always be, distinct in character. You cannot make a radical change except to improve it. Nature

226

has created all species for distinct purposes—nothing lives that has not a place and a purpose. Whether man understands, appreciates, and comprehends this fact or not, it is true. It would be the changing of a natural law to change species.

Evolution, then, starts on the earth plane with an atom of Universal Good, clothed and individualized in this sphere of development and of preparation for the real life, which only commences with physical dissolution. Evolution is forward, not backward. The atom of life-force, which finds physical expression here, prompted, urged, and taught by spirit-intelligences as well as by parental suggestion develops; and, at some time very early in life, comes to use reason: wants to know, thinks, looks upon the wonders of earth and sky and marvels. That life, so started upon its journey, growing to maturity, and passing to greater opportunity, by laws as irresistible as force, goes on and on, with but one opportunity for physical development, while he, a mortal being, journeys upon this globe. There is no coming back to live this life over again, no reincarnation, but everlasting and continued progress and development. Evolution springs from the desire to know, to see, to feel, to understand and to grasp all natural laws; and, as the individual grows, becomes more refined, and increases the ration of his thought vibration, he reaches higher planes in the progress of his earth development.

Evolution is not confined to life-force, but matter, as we use that term, develops in a corresponding degree. Of this we have material evidence.

There are three perceptible stages in the evolution of form: (a) Increase in the mass; (b) decrease in the stability of the molecules; (c) increase in the activity of the substances. The evolution of each material form comes by adding atom to atom in their dimensions, making distinct the unity of composition existing between the mental states, all pulsating at a higher and higher rate. There is positive evidence of evolution.

A spirit said:

**"Evolution means progress, higher development. Each vibratory atom must go through each stage of vibration before it can be fitted for the fullest perfection. The story of evolution may be seen in the grain of wheat. It is planted and then develops through each successive stage until it becomes nourishment for man, and thence its development is a part of a soul's progress; and eventually it becomes a part of the life-force, and generates life-force into another grain of wheat, and each new grain that reaches the life-force enriches it and makes**

227

**more powerful that force, so that, while it completes a perfect circle, yet it is always growing greater and more perfect. Thus evolution is constantly repeating itself on a larger scale each time."**

Wherever there is life-force there must be thought. There is intelligent action embodied in every seed that has a living germ. The acorn has sense enough to send its roots into the earth, its trunk and branches into the air, and to choose for food for root and branch, such elements as will make the oak tree, and to reject such elements as would be proper only for the pine. All grass has the same kind of intelligence in choosing food, and the power of choice must involve the power of thought. All the laws of nature, being universal in their application, apply to all life alike; what is true of the grain of wheat is true of man. The evolution of one is similar to that of the other, and is destined to increase the life-force of the universe. Knowledge is a pyramid with its base buried in the organic, towering higher and higher as it increases; and crowning the whole, embodying all of nature's handiwork, is the master-builder, man. What could be grander, more noble and beautiful, than the human mind at work under the guidance and suggestion of spirit-people, who have progressed beyond the comprehension of earth conceptions?

Evolution began with the primeval, nebulous mass, in which was held, potentially, all future worlds. Under evolutionary laws the amorphous cloud broke up, condensed, took definite shape and, in time, assumed a gradually increasing complexity. Finally, there emerged the cooled and finished earth, highly differentiated; and there was given us the breeding ground for the inception of life and for the organization of the elements into the first relation of sentient form. What has passed in history many know, but what evolution finally leads to in its progression, mortal man will never know. That is the province of spirit-people.

When they passed out of the earth conditions, because of evolutionary laws, spirit-people have beautiful flowers, far away hills, majestic mountains, leaping brooks, blossoming orchards, musical birds, the storm and lightning flash, the disturbed ocean, the clearing sky and the setting sun with tints of many colors. All that we have is but an imitation of the *reality* which belongs to their sphere only. Of course, what they have differs from what we have because of a higher and more rapid vibration, but the effect is similar.

The tendency of all life, wherever found or however clothed, is to perfect, improve, increase, and extend its sphere of usefulness.

228

This is evolution. It is a fact, a law and not a theory, and its possibilities are as boundless as the imagination. The work of ages begun by nature has no apex. Evolution is advolution. It does not stop with the organic; its future is greater than its past, and from spirit-people only can come such facts as will make the physical comprehend its possibilities.

## Materiality of the Universe

It is most difficult for the human mind to comprehend that anything which sight or sense does not disclose is material. The idea that what we call space is substantial and real, and composed of matter, the same as those things that are visible, presents a proposition difficult of acceptance—we know so little of matter's properties.

If those in the after life live and progress in a world as substantial and material as this, have houses and other structures and buildings, if that plane has forests and fields and growing grain, flowers, mountains, meadow lands and flowing streams, then that world is as substantial and real and composed of the same substance as this, varying only in vibratory action. As a matter of fact, these two worlds or conditions now blend, one with the other. What we see, feel and touch, only clothes visible life. Through *nature*, as we use that word, the spirit world functions and has temporary physical expression. This fact science is just coming to understand, but as yet little is known of the constituent parts of matter that fill the Universe, whether physical or spiritual.

Heretofore matter has been known in but three conditions—solid, liquid and gaseous. Sir William Crookes, the learned English chemist, while endeavouring to create a vacuum in a glass tube, discovered a fourth condition, which he named the *radiant state*. The atoms, freed by rarefaction, assume in this relative vacuum vibratory motions of intense and incalculable rapidity. They become flambent and produce effects of light and electrical radiations. This suggests a clue to most of the cosmic phenomena.

Variously condensed, in its three first conditions, matter *in the radiant state* loses a number of its properties, such as *density, colour* and *weight*; but in this new-found realm, it appears to be more closely and intimately related to the force which is life. This fourth aspect is another condition which matter is susceptible of assuming. The mind can picture a subtle, hyperfluidic state, as superior to the radiant condition as the radiant is superior to the gaseous, or the liquid to the solid. Science will, in the future, solve this problem and find an answer to such age-long and formidable problems as the unity of substance, or the preponderating forces of the universe.

Matter in its higher and more refined vibrations, becomes a fluid of infinite suppleness and elasticity, by endless combinations of which all bodies are engendered. In its primordial essence—invisible, impalpable, imponderable—this fluid, through successive transitions, becomes ponderable and capable of producing, by powerful condensation, those hard, opaque and weighty bodies which constitute the base of terrestrial matter. This state of cohesion is, however, transitory. Matter, reascending the ladder of its transformations, can as readily be desegregated and returned to its primitive fluidic state.

All matter is composed of molecules, atoms and electrons. The smallest particle that can be detected by the human eye through the microscope is about twenty-five times larger than a molecule. The molecule is composed of atoms which individually are about one three-hundred-millionth of an inch in diameter, while the electron—as the ultimate sub-division of matter—has a diameter 100,000 less than the atom. There would be thirty trillions of electrons to the inch, each one clothing life, that is force.

It must, therefore, be admitted first of all that nothing we see around us is absolutely solid. A mass of anything, whether it is metal, rock or other apparently dense and solid substance, does not exist as such. Cohesion of particles is relative only in proportion to weight, and each particle of a mass is relatively distant from the others, allowing space for the free passage of the ether, light—such as the X-ray-radio energy, which is life expressed in substance.

Professors Thompson and Tait say that if a drop of water could be magnified to the size of the earth, we should see the atoms about as big as oranges, and that electrons are about a thousand times smaller. Sir William Crookes, when elected President of the British Association for the Advancement of Science, in 1898, said in a remarkable address that all of the phenomena of the universe are presumably continuous waves, and "that we have good evidence that they range from one vibration to two thousand trillions per second, thus varying in their frequency and also in their velocity. As a starting point, he said:

"I will take a pendulum beating seconds in air. If I keep on doubling, I get a series of steps, as follows:

**starting point**
Step 1:   2 vibrations per second
Step 2:   4 vibrations per second
Step 3:   8 vibrations per second
Step 4:   16 vibrations per second
**sound**
Step 5:   32 vibrations per second
Step 6:   64 vibrations per second
Step 7:   128 vibrations per second
Step 8:   256 vibrations per second
Step 9:   512 vibrations per second
Step 10:  1,024 vibrations per second
Step 15:  32,768 vibrations per second
**electrical rays**
Step 20:  1,048,576 vibrations per second
Step 25:  33,554,432 vibrations per second
Step 30:  1,073,741,824 vibrations per second
Step 35:  34,359,738,368 vibrations per second
**unknown**
Step 40:  1,099,511,627,776 vibrations per second
Step 45:  35,184,372,088,832 vibrations per second
**heat-light rays**
Step 50:  1,125,899,906,842,624 vibrations per second
Step 55:  36,028,707,018,963,968 vibrations per second
**unknown**
Step 58:  288,230,376,151,711,744 vibrations per second
Step 59:  576,440,752,203,423,488 vibrations per second
**Roentgen, or X-rays**
Step 61:  2,305,763,009,213,693,952 vibrations per second
Step 62:  4,611,526,018,427,385,904 vibrations per second
**Radium rays**
Step 63:  9,223,052,036,854,775,808 vibrations per second

"It will be seen by the above that at the fifth step from unity, at thirty-two vibrations per second, we reach the region where atmospheric vibration reveals itself to us in sound. At 32,768 per second, to the average human ear, the region of sound ends. After the 32nd step vibration increases rapidly, giving us electric waves, then light waves at an unthinkable number of vibrations per second, until we reach the X-ray and finally, to us, the radium ray. The rays of radium are the results of quintillions of vibrations per second, and are also so subtle that they pass through all solids. It may be that the X-waves and the radium waves are only at the threshold of the wonders of the unseen universe. It seems to me in these rays we have a possible mode of transmitting intelligence, which, with a few reasonable postulates, may supply a key to much that is obscure in physical research."

Force, or energy, is life and is composed of and functions in matter on both planes. It is only when energy, or life, takes on a covering of gross material that it functions physically. Like all else in nature, it is indestructible.

Energy or life is found in and functions in every stratum. It does not begin at the earth's surface nor end in the air. Life differs in every condition of matter—in the earth, on the earth, and in that vast expanse which we ignorantly call space. The difficulty is that we do not as yet understand the various conditions and constituent parts of the matter in which the universe is expressed and functions. Until we do, we cannot understand how the so-called dead live and labour in a world material, tangible and real.

The subject is perhaps the most complicated of any in nature. Its mystery is a present beyond any man's comprehension. I but hope to create an interest in the subject, to set in motion individual thought. Others may, by research, work out some conception of the conditions in which those who have gone before live and work from day to day. We are coming to the conclusion that force and thought blend one with the other, that all are expressed in substance and are an expression of life force.

Water is a transparent, inodorous and tasteless fluid. It is a compound substance, consisting of hydrogen and oxygen in the proportion of two to one- by weight, two parts of hydrogen to sixteen parts of oxygen. These are both gases.

Atmosphere is likewise a gas, is inodorous, invisible, insipid, colourless, elastic and, being substance, is possessed of gravity. It is composed by volume of twenty-one parts of oxygen and seventy-nine of nitrogen, mixed, but not chemically united.

From the generic rock we see matter ascending in its vibratory condition, step by step, to the earth's surface; when the water with faster movement than air; then the ether, no less substance than are atmosphere and water, about which as yet we know but little. The component parts of ether are not known to certainty, but that it is substance is admitted. Ether, as we now know, fills all space and is the medium of light, heat and sound. It not only fills space, but passes through all solids, so intense are its vibrations. It is not strange that we do not see it, for we can not see atmosphere. The reason we see water is because of its slow vibration. We do not see electricity, except as we reduce the speed of its vibration. Therefore, it is not strange that we are unable to see ether.

Each stratum has its form of life. The earth has worms and crawling things, the sea fish and other marine life, the air man and animal life, the ether spirit people—each condition, each environment, is natural and real, and all are according to the divine plan. Today our physical bodies have a density, substantially corresponding to other substances, which limits our movements. Tomorrow, when the inner or etheric body emerges from its present housing, it will vibrate in accord with the finer etheric conditions, which are now invisible to us. All this is as natural to spirit-people as things of the world are to us.

What I am trying to explain is that the universe is substance, or matter, real and substantial. We are now clothed with physical substance; we function and work on one plane, the earth plane. The spirit people live and labour on another, a higher plane. They are separated from us, just as we are separated from various forms of life below us. This after life—Heaven, if you use that term—is substantial, composed of matter higher in vibration than the air in which we function. And in that vitalized, material condition, spirit people live just as we do, build structures of the varying substances, and grow things exactly as we do, though with greater freedom.

In calling attention to the constituent and chemical properties of our material, I show how little we know of matter, and lead, step by step, through its increasing intensity and vibration, or order that we may in a small measure comprehend the material conditions in which spirit people live.

We do not comprehend that substance called ether, and probably will not understand it until we become inhabitants of that plane, but we do know it is a substance and reality, as people live and labour in surroundings as real and tangible to them as the earth's substance is to us.

Another, speaking of the materiality of the next plane, has said:

**"Spirit ether fills the universe. It is a compound of two coexistent, co-eternal elements, the one positive, the other negative; one the male, the other the female element. These two primitive elements do exist, and always have existed, in union. Organic life is an aggregation of these primitive, spiritual elements. The law of chemical affinity, of every form of cohesion, of every human desire, of all love and affection, is but a manifestation of the affinity of positive and negative spirit ether asserting itself in organic aggregations of the positive and negative spirit atoms. Sun and systems of worlds**

are organic evolutions of this eternal life element. Spirit ether fills the universe. Life permeates and is inherent in all things. Nature expresses all there is of creative energy."

Another inhabitant of the next plane, speaking of matter spiritual and physical, says:

"Our world is composed of matter as real and definite as your own, but that matter vibrates at a higher rate, consequently your undeveloped senses can have but little cognizance of it. And, your own sphere being composed of matter at a low rate of vibration, it is almost as equally as difficult for us to manifest on your plane as it is for you to penetrate ours. Yet we have evolved from your plane, and have all the experience of that evolution, and it is perhaps easier for us to reach back and help you than it is for you to see forward. The principle of cooperation between the two planes is what we desire to establish, for this principle of cooperation is an essential and necessary condition for the development of the consciousness from your low and stagnant vibrations to those that are higher and healthier and more in keeping with the spirit's deepest longing, more in harmony with that process that is working for the ultimate and absolute destiny of the evolving spirit of man."

How little we know, and how much there is yet to learn of that which we call matter or substance in nature; until the mentality grasps in some measure this subject, life beyond cannot be comprehended.

## Nature's Laboratory

All the universe is the result of chemical action; this entire earth, and all upon it is one great laboratory wherein nature's forces are ever active, controlled by laws made and kept in operation by the Master Intelligence.

Nature abhors inaction and stagnation; life-force permeates every atom that goes to make up the mass which we call earth. We call the activity and expression of that force, energy. The ceaseless effort of this force to obtain development, coming into touch with other chemical conditions in nature's wonderful retort, is a refining process, working for the advancement of mankind. An interesting discussion on this subject by a spirit is as follows:

"It should appeal to you that each atom, or each element, and each molecular aggregation of sub-atoms, must possess distinct individuality. The scheme of nature, so far as so-called inanimate matter is concerned, is to allow a perfect expression of the individual characteristics of each separate species. The individual expression of those separate kinds of matter, be it in the atom or in that expression of associate atoms that produce separate effects, is to allow the steady and ever-occurring change that matter is constantly undergoing to bring about progressive conditions. As matter is ever undergoing a process of refinement in the great laboratory, it follows that, inasmuch as the rule must be an all-including one (for no exception is allowed by nature) a period of time must come when the material of which the human brain is fashioned will also be affected by the refining process.

"The time has arrived when this effect on the mortal brain is being observed by men, for the brain of the present day has reached the most sensitive state in the world's history. Being thus attuned by the gradual and ever-active process of refinement of matter, it is quickened in vibratory power, and thus is in more perfect accord with the vibratory activity of the people of the next step in progression, those who live without the clothing of the flesh. It is possible, also, for some few physical beings to be held in mental accord by certain spirit-people. The refined physical brain can adjust itself to the spirit-brain, so that the latter can dictate to the former comprehensive suggestions as to the proper method of procedure to grasp, harness, and control those subtle magnetic forces of fixed, ever-existing, steady, but pulsating, conditions of stress that are the perfect reflex of the ever-active particles of matter.

"It is a well-established fact, that substances of the same kind attract each other and are cohesive in a given mass in so called solid form, by a reduction of temperature. This kind of attraction has no relation to chemical attraction, but is mainly based on the physical characteristics of the substance, made possible by the similarity of the crystallization of the substance. Much has been told and explained to you about this subject of crystallization of substance. It is the true demonstration of the acute individuality of distinct elements and positive (actual) substance. A vegetablism and animalism assert their different species by the process just referred to, so all things in the world of matter likewise assert themselves.

"Different species of the vegetable and animal kingdom, by the fact of distinct crystallization (form), possess the power to give expression to all the fixed and distinct peculiarities that they possess, and to effect others of their kind, or of similar species, and mix and become assimilated with each other in their progressive action, and thus assert that subtle influence which you know as perpetuating life; the one nutrifying the other. Thus, they give expression to that power, which is the deep-seated principle of nature, that you explain as life, and that we know is the spirit. So also it is with matter. It is permeated with Spirit Life, and because of that fact, it is ever-active. If it were not for this fact, that it possesses Spirit or Life, matter could not undergo the ever-occurring changes, all of a progressive character, that it does; it could not change to unite and form substances and, after these new combinations have performed their duties, to break down and form some other substances which also fulfill their functions in the progression of nature's great scheme. Were the atoms dead, spiritless, they would of necessity be non-active, and hence useless for the work of the Master's hand.

"Matter, gross or fine, is but a vehicle for the use of the Spirit, and be it the invisible, theoretical atom of oxygen or of any other so-called element, or be it a perfect physical man, this atom of matter, or these aggregations of atoms used to form man, are but the Master's vehicles to work for, and act as the carrier of, the Spirit. The Spirit of man is the intelligence of man, and nothing more. This Spirit is the highest type that the Master has desired to create on your earth. It is the consummation of the workmanship of that great workshop, your earth; and it is the final result of the activity of all other spirit-forces that matter has for countless ages, as man records time, been manifesting.

"The final product of all of that ceaseless activity of matter is the one result that goes out from your earth as Eternal Life. Every other form of spirit-life is returned to the refinery for the further processes of refinement, until it is fitted for the last act of earth-life, —the creating of a sublime human intelligence, —and then it goes forth into the domain of Spirit, to be further refined and fitted for that purpose of the Master that is not clear to us in the Spirit-World, but, according to reasoning, based on such knowledge as is possessed by some of our most advanced intelligences, to be ultimately a power added to the great Intelligence that rules the universe. But be the further following out of the scheme what it may, of this truth you may be certain: God's use of this earth is to create human intelligence; and further, it is nature's constant effort to produce the best; and so, true is this, that, if you will but 'read' as you 'run,' you may note that people of your earth possess this knowledge as if by instinct (in reality by spirit suggestion) and they are constantly endeavoring, in their blind, groping way, to prefect themselves. Thus likewise it is with spirit-people.

"Clearly we see, clearly we feel, all that you see and all that you feel. As your sensations are the half-blind groping of a lower organism, sluggish, and dull as to the true facts that underlie real progress; so ours are the quick, clear, and fully-developed faculties for appreciating great truths. This refers only to those spirit-intelligences among us who have been awakened to a complete appreciation of our actual individual spirit-life as when in the flesh, and we have the same distinct personalities.

"Thus, knowing by quick perception, as we do, that only right is right, and that deception cannot succeed; that honesty only is a fact, and that dishonesty is a condition that brings about endless trouble that must be disentangled and made straight and absolutely honest by the causer; and, knowing that nature has established laws which are good, and, if adhered to, beneficial in their results; and which, if broken, must be mended by the breaker, —knowing all these things made possible by our power of rapid perception, (because those tantalizing desires of the flesh have no longer a hold upon us) we are ever and always anxious when we can come in touch with intelligence in the flesh, to give to such persons what we can of the truths that are clear to us."

## The Life Mass

I have thought a little and laboured long to comprehend the economy of Nature. I have found life everywhere, in trees and flowers and growing grains, in rapid brooks, and lazy streams, in the wind sweeping over the hills, and at rest in lonely places, in the majesty and glory of the dawn as the sun climbs the eastern sky, in the glow of evening and in the purple solitude of the night. I see life seeking better expression and individual growth in every birth, and rocked in every cradle. I see Nature working out its destiny, reproducing, increasing, and developing; and in such a presence I know that nothing, not even death itself, can diminish or stop the eternal progress of a single life, all a part of one stupendous whole.

We speak of inert matter, but there is no such thing in the Universe. Matter, the expression and language of which we do not understand, we term inert, —an error caused by our lack of knowledge. Nothing dead exists. We have little knowledge of the very small, and know nothing of the world of life forms invisible to the human eye, [Not then, in 1917. —Ed.] how they live, what they do, or how they communicate with one another.

There is a query in science as to whether every living thing is capable of thinking, and I am free to say that, in my judgement, wherever there is life, there must be thinking. I care not whether science accept or reject the theory; there is the power of intelligent action in every seed that has a living germ. The acorn has sense enough to send its rootlets into the earth, and its trunk and foliage branch up into the air, and select just such elements as will make the oak tree, and reject such as would be proper only for the beech tree. And the grass has the same kind of intelligence in choosing proper nourishment for itself; and the power of choice must involve the power of thought. Science is on the material and rudimental plane yet, and has much to ascertain.

Speaking of the life mass, one in the next life has said:

**"The basis of all matter is electricity; the basis of all electricity, for there are many kinds, is ether, —not that ether which is found in the atmosphere, but a subtle ether of which men know little or nothing. The basis of this subtle ether is spirit; therefore, all that there is of whirling planets, of brilliant constellations, suns, moons and satellites, all that there is in the physical Universe is ether clothed, in reality but an expression of spirit. It is the physical in and through which spirit functions, and in that way makes itself manifest to the external sense. When we once realize how infinitely great is the universe, how wondrous, how terrible, yet how beautiful in its simplicity, a feeling not exactly of awe, but of benign thankfulness must rise in our hearts at the knowledge that we are part of that stupendous system.**

**"Until the discovery of lenses and magnifying glasses, man had no idea of the world around him. He could not scan the heavens by night, nor did he know anything of atoms, nor of micro-organisms.**

**"If one is interested in geology—in the various rocks in the strata of the earth—let him take the hardest of these rocks—basalt—and in the basaltic rocks he will find a world of life. If he gets far away in the polar seas at the extremes of the earth, he will find life also. Thousands of fathoms down in the bed of**

the ocean there is life. In everything throughout the Universe life is found, and the germs of life are no less in the fire mists! The ink of the specks of protoplasm floating in the water. Look at them—examine them with a microscope. Then realize that at last, a long way off it is true, those specks of protoplasm develop into a Shakespeare or a Dante, Thomas Paine, or an Ingersoll. Nature is very wonderful!

"The atmosphere that you are breathing tonight contains organisms. You cannot see them with the naked eye, and even the most powerful lenses would fail to disclose some of them to you. There are microbes floating in the atmosphere, some of which produce disease. Most of them are unimportant. But apart from the germs, there are floating throughout this atmosphere, life forms which man may never be able to discover with any instrument that he may invent in the future. Near to Mt. Vesuvius there are a few pools or small lakes, which the internal fires round about make very hot. If tonight, I could take one drop from those pools and subject it to a close, rigid scrutiny by means of a more powerful glass than exists, we should find that in one drop of this hot water there is a world. We should find life there evolving and progressing towards perfection. Again, we should find in that drop of water, or it might be in a speck of earth—if we had the knowledge and power, and also the sight of an advanced spirit to disintegrate it—we should find that the speck of matter branches away into electric corpuscles. Searching deeper, we should discover that even the electricity of the corpuscles is made up of a subtle ether, impenetrable, something so rarefied that the sons of men cannot by means discern it. Had we the power and the knowledge that we shall have some day in an advanced spiritual state, we should find in the heart of that subtle ether something of wondrous power and influence—a continuous force which is indeed the Spirit of God.

"Therefore, in the physical we have a universe which at last touches the spiritual. In the infinitely great we have a universe which is controlled, inspired, kept steady, so to speak, and has its foundation, its very existence, in that force called Nature. And the spirit which you yourselves possess, is an emanation from God. This spirit, though manifest in many ways, and through many forms, is eternal. Matter physical is constantly changing, building up, disintegrating; it is scattered and reformed in the birth, the growth, the life, and the death of worlds innumerable. There is, in reality, no such thing as death. Men enquire from whence comes life? Life came from the Spirit, and when the spirit passes through the subtle ether, and the ether gets into the coarser electricity, it takes physical form—gross matter is then impregnated with life. That life never ceases, because, as I have said, it progresses and develops through the physical and is reabsorbed into the Great Spirit, the Source of all life—light, and power, and wisdom."

Another from the great beyond has said:

"In the whole universe right down to the microscope and beyond, life is found. There is no part of the universe where there is no life, nor where the creatures do not live in companies. It is not good for man, or anything to be alone; consequently all are set in companies, and there has been given to each individual a method and a way of understanding every other one, so that all may be happy in one another's company. Some will say that it is ridiculous to speak of inanimate things in that manner, but it is only ignorance which so asserts; it is inability to realize that the Divine Spirit of God is permeating everything. Walk upon the sands of the sea-shore, examine the tiniest grain; it is impregnated with that Divine Spirit which keeps the whole universe sweet.

"I cannot say much concerning the manner of communication that plants have, but I know from my side of life that they have this power, and do communicate. And the varieties of perfumes, how are they produced, and borne upon the breeze? The present hypothesis is that it is through some chemical atoms. First, the sun impregnated the plant. In the flower are found chemical substances—electrons—which are given off and float on the subtle ether. How do they float? Through vibrations. We have been a long time getting a little knowledge about vibrations, but the processes of Nature are carried on through vibrations. We have thought it most wonderful to set in motion electrical vibrations, and to convey to our friends a message hundred of miles away. That is but a childish effort, a childish accomplishment in comparison with what goes on daily around us, but of which we are ignorant. Realize first that there is the life of the plant, and there is the life of the animalcule, the life of the insect, the life of the animal, the life of man, and the life of creatures in the uttermost parts of Nature of which most men have no conception. Then we come to the sources of all life, —God. Cannot we understand that from Him flows the entire life of the Universe? When we die, as the expression is, though such a thing does not happen—when a dissolution of the material body and the spirit occurs, what takes place is this: there is a breaking up of a community—you and your body are a community interdependent on each other, —and at death, or dissolution, a colony, a company breaks up— I must for the time being use terms which will be understood—the etheric tenant vacates and goes on to a more glorious sublime plane. Paul said to the Corinthians, 'There is a natural body, and there is a spiritual body.' It is the earthly house of the tabernacle here which dissolves.

"The companies of insects, and of animals, though they make war on each other and may exist on each other, have a language. They know how to communicate, and in a measure they are dependent one upon the other. Is it not amusing to hear some people say that man alone has speech, that is, sound formed into certain word and syllables and sentences through the vocal organs. Let us, for instance, consider the birds. We see them and hear them warble and sing. That is their way of expressing joyousness; but that is not their language. They have a way in which they communicate with each other just as we have. Has the reader ever visited India? In the Burning Ghaut, where the Hindoos and others burn their dead, they carry the bodies up a flight of stairs to a high platform. The wood is already prepared, and the body is placed upon the wood. Look up into the heavens, calm and bright, the sun glaring down, not a speck in the sky. In two or three minutes the place will be black with carrion birds. Can we explain it? Yes, away perched on some high eminence or tree is the sentinel bird; perhaps miles away are his fellows. He speaks to them, the sentinel sounds the signal, and instantly they reply to him, and fill the air. Most people think that the world in which they live is a jumble. I grant that there are things that are abhorrent, which we cannot understand—the mystery of pain and suffering, of evil, for example, but I realize now that out of all that is evil, will finally come good. There is no confusion or jumble in the Divine Order. Everything is in its place, and ultimately it will be seen that in Nature, God has set the solitary in families, that his wondrous power is always recreating matter, and that there is never annihilaton.

"There may, however, be change of form. Take, for instance, the coral rocks on the seashore. Little creatures once swam in the ocean in tiny shells; they died in myriads, and the shells in time formed certain rocks. Old forests fall in decay, and the wisest man of the 20th century might have said: 'Show me the wisdom of God in this?' But today the coal farmed from these forests is used to give warmth and light, and all the processes of commerce are carried on through it. There is no death! Everything gives place to new forms of life."

And this is the fact that we must gather from our teaching: that out of the life contained in the mass, individuality has come; out of the mass of life, through Nature's process of constant change and refinement, every living creature that will inhabit this globe in the ages yet to come must be evolved. The highest form of life that is evolved from the mass is man—and to the highest, all lesser forms contribute. Mankind is the final result of evolutionary action.

## Beyond the Atom

We are told that atoms, through their power to change from one form into another, always follow the law of definite proportions; and that, in obedience to that law, they are amenable to the will of the intelligent force. Outside of the operation of this law, they are incapable of being controlled in any known way. This would place them beyond the category of mortal mind and make them, to some extent, superior to it. The atom holds within itself the properties of all forms and material things. It is the central point from which universal creative energy proceeds. It is the basis of all power that manifests form and force. It is indestructible in its nature; its existence is regulated by definite and fixed laws; and the substance into which it enters is held in position, as regards form, by the inherent energy of the atoms composing that form.

The atom, alone, has eternal duration of form, for it alone has the power to enter and dominate all other forms. It has no master except force, and to force alone it is amenable. Whether force precedes it, or is co-existent with it, is not now known; but, probably, the same force which impels the atom upon its course with unerring precision, precedes it in the province of creative evolution. Beyond the atom is an intelligence which has imbued it with these properties and powers.

Man, reflecting the image of wisdom, boastingly asserts his authority over the rest of creation; but he is ever subject to the power *vested in the atom*, and only as he reflects the activity of the elements in his own structure, is he able to rise to an intellectual status whereby he can comprehend the more simple laws of constructive energy.

This is one of the reasons why we are obliged to take into serious consideration the *existence of invisible intelligences,* who understand how to manipulate the forces distinctly pertaining to the evolution of the world of spirit. Numerous experiments have demonstrated beyond question that they exist. And that spirit-intelligences understand how to affect these forces in form, is neither untrue nor absurd. The failure to grasp this fact is really due to our own contracted minds, which are prone to limit all elements to the sphere of phenomenal physical conditions. We must conclude, then, that the same energy which controls and directs the movements of atoms and molecules, which sustains in position, and directs the course of stars and constellations, which finds life-expression in grass and in grains, in weeds and in flowers, in forest trees and in all vegetable growth, applies equally to man whose physical body, like all vegetable matter is composed of atoms.

As we ascend in the scale of conscious intelligence, the universe opens to our mental vision and gives us a basis for a broader conception of the intelligent force underlying the physical universe. When we consider the law of life, in all its varied relation to visible and invisible form, we understand how rational is the proposition that the great law of nature has its existence entirely above and beyond the physical realm. Theologians of the past, having no definite knowledge of creative energy, formulated a theory of the source of life ending in mere abstraction. Their logical position was this: "God is the source of life. God made the world and all upon it and in it, by a fiat, a decree, of His own free will." This is only a confession of gross ignorance and manifests a childish inability to produce satisfactory evidence concerning the subject. It shows the utter incapacity of the human intellect, dominated by superstition, to discern any relation of force beyond the range of physical senses.

Human progress may be rapid or slow, according to the effort expended; but the atomic forces are ever at our disposal, and we can move forward as we will, regardless of the craft of men or the position of ignorance. It must be acknowledged that the human intellect is unable to discern the relations of cause and effect in many of the problems that come before it for solution; and there lingers around the subject of the *life action of the elements* an idea that they are as far beyond the scope of intelligent explanation, as the *results* themselves are beyond the unorganized forms of the same elements.

What, then, is this energy, this intellectual force, which is back of the atom and expressed in or through it? What or who controls and directs its movement with perfect precision? Some call it energy; some force; some nature; and others call it God.

The word "God" is so indefinite! I doubt if those who utter the word with reverence, have ever formed any definite idea of the creator; and those who think He has personality, have little comprehension of the universe. If God has personality, in the accepted sense of the word, He must be a person with extraordinary powers and intelligence, for, by the law of comparison, ideas themselves must be formed.

God, I am told, means simply Universal Good. Apart from the philosophical signification of the word, this is its true philosophical import. Let me explain what I understand by the divine principle. The life force in all things, —the intelligence that directs matter in movement and works out the laws governing all things, —is but the intelligence of all those who have lived in this sphere or inhabited other planets, who, having progressed beyond the physical plane, have mastered all knowledge and are working in perfect harmony, as one mind, in a sphere of perfectly harmonious development; and in that sphere the mind power is universal, permeates all space, and finds individual expression in all life forms. The inclination within us to do right and to shrink from wrong is that atom of Universal Mind which, clothed with matter, becomes a man, while the same law that governs an atom, governs all mankind. The energy of the atom is its potential life-force, and the life-force in it or in us, is Universal Good working out its destiny.

Life-force dominates all matter. The whole physical world outside of planetary action and natural growth and change, may be largely governed, in it movement and direction, by man.

Matter operates on matter, and inert substances in the physical world move only when directed by the material mortal mind. The power of even one man's thought is beyond present comprehension. Man has taken iron, and fashioned it into machinery with which he moves great buildings. He has taken coal, and converted it into steam, which, confined and released, utilizes energy that will transport material to the limit of land; then, using like energy, he propels great ships over the sea, fashions sails and makes the very winds do his will. He has put a turbine under the waters, whose fall he directs; on the shaft a dynamo, which the waters whirl; he gathers and condenses the very ether into what we call electricity. Mind is all creative. The hands but fashion what the mind conceives.

Not content with dominion over matter sensible to physical touch, He reaches into the atmosphere and utilizes the very elements, —and the end is not yet. Only he who consciously progresses comprehends the possibilities of progress. Does the mastery of mind end with physical dissolution? Does death increase or diminish opportunity? Life would be futile if all the struggle for development were to end with earth-existence. While our conception of mind domination has its limitations, its possibilities are even now beyond our comprehension and one fails to appreciate the power of even a single mind. The energy produced in the electric current is as marvelous to the savage as the energy of the atom is to science, and as little understood.

We may follow, step by step, mind-power in mortal man, witnessing his control and his mastery over matter and the elements of the air; but, before we reach the limits of definite thought, we appreciate in a limited way that, if individuality and mind continue beyond the physical domain, man is still exercising his mental faculties, still studying and applying his intelligence to obtain greater control over matter in the conditions of the life beyond, —and the nucleus of all this action is the energy of the atom.

Whether we can appreciate this fact or not, it is true that, as men grow in knowledge in the after-life, they work in greater harmony with each other; many minds, in many ways, work as one, much more there than here, and accomplish greater results in a thorough, practical way. Science attributes these results to the unknowable; those of less understanding, to God. The individual mind, when released from its physical environment acquires greater mastery and power. Considering what men can do here and their control of the electric force alone; knowing that they live on in a constant state of progression, it requires no stretch of imagination to perceive that the same persons are ever exercising their reason and obtaining greater knowledge, increased efficiency, and usefulness, and, as this is being accomplished, their dominion over matter increases. Man creates nothing; the energy that he uses was dominant in the atom at the beginning; he, by combination or decomposition, only gets another and greater expression.

Beyond the atom we find minds, that have at some time lived in a physical body, working in unison and combining substances that will endow matter with energy which will give expression to life force in the material. In fact, all there is, is mind, matter is the substance used in its physical expression only; mind alone is creative energy. Men, who have lived in this or some other planet or constellation of the universe, who have passed out of the physical world that they inhabited, have, after countless ages of progression, reached the sphere of knowledge, and work as one, finding expression in every form of life and force. Thus, beyond the atom we find, not God, but mind.

I once asked a spirit: "What is the force that finds expression in the atom?" He replied:

**"It is the individual man, purified and developed to its highest capacity, and blended with other minds in a similar condition. Guided by the knowledge gained through vast intervals of time, and working in perfect harmony with each other, these minds are the controlling power of the universe. I say 'controlling' for they, in turn, are but instruments of the dominating laws of the universe. They make these laws, to be sure, but, these laws must be of one kind for nature aspires to good. They progress through a condition of intellect bounded by mortality, into a new development until the circle is completed, and a harmonious whole is formed. It is a vast subject to comprehend, and yet, once grasped, it is perfectly clear. What other theory calculated to satisfy rational mind, has ever been put forward, than that the intelligence should ultimately become so effective that, combined with all the rest, it should be the highest force for good? Everyone must feel, and appreciate, that thus only can the inferior order of minds be guided toward their ultimate goal. This is the only philosophy of existence which, when once fully understood, seems true, reasonable, and convincing."**

## Matter

All matter is composed of molecules, atoms and electrons. A molecule is made up of several atoms. For instance, a molecule of water is composed of three atoms, two of hydrogen and one of oxygen. The atoms are very small, about one hundred thousandth of an inch in size, and yet sufficient in number to make up the mass of all the planets composing the solar systems of the universe. These small particles possess a force so wonderful that it is utterly impossible for man to follow and examine them, for the reason that they are constantly changing in their rapid passage. They pass through the ether with wave-like undulatory motion, and, like human beings, have their likes and dislikes. When they find their affinity, we have what is known as cohesion, for every particle of matter has an attraction for other particles. These atoms have a force and a heat that all the furnaces of earth could not produce. Under certain conditions, however, there may be a loss of heat, and, if it were possible, in the laboratories of earth to expel heat entirely from the atoms composing matter, it would become practically lifeless and inert. This, however, is impossible; therefore, while they possess heat and force, they may b solid, liquid and gaseous, in which latter condition they may be said to bump against each other, rebound and move freely through ether which not only joins with the atmosphere surrounding this planet, but connects far distant worlds; and this ether, this subtle air, around and about us, permeates all substances.

In the wondrous atoms, with their likes and dislikes, attracting other atoms through the ether and in continual action, we have *force, motion* and *electrified heat.*

Atoms are split up and again sub-divided, and those small particles are called electrons; that is, they are electrified. In other words, they carry electrified points, not the electricity that we behold in the lightning flash or in magnet and coil, but a small, subtle electricity which mortal man does not yet comprehend. Electrons, then, are really the electrified points of the sub-divided atom, the polarized particles, not one of which could be spared out of the universe. A single atom can not be lost, it has its place, its power and its task to do.

The world of matter is a world of change. Molecules changing, atoms changing, electrons changing, but the subtle spirit which permeates them is never lost. Each possesses a spark of life-force from the great ocean of infinity which is immortal.

When we speak, ordinarily, of matter, we refer to sensible substances which offer resistance to the touch and to muscular effort, and which is indestructible and eternal, which reacts against external force, is permanent and preserves its identity under all changes. Again, matter is everything that possesses the properties of *gravity and attraction.*

While I am not able to state it as a fact, I am of the opinion, reasoning by deduction, that the laws of gravitation act only upon matter the vibration of which is so slow that it is physical; that when the vibration is increased to what we know as spirit or mind, the law of gravitation no longer acts upon it; then the law of attraction is the dominating force. The force of gravitation is in direct lines only; the lines of attraction reach in all directions. Gravitation then, acts upon the physical body only; attraction upon the mental state. And after separation from the body, the spirit, freed from physical substance, is free from the control and influence of the laws of gravitation, for which reason spirit people move freely and at will within the boundaries of their sphere.

There is not in the physical universe, as far as is known, a substance that is actually solid. A cubic inch of the hardest steel differs from a cubic inch of air only in the arrangement and position of its atoms and molecules. It is all a question of density and vibration. Could a magnifying glass be made powerful enough, what is known as solid matter would appear like dust floating in the sun's rays, for nothing is ever actually still. Nature abhors stagnation as it does a vacuum. All in the universe is matter, whether physical or spiritual, composed of atoms and molecules attracted and associated in varying degrees of density and therefore in vibration. All substance is, in fact, matter, whether it be visible or invisible, whether it be sensible to touch or elusive. In accordance with this theory of advanced science, all matter is progressing into modes of motion, dissolving into activity, and so shading off into that great reality that is all energy and life.

Can there be energy without substance? Does not everything that has expression necessitate substance? The idea that spirit-people exist but are unsubstantial is illogical and preposterous. The gases which compose water, taken separately, are as much substance as when united. The spirit body is as much substance as a physical body. Why should it be considered impossible for mother nature to clothe spirits with substance so that, when separated from flesh, both should continue to exist as absolutely as when joined together? When we pass into the spirit-life, we have the same features, the same general contour, the same proportions, and we carry that normal condition wherever we go. Our shape, size, features and contour are determined by the spiritual atoms forming our spiritual personality, and this continues through all spheres. Thus our identity, once established, exists in continuity with life, —remaining always the same, being always composed of the same personal atoms.

All that exists in positive condition is matter; intelligent forces permeate all material things, and are made manifest in motion. Motion is moving matter. Matter, in a very high state of vibratory action, may be, and frequently is, classed as immaterial; but, in reality, there is no immaterial thing; an absolutely immaterial thing would be absolutely nothing—so called immaterial things are conditions of matter in a very great degree of sublimation. We can not conceive of anything made of nothing.

Electricity and magnetism are highly sublimated conditions of matter; one step further finds us in the world of Spirit, which is a still greater degree of material sublimation as to be the connecting link between mind, or spirit, and matter; but we are not, as yet, able to grasp the condition of magnetic, electric, and spiritual vibration to any extent. Investigation causes growth step by step, until, by and by, we may understand the force of electromagnetism.

Matter disappears from our vision, but reappears to our senses. This thing called matter, which, in one state or another, is perfectly opaque, and will not permit a ray of light to pass through it, will in another form, which is spirit, become perfectly transparent. The cause of this wonderful change is beyond our comprehension. Science may say it is due to some attraction in the position or arrangement of atoms or molecules; but atoms or molecules, however confident the "scientists" may be of their existence and of the laws that govern their attraction and repulsion, are beyond the reach of the physical senses.

Substances dissolved in water or burned in the air, are not annihilated, for, by certain well-known means, they can be recalled and restored to sight, some in exactly the same state as before they became invisible, others in some other state or condition. Matter is indestructible; if there is matter, there must be spirit, for matter is only the substance that spirit uses for physical expression. Spirit, whether it finds physical expression or whether it exists apart from gross matter, as we use that term, is of primary importance and is the first subject for consideration, while the garment which makes life visible is only of secondary importance. One law, as we have shown, governs all conditions in the physical as well as in the spirit planes; and whenever we find life-forces, they are clothed with either physical or spiritual material, which is matter in different states of vibrations. So that the individual life, at dissolution, undergoes a change of vibration, like water changed into vapor; it is the same life still having form, feature, and expression, just as before, but changed in its vibratory action, the atoms pulsate at a higher rate so that they are no longer visible to us. Though matter still, they pass from our sight like steam dissolved in air.

Mind is matter, and day by day, and minute by minute, as it crystallizes, it takes definite form and shape; and its creations are clothed with substance. Some are given physical expression in works of art, inventions, books and buildings; but the great majority find expression in what we term spirit-matter, of which man comes to a full appreciation only as he passes into that sphere of usefulness. Matter, in this physical world, is changed and fashioned by hands or by machinery made by hands, so low is its vibratory condition; but, as we ascend in the scale of life, thought becomes such a wonderful force that it can fashion, model and mould substances that vibrate in similar waves into actual forms of its own creations. In this way, the environment that a spirit finds after dissolution is found to be one that he has, perhaps unknown to himself, been creating by his acts and his thoughts from day to day.[1]

Thought is the one great thing in the universe. Formed and fashioned in the human brain, it is projected into the ether, that permeates all things and all space, by laws we are not yet able to comprehend. It takes form and shape and awaits there our coming. The homes which spirit people have, and the condition in and about them, their very location, depend on the life-work and through action of the individual. Everything is governed by law; nothing happens by chance; cause and effect are as potent in the spirit plane as in the earth plane. These facts must be borne in mind: All is matter, here and hereafter; spirit people have bodies; their identity never changes; they have homes; they are real; they are people; and they live after what we call death.

On this subject, I am told:

**"Spirit is ethereal matter—matter whose home is in ether, which is higher in vibration than the atmosphere in which it formerly existed. Each change into another sphere is a higher, more vitalizing vibration, until the emancipated spirit reaches a sphere of most intense vibration, which holds the power of life. Then it can impregnate matter in a lower material condition, and give it an atom of spirit to develop. The reason that man is continually growing in spiritual thought, is because as this force, this life-giving force, increases, it becomes stronger, and man is being equipped for the development of his spiritual being.**

**"Matter includes all things that have continued life, —and we know that nothing can die. Ether is the atmosphere of spirit-people. From each man in his natural condition emanates spiritual ether. It is because of this atmosphere that we are able to come close to him, and thereby reach his subconscious mind."**

Spirit-material is nothing more than earthly matter raised to a higher degree of activity; while spirit-force is pure force. The physical world is a counterpart of the spirit world, but the latter is the reality.

---

1 This is the very basis of the natural laws which underlie the science, philosophy and religion of Spiritualism.

There are more than five avenues of knowledge. There is much about matter that we do not know. It is possible to pass matter through matter. Recall the flowers heretofore mentioned, brought from a distance, passed through the walls of the room in which we were, and reconstructed. How was it done? Spirit chemists know how to use this subtle electric power to reduce the atoms that are solid, to a gaseous state. Oxygen at low temperature and under pressure, can be transformed into a solid; it can also be reduced to a liquid and changed into ether. Physical substance, under such treatment, becomes gaseous and etheric, and may, by a similar process, be restored to its normal conditions. In this manner the flowers were dematerialized and again materialized. The process was simply a chemical change.

Savages rubbing sticks to produce fire, looked upon the traveler with suspicion, with fear; but when they saw him produce fire with a match, their souls were filled with wonder. Spirit-people look with sorrow upon the people of this generation, for the great majority, in their simplicity, are still rubbing sticks to obtain light, though the sun shines in the heavens.

## The Subconscious Mind

The physical and the spiritual universe are closely interrelated. There is a physical brain and there is a spiritual brain, and they have relations to each other which can not be ignored. All that is physical has its duplicate in spirit, but all that is in spirit does not have its duplicate in the physical.

It must be forgotten that the earth-sphere is a natural world; and that the spirit-world is also a natural world. The relation of the one to the other is, therefore, natural. In a physical sense, mind is memory, thought is that which feels, which wills, —the conscious subject. Again it is the ego, the soul, the spirit; it is all these and something more; *it is something that catches suggestion from the intelligence of other spheres and expresses it in this sphere.*

Let us now deal with the world of mind, with special reference to the subconscious mind, which immeasurably transcends in importance the physical domain. Science has tried hard to explain many things on the hypothesis of "mental telepathy," "secondary personality" and "subliminal consciousness" in its efforts to understand spirit-phenomena; when, as a matter of fact, it knows but little about the subject. Suppose one mortal should try to send a thought message to another at a distance. What natural law is used? No wire; no wireless instruments; merely a sentence sent out through space, encountering in its passage countless millions of

251

other thoughts of different kinds. What is the motive power? What directs its course? And, if it should, by chance, reach the ear of the person intended, by what process will he hear something that comes in the silences, but not out of it? Why advance a theory that is not based on a single known law? The Marconi system has instruments perfectly adjusted and in tune with each other, and, by laws that are understood, are able to receive a signal sent by the sending to the receiving instrument. We, too, have an instrument, to wit—the human brain—far more complicated and wonderful, and the time may come when mental telepathy is practical, though it is not now.

I know that thoughts and messages are at times carried from one mortal to another, but it is a rare occurrence. Ordinarily someone in the spirit-world hears the message, and becoming a messenger, finds the person for whom the message is intended, and impresses the words on his subconscious mind. This will be easily understood when human beings come to appreciate this community of spirit-people who dwell about, yet not with us. Mental telepathy is, in fact, suggestion, much used by spirit-people. In aiding and directing the conduct of mortals such practice is common with them, and it is hard for us to differentiate between self and spirit-suggestion, so vague is the borderline. Thought-suggestion between mortals is possible, but unusual.

There is but one self, but one individual atom of good in any person, and though that person may, at times, do and say things of which he has no knowledge and which cannot be accounted for by any known physical laws, the fact does not double or change his personality. This is called "secondary personality." It is possible for spirit-people, upon rare occasions, to take a mortal out of his body, and entering into his living body, use his vocal organs. This is not uncanny, but simple and natural. If one, under proper conditions, tells of things of which he had no previous information, which, upon investigation, are found true, it was not another self but someone else talking; for by what law could that second self know what the first self did not know? And so with "subliminal consciousness," that is, something below sensation: the doing of acts without being aware of it. These words, coined by men seeking a material solution of problems not understood, have not justification in fact, they are misleading and the theory is erroneous.

When those who coined the words "mental telepathy," tell us what law is used in its operation; when they tell us how it is possible to have two personalities; and where the one is and what it is doing when the second self is present; and a little of what is meant by "subliminal consciousness," they will be entitled to more consideration.

The answer to these last two propositions is the spirit-hypothesis based on fact and founded on natural law. The subconscious mind, when understood, will eradicate those senseless words from the vocabulary, and solve many problems with which man is struggling.

I asked one far advanced in spirit-life to tell me of the subconscious mind from his point of view, and he said:

**"The conscious mind is one controlled by yourself. In it are held all the material parts of your thoughts, —I mean those connected with and controlled by, earth things. The subconscious mind is the one controlled by psychic forces entirely. It is the spiritual brain of man. I mean, that it is subject to the laws of vibration, which the other part of the brain is not sensitive enough to catch. It is the subconscious mind that gets suggestion from spirit-people, the connecting link, or battery, that for an instant holds the suggestion, and passes it on, to grow into a thought or impulse. The subconscious mind does not retain suggestion. It is the embryo thought, which takes definite form only as it reaches the conscious mind."**

From this concise statement of fact it is evident that all the strange phenomena, which science has been trying to solve and to which it has given many names, consist, ordinarily, of spirit-people hearing the spoken words or seeing the written message, then finding the person desired and impressing the words or message on the subconscious mind or spiritual brain. When the conscious mind catches the suggestion and makes it a part of the material thought, we have what is called mental telepathy, which, in fact, is except on rare occasions, all accomplished by spirit-people acting upon the subconscious or psychic brain.

Speaking on the subject generally, one in the world beyond said:

**"It is well, always, to consider that a result is equivalent to the effort put forth. The intensity and constancy of a thought are a positive force. A thought, bearing upon any particular subject, having been thoroughly established in the brain, grows just as a plant grows from the seed. As the development of that seed will be proportionate to the conditions of the soil and the amount of sunshine and moisture, so is it with the growth of thought.**

**"Thought is planted in the human brain by the next great power beyond mortal man, sown in the form of suggestion,**

and, as with the seed sown by the master hand of man, so it is with the suggestion sown, largely, by the master hand of spirit forces. Some are given birth and grow and fully develop in all their importance and beauty; but many—by far the great majority—fail of birth. Where the latter condition prevails, the human brain must, by a process of purification, be made receptive until it can catch and give birth to the seeds of suggestion sown.

"Progress is the grand object of nature. This word 'progress' is one of mighty import to the material world, and true progress is possible only when those who have advanced to a higher plane help those who are still struggling upward. This applies to all things, material, intellectual, and spiritual. Nature has imposed upon us spirit beings the duty of assisting those mortals in the body by such suggestion as we can impart to them through the subconscious brain; and so, likewise, there are some among us to whom suggestions are imparted by those in the grade immediately above us.

"As on earth there are weeds, as well as useful grain and beautiful flowers, so among your people are there apparently worthless mortals; but who can say when or how the weeds, following the great law of progress, will evolve into useful or beautiful plants; and yet, as simple weeds, may they not serve a great, if hidden purpose? And so with those among you, who according to your judgement, appear worthless, do not forget that the same Master-hand that created them, created you; and that it is better not to criticize, but to endeavor to get an expression of the intent of their condition. Always have charity. If you do not possess it, secure and cultivate it.

"What I have said this beautiful Sunday mourning, is a sermon to you, the lesson of which is: Let those thoughts that come as suggestions flashed upon the sensitive plate of your brain, upon your subconscious mind, grow. Cultivate them. As they develop, they gain in strength, and as they become strong in themselves, they can by their own strength, and because of the emanations they throw off, accomplish deeds. Whatever comes to the subconscious mind must be at once grasped and held, if you would make it your own. Then the thought is fashioned and developed to become again a part of the universal stream that flows into the Eternal Mind."

The average so-called man of science seems determined not to accept the spirit hypothesis of psychic phenomena, and offers many other explanations while going through its erroneous process of elimination; but truth existed before, and will be after, this futile struggle is over, and we many be among the last to understand this simple law.

Sir Oliver Lodge, the foremost scientist of the present day, (circa 1908 —Ed.) who acknowledges the existence of an invisible world of spirit people and has proved it to his own satisfaction, says: "The object is to get, not something dignified, but something evidential." It seems to me that when one has proved the existence of a thing, he would like to know something about the thing proved and not try to prove it again. Having long ago proved the existence of the invisible world of spirit-people, I have not sought for an accumulation of evidential facts, but rather for something dignified from the inhabitants of that world. Whether or not such facts have been given me these pages will answer.

## Spirit Suggestion

Have spirit-people any influence on our daily thought and action? If so, to what extent and by what process?

To bring ourselves intelligently to the question, we must appreciate, as we have never done before, that those out of the physical body are people, —as they were before dissolution; that their bodies are composed of matter differing from ours only in vibration; that they live and inhabit what we know as space; move over and walk upon the city's busy streets; go into and out of homes, as freely as before; and are silent witnesses of our daily thought and action. They travel at will, along the old highways, stay about the homes they loved and built with infinite care and ceaseless toil; see us and know our daily wants, desires and ambitions; and are acquainted with the discords, as well as the harmonies, of our lives. By law many become co-workers in our struggle for development. I know the limitations of the human mind and its inability to grasp this simple proposition, more important than the accumulation of wealth, and wish for many tongues that I might speak in nature's dialects and languages, and bring this simple fact home to all the men and women who inhabit this globe, for it would revolutionize the conduct of mankind and enrich the world.

There are some truths that cannot be told too often; there are truths that, no matter how often told, seem to make no impression; there are some soils which no matter how perfect the seed or how thickly sown, give little return; and so, in many ways, we tell over and over again what follows dissolution, finding now and then a fertile brain.

All knowledge is the result of suggestion, which may be divided into three classes—physical, mental and spiritual.

(a) *Physical:* that which is objective. Everything we see or hear in nature makes its impression on our minds. Something is by that process suggested to our senses, and, to the extent that we grasp and understand, we make it our own and thereby the sum-total of our knowledge is increased. One in spirit-life, who has given many lectures, said on the subject:

**"Come with me through the walks of life, and see the manner of men we can help. It is not the arrogant fool who says in his heart: 'My way is the only way,' nor yet the man who weakly fears to trust his own instinct and vacillates falteringly between the opinions of man; but it is the sane, quiet thinker, who is willing to listen to all arguments and to choose wisely those that appeal alike to his heart and brain. Such we can assist by spirit-suggestion. Without his being conscious of it, we can often guide his thought along right lines, because he is fair minded.**

**"Suggestion is one of the strong factors in the life force. As you said this mourning, all things have their power of suggestion. Does not a low saloon throw out its vile suggestion to all men? Whether this emanation entices or repels, depends upon the man, but its surrounding influence is felt strongly, and the suggestion is evil. A beautiful rural scene is helpful with its suggestion of peace and harmonious coloring. And so it is through all phases of life. Hence all should seek the best, and, unconsciously all do aspire to it."**

(b) *Mental:* that is, by deduction or reasoning from one known cause to its effect, something more is suggested. By this method we prove facts previously unknown. An illustration of deductive reasoning is found by accepting what is known as a fact that "Nothing in nature can be destroyed." From this proved hypothesis, we find that our mind, or soul, is a part of nature just as much as the earth itself, and more important. The Master-Mind that created all things has not planned the annihilation of its higher forms, and preserved the lower. That would be at least an injustice. Man has proved that it is impossible to destroy an atom. We prove by the process of deductive reasoning, which is really the highest form of demonstration, that a human soul cannot be annihilated; and, having reached that stage of mental development, it is only a step to prove, by laws as certain as those pertaining to the physical, that the spirit of man, as a fact, is not destroyed. This we know because, with many others understanding the elementary laws of vibration, *we have talked with them.* The inductive method will help to confirm the conclusions of the deductive on the subject, for if the spirit of man be indestructible, why should it be impossible for earth-dwellers to communicate with those who have left the earth? Franklin was able to demonstrate the two methods; inductively he showed that lightning and electricity are identical, and, deductively, that houses may be protected by lightning rods. If spirit be seen by induction to be identical with mind, deduction will enable us to conclude that spirits, still in the flesh, can have direct relations with spirits out of the flesh.

(c) *Spiritual:* With spirit-people, thought is such a positive force, and takes such definite form and shape, that it is visible. Their language is a thought language and is as well understood among them as words among us. They soon lose all desire for physical touch or expression, finding the purely mental so much more intense; and, as they move in and out among the people of earth and see when and where they can do good, they, by a purely mental process, often suggest to us what to do or what not to do. Thus the suggestion of those who have passed out of earth-life comes to us as a moral guide, whose true origin many ignore because so many have absolutely no knowledge of what happens after dissolution. This form of suggestion we call intuition, impulse, inspiration.

Spirit-suggestion comes through our subconscious mind. Mind, whether in or beyond the physical, is a positive force in nature, more in fact than action, which is the result of mind; and spirit-people, desiring to influence our conduct to some desired end, retard their mental vibrations, and, at the same time ours increase until our vibrations and theirs pulsate more or less in harmony; then it is possible for them to make their thought our thought, and when we, guided by their suggestion, do some good deed with their cooperation, we increase in some degree the sum of Universal Good. But, because those beyond the physical are not always spiritual, some being on the contrary, of a low order of mentality, often depraved, as when in the body, with low instincts and base appetites, they, if our thoughts and desires are of a similar character, can reach our subconscious mind, and suggest that which will satisfy their desires and the results are base actions produced by both factors. Man is not a mere automaton, but a personality, deriving his progression from suggestions of people both in and out of the body; and it is difficult, so subtle is spirit suggestion to tell with any certainty whether the thought that preceded the act was our own conception or that of some spirit working through our brain to do good or to satisfy his own selfish desires. For this reason one should weigh well what he has an impulse or desire to do. Good always precedes evil. First impressions are better than those which follow, because they are more spiritual.

The whole process of thought is the result of suggestion, without which ideas could neither be formulated nor expressed. Knowledge would be unknown and evolution impossible, were it not for suggestion. The influence of the spirit-world is far greater than any mortal can comprehend because we are unable, so faint is the line of demarcation, to tell the origin, or source of any thought.

In formulating this philosophy, I am unable to say to what extent intelligences beyond the physical have influenced my mind. My brain may have been, so to speak, a conduit of thought, and my hand an instrument to give physical expression to natural laws not generally understood by man. I cannot tell; I have not been conscious of any suggestions; but, knowing, from my conversations with spirit-people, the subtle power of suggestion, I would not say that they have not had a very great influence in shaping this work. I have the greatest respect and love for many who have, voice to voice, proved their identity, and given me their knowledge. What they have taught I know; to just what extent they can influence our daily conduct and thought depends on their mental condition and ours. It is, therefore, largely an unknown influence, but an important fact, which man should understand.

The life of spirits is intensely active and real; they have their work along those lines for which their experience in earth-life has best fitted them; they labor where there is the greatest need, where most good can be done. The ignorance of those in the physical world on this subject is very great and, as a result, their condition is so inferior to what it might be, that spirit-people, realizing the deplorable situation, spend much time in the earth-plane striving to enlighten mankind and to make them live better individual lives, a task which increases their labors and impedes their own progress.

I recall listening, not many years ago, to a boy not more than fourteen years old, playing the great masterpieces on a violin with marvelous technical skill. His intellect was not above the average, nor had he received any special artistic training, yet he could execute the most difficult music. One of our standard law-books, recognized as an authority, was written by a boy while at college. Fiske wrote philosophy in his teens. We have always had prodigies who were able, without much education, to accomplish great things; but there is nothing remarkable in this, after all, it means only that a master in spirit is able either to suggest and to work through their subconscious brains, or, in some instances, like the boy violinist and Blind Tom, to take actual possession of the body and brain, which, for the time being, is used as an instrument by a master-mind to give physical expression to his attainments.

What is true of the boy, is true likewise of the man. It is difficult, so great is the power of spirit-minds, so fine is the line of demarcation between self and their suggestion, to tell, at all times, what is self and what is suggestion. This mind of ours is like a stream having its source among the hills and flowing toward the sea. A thought to the right finds its way to the channel; another one comes from the left, and joins the current, adding volume and character; and when the stream reaches the sea of expression, it is hard to say how much of it came from the original source, how much is our own, or how much flowed in from surrounding conditions.

We hear a voice calling our name; we turn and listen; it suggests that some one would speak to us. We hesitate while the thought finds lodgement in the brain; and it, too, sets in action a line of conduct. That thought may have been generated by a process of reasoning, and, again, it may have been the suggestion of some spirit interested in our welfare. Spirits can call as well as those in the physical body; both can be heard, the first by the mind itself, and the last by the physical sense of hearing. And it is difficult for anyone to say, such is the feasibility and possibility of spirit-suggestion, whether one originates or obeys. Inspiration is spirit-aid and suggestion, nothing more.

### Power of Suggestion

The inhabitants of this invisible world influence and in some measure control the thought and conduct of every individual. They are more progressive than we, and having no incentive to accumulate money, devote themselves to the acquisition of knowledge. They delve deeply into the forces of Nature, and dealing with matter in greater refinement, make from time to time discoveries, some of which are utilized on the physical plane.

Faraday, who first made practical the force known as electricity, did not cease his investigation with dissolution, but has been a potent factor in its development through suggestion to those who devote their time to the utilization of that force. Raphael did not cease to portray upon canvas his wonderful creations, nor did Michael Angelo lose his ability to chisel marble into forms of beauty when he ceased to inhabit this plane. The years that have elapsed since they went on, have been years of opportunity and progress. Mozart, Beethoven, and all the other musicians who gave us our great compositions, have they gone down into the silent and relentless darkness, or have they continued their work, impressing on others from day to day new music that enriches the world? Milton, Dryden, Pope, Goldsmith, Moore, Wordsworth, Burns, Browning of modern times, Seneca, Pliny the Elder, Plutarch, Epictetus, Tacitus and Cervantes, of an earlier period, were all their wonderful writings and philosophies produced without suggestion from the master minds in the more advanced spheres? I know this one fact, that people in the after-life are so close, so in touch with our thoughts that it is difficult for any one to say that this or that is the product of his own intellect. Progress owes much to the invisible.

Robert G. Ingersoll, well known to me in the after life, speaking on this subject said:

**"Let me give the most remarkable illustration of spirit suggestion—the immortal Shakespeare. Neither of his parents could read or write. He grew up in a small village among ignorant people, on the banks of the Avon. There was nothing in the peaceful, quiet landscape on which he looked, nothing in the low hills, the undulating fields, nothing in the lazy flowing stream to excite the imagination. Nothing in his early life calculated to sow the seeds of subtlest and sublimest thought. There was nothing in his education or lack of education to account for what he did. It is supposed that he attended school in his home village, but of that there is no proof. He went to London when young, and within a few years became interested in Black Friars Theater, where he was actor, dramatist, and manager. He was never engaged in a business counted reputable in that day. Socially he occupied a position below servants. The law described him as a "sturdy vagabond." He died at 52.**

**"How such a man could produce the works which he did has been the wonder of all time. Not satisfied that one with such limited advantages could possibly have written the masterpieces of literature, it has been by some contended that Bacon was the author of all Shakespeare's comedies and tragedies.**

**"It is a fact to be noted that in none of this man's plays is there any mention of his contemporaries. He made reference to no king, queen, poet, author, sailor, soldier, statesman, or priest of his own period. He lived in an age of great deeds, in the time of religious wars, in the days of the armada, the edict**

of Nantes, the massacre of St. Bartholomew, the victory of Lepanto, the assassination of Henry III of France, and the execution of Mary Stuart; yet he did not mention a single incident of his day and time.

"The brain that conceived "Timon of Athens" was a Greek in the days of Pericles and familiar with the tragedies of that country. The mind that dictated "Julius Caeser" was an inhabitant of the Eternal City when Caesar led his legions in the field. The Author of "Lear" was a Pagan; of "Romeo and Juliet" an Italian who knew the ecstasies of love. The author of those plays must have been a physician for, he shows a knowledge of medicine and the symptoms of disease; a musician, for in "The Two Gentlemen of Verona" he uses every musical term known to his contemporaries. He was a lawyer, for he was acquainted with the forms and expressions used by that profession. He was a botanist because he named nearly all known plants. He was an astronomer and a naturalist and wrote intelligently upon the stars and natural science. He was a sailor, or he could not have written "The Tempest." He was a savage and trod the forest's silent depths. He knew all crimes, all regrets, all virtues, and their rewards. He knew the unspoken thoughts, desires, and ways of beasts. He lived all lives. His brain was a sea on which the waves touch all the shores of experience. He was the wonder of his time and of ours.

"Was it possible for any man of his education and experience to conceive the things which he did? All the Shakespearean works were, beyond a doubt, the product of his pen, but the conceptions, the plays, the tragedies were the work of many brains, given Shakespeare by spirit suggestion. He was but the sensitive instrument through which a group of learned and distinguished scholars, inhabitants of many lands when in earth-life, gave to posterity the sublime masterpieces of the Bard of Avon."

The writings of Swedenborg were produced in the same way. Sardeau wrote by spirit suggestion, and as a fact many of the best works of so-called great men have been in part the action of the minds of those beyond our earthly plane, who, working in conjunction with man, do something for the uplift of the human race.

Knowing as I do the potent influence of spirit people upon the world's thought, and how in every way they seek to enlighten us to the change called death, I have wondered what spirit impressed this poem on a mortal mind:

261

As the faint dawn crept upwards, grey and dim,
He saw her move across the past to him-
Her eyes as they had looked in long-gone years,
Tender with love, and soft with thoughts of tears,
Her hands outstretched as if in wonderment,
Nestled in his, and rested there, content.

"Dear wife," he whispered, "what glad dream is this?
I feel your clasp—your long-remembered kiss
Touches my lips, as when you used to creep
Into my heart; and yet, this is not sleep-

"Is it some vision, that with night will fly?"
"Nay, dear," she answered, "it is really I."
"Dear heart, it is you I know!
but I knew not the dead could meet us so,
bodies as we are—see, how like we stand!"
"Like," she replied, "in form, and face, and hand."

Silent awhile, he held her to his breast
As if afraid to try the further test-
Then, speaking quickly, "Must you go away?"
"Husband," she murmured, "neither night nor day!"
Close to her then, she drew his head,
Trembling, "I do not understand," he said.
"I thought the spirit world was far apart . . . "
"Nay," she replied, "It is not now, dear heart!"
"Quick, hold fast my hand, lean on me . . .
so . . . .
Cling to me, dear! . . . 'tis but a step to go!"
The white-faced watchers rose, beside the bed;
"Shut out the day," they sighed, "our friend is dead."

This is a substantial description of what is actually occurring
from hour to hour. In the change as the individual catches his
breath in the etheric atmosphere, and his vision is clarified as a
result of throwing off the flesh tissue, he sees spirit people, "like in
form and face and hand," so natural, so unlike what one has been

led to believe that it is hard to understand. But let us remember that the change is a natural one, that all Nature's changes are for our good, planned by the Master Intelligence, in order that our opportunity for development may be increased, and we may grow more God-like. Knowing this we meet the dawn of the new conditions with confidence and courage.

Man is a part of Nature; his intelligence being developed and refined to a greater or less degree, he is an integral portion of that force which we term God. It is not necessary that we bend the knee and worship at any shrine or altar, but knowing that we are a part of that intelligence force which holds dominion in Nature, it is incumbent upon us to do no act unworthy of our position, to live where the best thoughts grow, day by day to strive to maintain the integrity and standard set for us, and ultimately to do our utmost to increase that force called good, or God.

In all ages Man has pursued happiness by countless paths and innumerable roads. Some have thought that within the hollow crown that rounds the mortal temples of a king, it kept its seat; some have thought that on the throne it sat and smiled, and have waded through seas of blood to reach it; some have thought that behind the walls of splendour it made its home; others, despairing of finding it there, have pictured a world beyond, where happiness could be found perfect and complete. But let us realize that there is only one royal road which leads to happiness, and that is to practice the plain, old, yet incomparable maxim, "Do unto others as you would have them do unto you." These sacred words uttered in different form six hundred years before the alleged birth of Christ, fell from the lips of the great Confucius, and are to-day found in nearly every sacred volume of the world.

## Truth and Appearance

Truth is always an achievement; it becomes such by reversing appearances, turning rest into motion, solids into fluids, centers into orbits, and by breaking up enclosing firmaments into infinite space. The sun, the moon, the stars seem to revolve, but they do not. We feel that the earth is motionless; that idea is erroneous, too. We see the sun rise above the horizon; it is beneath us. We touch what we think is a solid body; there is no such thing. We think we hear harmonious sounds; but the air has only brought us silent undulations. We admire the effects of light, and the colors that bring vividly before our eyes the splendid scenes of nature; but in fact there is no light, there are no colors. It is the movement of colorless ether striking on the optic nerve which gives us the

263

impression of light and color. We speak of heat and cold; there is neither heat nor cold in the universe, only motion.

Once it was said "this is as it appears." Now we say "The reality is not according to first appearance, but usually the reverse." Knowledge has reversed these beliefs, and the contrary is now proved to be the fact. The energy of an active agent seems to end with disorganization, but it really passes into another form. The appearance of nature is almost always elusive; and our first interpretation of natural conditions is usually the reverse of the reality. Of course this must be so; *it is the wisdom of creation and the secret of the world; else knowledge would be immediate and without process.* Nature has put reality at a distance, and, by labor and study, to distinguish reality from appearance.

Dissolution in no exception to the universal law. It is not as it appears, but the contrary. Death is only another birth into a more active condition. Those whom we call dead simply move into a new community, leaving mankind, because of their unenlightened condition, appalled at the change. There is nothing in the great scheme of nature that, when understood, is not simple, harmonious and beautiful. Many look at dissolution with horror because they do not understand what it is and to what it leads. Fear is the lowest of human emotions, and the child of ignorance. When we all come to such a stage of mental progress that we can understand, we shall appreciate the wisdom and necessity of dissolution. Were it not for death, as we call it, this world would be crowded to starvation. Were it not for pain, we should not be warned against danger nor should we know how to avert it. Sickness is a necessity; and all punishment that results from violation of nature's laws, is disciplinary. Dissolution only shifts the scenes, and transfers the individual from a material to a spiritual stage of action, without taking from or adding to his moral or intellectual capacity. In the next sphere of action, he no longer sees with half a vision, but is brought face to face with himself, which gives a higher, broader, and more comprehensive view and understanding of the economy of existence, which is evolution—a law as unalterable and indestructible as the mind itself.

If a man never becomes more than he is now, the whole process of evolution, by which he has come to be what he is, turns on itself. The benevolent purpose, seen at every stage as it yields to the next, stops its progression, dies out, and goes no further; the little bubble of existence that has grown and distended till it reflects reality in all its glorious tints, bursts in a moment into nothingness. Life has been given to us forever; it is the only one of all the gifts that nature will never take away from us. This body of ours may decay on some desert or plain, it may mould and go back to dust from which it came; but the life will never be extinguished. The breath is not the life of man; it only keeps in motion the wonderful mechanism that holds spirit in the physical plane. The soul, the spirit, the self, never dies.

Life beyond the grave is the promise that hope has ever whispered to all who have lived; but it has taken more ages than those of which we have a record for evolution to develop the mental faculties so that they can grasp these more advanced conditions where evidence is obtainable, and to demonstrate the fact. Time was when every cradle asked us whence, and every coffin asked whither, and this generation, for the first time in history, answers these questions intelligently. Unfortunately, the average individual has formed erroneous conceptions concerning the after-life, and these must be corrected before he can appreciate the sublime standard of natural law, and stand erect beside the column of knowledge, from which flares the inextinguishable torch of reason.

The sovereignty of the individual must be gained by effort in the manner nature has decreed. The mind is so constructed that truth and error can not occupy the same place at the same time; and when one attempts to understand a new condition, the one must be ejected before the other can enter. It has ever required greater effort to get rid of the false than to acquire the true. The weak must be taught. The strongest at some time must bend and obey. Should anyone who reads this new philosophy fail to grasp these laws, let him ask himself the reason, and see whether these are not two causes: (a) preconceived notions based on what one has been told, of which there is no proof; and (b) unfamiliarity with the conditions and laws in force beyond the physical.

No man, however well he may have mastered the laws of the material universe, should consider himself qualified to pass judgement on the conditions following dissolution, until he knows something of matter in its higher vibratory conditions; for in this domain only is intense life found. These laws, like those pertaining wholly to gross matter, can not be comprehended until the mind is free and open to conviction, and has evidence from which deduction may be drawn. The eternal dome of thought is high and broad, and each should do what he can to change the night of intellectual darkness into perfect day. Every man who discovers a fact adds something to the knowledge of the world. "Why," I asked a spirit, "is knowledge not immediate and without process?"

**"Because,"** was the reply, **"knowledge is worth more when it is gained by self-effort. To every mortal who thinks rightly,**

Nature's laws become natural laws. It is only the ignorant who are blind to all that is going on around them. Each change in spirit-existence is partly hidden from the plane below, because the conditions of each change make it best for the soul to fit itself for the next, without absolute knowledge of the the next step. All that is necessary is given to the soul when it is ready. As you, in earth-life reach out for knowledge, much can be given to aid you to govern your earth-life rightly, but not so much as to make you impractical in your daily work. Life in each sphere must be lived according to the laws of vibration that govern that sphere.

"When the right moment comes for the unfolding, the light breaks into the dark recesses of the mind, and the sudden radiance is dazzling. I keep telling you to live rightly and to teach others so to live. That is what earth-people must learn, but they are doing it very slowly. I tell you that the majority of souls on earth are sometimes centuries coming out of the deep shade of ignorance and sin. Learn to think good, pure, charitable thoughts. You can not know the reward the future will bring."

## Never a Secret in The World

There has never been and never can be a secret in the world. This is an entirely new proposition, which, if understood, would prevent much crime and unhappiness, and would enrich all mankind. There has always been an idea that many things can be done secretly; that, for instance, one can lie, and it will never be known; that one can cheat and defraud another, and not be found out; that a thief can enter a home without detection; that immorality can be carried on without the society being the wiser. All these wrongs are being done under the belief that they can be accomplished secretly, and most of them are done in this manner so far as our world is concerned. Mankind has been taught that God sees all and knows all, but man and women do not believe it; otherwise crimes would not be committed, and the moral code would not be violated.

Pride and speech of people have a great influence on conduct. Now, suppose the thief knew that if he took the property of another, his act would, beyond preadventure, be exposed in the mourning paper, and he would be under immediate arrest. With conviction absolutely certain, would he commit the crime?

Suppose the business man, or captain of finance, knew that if he formed unlawful combinations and defrauded the public, he would certainly be imprisoned; suppose that men and women knew that violations of the moral code would be known and censured within the hour—would wrong and crime go rampant through the land? Men and women do these acts in the belief that they are discreet enough to so cover them, that they will never be known. Such people have little idea that every act—I will go further—everything is known by those in the after-life who are interested in our welfare. But they arc far away, one says. No, they touch elbows and walk beside us day by day. One can not comprehend God as a personality witnessing each act and knowing the individual thought of over 400,000,000 of people, but one can comprehend the fact that the after-life in inhabited by those who have passed through the earth-life, that they improve their condition by helping those in need of assistance, that by their silent suggestion through the subconscious brain, they try to aid us, keep in touch with our thought, and are silent witnesses of all of the wrong in the physical world.

I do not mean that all the inhabitants of the after-life know each wrong act. What I do mean is that every man, woman, or child has loved ones in the after-life who take a deep interest in his or her welfare, be their position high or low. In other words, the ties of blood, the bonds of love, the interest of friends are not severed by dissolution. As the father, mother, brother, sister, wife, or child, know by experience the awful effect of wrong-doing, and are able to come about us and witness our conduct, note our mental vibrations and so read our thoughts, is it not the most natural thing in the world that they should try to stay our evil acts? If mankind knew this fact—that nothing is ever really done in secret—would wrong be committed at all?

Men and women are restrained often by pride; they only stray from the path of rectitude when they think that they go in secret. Teach men the truth, and it will help to make the home sacred, to empty the prisons; it will add more than any other one thing to the sum total of human happiness.

Again, the churches teach in substance that though our sins be scarlet, yet we can become as white as snow, and that there is forgiveness for all sin. One sect goes so far as to vest that power in the church. The practical result of such teaching has been—and is—to license wrong and crime.

Men do wrong under the impression that in some way they will escape the just consequences of their wrongful act. I have said before, and I will say again, that the world is not a jumble, but controlled by law; for every effect there is a cause, and that cause is governed by law. Every act produces a result. Every thought being material creates a condition about us, and is retained in one of the sixteen or more million cells of the brain. When, therefore, any one goes out of this life and enters the etheric where everything, the good and the bad, is intensified beyond mind-measure, the storehouse of the brain is opened, and he or she is confronted with the record which has been made. Nothing is forgotten; the good get reward, otherwise courage would be lost; punishment for wrong-doing is terrible beyond words. Everyone must bear his own burden, must meet again every wrongful act and make in ways that are provided complete restitution. This is very difficult, and the way is very long.

One who believes that the world of men marks the beginning or the end has no more comprehension of the true situation than the mole, following the path which it has made under the dead grass in the meadow-lands, knows of the physical world.

I have been told two most important truths by those who have honored me by their teaching: that there has never been and never can be a secret in the world; that man has no saviour but himself, and that the wrong which he does, he must undo. Whatever obligations he contracts, he must meet. I have had other teachings that have appealed most strongly to reason. One of these is "do no worry," but fit yourself to met situations from day to day. The obstacles which we meet are of our own making. If we possessed all wisdom, we would then be Gods, and not make mistakes. No one is perfect in this world or has reached full development, and until such time every one as a result of lack of wisdom and judgement will continue to make mistakes and create obstacles over which he will stumble. But that is not misfortune; mistakes are necessary, and it is only by creating and overcoming them that we gain wisdom, and know how to avoid the same conditions again. They are the stepping stones to the heights of understanding, and are good for us. Let us meet them cheerfully and appreciate the lesson each teaches. Ordinary errors ought not to cause us anxiety, for it is only through them that we make progress. A just and full appreciation of this fact would take from the mind the useless burden of worry. Calamity is Nature's spur; trials are not only essential, but are disciplinary; misfortune is opportunity.

Other desirable things which I have learned from this unusual source are: We have no right to burden others with our sorrows; all Nature is optimistic, all tending toward good; as one thinks, so he is. There are some men so pessimistic that given the choice of two evils, they insist upon taking both; they see no good in anything and are ever looking upon the dark side, anticipating misfortune. The mind is a wonderful force, its influence extending much further than we have any idea of, and one can do very much to make the world happier. On the other hand, one can do much to make others unhappy by throwing upon them one's own mental condition, and many people by force of habit do this, unmindful of the result.

I recall not long ago a mourning in the spring time. The sun was warm, the air balmy, dandelions bared their velvety bosom to the sky, tulips and daffodils fringed the borders. The lawns were carpeted with green, birds had returned from the south and were building nests and singing. It was a mourning when a temperament that could not respond to environment was poor indeed. As I stepped out upon the avenue on my way to my office, I saw a prominent citizen approaching. His head was bent, his eyes were fixed on the stone walk, his mouth was set; dissatisfaction and unrest showed on his face. The impression, as his mental condition touched my own, was most depressing. I knew the man well; involuntarily turning as I met him, I said:

"Don't take that down into the city to-day."

"Take what?" he answered quickly.

"The countenance you are wearing this mourning," I replied.

He looked at me in amazement for a moment and inquired, "What is the matter with it?"

I spoke with kindness saying, "It is full of discontent, unrest, and worry; you look at war with all mankind. You will make miserable every man, woman, and child who sees you with your present expression."

"Have I made that impression on you?" he asked.

"Yes," I answered.

"I would not like to create that impression," was the reply. "I have never thought that my mental attitude affected those with whom I came in contact. That is a new idea to me."

"Have you observed the mourning?" I asked.

"No," he answered, "I have been so engrossed in thought that I have not observed the day."

I then said, "I want you to forget the things you are worrying about. Look up and see how beautiful the world is, and feel what a privilege is ours to be part of it. Listen to the songs of the robins, watch the blue birds, respond to the flowers, get in harmony with it all, and as we meet those we know greet them cordially, and watch the effect on them and on yourself."

He walked for a little way in silence; the suggestion was working, his jaws were relaxed, the frown had left his face; his eyes had kindled, his lips smiled. With his expression wholly changed, he walked, a different man, and as he met his friends and acquaintances with a cheery "good mourning," his joy and happiness radiated. Others caught the charm of his personality, the world was happier, and so was he.

## The Attitude of Science

We are apt, with our physical environment, to stand in awe of so-called "men of Science," and expect that all progress, spiritual as well as material, will come through them.

I have never agreed with the method adopted by them to prove the continuity of life. Many attempt to build their structures by tearing down; to establish a fact by a process of elimination; they try to prove a thing is so, by proving it is not so. This method, I am led to believe, is erroneous in dealing with forces beyond the physical plane.

The judgement of spirit-people, with their greater knowledge and experience, is interesting. One now in spirit-life, who has advanced far, made this startling statement which I have hesitated to publish:

**"All proper respect is due and payable to the man of learning. But when learning, be it the result of book-study, of experimental investigation, or of knowledge imparted from one to another, has the effect of making men self-important, so that they adopt such an attitude towards others as to imply that all wisdom and knowledge repose solely and entirely in themselves, then I say that the so-called men of learning only make themselves ridiculous, and that the institutions which produce savants of this type are defective, and antagonistic to real intellectual progress.**

**"No one has a greater feeling of respect and admiration than I have for men who have, by constant and patient effort, sought to unravel and explain those great laws of the universe, the proper understanding of which tends to help and to advance their fellow-men. We all salute the man who does things; but we also feel contempt for that egotistic group of socialists, to be found in every country, who are always seeking to surround the laws of the universe with a hidden meaning, and to throw a halo around themselves and the cult they seek to organize, by erecting an artificial superstructure of baseless theory upon the facts already explained by the earnest worker, who has by toil and study revealed some hitherto unknown law. The genuine scholar is a plain man of simple ways, somewhat reserved in his expressions and criticisms,**

because what he knows makes him diffident about speaking in an adverse manner of new propositions which he has not investigated. But the self-satisfied man, who, because of the fact that he, by some chance, has become enrolled among the members of a cult, pretends to know everything and dares to doubt everything, while in reality too shallow for thorough knowledge, is often found among so-called scientists.

"Are there not notes in the scale too high in their vibration for mortal ear? Are there not colors belonging to the rays of the spectrum, too rapid in their vibration to be detected by the mortal eye? Yes, of course. Why 'of course?' Because science has proved it! Nonsense! Let me ask ourselves, what is science? I will tell you what science is. It is the result of the determining of the why and the wherefore, of a few of nature's laws that existed for ages before this word science was invented. Poor mortal man! His opportunities for advancement have been one long succession of trials. First he was obliged to overcome his visible enemies and the fear of the wilderness, then, when he had gained a little confidence, a combination of men arose and ensnared him by fear of the so-called supernatural; and then, when he dared not tell that set of men, 'Begone' so that he might think alone; behold! another set of men arose, who told him that he could think only as they should decide.

"Pray, tell me, what has any man of science, no matter how arrogant his claims may be, accomplished to entitle him to say that he holds the key to all knowledge? For each discoverer of a new scientific principle by which the world is benefited, there are a hundred, who, if they had been guided by 'science' only, would have remained all their lives in intellectual stagnation, but who have, with spirit-assistance, been able to enlarge the boundaries of human knowledge by a proper application of nature's laws. If the word 'science' be confined to knowledge of the laws of the physical world merely, it covers only a small field. The laws of spirit are far more important than the laws of our bodily structure. Man's spiritual future is a grander field of inquiry than the principles of mechanics."

Another said:

"To treat the subject of psychic phenomena by analysis, as you would treat matter, is not within the province of mortals. The soul is the spirit, and can be apprehended by mortals only by the operation of a thinking mind. 'Whence comest thou?' 'Wither goest thou?': These are the two great questions for all, and all must some day have the power to answer them. Would not a comprehensive knowledge of these questions be of inestimable benefit to you in your earth-life? Many a great and grievous error might have been avoided, and many who suffer might have been made happy, had it been universally realized that the earth-life is but a preparatory school for a future condition, where progress or retardment of progress is the result of one's own actions.

"It is well that mortals should live the earth-life in accordance with the laws of nature, and not spend too much time in speculative thought as to the why and wherefore of his being; but good being the desire of all, or the necessary condition of all for advancement, a true knowledge of the future state of the spirit is necessary that errors of life may not occur, through your own unguided actions.

"A knowledge of the continued life after passing from earth, can not be determined by weighing, measuring, or comparing as is done with material things; but by an acceptance of truth, manifested by the power of mind. There having been no beginning, there will be no ending of nature or of natural laws. Is it then to be said that mortal man is to be the sole exception in this eternal order of things? As you are, so shall you be. Your path lies onward; death, as you term it being but a single step, an unimportant change in the journey. Everything moves forward, nothing backward. The ending of mortal existence is but the first change to usefulness. You must not consider that the law that applies to constant improvement, does not apply to the lowest as well as to the highest in life.

"The principle that leads some men of science to hold that the only true laws are those provable by his deepest investigation and research, is a great error. After the limit of investigation has been reached, there are many more questions to be answered that are as yet unanswerable; this being so, you must seek for the answers by a process of philosophic reasoning.

"Great minds require proof of small things, and this is right; but it does not require that great truths should be placed before great minds. Many minds, of more simple attainment, grasp great truths much more easily than do minds which possess the quality of greatness."

272

Another, who while in this life was a well-known preacher, says:

I should like to add my mite to your epistle to the 'scientists' and to tell them that the life for which they try to find a scientific, materialistic reason, is as wonderful and as eternal as the universe; they cannot end it by death, any more than they can produce it by artificial means. Life comes from the great force of a mighty blending of souls which permeates all things and all space; life enters in, and is taken by the material atoms, when nature's law, which governs all things, deem the conditions in a productive state. The amount of this great force, which is retained by the being as it develops, depends largely upon the condition of the soil in which it is planted.

"All the talking, thinking and surmising, of all the minds in the world, cannot bring about the birth of a soul; and the great power that can generate a soul may be trusted to look after it justly and carefully after death. That death is the end, is a belief that a well-balanced mind cannot accept. Life would be but a futile thing, and all effort useless, if the future did not stretch before us endless and unlimited in its possibilities. Believe me, the justice that meets the naked soul, on the threshold of its spirit-life, is terrible in its completeness! If the understanding of this truth could only reach people during earth-life, they would escape much sorrow, —sorrow intensified to a degree greater than earth-dwellers can conceive."

Great was my gratification to receive the following statement, from a man well-known on earth, which I here give word for word:

"Tell your fellow-workers for me that I was working on a material plane all the years of my earth-life; that since I passed out, I have found that the material is but a fleeting thing in the real existence of the soul; that the nearer a man lets himself come to the spiritual, so as to accept suggestion and help from a higher source than the material, the nearer he will come to an understanding of life in its true sense. All these theories about another sense are ridiculous and were begotten in the brains of clever men, who were unable to give up their own petty ideas. They wanted to create, to make the laws that govern the universe; but I tell you that those laws have already been made, —they are fixed and unalterable, and the sooner the mass of mankind realizes this, and comes to a true and definite conception of the simplicity and justice of the laws, the sooner will they live lives fitted to carry them up the next step of progress. They must accept life and its governing forces as they are, at some period; therefore, the sooner the better. I am anxious to be the means of bringing light to some brilliant minds. But they must learn to accept the truth, to put themselves aside, and to realize that as it was in the beginning, it is now, and ever shall be. I am profoundly impressed with this fact: either men of science must grasp these higher laws, or let this new thought fall into other hands."

I do not mean, by quoting from the speech of spirit-people, to attempt to belittle, if that were possible, the achievement of modern scientific men, for they have done a great deal for material progress. But I do say that they have not done everything; for many great discoveries of nature's hidden laws have come from unknown and unclassed sensitive brains subject to spirit suggestion.

The "scientists," as a class, are materialistic and know little of any forces outside of matter in its lower manifestations. But these men have made psychics respectable, and the world will ever remain indebted to them, for, by their personality, they have dignified research.

Men like Alfred Russell Wallace, Sir William Crooke, Sir Oliver Lodge, Camille Flammarion, Dr. Charles Richet and others have had sufficient greatness of mind to break through the limited bonds of physical science, and to tell the world that there are laws in matter, and beyond matter, of which they have evidence and that life continues beyond what is known as dissolution.

This has also been said to me:

"If men of science, with all their knowledge and eager quest for the how and wherefore of all things, would only consent to learn a little of something beyond their actual touch! I know some do not deny the existence of life after death, but they spend all their time and effort in proving to their own satisfaction, whether a few insignificant spirits really are whom they claim to be, instead of making their investigation dignified and useful by learning something of that future life, and the best way of getting ready to enter it."

The present attitude of science is of no importance except in so far as it presumes wholly to preempt this field of research, which is the domain of the individual. We can come as near to the heart of nature, and can understand the simple laws of life that find no physical expression, as they can who formed the hypothesis of the molecule and measure the stars. We have eyes, and we see what nature has created; and ears upon whose drums fall all the wealth of sound. We taste the fruits and smell the perfume of all that grows, and with our hands fashion and build what the brain conceives. The man of science has no other senses, and can do no more.

I do honor those earnest men who have done so much for the material progress of the world. Their mastery of the physical side of nature has challenged the admiration of all, and the future, in so far as it relates to such matters, is largely in their keeping; but, in this field of psychic research, they are as yet trying to prove an axiom. I do question the methods adopted by them. The Master Mind has not reserved to any class the exclusive privilege of discovery. The University of Nature is the greatest institution in the world; its doors are thrown open to all who seek to know her ways, to which no coterie hold the key. Her vast treasure-house is full, and she gives with a prodigal hand. All who know her wondrous laws, and thereby enrich themselves, must, by a process of elimination, free their minds, and, like children, approach the throne of knowledge. They must say these facts are not accepted by science, that I cannot demonstrate them by their man-made rules, that they are not evidential. This may all be true according to their understanding: but I answer: many facts in nature are provable by laws in common use by those who have studied metapsychics, and it is the great desire of individuals in the great beyond that men of science adopt those laws, applicable only to matter in the higher conditions of vibration and discard in this field of investigation those laws that only apply to matter so slow in vibration that it is physical. If this is done they will enrich the spirit as they have enriched the material world.

## Vibration

Science can measure the velocity of the wind, of the stars and constellations, and of rays of light; but who shall attempt to measure the velocity of human thought? We cannot demonstrate spirit-forces and the conditions governing them, by the same rules that are applied to physical science. This is simply because there is a difference in the rate of vibration between things material and things spiritual. As long as matter is sensible to touch, science can measure it, analyze its substance, and learn its component parts; but when it reaches a certain vibration, where activity increases beyond their knowledge, the "scientists" are lost in the wilderness which they call "the unknown." This is where the philosophy that we term "metaphysics" commences. We, of this new school of thought, are no more qualified to enter into the domain of physical science than the physical scientists are to come into our domain, and it would be most profitable for each school to confine itself to its own field of usefulness.

Sir William Thompson, led by a hint of Faraday's advances the theory that "all properties of matter, probably are attributes of motion." I am told there are but two elements in the universe. This must be so: the positive and negative, male and female; else how could we have the harmony of the universe and the tendency to final equilibrium of inharmonious conditions and things. All other conceivable elements are not elements, but compounds. Vibrations are slowest in the basic or generic rocks; the atoms and molecules composing them lying close, of necessity, movement is slow. The basic rock, where it has not been changed in its position by upheavals, is most removed from the earth's surface. It has changed but little from the condition it assumed when this planet cooled and substance came together in so-called solids; but, starting from this generic rock as our basis of comparison, as we come up through the different strata in which are recorded the earth's ages, we observe the vibration gradually quickening as matter changes in its formation, resulting in greater motion; the vibrations intensify as we reach the soil and growing grains and trees, the plants and shrubs, and, finally, the flowers, bringing motion up to the highest pitch in the vegetable kingdom. But vibrations do not cease there; as we reach man they increase. After the physical comes the spirit-body, still matter, still vibrating, which progresses on and on among spirit-spheres with ever increasing action, in spirit-planes its refining process never ceases increasing, any more than man ceases progressing.

Vegetation has life, the same character or kind of life as human beings, but, its vibration being slower, it cannot move of its own volition. The only thing that makes it possible for man to move at will, is because he is in a higher or more rapid state of vibration, but with movement limited, —for all things have their limitations. We cannot pass through solids; but spirit people, living in a higher state of vibration, can. The spirit, while in the body, whose vibrations are slower and heavier, is impeded in its movement by the material; but at dissolution it escapes physical impediments, its molecular or atomic action increases, and it can do more at will. There is quite as much difference between the vibration in and out of the body as between the physical body and vegetable kingdom. Dissolution, then, is only the changing of vibratory conditions. It has been illustrated to me in this way:

**"When the body, from disease or long inhabitation, becomes a broken shell, the intense vibration of the spirit**

breaks through the limiting space to which it has become accustomed, and reaches a plane of higher vibration. The soul-sense dominates all our thoughts and actions; and, consequently, it is held in check only by the physical limitations of the body. When, as I say, the body becomes unfit to hold the spirit, the spirit breaks away at the first opportunity, and seeks the sphere best adapted for its expansion. The heavy vibrations of the body, unless quickened by the presence of the keener soul-vibrations, fall back into the still-heavier vibrations of matter, which is earth and vegetation. Nothing remains stationary, and if one part goes onward, the other goes backward. These are the elementary laws that govern change and evolution, and they are the A B C of spirit-knowledge. As this is becoming more known among those in earth-life, it tends toward their ultimate benefit.

"There are always vibrations depending upon the subjection of molecules that are not so free in expression. I mean they are taken into the life-principle, and given their proper position they change only to go into the vibration that is gradually made for them. They do not have the sudden release that comes to the soul, but slowly glide from one form into another, all in the same series of vibratory action. The soul's change is usually so sudden as to be a shock; for it is hard for a spirit to accustom itself to the intenser vibration. This is the reason why at a death-bed there is always a gasping for breath. It is not the physical body that is striving to breathe; it is the soul emerging into that higher atmosphere of spirit, unconsciously trying to adjust itself.

"Spirit-material is only earthly matter raised to a higher degree of atomic activity. Chemistry shows that when two elements, having a different degree of atomic motion, come together, there is an attempt at equilibrium, which, being accomplished, produces a new form of matter, and in the spirit-world there is no change of law."

In the progress of matter from the simplest elemental state to the most complex organic compound, there is constantly (a) increase in the mass, (b) decrease in the stability of the molecules. This is well known in physical science, but a new condition is discovered: (c) with all these changes there is an increase in the activity of the properties which continues, not only as long as matter is sensible to touch, but through all the planes of life beyond the physical. There is not one law for the physical and another for the spirit, but one law for both.

Vibrations increase in geometrical progression, and it is a well-known fact that there are long skips in the scale where mortal ear hears and eye perceives, for motion becomes so rapid that it is lost to sight and sound. Watch the spokes of a locomotive wheel as the speed increases, they appear first blurred, then continuous. As the speed still increases they pass from our vision, as completely as spirit form does. Both are governed by the same law. We do not see the spirit-forms of men or animals simply because of their vibratory condition; that is to say, the average mortal does not; but there are some men and women who can catch sounds from the spirit-world and others who can see spirit-forms; that is, they are psychic; they can see things and hear sounds that the average mortal cannot. This is termed "clairvoyance," and "clairaudience." Then again there are two forms of each one, the outward and the inward: (a) the outward form is where the psychic sees the form of a person, thing or object, or hears sound produced in the ear; this is a question of being attuned to higher than ordinary vibrations; (b) the inward form is where a spirit is able to impress thought on the subconscious mind. The latter form is generally called impression or inspiration, but this too, is only a question of vibration. A psychic is also known as, and in fact is, a "sensitive," who is able, to an extraordinary degree, to catch sights and sound that the average individual cannot.

There are birds whose homes are among the crags and high altitudes of the Andes, who's song mortal ear has never heard; yet many men have seen their bills open and close with lightning rapidity and their throats pulsate, but the song is pitched so high that it fails to vibrate on mortal ear. Again one said:

**"All life is the expression of the overmastering energy of atoms. Vibratory action in the physical world is the ceaseless action and reaction of one force upon another—one undulating wave on another undulating wave. There is never an instant when this action ceases. It is at once the process of elimination, rejection, propulsion, discord and harmony. Nature is apparently relentless. The sweeping storm, the force of the fire and tornado, destroy alike the gnarled oak and the perfectly formed landscape. Mortals with limited physical vision look with horror upon the devastation wrought, but we who have clearer vision see that this is only nature's mode of house cleaning. Out of the chaos, the great law of vibration produces harmony. A universal peace and calmness follow the ravages of the destructive elements. Why should this be so? Because all atoms have been brought together, governed by**

this law, then as quickly separated: and, after having been hurled apart and crashing here and there, the similar particles fall into harmony once more.

"I am fully conscious that any other statement of this law of vibration must, of necessity, be closely related to the theories of creation. It must fulfill a triple purpose; it must be not only cause and effect but the strange, indefinable, intermediate step that is the growth, as it were, of the real into the unreal. This triple purpose is revealed in the ceaseless action of the positive and negative qualities of every atom. In its power of repulsion and attraction, in its differences and similarities, this law governs the slowly-dissolving elements of every period of the earth's formation from nothingness, nameless ether, into harmony of activity; from this activity into form; from form to organized being; from organized being into other forms of being which again dissolve, and again form, completing a circle back again into nameless, nothings, ether, and the essence of force. When the vibrations grow gradually less, the form begins to be manifested and we have the atom, the molecule, the electric spark, the physical expression of life.

"The freed spirit comprehends the laws of vibratory physical action. To know is to be outside of; hence, not until we have become disembodied, do we truly know. As disembodied spirits we cannot experience. That belongs to earth-life alone; it is an illusive teacher. Not until we cease experiencing, can we grasp the law that governs. The subconscious mind, governed by this law, grasps it, adds to it, repels and attracts, and moulds itself over and over until, finally, you of earth-life, get a little appreciation of it."

This is a new theory in the philosophy of man. But towards its proper comprehension the thought of the twentieth century will be directed; and, with the mastery of the elementary principle, will come greater appreciation of the future condition of man, in the life beyond the physical.

## Facts Well to Know

"Are you ever told by those in the after-life anything you did not previously know?" I am often asked.

Yes, but future events have never been foretold, for the simple reason that the future is no more known to them than to us. I have been told many things I did not know, and some beyond my comprehension now.

279

One speaking of the human heart said, **"It is the chief organ of the body. It pumps blood every second to the extremities, to the feet as well as to the brain. Every thought breaks down tissues, every movement produces waste. Let it stop for one moment, and dissolution takes place. It is sending life to every part of the body."**

"We all know," I replied, "that it takes energy to keep anything in motion, and whenever there is motion, there is waste. What then supplies energy that keeps the heart in motion?"

Michael Faraday coming in said:

**"You have been told that by the process of decomposition of waste you obtain electricity. This proposition you can demonstrate to be a fact. Now oxygen is one form of electricity; hydrogen is another form of electricity called negative electricity; magnetism is in fact negative electricity.**

**The tremendous power in Nature's compounds called chemical affinity is due to the union or attempt at union of positive and negative electricity concentrated in the atoms composing the different so-called elements of the compound. Chemical affinity is the affinity of electricity and magnetism for each other. Electricity and magnetism are both matter in its simplest yet highest or greatest degree of atomic activity. But beyond the electro-magnetic is yet a greater degree of eliminated refined atomic activity which is the realm of spirit.**

**"Electro-magnetism in true equilibrium is etheric, the dwelling place of spirit and the connecting link between spirit and the material compounds in various states of atomic activity. Electricity and magnetism are the male and female elements in the universe. From the oxygen of the air by pulmonic process the blood gets electricity. From the hydrogen of the water by the digestive process the blood gets magnetism. The oxygen of the water is absorbed by the iron of the blood. By the nitrogen of the air partly mixed with the blood at the lungs, and partly by the nitrogen of the food taken into the stomach, the flesh compound is formed.**

**"Hydrogen and carbon form fatty compounds. One set of blood discs are electric, the other magnetic. The electric discs have an affinity for the magnetic discs when out of equilibrium. But at the lungs they are in equilibrium and hence repel each other to the left auricle, then into the left ventricle, the valves preventing back-flow; this repulsion of the discs to each**

other must carry the whole crimson mass forward while the equilibrium is maintained to the capillaries.

"The electro-magnetic equilibrium of the two sets of discs is lost in the capillaries and becomes less and less to the right auricle. Of these discs the set nearer the heart because of the inequilibrium, attracts the ones next behind, all the way from the capillaries to the right auricle where, by electric action from the brain in moving the heart to contraction, the equilibrium is again practically established.

"Now the two sets of discs repel each other to the lungs and through the pulmonary capillaries where the equilibrium is more perfected so that the repulsion of the discs carries the blood into the left auricle; thence my muscular action into the left ventricle and by further muscular action into the aorta. The heart being in equilibrium to arterial blood and positive to venous, attracts."

Knowing as I do that everything in the Universe is composed of matter varying in vibration only, and that the spirit-body is composed of ether, electric, and magnetic in its composition, one evening I inquired of one in the plane beyond the physical, one versed in the action of electricity, how it was that electricity could by its action destroy life, and I recall very distinctly his answer.

"You are aware," he said, "of the voltage used in the various prisons when they put a criminal to death. You are also aware that frequently a current with many times the voltage used in electrocution passes through a body without serious injury. It may startle you to know that any person who has been electrocuted, or who has suffered a lightning shock, or who by accident has received a charge of electricity that has apparently produced death, could be restored to life by proper treatment. The charge of electricity, as applied in our prisons, paralyzes the heart action, all the bodily functions, and the person is apparently dead. But you have probably observed that wherever and whenever a person is put to death under sentence of the law, a post-mortem follows. Death was and is produced by the post-mortem and not by the electric shock. In the beginning, surgeons were anxious to know the effect of the force, and undoubtedly made very careful post-mortems. You would be astounded to know as we know, that post-mortems have lost interest and that frequently they now consist of jabbing a knife into the apparently dead body and passing it on for burial.

"When a person receives an excessive charge of electricity, either by accident of design, and the bodily functions are thereby temporarily paralyzed, if the body were immediately stripped, laid upon the fresh earth and sprayed with water, the electricity would be drawn therefrom, and would pass into the earth. If then, artificial movement of the arms and stimulants were resorted to, the heart action would be resumed, and one apparently dead would get up and walk away.

"Persons die from electric shock because they are not properly treated. When the bodily functions are paralyzed and the electricity is not immediately drawn from the body and the action of the heart is not started by artificial means, death will, of course, ensue in a short time. If the treatment described is administered in time, there is no occasion for dissolution from electric shock. Electricity is life, and life will not destroy life. In this day, where electricity is in such common use, countless lives could be saved if the facts that I am not giving you were known and the treatment applied."

I received this information some years ago and thereafter arranged with one of the wardens of a prison in New Jersey to undertake to resuscitate a convict who was to be electrocuted, but the plan came to the attention of the authorities and was forbidden upon the ground that it was interfering with the due execution of the law.

Society must, of course, have protection from the acts of the vicious, and laws are properly made to imprison those who cannot be controlled, but the representatives of the people assembled in the various legislatures have not the right to prescribe the penalty of death. There is a limit to their sovereignty. What right have we as people to electrocute one who has committed murder? The life of every individual comes from God and though may have strayed far from the path of rectitude, yet the people have no more right to take that life than the murderer has to take the life of the murdered. What right have we as a people to electrocute a depraved criminal and by so doing, liberate him in another sphere where he may continue wrong-doing? If the public understood what dissolution leads to, they would stand aghast and horrified at the mere suggestions of electrocution.

Again I am asked, "Do you get teachings from the invisible world that are worthwhile?" Let me answer by giving just a few among thousands received:

"Immortality is the first promise of which man is conscious; but, as he acquires that which he considers worldly knowledge, he tries to rid himself of this promise. It stays with him, however, and, no matter how often he may deny the fact, his everyday life keeps before him the claims of immortality. The fields, the fireside, the love, and companionship of his fellow beings all suggest Immortality. The very thought that death ends all, causes him to shudder. Life would, indeed, be a hollow mockery if the earth-life, with its joys and sorrow, its lights and shadows, were the end. Every heart-throb is a protest against such thought. Nature not only promises eternal life, but fulfills that promise, else we would not be here tonight encouraging you to better efforts.

"Ages were required to develop men so they could discuss rather than fight over the matters concerning which they differ, and adjust them in the forum instead of on the battlefield.

"If you live a good life, the day of your death will be a great day; for, it will be a day of liberty; but, if you do not live as you should, the day of death will find you in bondage, bound by fetters of your own making. The manacles of earth are not nearly so binding as these will be. Follow where the light of spiritual guidance beckons, and do the things you find to do, upon the way. Many tasks will be disagreeable and not to your liking, but they will be the very tasks you will need to perform.

"I feel that it is my duty to help those who try to help themselves. There are many on the spirit side of life who are so densely ignorant that they have no ambition to become better. They continue on in the same old rut in which they were when on earth. Such spirits are of no benefit to the people on earth as they cannot bring useful knowledge to them. If you were able to see and know the conditions of the spirits in the lower spheres and could contrast their condition with that of spirits in the higher spheres, you would understand how important it is that people should be enlightened upon this subject while they are still upon earth.

"Friends, there is one God, the God of Nature; or rather, the God Nature. This God permeates everything and has absolute dominion over all that exists. You are all children of this one God under whose dominion you are here; and you are here, because you could not help yourselves. You had no say as to that part of your destiny; and you will leave the earth-life under the same dominion—Nature—and you cannot change the destiny Nature has marked out for you. Nature's mode of reform is development.

"What is the use of pictures to a person who cannot see, or of descriptions to those who cannot understand? The description of the higher spiritual spheres, even if it were given by one of the highest spirits, would be unintelligible to mortal mind.

"It affords me pleasure and joy unspeakable to know that I am still a man and can disclose in my weak way to some on earth the great fact that life continues, and that mere theories cannot stand out successfully against eternal fact. I was ignorant and weak when I came into this unknown country, and was not prepared to advance, until I learned here what I should have known before.

"What you have gained, what you need, will be yours in the spirit spheres. There is the closest love and quickest sympathy between the earth-plane and the spirit world, but we cannot make you understand what our lives really are, without becoming exact counter parts of each other. You will each find a different home, suited to you and your work. Your sphere now lies upon the earth-plane, and it is for you to perform the duties allotted to you. You may not be able to give the ignorant learning or the hungry food, but you can inspire their spirits to nobler and better deeds, while someone else, who is able, provides food and shelter. Let them feel that they have your love and sympathy and let them see that, even if the clouds of adversity hang low, your soul is able to ascend to higher spheres. It is good to know that you do not travel the stony path of life alone; to feel that, no matter how rough or dark the way may grow, you can, if you will, stretch forth your hand and feel an answering clasp—a clasp that makes your heart grow braver. The Creator seems so far away to most that, unless they can have the love and help of each other, they feel deserted. It will always be impossible for the finite to grasp the infinite. There are thousands who walk secure in the consciousness of 'leaning on the strong arm of the Lord' when in reality, they are cheered and guided by some unseen friend. It is this spirit that gives to them the feeling of strength that so ably assists them through life. The inhabitants of the spirit world are not bound by dogmas or creeds -that is, those who have been there long enough to get rid of their earth ideas; and they go forth to do good wherever they find opportunity. The main thing is to be honest with yourself, and just to others.

Your ideas of good to-day may not be the same to-morrow. Therefore, do not attempt to lay down a rule for your friends to follow. Let each be a law unto himself; for each must answer for his own actions and not the actions of others.

"It is not what a man does that makes him great, but what he is. Action is merely thought dressed in physical garb. Being must ever precede doing."

In this manner I answer the two questions so often propounded.

## Development Through Charity

Charity, in its general acceptation, has been identified with alms-giving. Spirit people, with their higher intelligence, contend that charity means giving to those in need of our best and purest thought; and they have pointed out that on the earth plane it is rather a mechanical than a spiritual action to distribute material things to these. How many, when they help those in need, give their best thought as well as material aid? True, material assistance is often indispensable; but nevertheless, it should be only a stepping stone to something higher and nobler. A charitable thought, sent out and transmitted by waves of psychic ether, will reach many souls in despair; and, perhaps, lift them to higher conditions in the material as well as in the spirit spheres. There are persons in earth life who are too poor to give material aid, but who, out of the richness of their benevolent hearts, give that which is better, more precious, more God-like, loving words and kindly deeds.

Such as these are never too tired to offer sympathy, never too weary to speak a cheery word to struggling neighbor. Such persons radiate happiness around them, and are continually sending forth the purest and best of which a soul is capable, and, when they go out into the after life, they find that the bread of thought cast upon the waters does return.

It is my custom to ask of spirit people to give some expression of their views on subjects under consideration, and in reply to an inquiry about charity one said:

"And the greatest of all is charity of thought, without which the utmost gifts of money become as pebbles in the mouths of the hungry. Think of all as you would have all think of you. A thought once born grows to its fullness, not only by the good done to the individual, but by this strength and goodness. It circles around, and after encompassing many in its kind embrace, rebounds to enrich the originator. Cultivate the desire to think kindly of your fellow men.

"Some thought dominates all actions. Those who have evil thoughts are in danger of becoming evil themselves, though they may be unconscious of the fact. The mind flings out a radiance which, to some extent, sheds light on every avenue of life. If that radiance should grow feeble and your life selfish, you would long remain in the twilight, and your outlook would be limited. But, if kindness and true charity dominate your thoughts, the radiance will continue rich and bright till its emanations reach the boundaries of hope, and your soul is illumined by the crowning sun of happiness.

"The best way to judge character is to watch the faces of children who turn toward men. A good man loves them and has patience with them, and they turn to him as naturally as a flower follows the warmth of the sun. A bad man realizes their helplessness, and brutally vents his malignity on their small defenseless heads. Such a man is not to be trusted in any walk of life.

"Again be generous to those to whom nature has limited her gifts, for nature compensates, and the time will come when all shall be equal. The poorly-equipped for earth life will more easily acquire the lessons to be learned in the next, for those of patience and humility are learned already. Those who think differently are to be enlightened, not censured or ridiculed, for all who understand this truth of life's progression are entrusted with the great responsibility of teaching all who can understand; and you must get as close as possible to the lives of others, that your words may have weight.

"Let your hearts be fallow ground, plant therein the seeds of love, charity and purity; nourish them daily with the clear water of tenderness; and you will have a wonderful garden filled with fragrance and white with blossoms, and your life will become a part of the great life principle."

A spirit, well known when in earth life, said one evening to a gentleman who worked with me, and who helped obtain the information now given the public:

"The intense satisfaction that is the constant result of right doing, based on honest purpose, is, in itself, sufficient reward for action. Of all the trite sayings of the Bible, the one that reads, 'What shall it profit a man, if he shall gain the whole world, and yet lose his own soul?' is one with the greatest meaning.

286

"Wealth brings many opportunities for good and for evil; in fact, there are more for the latter than for the former, as the besetting sin of mortal man is selfishness and the possession of great riches allows free expression of that greatest of all sources of trouble. The true and full meaning of the word 'selfishness; is in every way opposite to the most beautiful word in your language, 'charity.' Shorn of their meaning, as applied to money, they are the negative and positive of man's character. The fullest opportunity of giving expression to these two opposite words comes with the possession of great wealth. The understanding of the full meaning of these two words is the truest index of a man's character. The ability to make one's life the embodiment of that wonderful word 'charity,' and to understand that other word 'selfishness' so as to avoid it, is the true test of mortal man's ability to control himself.

"Self-control is man's perfect condition. To know charity and practice its meaning; to know selfishness and keep it from you; this is self-control. This state of existence is as near perfection as the earth-tied mortal can hope to get. You have been chosen one among many on your side of life to bring certain great truths to the people of the world. In advance of time, you are to be prepared for the time of your usefulness, and this is one of the moments of laying before you certain truths. To teach the truth, the teacher must be truthful; to induce others to accept pure and honest principles, the teacher must be pure and honest himself; to set certain facts before others, the teacher must be above criticism.

"You may honestly atone for those things that have so far occurred in your life, by making amends to those to whom you are indebted. So far as the errors of your past are concerned, you have well and strongly conquered their chief cause, and you need no longer fear them. You have henceforth no excuse to do otherwise than follow the honorable and ennobling instincts of your nature. Guard well your actions, that they may not be open to criticism from others; and particularly from the one of all others from whom you cannot escape, —your own self. You have been, and you are being, weighed in the balance; and so much is expected of you, that you must not be found wanting.

"Remember that wealth brings the opportunity to give expression to what is best in your nature, and that you will find the only reward for doing good is that intense feeling of satisfaction that can come only as the result of a good deed, unselfishly done. It is well that man should earn his daily bread. It is the intention of nature that every mortal should struggle, for by no other means can he progress in the scale of being. This being so, one so situated that he can live without a proper exertion on his part, is unfortunate. Never forget this principle; the waste of money is not charity, but foolishness. You will find many practical ways to do good and to do it in the right way. A clean tenant demands a clean habitation. A pure heart and a pure mind are the results of your own efforts so to keep them.

"Charity is not a formula; it is a thought, clothed with a kind act. Cultivate charity in judging others; try to draw out the latent good in them, rather than to discover the hidden evil. We must do this if we would rise to the full glory of our privilege, to the dignity of true living, to the supreme charity of the world."

## The World's Desire

This is an age of greed. We, as a people, have drifted out upon the sea of selfishness, egotistic desire and devouring ambition, and set the main sails to woo the winds of fortune. This is the age of money. Every nation and every people have erected a throne on which wealth sits in state; they have placed upon its brow a crown of gold, and have decreed that the possession of money, with little regard to the manner of acquisition, should be the only qualification for this kingship of modern times.

Man, at the dawn of physical development, is shown this goal, and taught that money is power and the world's desire. He enters the strife and bends his energies, as others do, to grasp the greatest amount of wealth with the least possible effort, matching his cunning against labor, —mind against muscle, —artifice against simplicity, —and directs his thoughts towards wrenching from the hands of honest toil, a portion of its legitimate earnings.

Does wealth ever ask what claim it has on the savings of labor? Why is it adding to its already vast store, while other hands are growing feeble from want, and shadows are falling on poverty stricken homes? Does capital ever contemplate the privation and suffering that must follow close upon the heels of cupidity and deception? Do captains of industry realize that, by directing their ability towards the concealment of base designs under the veil of enterprise, and by the misappropriation of the proceeds of honest toil, they are, according to a higher standard of ethics, guilty of larceny? And that by a law, as fixed as gravitation, the time will come when them, through laboring and suffering, in the life beyond the physical, must make compensation for every dollar acquired unjustly.

Consider what a future awaits those who make ambition their goal, and who succeed in seating themselves upon the throne of wealth by modern methods! It is a great misfortune to have false ideals, to worship at the shrine of money; but it is a far greater misfortune to succeed, and to hold unlawful gains, or more of nature's store than a simple life requires. That all should work and save against old age is proper; but that accumulations should greatly exceed the needs of existence was not intended by the intelligence that planned all things. We see men in the morning of life preparing for the strife: so fast they rush, so eager is the struggle, so crowded the field, so elusive the object of pursuit, that each one thinks only of self. Like men in actual battle, they fight for mastery, never hesitating to push aside those in front or to trample on those under them; and what is the end for which they strive? Wealth? Yes, but not all, for with the advantages that money brings, come arrogance, pride, greed, and increased selfishness.

Of what real benefit to the world are the very rich? Some few do good by gifts that help the poor and needy; some endow hospitals where suffering is reduced; some give libraries; others build churches and cathedrals. But the great majority hoard their gains and count their money; the love that should encompass all mankind is given to wealth. The greater portion of their thought has been spent in accumulating their hoard, and consequently they love it. This is the old age they have been preparing for, and, like the miser in his tower, they sing and chuckle as they count their gains and the gold coins slip through their fingers. So intent are they on accumulation that they are deaf to the call of charity. Surrounded by luxury, they have not come into contact with suffering; so busy and self-centered are they, that they have not had time to give encouragement to others. Nothing but self has found lodgement in their minds as they have been preparing for the future. What future? "Old age," one answers; but I answer: The future lies beyond the world of men! Will this gathered wealth support you through the coming ages? If another life follows dissolution; if natural conditions prevail, in the great beyond, and one has necessities there as here, what wealth has been accumulated for support in the community after this? Money, being a material substance, is not taken, nor indeed can it be, for we see its distribution here. What, then, has been accumulated for support and maintenance out in the after-life where money is not king? All the wealth one can take with him into the after-life, is that which he gave away in this.

The thought that the *rich man here* may be, and usually is, the *pauper in the after-life*, is startling in its possibilities and dreadful to contemplate. A man who has made money his God and worshipped at the shrine of gold, having no other thought, ambition or desire, in earth-life, is poor indeed if his hoard cannot be taken with him, for poor he is in all else, in a world where kind and thoughtful acts are the standard of wealth.

When the fact can be driven deep into the human heart and brain that after the material life, out in the great hereafter, one lives a life similar to this, and that he has necessities, actual wants, and desires that money will not satisfy; appreciation of what true wealth is, and how to gather it for one's eternal good, may dawn upon the minds of men.

Contemplate the after-life, where money is not used! The occupation of most people will be gone, they will find themselves disqualified for any other position, ignorant and helpless in a world of activity; then will come appreciation of the lost Atlantis men call opportunity. Upon the pages of memory will be written: wasted energy, false ideals, worthless ambitions, erroneous conceptions, ignorance of the simple laws of nature, —and selfishness will find itself a pauper, in a world of plenty.

In the next life, I am told, the only way to gain advancement is by helping others; in this way only is knowledge gained, for by contributing their efforts to greater good, the Master Intelligence has provided for the individual advancement of spirit-people. Each builds his own stairway to the heights of knowledge, —"all for one and one for all," -that is the law of their progress when they have emancipated themselves from earth conditions. Material wealth is only for a day, as time is counted. What the good man does enriches him here, and becomes a part of his own self for all that we call eternity.

If "doing good" is the only wealth that one can carry away into the after-life, how shall it be with those who have thought only of money, grown indifferent, cold and hard, and have lived this life for self alone? A picture of the condition of those in that class, whom we have talked with in the life beyond, is too terrible to describe.

In earth-life, they draw about themselves a mantle of arrogance and pride, closely woven of selfish thoughts and greed. Such is the garment that covers these naked souls as they journey on. Upon many, not one ray of light shines; there is only darkness and despair; nothing penetrates the gloom but the chill of death and dissolution. The selfish worshiper of wealth is not only a pauper in a world of wealth, but an outcast in a world of harmony. The good men do "lives after them," their earth career becomes a part of them, and they a part of it. Good radiates light; selfishness is darkness—the absence of light—and so condense the thought emanations as to encompass and obstruct one's vision. And so, on going out into the next life, the selfish enter into a condition they have created, there to remain, until, through suffering, the wish shall come, from within, to make restitution for a life of greed. Then will come the desire, unknown during earthly existence, to become a worker to help others—just for the joy that comes of doing good—and to find in this way only that "peace which passeth all understanding."

The wealth that all in this physical world should seek has not the ring of gold; it is gathered by right living, by helping others to live right, and by doing something each day that will bring joy to hearts that are sad, encouragement to those who falter, good cheer to those who are depressed, bread to those who hunger and clothing to the naked. Do something each day to make some mortal happier, and with each act let love go hand in hand. Thus only can mortals be enriched here and hereafter, "beyond the dreams of avarice," for one good act, sent out with love as its companion, will reach beyond the confines of the stars, and touch eternity.

## Progress

To the average mind that has given no thought to the problem of life after this existence, and to its great possibilities, the suggestion that those out of the body can communicate with us at all, is startling. The fact that any conditions have been made where they can speak in their own voice so as to be hard distinctly in our atmosphere, is beyond their comprehension. That spirit-people control the physical brain and hand to write, is beyond all understanding. The fact that millions of human beings have not heard or spoken to spirit-people, or seen them use the hand of a sensitive to write, does not even tend to prove that I have not had such experiences or that these are not facts. Knowledge is positive; ignorance is negative. I have seen the one and have heard the other again and again, and I know both to be facts; I have had taken down in writing many discussions and lectures on problems that are of vital interest. Let me give the words of a spirit on the subject of progress:

"In the great theater of the universe all is harmony that pertains to the management of the play. The one touch of discord exists with players only. Gradually, but steadily, the players acquire a perfect knowledge of their various parts, and, as they learn to conduct themselves so as to allow the play to go on smoothly, the entertainment becomes more agreeable. But much rehearsing is required before a satisfactory exhibition can be given.

"That all who wish may enjoy that to which they are entitled is nature's full intent, and gradually mortals are coming to realize that such is the case. An appreciation of universal good for the benefit of mankind at large, can come only when the single and separate individual can clearly understand that he is entitled to those gifts of nature which his senses tell him may be had for the demanding. Until recently it was an almost universal belief that there were special privileges for a certain number of the supposed elect of God; but when a few who were barred out of those privileges, fearlessly raised their eyes and studied nature as it is presented on the stage of the universe, and learned that the only true supremacy and greatness lies in the difference of intelligence, and not in any distinction that can be marked by heredity, there came an awakening; and since that day, the scenes on the stage of your world have changed rapidly, and each succeeding on has shown an improvement over its predecessor. And when this appreciation of the only true mark of greatness among mortals has been realized, then and then only, will the chord of harmony be struck, and the play shall be so thrilling that the doors shall be open to the universe at large, and all the different constellations will ring with applause as they see one more evidence of the splendid work of the master mind.

"Knowledge is the key that shall open the door for this great production. Knowledge is the magic key to progress. With knowledge comes confidence; with confidence comes a strengthened desire for more knowledge. When the creeping babe first pulls its body to an erect position by its hands and arms, and finds that it can stand erect on its little feet, confidence in the power of its being is established, and the first forward movement of its feet gives it further knowledge of its power, and, as step by step, its feet carry forward its little body, knowledge of its power begets confidence, and confidence begets the possibility of acquiring further knowledge;

292

and, until something occurs to weaken that condition, the forward and onward movement to acquire more knowledge is continued. As it is with the creeping, toddling child, so it is with the adult; until something occurs to stop that onward movement of gathering knowledge, progress is constant. What, then, is more terrible to contemplate than any system of teaching that can beget, or has begotten fear, the great destroyer of confidence? Like one who sits upon a great height and has an unobstructed view of what is happening on the plains, we, of the spirit-world, can look with unobstructed vision down the long vista of the past, and see the terrible crimes that have been committed against our fellow spirits and earth mortals by those bands of men who dared to intimidate their fellow creatures, and to hold them in subjection by writing and preaching about things of which they were utterly ignorant. Some were mere fanatics; but in the main, they were mean, low, and unscrupulous men whose only thoughts were of personal gain and personal advantage. Awful will be the punishment of such men. Some are now undergoing their punishment in the spirit world, and others are clinging tightly to those whom they have deceived, and, by suggestion, are still doing their harmful work."

When the intellect ceases to be enslaved, then is the body free. When the knowledge holds full sway, then the intellect is free. Knowledge gives one the power of self-control, and when one has learned self-control, knowledge increases rapidly. And as one acquires knowledge, he gains self-control in like degree.

"Let fear and superstition and dread of the future be banished from the minds of men, so that they may see clearly and understand nature perfectly; then will knowledge come to them, imparted by those who have journeyed into the next stage of progress, the spiritual or stage of acute intelligence."

# CHAPTER 10
## *Fragments*

*Our object in life should be to accumulate a great number of grand questions to be asked, and resolved in eternity. Now we ask the sage, the genius, the philosopher, the divine, but none can tell; but we will open our queries to other respondents—we will ask angels, redeemed spirits, and God. —Foster*

## Psychic Truths

Not withstanding the many years of this research, we were always careful to utilize our strength to the best possible advantage. Little time was spent with tests and personalities, none with frivolities. It was a dignified, scientific work, wherein we sought knowledge to the utmost.

At times there would come concrete and definite statements, with great rapidity and tremendous import. It seemed as if the group of spirit people wanted to say as much as possible in the fewest words. Frequently, I asked slower speech, so that my stenographer might get the statements correctly, and I recall being told that it was impossible at times to slow the message; when conditions were right, they had to send them through or lose the opportunity.

I have gathered from my records short, terse statements from various communications received from those in the after life, some beyond world teaching, that seem worthy of publication. The following are but a few of the thousands, mere fragments of spirit philosophy:

1. "Force wherever found or however expressed is life."

2. "Each plane in spirit existence is partly hidden from the plane below, because the conditions of each change make it best for the soul to fit itself for progression without absolute knowledge of the next step."

3. "When the intellect ceases to be enslaved, the body becomes free."

4. "The supreme need of each man is to reason and to remain, ever after, true to his convictions. Where reason leads, each should follow publicly and openly. This is the highest conception of duty."

5. "Man's conscience is his judgement seat, and reparation for wrong cannot begin too soon. Love for humanity is the basis upon which mankind must stand to gain ultimate good; that to help a sprawling beetle to gain its feet is an act the result of which will follow one through eternity."

6. "Dissolution is simply the throwing aside of the physical garment, the outer covering composed of flesh compounds, whereupon the individual becomes an inhabitant of another sphere of usefulness, differing only in its intensity."

7. "Inhabitants of this material world cannot see the spirit form while in the body; neither can they see it when separated from the body."

8. "All life has intelligence; all intelligence has language; all language, expression."

9. "One who does right and has the courage of his convictions, will find in the after life a radiant happiness, and the censure of this little world will fail to sting."

10. "A thought born in your mind is for good or evil, a thing to be reckoned with again in the after life, when it will confront you face to face, and claim you as its author."

11. "Do you not think that the great intelligence that planned millions of worlds, and made them move with perfect harmony and precision, that peopled them, that fixed and marked each one's course, and lighted its pathway in infinite space, knows what's best?"

12. "At dissolution, each sense is quickened, and all that fills space is visible to the spiritual senses and tangible to spiritual touch and brain. Space must then take form, substance and reality, —a world of thought, boundless and endless."

13. "The rains will come when they are timed. They will replenish the green of the harvest and make it richer. The storms of life may beat upon you, but you will find they only break down the dead branches, and you will be more straight and fair for their passing."

14. "All about this material world there exists actually the psychic or spiritual universe, more active and real than this, peopled with all the countless dead, who, no longer burdened with a physical body, move at will within the boundaries of their sphere, in what appears as space to mortal man."

15. "In the kingdom of the mind there can be no personal dictation; there is no God but universal good; no Saviour but oneself; no trinity but matter, force and mind."

16. "Life beyond the grave is the promise that hope has ever whispered to all who have lived."

17. "The sovereignty of the individual must be gained by effort. The weak must be taught; the strongest at some time must bend and obey."

18. "To every mortal who thinks rightly, Nature's laws become natural laws."

19. "Dissolution is a step in evolution, and involves no mental change, adding nothing, subtracting nothing, but simply increasing the opportunities for observation and learning."

20. "Men who deny to others the right of public speech are not qualified for speech themselves."

21. "If you would impress your thought on others, and spread the truth, make that thought the highest expression of truth."

22. "Make yourself attuned to the most harmonious vibrations, so that your impulses will be good, and then obey them. They are apt to be the suggestions of a fellow-soul working out his salvation."

23. "Mind is the aggregate of all thoughts. Mind is the universal thought. As a drop of water signifies but one infinitesimal part of the great ocean, so a thought is but one infinitesimal part of the great ocean of the mind."

24. "Deeds are thoughts grown to maturity, and yet a thought unspoken or unlived, will exist through all the ages, as though expressed."

25. "Everything is governed by law; nothing happens by chance; cause and effect are as potent in the spirit plane as in the earth plane."

26. "There are sounds that our ears have never heard; there is light that our physical eyes can never see; there is an invisible world filled with people that few have ever imagined.

27. "Life would be but a futile thing, and all effort useless, if the future did not stretch before us, endless and unlimited in its possibilities."

28. The justice that meets the naked soul, on the threshold of its spirit life, is terrible in its completeness."

29. "The tendency of all life, wheresoever found or however clothed, is to perfect, improve, increase and extend its sphere of usefulness. This is evolution. It is a fact, a law and not a theory, and its possibilities are as boundless as the imagination."

30. "The atom, alone, has eternal duration of form, for it alone has the power to enter and dominate all other forms. It has no master except force, and to force alone it is amenable."

31. "The wealth that all in this physical world should seek, has not the ring of gold; it is gathered by right living and by helping others to live right."

32. "It is far better to have committed an honest error and reaped no profit, than to have great profit and to have honesty gone from your own heart."

33. "Selfishness in the human heart is the cause of all evil; where selfishness dwells, love can not abide. Selfishness and love can not occupy the same place at the same time."

34. "An atom from the great ocean of spirit finds lodgement in a physical organism—and behold, a man!"

35. "Mortal needs spirit suggestion, but spirits indeed of mortal thought have just as great a need."

36. "Life enough is given to rule each day in our kingdom, but not enough 'for tomorrow.'"

37. "Wisdom is born in the soul of man when he recognizes that natural law governs and accounts for all things."

38. "If a man is clean, he feels clean, and keeping clean inspires him to clean deeds."

39. "Wisdom, power, beneficence, and the peace that passeth all understanding—these come not from above, but from within."

40. "If a man can make himself habitually right in his thought and desire, right in his will and purpose, he must become right in the tissues built up out of the mind's action."

41. "Power is born of desire; no man can earnestly desire to live upon a high plane and yet be compelled to live upon a low plane, since we live in that state of development that we create for ourselves."

42. "Every life is placed exactly where it should be, and is in touch with the environment needed at that hour to unfold itself."

43. "It is thought that builds the body. Thought is food, thought is force—the motor power, by means of which the soul expresses itself in physical form."

44. "Why are old experiences repeated? you ask. Because the tangle of life must be made right, and it must be made right by the individual soul. This is the truth I taught. Only a few are ready for it, and even today only a few enter into my sphere. There are those in earth-life with whom I daily and hourly commune; there are those here who still seek expression through some form of earthly religious belief; few are willing to stand alone and think."

45. "Nature is an open book, with language simple and easy to comprehend; yet man, with all his boasted knowledge, has read but few pages and mastered less. Its lessons are written in rocks, in earth, in minerals and grasses, in grains, in flora, in trees, in bursting bud and growing things, in mountains, in snows and glaciers, in sun and stars, and in all movement and evolution of matter, gross and refined."

46. "Literature, art, all the great work of masters, all the products of the genius of the present and the past, will come to the assistance of those who call. We are here to aid, to comfort, to uplift and to support all who ask for help. Only a few here have a faint glimpse of a life beyond the satisfaction of earth-desires. Like tendrils clinging to a wall or to a decaying tree, through disappointed loves and blasted hopes, they keep tenaciously struggling with the problems of mortal life."

47. "Open your eyes and you shall see the new heaven and the new earth, all invisible to the physical eye, which sees only that which it wants to see, but it sees nothing of the eternal harmony, of which mortals express only a counterpart. Awake to the truth of the joy of being! Awake to the infinite cause of all happiness! Awake to the omni-active energy that surrounds you!"

48. "All beauty is expression in a varied language—not of words, but of pure ideas, hopes and joys. Emotions have a language not yet comprehended, and yet to be given to a listening, waiting, longing world. Be filled with joy! That is the expression of God. If you would impress your thought on others, and spread the truth, make that thought the highest expression of truth! Make your life a continual song of thanksgiving for the good you find, and the good you give to others. Be consistent, looking to the harmony of natural law to guide you, and build your life on the same simple principle. This life means to the true thinkers a wonderous unfolding, beginning with a child's first conscious look, going on and on until the individual is taken into that one great scheme of indivisible good. This is the ultimate end of all."

49. "The universe is teeming with life, —beautiful, abundant life. Open your soul and stretch out as it were with eager hands, and let the spirit of Good enter, and abide. Like dew upon the thirsty, famished flower, it will make a sick soul well. It is the same force

that is in the dew; only to the flower it must come in the form of dew, rain or shine; while to mankind it comes as a suggestion, enters into the mind, makes it strong and courageous; for a mind filled with the uplifting principle, which is Good, must be a pure one, one able to lead others to the great book of nature, there to learn to obey its laws—steadily, insistently, working for each blade of grass, each soul of man."

50. "Beware of criticism. It kills naturalness in yourself and others, and the best impulses are suppressed by the frost of self-criticism. Attune yourself to the most harmonious vibrations, so that your impulses will be good, and then obey them. They are apt to be the suggestion of a fellow-soul working out his salvation; and, by letting the impulse hold sway over you, you not only do a good act, but help that struggling soul one step farther on his way."

51. "When the end drew near and I knew my judgement was at hand, my spirit shuddered with horror. I knew I had not lived according to divine good. I had deceived, and, more than that, I had lied and abused the confidence of many who looked up to me. Will I ever be able to complete the restitution necessary? Sometimes my soul sickens under the burden of sorrow and suffering I have caused, and I am afraid. I want, by these teachings I am privileged to give you, to gain much for my own advancement. Perhaps you and I together may grow in greater harmony each day so that much good may come of it. Call me when you will, I will be watching, eager to take up the work."

52. "Beyond the great divide, await all those for whom you mourn; all unsatisfied ambitions, providing they are tending toward progression, you will have the power to gratify by work and application."

53. "There is no such thing as space; what seems so to us, in fact, contains all the elements that produce objects."

54. "Mind, I mean thought, not the habitation of thought, when the earth-life is over, becomes the entire being. It is the only part in man that is of such vibration that it can enter in and progress to spirit-life."

55. "Nature is God, is always good, always smiling, even in her storms nature is but fulfilling her promise of future plenty, as a mother goes through the storm of childbirth that she may replenish the earth."

56. "Nature is natural in all her changes. The God-spirit is breathing through every fold of the rose, every leaf and ear of corn."

57. "All Nature's laws are natural laws. Those things that to mortal minds are mysterious, are called phenomena. But Nature never made anything phenomenal. Things seem so to the undeveloped mentally."

58. "Truth is always an achievement; it becomes such by reversing appearances, turning rest into motion, solids into fluids, centers into orbits, breaking up enclosing firmament into infinite space."

59. "The appearance of Nature one nearly always finds to be not false, but elusive; and our first interpretation of natural conditions is usually the reverse of the reality. Of course, this must be so; it is the wisdom for creation, and the secret of the world; else knowledge would be immediate and without process."

60. "Time was when every cradle asked us whence, and every coffin whither; this generation, for the first time in history is able to answer these questions."

61. "The eternal dome of thought is high and broad and each should do what he can to change the night of intellectual darkness into perfect day. Every man who discovers a fact adds something to the knowledge of the world."

62. "Back in the past centuries, when the world of spirit had not its present development, there was little original inventive thought. Man built a shelter, killed his food, and fought his enemies, as any animal does. As the spirit-world progressed and became more intelligent; as it obtained greater understanding, and grasped with greater power, the life-forces, in other words, more power of thought and more ability to help mortal development, then, by reason of spirit-suggestion, acting through man's subconscious mind, he began to feel an awakening for something better, and the progress of civilization began."

63. "Gravitation acts upon the physical body, attraction upon the mental state. Gravitation in the physical world, attraction in the spirit world."

64. "One law governs all conditions in the physical as well as in the spirit planes; and whenever we find life-forces, they are clothed with either physical or spiritual material, which is matter in different states of vibration."

65. "Thought is the one thing in the universe formed and fashioned in the human brain; it agitates the ether, and thus permeates all things and all space."

66. "Everything is governed by law; nothing happens by chance; cause and effect are as potent in the spirit plane as in the earth plane."

67. "Savages rubbing sticks to produce fire, looked upon the traveler with suspicion and fear; but when they saw him produce fire with a match, their souls were filled with wonder. Spirit-people look with sorrow upon the people of this generation, for the great majority, in their simplicity, are still rubbing sticks to obtain light."

68. "To the masses, spirit-life is a mystery; death a hopeless problem; while the world of the invisible, just another community all around us, cannot be comprehended by the average mortal mind."

303

69. "The genuine scholar is a plain man of simple ways, somewhat reserved in his expressions and criticisms, because what he knows makes him diffident about speaking in an adverse manner of new propositions which he has not investigated."

70. "Great minds require proof of small things, and this is right; but it does not require that great truths should be placed before great minds. Many minds, of more simple attainment, grasp great truths much more easily than do minds which possess the quality of greatness."

71. "That death is the end, is a belief that a well-balanced mind cannot accept."

72. "The Master's great purpose is the gradual, yet positive, improvement of matter until an observant and grateful mortal is the final result."

73. "Evolution is but the action of that great power called by mortal man, God, but which really is the process of refinement and purification of gross matter until the resultant product is living, thinking, mortal man, and then the intellectual man. The next step in that ever-changing, ever-progressing evolution, is the endowment of that physical intellectual man, with what we call spirit."

74. "The atom, alone, has eternal duration of form, for it alone has the power to enter and dominate all other forms. It has no master except force, and to force alone it is amenable."

75. "Beyond the atom is an intelligence which has imbued it with these properties and powers."

76. "What then, is this life, this intellectual force, which is back of the atom and expressed in or through it? What or who controls its movement with perfect precision? Some call it energy; some force; some nature; and others call it God."

77. "Beyond the atom are minds, that have at some time lived in a physical body, working in unison and combining substance that will endow matter with energy which will give expression to life force in the physical."

78. "The conscious mind is controlled by yourself. In it are held all the material part of your thoughts. I mean those connected with and controlled by earth things."

79. "The subconscious mind is the one controlled by psychic forces entirely. It is the spiritual brain of man. I mean, that it is subject to the laws of vibration, which the other part of the brain is not sensitive enough to catch."

80. "It is the subconscious mind that gets suggestion from spirit-people, the connecting link, or battery, that for an instant holds the suggestion, and passes it on, to grow into a thought or an impulse."

81. "The subconscious mind does not retain suggestion. It is the embryo thought, which takes definite form only as it reaches the conscious mind."

82. "On earth there are weeds, as well as useful grain and beautiful flowers, so among your people are there apparently worthless mortals; but who can say when or how the weeds, following the great law of progress, will evolve into useful or beautiful plants; and yet, as simple weeds, may they not serve a great, if hidden purpose?"

83. "The poorly-equipped for earth life will more easily acquire the lessons to be learned in the next, for those of patience and humility are learned already."

84. "Charity is not a formula; it is a thought, clothed with a kind act."

85. "Wisdom sits in the presence of a theory, but stands in the presence of a fact."

86. "Character is the product of trials, conscience is born of suffering."

87. "Man cannot be saved by proxy; he must be his own Saviour, there can be no remission of sin through faith or prayer."

88. "Evil is not an inheritance; it is the result of ignorance of natural law."

89. "Matter is an outer crust, a crystallization of Mind."

90. "The trees and solids of which our earthly furniture is made were once full of sap, which is life. They came out of the invisible by a process of growth. They will disintegrate again, and be worked up into other forms by the permeating Spirit—the resistless Energy of the universe that is constantly changing all things."

91. "Different rates of vibration give us different planes of consciousness. On the physical plane, one rate gives us sight, another hearing."

92. "Be true to conscience, which is God's voice."

93. "Another name for vibration is motion."

94. "When I hear music or sounds of any sort, I know that I hear only because sound travels. It moves in waves, just as light does, but the sound waves take a different direction, and are of different length than the light waves. Therefore, light and sound are simple energy, or force, moving at a different rate of vibration, and in different directions. All force is motion."

95. "Our progress is through the relative to the absolute, through the finite to the infinite, through weakness to strength, through bondage to freedom, through man to God, through death to life."

96. "When the thought is fully focused by the will on the thing desired, force must be put behind it, else it is like an engine without steam trying to pull a train of cars. Though fully equipped with masterful machinery, it will not budge an inch till the force is applied."

97. "Love is to thought what steam is to the engine."

98. "Thought is a power that must be recognized in the divine economy."

99. "Man has made his own condition; yet the blunders and crimes he has fostered and committed have been ignorantly ascribed to Providence."

100. "Will is an architect; intellect is a builder."

101. "Founders of great enterprises and promoters of philanthropic causes do not lose their interest in this world's affairs, because they have cast off their outer sheaths of personality."

102. "A rational view of life's continuity and a clear statement of what awaits them in the Beyond are among the greatest and most truly answerable demands of the twentieth century."

103. "The seeker for Truth should expect to find it everywhere. Thus alone will he realize the brotherhood of souls, the unity of religions; for Truth cannot be confined within the limits of a creed, or restricted to the necessities of a few, this is the New Thought."

104. "All things work together towards a high ideal in the kingdom of the spirit."

105. "Living without the light of the New Thought is like having a grand musical instrument in the house without the ability to awaken its magnificent melody."

106. "Every soul is a law unto itself, and would outrage its own sacred birthright, should it accept the criterion of another instead its own."

107. "There should be less worship and more work among men."

108. "A God whom limited intellect could comprehend would not be a God; the intellect would be the greater."

109. "The only religion that will save the world from its sin, and raise it from its degradation, must find its way to the hearts of men through the filtering process of human reason. Science and philosophy will be its handmaids, and eternal laws and immortal truths its gospels."

110. "The imagining faculty, which we all possess, is our creative faculty."

111. "With successful people in all walks of life, thought is concentrated on particular aims; but with the masses of mankind, it is but a wandering vagrant loitering upon the outer wall of circumstances."

112. "The spirit world is the thought world. And as thought lives within the physical man, so the spirit world interpenetrates the material world."

113. "Knowledge is merely a cultivation of that divine spark of wisdom inherent in all."

114. "The goal of yesterday we only reach to be lured to a grander view."

115. "First, the natural, afterward, the possible."

116. "When will the popular mind be taught that there is no age, except as we permit it to affect us? We should put behind us all the thoughts of a life 'here' and a life 'there'; there is but one life, and that is eternal. Then, why reckon upon 'age' at all?"

117. "There is not in the universe a single great problem that man can truthfully say he has mastered, and concerning which nothing remains to be found out."

118. "The law executes perfect justice everywhere and at all times. Universal law is universal justice. Without law, or without justice, the universe could not exist a day."

119. "Those who, through ignorance or prejudice, decry a new discovery, and so prevent fair consideration, are enemies of civilization."

120. "Truth has neither youth nor age; it is, and ever has been, a brother to reason; it does not need the assistance of fame or science; it has never been in the keeping of any particular class of men; it is the heritage of all who live."

121. "I look into the future and see the creeds and dogmas, that for centuries have enslaved the human race, dead and obsolete laws in life's great statute book. I see knowledge take the place of faith and superstitions; I see the awful fear of death banished from every human heart and mankind at peace. I see a world of thinkers, honest and free, teaching the gospel of truth, the religion of nature, and philosophy of meta-psychics, the new science of matter."

122. "Let this fact sink deep into every human heart: the individual thought must at all times be kept clean and pure, for this wondrous and ever-active mind of ours is from day to day throwing the shuttle through the web of life, incessantly weaving the fabric of condition that will clothe the naked soul on the threshold of the after-life, and those in the great beyond watch beside the loom."

## An Interview With a Spirit

All life is infinite and of God; this earth is but an incubator, developing and increasing the sum total of life force. Who shall say that ultimately all who live may not become a part of that Infinite Intelligence, and work as one with the force that fashions worlds? I do not know, and those with whom I have been privileged to discuss the question do not know. They do not know what is beyond them any more than we know what is beyond us. They receive and accept teachings from those who are in planes beyond themselves, the same as we do. Discard, if you will, my experiences, treat what I am saying as theory—but does it not seem natural? Does it not appeal to your reason?

"From whence comes all life-force of the Universe?" I asked.

This was the answer:

**"There is a great central force, the emanating rays of which are gradually lessening in their vibratory action, reaching the lowest ebb in the center of your earth.**

**"This central vibratory action is in the highest sphere we know, so intense and so high in vibration that souls who are in the highest state of development are the only ones who come near its circle. It is the apex of the universe, from which the rays lessen as they go out through infinite space to all spheres.**

**"Some of the other planets are much higher in vibratory action than is your earth, so that if one, retaining earth conditions, were to go to them he could not see any life, because his sensitiveness to vibration is so much lower.**

**"This condition is apparent when once one has grasped the immensity of the universe and the harmony of its laws. If you were able to see all the conditions and people beyond you, life would appear as chaos and confusion—each sphere mixing with another—no regulations, no harmony anywhere. As it is, each has its own place in the scheme of progression; the invisible wall of vibratory force is a safety guard to continued rational living.**

**"Those who pass through each stage of the soul's progression are slowly but surely becoming a part of that great force. It is the contention of many here that individuality is lost in the immensity of that great harmonious force, and becomes in turn a tiny part of the new conception in the earth form. It is a part of this force that creates life in earth form, and that part is taken from the infinite whole."**

310

"What determines one's condition, position, and environment in your plane of activity?" I asked.

The answer came:

**"Character, and in this regard there are many factors to consider. With you in earth life, wealth and birth have much to do with your position. Education and social status also are factors; one may be selfish and cruel and yet hold place and power, but in dissolution, stripped of gear and gold and all things physical, he comes naked into this world of ours. Before transition one may hide, dissemble, and deceive, but with us character—that is the soul body—is visible, so that as we come in contact with one who has passed the portal, we know at once what he is."**

"What law," I asked, "fixes and determines one's status there?"

The reply was:

**"The dominant law is one of harmony. It may be said that the law of attraction with us corresponds in principle to your law of gravitation; as your physical body is subject to the latter law, so are you, when separated from its flesh garment, subject to the law of attraction. When one comes here he is irresistibly drawn into that condition and company for which he is fitted by character. So the selfish are together; the immoral and cruel have like companionship; thieves and murderers are among their kind. Also the charitable, the kind, the devout, the spiritual, are drawn to congenial souls, among whom they work in harmonious accord. This is one of the laws, fixed and forever in force."**

"What of opportunity for advancement?" I asked.

**"That, too, is provided for. A spirit may work out of his environment, no matter what it is, and may climb the heights. Indeed, all must ultimately progress; but the way for some is dark, dreary, and lonely. Only by one's own effort can he advance to higher planes; through work, that is by helping others, the soul of the individual spirit becomes developed, refined, more spiritual. The same law that fixed his status on his arrival will advance him to whatever condition he earns, so that he may constantly be in harmony with his associates.**

**"Every wrong act in earth life must be lived over here, and lived right, before one can progress. If your world knew this fact, incentive to wrong would be counteracted, so that you would have a better world and a happier people. As you are**

developing character every hour of your earth life, you see how important it is to build it right."

"Our thoughts, then, build character?" I asked.

**"You have so little knowledge of true psychology that it is difficult to explain the process. First of all, you have a mind that functions in and through your etheric brain; it receives impressions and suggestions from our side; it formulates what you know as ideas by catching spirit suggestion, and through observation. It is colored at times, unfortunately, by heredity, selfishness and desire, but it has perfect freedom—limited only by the laws of your society—to express itself, and so to build character.**

**"You are answerable to the State for violation of the laws of the State, only if you are discovered; but you are answerable to the higher laws for every act and deed without exception, for your world holds no secret from us. I do not mean that a personal God watches you from day to day, but I do know that those who love you and are interested in your development can witness your acts, and do know your very thoughts. When in the death change you come here, your character is visible to all, so that your personality becomes common property."**

Another said:

**"Thought is material as granite, differing only in vibration. It takes not only form, but color; a thought is as real in itself as though it were expressed in the physical, for of necessity the thought itself precedes the physical expression of it. As thought is real and lives forever, you can see the importance of keeping it clean.**

**"One who conceives low, selfish, and beastly thoughts, is even now surrounded by a dark and filthy mental condition, in which foul conditions he will find himself when the flesh garment that hide from your eyes the real self is cast aside. Where else could a wise and beneficent Providence place him? Should such a character mingle with those who are clean and pure?"**

"Explain, if you please, how thought molds one's personality?" I asked.

**"Let me illustrate if I can. Consider for a moment the brain as a machine, through which passes mental fabric. The results**

may go far and wide, but the brain is yours, never for one moment to be lost or destroyed. It creates what is called an aura—that is an integral part of your spirit body.

"We even now can tell the character, and know the extent of your spiritual development, by the color of the emanations that come from your soul center, and find expression in acts and deeds. Your soul body is a thought body; as all thought is material, so your inner or etheric body is molded, fashioned, and tinted by your thoughts from day to day."

Our thoughts from day to day, then, are woven like tapestries, in patterns involved and strange, with dreams and fancies interlaced, with harmonies that go from us and return to catch the pulsations of life's great theme, as wonderous as traceries in frost, wrought on grass by winter's subtle art.

"What of memory?" I asked. "Do we retain for all time consciousness of this earth life?"

One answered:

"The images that are impressed in one's soul during earth life are so persistently real that it is almost impossible to change them. Thoughts make those images, but few realize that they are building something so real and lasting. Here, one lives with these images, until one is able, by effort and strength of purpose, to change them into something more worthwhile.

"The time will come when one must have about him only what is lovely, beautiful and harmonious, for without those conditions, there can be no real progress; then all the old images of deceit, jealousy, and unhappiness must be torn down and destroyed. They are not pleasant things to find in one's home-life here. The home including any of them can never be beautiful or properly built.

"Come to us with as little of the discord of earth life as possible; it will be so much easier to get used to conditions here, and there will be the less to get rid of."

# PART III

## Emily S. French Solves the Psychic Riddle

The Powers of Emily French are Tested in New York City
by Dr. Isaac K. Funk, May 29th to June 10th, 1905

# CHAPTER 11
## Tested in New York City, 1905

*And when they heard of the resurrection of the dead some mocked;
and others said, "We will hear thee again of this matter."*

—Acts 17: 32

### The Psychic Riddle / Isaac K. Funk, D.D., LL.D
### Chapter IV—The Phenomena Known as the Independent Voice

In the early part of 1905 I received a letter from a prominent
lawyer in Buffalo, N.Y.—Mr. E.C. Randall, head of the firm of Randall, Hurley & Porter requesting that I investigate "a remarkable
medium" of his acquaintance, by name Emily S. French, through
whom come independent voices and for whose honesty he would
vouch. Said he, "About fourteen years ago I became acquainted
with this woman. I was sure her phenomena were the result of
fraud and I determined to expose it. After many sittings and exacting experiments, I became convinced that they were genuine, and
finally at the suggestion of the spirit intelligences, I had fitted up a
seance-room in my own house in which my wife, the medium, and
myself held seances, and we have done this now for more than a
dozen years. I have tested Mrs. French in every way I can think of,
and am thoroughly convinced that the phenomena are what they
claim to be. The talks are exceedingly instructive and I have had
many of them taken down in shorthand. I wish you would do me
and others here the favor to investigate thoroughly these manifestations, and I would be very glad to have you visit us and remain as
long as you desire at my home for this purpose. Every facility for
thorough scientific investigation will be granted you. Rest assured,
you will find the phenomena exactly what I tell you they are."

About the same time I received an urgent letter from an editor of one of the leading dailies in the western part of the state, urging "a scientific investigation of some extraordinary psychic phenomena that come through a Mrs. French, and which are perplexing some of our best minds. The phenomena are much out of the ordinary, and the medium is not a public medium who exhibits for pay."

Shortly after this correspondence Mr. A.W. Moore, the secretary of the Rochester Art Club, wrote to me as follows—I quote very fully from his letter as its story is interestingly told:

"My attention was called to Mrs. French's phase of mediumship about twenty years ago, when I was on the editorial staff of the *Union and Advertiser*, Rochester, New York.

"At that time I was not only an unbeliever in spiritual manifestation, but prejudiced against it, believing it nothing but fraud. In reporting of it to the press, I always treated mediumship with ridicule and sarcasm.

"One summer's day I had occasion to visit Hemlock Lake and there met by chance J. Nelson Tubbs, the well known civil engineer, and now inspector of the Erie Canal. Our conversation drifted into Spiritualism which I firmly discountenanced and ridiculed that he asked when, where, and how long had I investigated the subject. I had to confess that I had really investigated the subject very slightly. He pointed out the inconsistency of my condemning mediumship and taking such strong grounds against it without ever having taken the trouble to examine into the subject, and he warned me to be careful in writing about it until I got better posted. Mr. Tubbs then gave me an account of his investigations carried on during a series of years which resulted in his being a firm believer in spirit return. He gave an account of his experiences with various mediums and particularly the phase of manifestation peculiar to Mrs. French, viz.: Independent voices. He advised me to have a talk with Judge Dean Shuart of Rochester, who was for many years judge of the Surrogate Court of Monroe County.

"The fact that two such level-headed men—one an eminent civil engineer and mathematician, demanding 'weight and measure' in his profession, the other, a learned jurist and man of such impeachable character that he had been repeatedly elected to the responsible office of Surrogate Judge—had professed their full belief in spiritism, caused me to reflect deeply. I, therefore, on my return home, sought out Judge Shuart, and that gentleman told me many things that set me to thinking. He spoke of Mrs. French and arranged for me to attend a private seance at the house of a mutual friend.

"I attended a seance as arranged by Judge Stuart. There were present, besides my wife and myself, Mr. and Mrs. Austin (our hosts), and Judge Shuart and one or two others. We met in a small room upstairs and after being seated and taking hold of hands in a circle, the light was extinguished. It was explained to me that it was absolutely necessary that not the slightest trace of light be allowed to enter the room. Judge Shuart asked all present to sing, saying that vibrations were necessary. We, therefore, sang several familiar songs and afterward talked on various subjects, when all at once, a voice, loud and sonorous, high above our heads, exclaimed: **'I greet you my friends!'** The suddenness of the voice startled all present into silence, and the speaker continued to talk. After continuing for a while, the voice said: **'Ask any questions you may wish and I will answer them to the best of my ability.'** I asked, 'What is your name?' The answer came, **"I was known as Red Jacket when in the mortal."** I then asked him to describe conditions in the spirit-world and the passing of the spirit out of the body. In reply, Red Jacket gave a long talk on his own experience. He said at the time of his passing out he was in a very low spiritual condition, due to the excessive use of 'fire-water' which the white man had taught him to indulge in, and also to his intense hatred of the 'pale faces' on account of their having robbed his people of their hunting grounds, etc. He then described some of the ordeals his spirit had to undergo in order to overcome the desire for strong drink which still clung to him, and to turn his hatred of the white man into love.

"I can merely touch upon my experience at this seance. Other voices came, male and female. My impression at the close of the seance was that the whole thing was an imposture, and I determined to find it out somehow. I told Judge Shuart frankly that the voices were made by some living person, and that if he would examine the cellar of the house he would find a pipe leading from thence to the room. The Judge immediately requested me to go with him into the cellar, a damp low-ceilinged place, full of cobwebs, but we saw not the slightest indication of a speaking tube. I then fell back on ventriloquism and accused Mr. Austin of doing the business.

"To all of this Judge Shuart listened kindly and suggested that I follow up my investigations until I had discovered the fraud. 'If there is fraud in Mrs. French's circles,' the Judge said, 'I would like to know it, because my time is too precious to waste by attending these seances.' Continuing, he said, 'I have been sitting with Mrs. French from time to time for the past five years and tested her in every possible way that my mind could suggest, but I have not discovered the slightest trace of fraud. My friend, you will, if you continue your investigations, be compelled to acknowledge that Mrs. French's voices are occasioned by a power beyond the material, and the only conclusion you can arrive at is that they are, as they claim to be, Spiritual.'

"To be brief, I will say I attended another seance at the house of Mr. Austin, with the full conviction that I would be able to detect Mr. Austin as the ventriloquist. But on arriving at the house I found that he had been telegraphed for by his son who was mayor of a town in Colorado. Consequently, the seance took place without the presence of the man I suspected. The voices came as usual and stronger than on the previous occasion. I was placed next to Mrs. French in the circle and took hold of her left hand, her other hand being taken by Judge Shuart. When the voices came Mrs. French placed her mouth on the back of my hand until the spirits ceased talking.

"While Red Jacket delivered an address his voice suddenly seemed to die out like the notes of an organ when the wind fails, and he exclaimed **'Sing!'** When his voice came again he explained that the cause of his voice failing was lack of vibrations, and he entered upon a discourse regarding the wonderful atmospheres, electrical conditions, ethers, and vibratory forces of which mortals were quite ignorant, that formed the conditions that enabled spirits to throw their voices into our atmosphere. At the conclusion of this seance, I was just as skeptical as ever, and still more determined to fathom the mystery of the voices.

"I went again and again to the seances held by Mrs. French and I took with me one of the chief skeptics in the city, Mr. J. McCall, who denounced the whole proceeding as a fraud, but he failed to point it out. His vehement denunciation of Mrs. French aroused me to protest, and I said, surely before you are so loud in your condemnation you ought to point out where the voices come from. 'The fact is,' I said, 'I am beginning to think that they may be spirit voices, because I have exhausted every device for detecting fraud and failed.' 'Did you ever have Mrs. French give a seance in your own house?' asked McCall. 'No,' said I. 'Then,' replied he, 'if you can get her to produce the voices in your own house you will find, if she accepts your invitation, that the thing won't work.' I asked Mrs. French if she would come to my house. She replied that nothing would give her greater pleasure. A few days afterward, Mr. McCall and his wife were at our house and I suggested that it would be a good opportunity to have Mrs. French over. I walked to her house, a short distance away, and brought her back with me. We sat in my study, and there were present on the occasion Mr. and Mrs. McCall, a nephew of mine just arrived from England, my wife, and myself. We had no sooner turned out the light when Red Jacket said in the loudest tones I had yet heard: **'You see Brother Moore, I can come to you even in your own house!'** He then went on to describe the work he was doing as a missionary spirit. It took him a long time, he said, to outgrow earth conditions and appetites, in order that he might try and undo many things he had done in the flesh. His great anxiety was to come and return good for evil among those whom he called the 'pale faces.' He was happy when he attracted the attention of the white men so that he could teach them something of spiritual law. He said the spirits are working very hard to bring about conditions by which there can be an intercommunication between the two worlds, and the time is coming, said Red Jacket, when materialized spirits would appear upon platforms and address large audiences. The reason that Indian spirits took a large part in spiritual manifestations is because America was their hunting-ground and the red men lived close to Nature and were thus tremendously magnetic.

"Well, in brief, the seance was most wonderful; not only did Red Jacket come with great power, but several other spirits who spoke on different topics.

"The result of this seance was, that Mr. McCall shook hands with me and said, 'Moore, I believe the voices are spiritual!' From that date Mr. McCall became a thorough believer and prominent in spiritualistic circles.

"Since that period I have attended so many of Mrs. French's circles that it would be impossible to give in a letter the many wonderful communications I have had . . . I think I can say that I have attended in the neighborhood of one thousand of Mrs. French's seances in the last twenty years.

"I have learned enough wisdom from the old Seneca Sachem Red Jacket regarding spiritual things to fill a large volume. His sermons are at times full of pathos and beauty, and I have known the circle to be brought to tears by his eloquence. He lays great stress on the necessity of living lives of purity, temperance, and benevolence. He admonishes us especially to be charitable toward those who oppose the spiritual philosophy and cling tenaciously to dogmatic theology. He tells us not to try and convert people, but by our example and words draw them to inquire into that which gives blessings and peace to us.

"I might add many things to this testimony regarding Mrs. French, whom I believe to be a most honorable and trustworthy lady, who would scorn to do a dishonest thing, and would never for one moment give herself over to fraud and deceit. The fact is, she does not have to, as her manifestations are among the most wonderful and instructive to be found in the world today."

Mr. Moore in his correspondence again and again urged that I undertake a serious investigation of the psychic phenomena as manifested through Mrs. French.

Earnest as were these and other urgings, I said no, having so often been led on wild-goose chases in hunting up phenomena of this class and classes similar to it, and besides I long since had made up my mind to accept no phenomena as genuine when the conditions were not wholly under my control, and these, it seemed to me, would not be, especially as they were produced in the dark.

Finally, I was visited in my New York office by a lawyer from Rochester, a man whose integrity and levelheadedness are nowhere questioned and who is a lawyer of state-wide reputation. He came to urge me to the same investigation. He told me that he also had known Mrs. French for many years, and had visited her sittings very many times the past five years; that his partner, now dead, who was also a prominent lawyer and a judge was thoroughly convinced of her honesty, and was convinced that the phenomena were of spirit origin; he declared that he himself was not a Spiritualist, and hence did not wish his name mentioned in connection with the matter, and finally suggested that he should try to induce this aged woman to come to New York for two weeks, and to be wholly under my direction, for the most thorough investigation that I would care to make. He said it would be best, however, for him to send with her a lady friend of his, as Mrs. French was now over seventy years of age and was exceedingly feeble, being afflicted with heart trouble which made it unsafe for her to travel alone. He assured me that she gave no sittings for pay, that she was a refined, well-bred woman, a delicate lady in every sense of the word, and that the friend whom he would send with her as an escort was one that he had known for nearly a quarter of a century, and for whom he would vouch in the strongest possible way. I finally assented, and the conditions agreed upon were as follows:

1. No one was to come with Mrs. French except the one lady escort.

2. Both ladies should stop at the home that I designated.

3. That the sittings should be at such homes as I would make known to them *after* their arrival in New York, and this house was not to be visited by the medium or her friend except during our sittings, nor by any person representing them.

4. Both women were to follow my directions absolutely while in New York City.

These terms were cheerfully accepted.

The unconditional acceptance of the requirements made the series of tests a very interesting case.

In the first place, there was nothing doubtful in the history of the medium. The testimony from those who knew her showed that she was most highly respected, that she had in her favor the verdict of the jury of the vicinage where she had lived over three-score years. This rightly counts for much in one's favor. Among those of whom I have since inquired concerning her history are many who have known her for many years, all at least five years, and one, a man who had been acquainted with her for over sixty years. She has come of good stock, and that is also an element that counts; she is a Pierrepont, one of the most noted families of the State of New York; in short she is what the old-fashioned novelists would call high- or lady-bred. Those of whom I have inquired—several of whom are not Spiritualists—are unanimous in telling me that they regard her as person incapable of deception or falsehood.

But, in the acceptance of so uncommon a phenomenon as that of the independent voices, our proof should be of a sort that does not depend at all on the honesty of the medium. People of good reputation, even "Sunday-school men," have been known to lie. Proof that measures up to the standard required must be of a kind that implies an absurdity to suppose the phenomenon is not what is claimed for it. (Astonishing, is it not, that Dr. Funk completely disregards the testimony of others. Learned men and women who have tested Mrs. French in every known way they could devise and have been convinced beyond question. —Ed.)

Still, it was a satisfaction to have, for testing, a medium with an unblemished reputation, and to have for point two—a seance-room that made trap doors and confederates impossibilities. A close friend of mine, a wealthy businessman in New York, whom I have known for over thirty years, consented to permit me to use a room in his family apartment for this series of seances. It would be difficult to conceive of a better room for this purpose. The windows of the apartment are so arranged that they all open out about fifty feet above the surface of the ground. It is entered by two doors, one from the hall which leads to the elevator, and the other from the fire-escape. The latter at all of our sittings was locked and chained from the inside, and in addition, a heavy trunk rested against the door. The hall door was also locked from the inside. At several of the series of sittings I kept the key of this door in my pocket during the entire time. The persons at the seances were this friend whom I will call Mr. Z., his wife and daughter and myself, the medium and her lady escort—these comprised all of the persons who were in the apartment; not a servant, not even an animal pet of any kind was allowed in the apartment during the sittings, except on two occasions—once we invited an outside friend, and once a friend and his wife.

Mrs. Z. had often investigated Spiritualistic phenomena with me during the last twenty years. She is an expert at this kind of detective work. Her daughter also had attended a large number of seances, and withal is an author of reputation. Both Mrs. and Miss Z. are very skeptical as to the Spiritualistic hypothesis and are, in my judgment, keen investigators and have a lively knowledge of human nature, especially of the woman sort. Mr. Z. himself has been for years a student of psychic matters and has had no little experience with the tricks of mediumistic fakers. I know of no house or family better fitted for the work I here and then undertook.

There is another fact to be noted. After my attention was first called to Mrs. French, I had a friend who is an able expert in psychic matters go from New York to Buffalo to attend some of Mrs. French's seances and to make report to me. He did so, and his report on the whole was unfavorable, basing his conclusions mainly on the darkness of the seance room, the possibility of the medium producing the voices herself, and also on this other fact, that one of the voices spoke of a physician who was sick at a distance from Buffalo, a fact my friend afterward discovered was known personally to the medium. The opportunities for investigation by this friend were not of the best, and the time was brief and, as he afterward informed me, he was not acquainted "with all the facts that are favorable to Mrs. French." I had the detailed written report of this friend for my guidance in my own much-larger series of sittings. Having the medium in the house of my selection gave me also a great advantage.

I trust my readers will pardon me for digressing at this point a moment in reply to certain critics.

Again and again Spiritualists lose patience with me, one saying very vigorously that I am not a medium and hence cannot be competent to judge of mediumship. The conclusion may be sound, but it is a non-sequitur. I believe that I am better fitted to pass judgment on mediumship than a medium can possibly be, who is always super sensitive and often in a trance. John B. Finch used to say, "I can not lay an egg, but I am a better judge whether an egg is good or bad than all of the hens in the country."

J. R. Francis, the editor of the Progressive Thinker, a Spiritualist paper published in Chicago, has done more—I am sure I am well within bounds in saying it—to free Spiritualism from fraud than any other man in America. Mr. Francis has been pleased in writing recently to declare that he regards me as "an ideal investigator of psychic phenomena," and that he regards my methods as being exact and far-reaching and altogether fair. I think it well to say these things at this point so as to help lead my readers to free their minds as far as possible from all prepossession against my testimony concerning the extraordinary facts I record in the following pages.

## The Testing of "Independent Voices"
## First Sitting, Monday May 29, 1905

Mrs. French and her escort, Mrs. Blank, arrived in New York on Monday evening, May 29, 1905, at about 6 o'clock p.m. At 7:30 they were escorted from the boarding-house by Miss Z. to the apartment which I had selected for the seances. The room off the parlor had been fitted up by Mr. Z. as a seance room, simply by arranging the one window to the room so as to exclude the outside light. The size of this room is about twelve feet square. We were seated in a semicircle around a small table in the order indicated on the diagram.

It was decided that our series of meetings should be held in the evenings, beginning promptly at 7:30 o'clock and that the sittings were to be strictly private.

I dislike the condition of absolute darkness in the production of psychic phenomena, as it immensely increases the difficulty of making absolute tests. I asked a "control" at one of our earlier meetings the reason why they could not produce their phenomena without darkness. The answer was:

**"The nature of the phenomena and the physical condition of the medium make any other course impossible. Were the medium in good health we might carefully experiment, but now we can not. To try would be fatal to the medium. We**

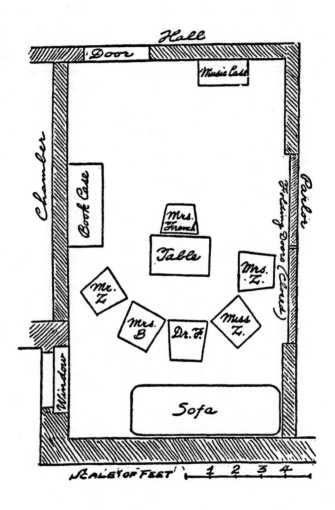

The room where the "independent voice" experiments were made.

**understand your wishes and the reason for them, but you must believe us when we tell you that you ask what is impossible."**

This, of course, proved nothing, nor did it help us over the difficulty; yet, of course, it is true that light has a certain dynamic power. Every second, millions of light waves strike blows where they are admitted, and there are processes in nature from which it must be excluded. As has often been said, the prenatal child matures in absolute darkness, and light must be excluded from the photographic plate.

Prof. Charles Richet, in his address published in the January (1905) number of the Annals of Psychic Science, says: "Moreover, there is nothing unreasonable in the admission that light may exercise an inhibitory effect upon certain kinds of phenomena. It is often alleged: 'Darkness is required by spirits only because all kinds of trickery are possible in the dark,' but this conclusion is absurd." Richet further holds that if careful precautions are taken "it is rather foolish to consider worthless all experiments made in the dark."

Absolute darkness calls for special care, but it is not a sufficient reason to refuse to investigate.

This evening before we entered the cabinet-room we observed that Mrs. French was exceedingly deaf, so deaf in fact, that it was difficult to make her hear in conversation except the voice was considerably raised, and this even when we were removed from her not more than three feet. This fact became an important one in our testings, and hence afterward I sought for fullest confirmation of her deafness by correspondence with several physicians who have attended her—including Dr. Alvin A. Hubbell, of Buffalo, a specialist in eye and ear diseases recognized as an authority of much weight; especially is his testimony here of special importance as he is not a Spiritualist. The testimony of these various doctors leaves no doubt in my mind as to the genuineness of this serious defect in the hearing of Mrs. French. (I have added in the Appendix at the end of this book some of the physicians sworn testimonies to Mrs. French's deafness. —Ed.)

We waited in darkness about twenty minutes, having joined hands. It will be observed by the diagram that Mrs. Blank was placed between Mr. Z. and myself, he having hold of her left hand, and I having hold of her right hand; and Miss Z. was next to me and Mrs. Z. next to her. Mrs. French sat at the table directly in front of myself, about four feet distant.

(I would like the readers to take careful note of, once again, the following points, before Dr. Funk's descriptions of what took place begins:

1. Mrs. French: 72 years old, extremely feeble and frail, a very sensitive and dangerous heart condition, almost entirely deaf.

2. Sitting for Dr. Funk with barely any time to have had to rest after the long journey from Buffalo to New York.

3. Surrounded by people—and their corresponding vibrations—whose intentions are to detect her in fraud.

4. Mrs. French is sitting right across from Dr. Funk and not moving. —Ed.)

The first voice that came was an exceedingly loud masculine voice which, we were informed by Mrs. Blank, was that of one of the controls, the Indian chief, Red Jacket—the inevitable Indian! The voice spoke consecutively about ten minutes on the work the "forces" wished to do at this series of meetings—he and those with him. They were exceedingly anxious, this voice assured us, to make us know, and make those with whom we came in contact know—not believe, but *know*—that life is continuous.

**"We live,"** he said, **"as real lives—more real on this side than we did on earth. The laws that govern life are the same here as with you. In fact, everything here is so real that many who come over—die, as you call it—do not know for a long time that they are dead. A great part of the work to be done here is to instruct the dead in the true science of progress. To the circles held by this medium we often bring dazed and earthbound spirits, so as to be able to reach their consciousness through earth surroundings. We and they are then brought to the same place and we then can better make them understand their condition, they at these seances often recognize the voices of those whom in earth-life they knew, and who are in the circle. Many of you people in the flesh think that those who die are done with time and with earth, but it is still time and it is still earth after we pass over. We have not reached the outlines of time nor of the material world. Life on both sides of the grave is part of the same plan and has the same object and is governed largely by the same laws.**

"Think not that the spirit world has not a language of its own. We have a language compared with which the earth languages are blundering. It is heart-and-mind language. You have what you call telepathy. Do any of you know what that is? When you find that out you will know somewhat about our language.

"It may be said that the spirit hears what it wishes to hear, and that it makes its own world. Each spirit is a creator. You have faculties that are now only faintly imagined by you. There is reality. The Great Spirit is reality. We can not explain these things to you. Only the most developed among us know the beginnings of these things. We blunder here as you blunder on the earth, but there is great progress. You must not believe every spirit any more than you believe every man. To some this is a dream world, or rather dream worlds, for there are as many of these worlds almost as there are individuals. But this spirit world is also subject to law. It has its environments and its developments. It has its scientific basis and limitations as you would call it. You must learn to think of this world and of the people in it as real."

The various talks of Red Jacket this evening in all must have covered one hour, bearing largely on the main thought running through the above talk. This kind of talk is not new to those who frequently attend the better class of seances. If we can believe these "spirits," death is not a barrier, but a highway, like the sea was to the Vikings. But the thoughts expressed had comparatively little interest to me, for I already believed these truths, and some of them seemed to be but an echo from my own mind and might have been gathered by any bright medium through reading my mind. What I wished to know was whether this loud voice was produced by that feeble little woman sitting at the table; or whether the voice was produced through extemporized vocal organs by a foreign intelligence—this latter alternative seemed to me extremely improbable.

The thought expressed by the other voices during this first evening was all of an exalted kind, and they were always ready to answer the questions which we asked.

Some of the voices were bright and one or two even "snappy," but the voices of Red Jacket and Dr. Hossack, another of the principle controls, were exceedingly serious, impressing one that their owners were intelligences of great earnestness.

It was quickly evident that one of two hypotheses must furnish the explanation of these phenomena. Either they were produced through conscious fraud on the part of the medium, a fraud which has been continued now for more than two-score years, or they were produced by foreign intelligences. Let it be remembered that the hand of all in the circle were joined together, except the hands of the medium, I having hold of the right hand of Mrs. Blank and Mr. Z having hold of her left hand. We frequently talked to Mrs. Blank while the voices were talking. Mrs. Blank was in this way practically eliminated from the problem. The voice of Red Jacket appeared to come from a point some four feet above the head of the medium, and about three feet to the left of her as she sat facing the members of the semicircle.

After I had fully fixed the locality in my mind, I asked one after another in the circle to locate the point in the room from which the voice came. This I did without telling my own impression. All located it at about the same spot that I did.

It must be remembered that it is not an easy thing to locate from whence a sound comes in darkness. Those who have never tried it will find it an interesting experiment. At my request, the voice of Red Jacket changed to different parts of the room. This it did *always on the side where the medium was sitting*. In a reply to a question why he could not come behind those of us who were in the circle and speak, he said: **"It is necessary for us to be near the medium, as we draw force from her"**—a possible, but an unfortunate necessity. Had the medium stood on a chair or used a long-jointed megaphone she could herself have made the voice come from the point whence it seemed to come—that is, if possessed of the power to produce the voice.

We sat in the circle about one hour and a half, and as the medium was fatigued by travel, it was suggested by one of the controls that we close the sitting for the evening. Instructions were given us by the controls to have the room on the succeeding nights the same as this night, and to occupy hereafter the same seats. This voice was introduced to us as that of Dr. Hossack, a physician who, we were told, when on earth was a professor in Columbia College, New York City and, who claims to have been the physician who attended Hamilton after the fatal duel with Burr. There seemed a trace of Mrs. French's voice in that of Dr. Hossack, but none of us could discover in the voice of Red Jacket any semblance to the exceptionally feeble voice of Mrs. French. We determined hereafter to watch carefully for this similarity, believing that in it we might get the key to the mystery. Mrs. French is a frail woman of about one hundred and seventeen pounds weight, seventy-two years of age, with a pulse that indicates quite a weak and irregular heart. Immediately after the sitting I felt her pulse, and found it sixty-eight to the minute, missing every third or fourth beat. It is not often that one hears two voices more unlike than that of Red Jacket and Mrs. French.

## Second Sitting, Tuesday, May 30, 1905:

Immediately upon the arrival of Mrs. French and Mrs. Blank, we entered the seance room, and were seated as on the first evening. It will be remembered that neither of these two women were permitted to visit the home of Mrs. Z. except at the time of the sittings.

Before the lights were turned out, we all carefully marked the exact location of Mrs. French, and also trained ourselves to locate by the sound, the distance and direction of a voice, observing how, when the head is turned in any one direction, the voice seems to proceed from a point toward the side of the room to which the head is turned. In that way a voice can be made to appear as proceeding from a point near the ceiling or a point near the floor, or to the right hand or left hand, or back of the one speaking.

When Red Jacket's voice came, he directed, upon my suggestion, that the left hand of Mrs. French, and the right hand of Mrs. Z, be joined. This made it more possible for Mrs. Z. to detect any movement of Mrs. French. It should be remembered that Mrs. Z. is not a novice in psychic investigation, and is keenly alert to the tricks of fake mediums. Both Mrs. Z. and her daughter are very skeptical as to the spirit hypothesis, and hence are keen to suspect and detect fraud.

The voice of Red Jacket appeared to be of the same *timbre* as the night before, and it seemed equally high above the medium's head, about eight feet from the floor, and toward the sliding door between the two parlors. Our various tests again confirmed our partial conviction on the night before—that Mrs. Blank had nothing whatever to do with these voices. This we proved by talking to her and having her talk to us while the voices were speaking. Our tests also eliminated the theory that Mrs. French left her seat or stood up. All of these possibilities had been thoroughly canvassed by us prior to the coming of Mrs. Blank and Mrs. French this evening.

The theory of a megaphone manipulated by one hand of the medium, and the theory of the medium being an accomplished ventriloquist remained. To test these theories, I requested the medium to talk at the same time Red Jacket talked. If this could be done, it would help us also to locate the whereabouts of the medium when her hand was not being held by Mrs. Z. We were told by one of the voices that we must recognize the possibility of failures in this simultaneous talking because of the complexity and difficulty of the phenomena: **"You do not fully realize,"** said Dr. Hossack, **"how exceedingly delicate is the organ** [medium] **we have to work with. She is very frail. Many times we have kept her in her body when even her physicians were sure that she would pass out. She is of very great importance to us as an instrument, and you must not ask us to take undue risks; and yet, on the other hand, we understand perfectly the value of the experiments that you are making, and will do everything in our power to help you make these experiments satisfactory. It is far better for her that she keep quiet while the other voices are talking and are thus drawing upon her strength. We have here a band of medical experts who are watching closely the heart and mind of the medium, and we have also with us a chemical expert and a band of what you would probably call electricians, who are adept in the manufacture and control of the vital currents. It may seem to you an easy matter that the medium should talk simultaneously with us; but I assure you it is an extraordinarily difficult and dangerous thing; and I again assure you that we have come here to do all that is possible to do to satisfy you of the genuineness and the significance of these phenomena."**

"Yes, yes," said the medium. Her "Yes, yes" seemed to be simultaneous with the voice, yet we were not all absolutely certain of this. During the remainder of the evening, a score of times the medium *seemed* to talk at the same time that did the other voices. Some of us thought Yes, others of us were slightly in doubt, believing that there was a fraction of a second between the voices. Mrs. Z., who had Mrs. French's hand, was fairly sure that the voices were simultaneous. To us all it seemed very hard to believe that any human being could have spoken in two different voices so nearly simultaneously and so often, without sometimes using the wrong voice; and also the conviction was constantly growing upon us, that the feeble, quiet, delicately refined voice of Mrs. French could not have produced the strong masculine voice of Red Jacket even though assisted by some mechanism. Another point to be tested was whether the defective hearing of Mrs. French could catch our questions asked of Red Jacket when uttered in low conversational tones. We found that Red Jacket responded to our questions and remarks, no matter how low our tones were. This is a very important factor in the problem of determining the origin of these voices.

As to Dr. Hossack's suggestion that the phenomena is difficult to produce, when we come to think of it, what reason have we to conclude that the spirit world is a simple and easy state of existence? Analogy tells us the contrary. As we progress the problems of life, of thinking, and of acting grow more and more marvelous and difficult. Water seems to us an easy substance to handle, but as we go upward to hydrogen and oxygen, and then back to atoms and electrons, and the combining of these in many ways—well, who cares for all this? We cut the Gordian knot and say "God directs." Why may it not be that there, as here, God works through others these countless marvels, and that among these others are the spirits of the generations that have gone before, and that there as here the doing of things must all be learned in natural ways, and the human faculties developed gradually by exercise, so that there as here all are degrees of perfection and imperfection? This, of course, is only a guess, and yet our unbelief in the immensities of the universe leads us into countless absurdities. Only a few centuries ago, the sun, moon, stars, were believed to be only so many lamps that rose in the east and crossed the sky of the stationary earth to the west, and thus in childlike simplicity, we settled it. Now we seem immensities upon immensities, and complications untold.

The seance lasted this evening two hours, about one hour and a half being taken in talks by some half a dozen different voices. About fifty minutes of this time was taken in a talk of a most serious sort, by Red Jacket, urging the human race to brotherhood and to labor for others, insisting that each one make his life harmonize with truth, and saying that if we did this, we would be well advanced when we entered the other world, **"for,"** he declared, **"all real growth springs out of a desire for the welfare of our fellows."**

Ventriloquism or a megaphone still seemed a possible explanation. Mrs. Z., who kept her hand during much of the evening on top of the hand of Mrs. French, declared that she could not detect the slightest tremor of her hand when the loud, voice of Red Jacket was most earnest. Nor could she detect the slightest movement that it would have seemed necessary for her body to have made in manipulating a megaphone. Of course, either of these hypothesis meant conscious fraud of a very depraved sort on the part of the medium whose personality and truthfulness impressed us more and more every time we spoke to her. She seemed an ideally refined, well-born, well-bread, and an ingenuous big-hearted woman.

332

I urged Mrs. Z. and Miss Z. to study both women very carefully during the day, by calling upon them, giving full play to the intuitive knowledge which women are said to have of womankind. Red Jacket talked very much about himself during the evening. He seemed to understand himself quite well, and it may be, after all, the Irishman wasn't far wrong when he said, "We get the best view of our lives after we are dead." This seemed to be true of Red Jacket's post-mortem of himself.

### Third Sitting, Wednesday, May 31, 1905:

We added to our circle this evening Miss H., a celebrated author. She sat between Miss Z. and myself. The position of each sitter in the circle was otherwise the same as on the two previous evenings.

When Red Jacket's voice came I told him that the theory of the megaphone or speaking-trumpet would be used by the critical public as a possible explanation, also that ventriloquism would be urged in explanation, and asked him, if he could, to give us some experiments that would exclude both of these hypotheses. His answer was, **"We will do whatever the strength of the medium will permit."** In reply to a question whether he would not tell us his experiences upon his entrance into the other world at death, and also let us know what his present work was in the spirit-world, Red Jacket for fifty-five minutes, as nearly as I could judge by noting the striking of the clock in a nearby room, spoke in his usual loud masculine voice.

My purpose in putting these questions to Red Jacket was to have him make a long speech, believing that such an effort would test greatly the physical endurance of Mrs. French, provided she produced the voice. I have had much experience in judging the carrying capacity of voices, and I have no doubt that the voice of Red Jacket, as we listened to it this evening, would easily have filled a hall with a seating capacity of two thousand people, while Mrs. French's voice, at its loudest, so far as I have heard it, would not fill a parlor twenty feet square. An address in a loud voice, lasting fifty-five minutes, is an exhausting strain upon the average strong man. Immediately after this speaking I felt Mrs. French's pulse, and found that it was as usual, weak and irregular; but not noticeably so beyond what I had found it when she first came into the room.

At the beginning of the seance Mrs. Z. was requested by Red Jacket to put her hands upon *both* of the hands of Mrs. French. This she did throughout the speaking. Under these conditions the megaphone theory became wholly an impossible one. Mrs. Z. knows well the trick of a medium covering both hands with one, so as to make believe that both hands are being accounted for. She assured us that she covered fully each hand of the medium with her hands. Frequently at this sitting Mrs. French replied in a natural voice, that certainly *seemed* at times simultaneous with Red Jacket's speaking. During the whole of the talking one of Mrs. Blank's hands was in Mr. Z.'s hand and the other was held by me. The sitting lasted one hour and forty minutes.

### Fourth Sitting, Thursday, June 1, 1905:

Red Jacket invited me to sit immediately in front of the little table at which Mrs. French is accustomed to sit, and to place my hands on her two hands. I separated her two hands about twelve inches, so that the one hand of the medium could not possibly be mistaken for two hands, a trick that I have known to have played successfully in a dark circle. I put my hands straight out from my body, so as to have the width of my body between the two hands. I again requested Mrs. French to talk much. Her face could not have been more than twenty-four inches from mine. I could hear her breathe as well as talk. Red Jacket and the other voices talked freely, and Mrs. French frequently spoke, seemingly at the same time. This test probably lasted ten minutes. It made it impossible for me to hold longer the megaphone theory, and it is difficult to see how it was possible to explain the phenomena by ventriloquism.

As nearly as it was possible for me to detect, Mrs. French breathed naturally and talked in her usual low tones, at the same instant that the explosive voice of Red Jacket spoke. Her breath came regular during the sentences of Red Jacket, whether they were long or short.

**"Sit back!"** Red Jacket suddenly thundered in an explosive voice that seemed to shake the room. I sat back. He afterward explained that the heart of the medium had begun "to thump," and that there was danger to her if the test continued longer. Just before the command, I was told I would feel the passing of a spirit over my face. I felt a cool breath of air. But this could have been produced by the medium, if she had so desired, for if you blow in the face of another at the distance of fifteen or twenty inches, the air will feel cold.

After I had resumed my seat in the circle there came a strange, laughing voice, very loud, which seemed to come from the neighborhood of the door that led into the hall, or from out in the hall, some six or eight feet distant from the medium. This loud laughing voice was a curious phenomenon, and seemed to startle greatly the medium.

The voice came at our request repeatedly, some ten times in all, each laugh averaging possibly a dozen ha-ha's, and varying from a deep basso to almost a treble. We were told by Red Jacket that this phenomenon was permitted to show the impossibility **"of the medium producing these voices through ventriloquism, as it must be manifest to all here that it is wholly beyond any conceivable compass of a female voice, and especially of so weak a voice as that of Mrs. French."** The location of the voice seemed to change from place to place at our request, sometimes it sounded as if near the floor and then up high near the ceiling, and then about six feet to the left of the medium and then to her right, and then back of her, and then again immediately in front of her. This suggested the art of ventriloquism together with the turning of the head from side to side; but the utter physical weakness of the medium, and her exceptionally feeble voice added to the other tests that we had previously made, seemed almost conclusive—if not altogether so—against this theory.

At times when the laughing voice took place, Mrs. Z., at our request, took hold of both hands of the medium, and Mr. Z. and I held both hands of Mrs. Blank, so that the use of megaphone was again wholly impossible. It is well again to remember that for Mrs. French to have produced the laugh that we heard, requires us to believe that she possesses extraordinarily well developed lungs and vocal powers, while the truth is, her whole physical build is after a most delicate, feeble feminine model. It is as easy to think of a rabbit barking like a bulldog or bellowing like a bull, as to think of one physically made up as is Mrs. French producing such a laugh.

It should be remembered that Mrs. Z. and Miss Z. and I are all seasoned investigators. I myself have been at hundreds of seances of all kinds. The reader can take it for granted that not one of our company could be stampeded or excited by the novelty or weirdness of this sort of experiences. (How any individual, no matter how scientific or dispassionate, could not be excited by the very proofs of immortality unfolding itself right in front of them is almost beyond belief and was very questionable to say the least. —Ed.)

During the evening their were female voices as well as male voices other than that of Red Jacket's. The phenomena continued until 9:30. The theory of collective hallucination it would be very difficult to apply to this series of phenomena. We did not expect the laughing voice; we had not heard that anything of the kind ever occurred at Mrs. French's sittings. On inquiry I found it had not been heard at the sittings in Buffalo or Rochester. We criticized it one to the other, talked about it, and talked to the spirit's personality, and he responded. We talked in a low voice also to the personality, and were correctly answered. Mrs. French seemed very much amused at the voice, and often laughed in her quiet way, but so loud that we could all hear her laugh, seemingly at the same time that this loud laughter occurred. A transmitted subjective impression is likely to have marks of subjectivity, while this voice had all the marks of objectivity. After listening to it on the other evenings, I have no doubt whatever as to the inapplicability of the collective hallucination theory.

The following question was asked of Dr. Hossack during the evening: Why can not every one be a medium? Why does the spirit-world pass by some of our most excellent people, and chose sometimes unworthy ones for the mediums? This was asked also to test the mental caliber of the personality who talked. The answer was: **"Can you tell me why it is that copper is better than gold to carry the telegraphic message, or why it is that one material is better than another to hold the picture on the photographic plate, or why is it that radium is to be found in pitchblende and not in silver or gold? It is, my friend, a natural law, and it is not for us to quarrel with natural laws, but to conform to them. It is only by conforming to them that we can get anything from nature."** This talk was written down from memory several days afterward and may not be verbally correct, but the thought is. In nearly all other incidents in this series I wrote out the talks the same evening.

### Fifth Sitting, Friday, June 2, 1905:

For about forty minutes no voices came. At all of these meetings Mrs. French claims she sees, somewhat over our heads, a string of lights which at first are disconnected, and, when conditions are perfected for the voices to come, the lights join. To-night she reported the lights are coming very slowly and as being very loath to connect. The weather conditions were reported unfavorable, as it was stormy, and the atmospheric pressure heavy. The voices, however, finally came. Red Jacket delivered a talk of about half an hour in length, a well-sustained and connected talk. His addresses on these occasions are all remarkably free from errors in grammar. Sometimes he will ask for the proper technical word. The following is an outline of his talk as written down the day following by Mr. Z. at my request—it is as unlike as can be to conversations I have had with Mrs. French out of the seance rooms.

**"Friends, I greet you! I wish to call your attention to some of the conditions used by this medium in making communications possible.**

**"Referring back to many moons ago, or as the Pale Face says, years ago, after my entrance into spirit-life, a number of earnest spirits, anxious to help mortals by imparting more accurate information about the conditions of life here and how life on your side affected life here, held meetings in an assembly-hall here called "The Hall of Truth." We decided to search among mortals if we could find any sensitives suitable for the special purposes that we had in view. We found but three, and one of these soon passed over to this side. Later we found that the kind of sensitives we had selected would not answer. We needed a different and higher grade. We made other examinations, testing other mediums. Finally we found the medium we have been using now for so many years.**

**"You understand the mind works through the brain. But to the mental force is added what may be called the vital force which is more closely connected with the entire nervous system. These forces produce what may be called electro-magnetism. Follow me closely. Now, we have found that there are some mortals born with a double spinal cord. This is very rarely a fact. This second spinal cord generates the force we need for our particular purpose, that is, to produce the vibrations which you call 'voices.' So delicate and important is the force produced by this second spinal cord, that a medicine man stands behind this medium all the time we use this force, and brings a pressure to bear at the end of the cord, near the base of the brain. This explains why this medium says she feels a tapping going on at the base of her brain while we are talking."**

The curious explanation of the phenomena by Red Jacket was drawn out to a considerable length, and became very technical.

In answer to a question, Dr. Hossack replied that when he was practicing medicine on earth, he read the report of a case of the finding of a double spinal cord. This was found in dissecting the body of a Scotchman in Berlin, Germany. It was then regarded by the medical authorities as a mere freak, and little attention at that time was paid to it.

Suddenly in the midst of our talk there broke in a voice with a very pronounced Irish brogue. He seemed to pass to the right and then to the left of the medium again and again, and kept up a rattle of quaint remarks for about five minutes. We were afterward told by Dr. Hossack that the object of this interruption was to get us less intense, so as to make it easier for the spirits to use the vital forces of the medium and of the members of the circle. This voice had all the quaint humor with which we associate the typical Irishman. It is quite evident, if these phenomena are what they claim to be, that national and individual characteristics persist beyond the Great Divide.

Of course, the apparent change of location of the voice could be produced by a medium, if tricky, by turning her head as already indicated. The left hand of the medium was held most of the time by the right hand of Mrs. Z. Mrs. Z. reported that the medium seemed to be wholly passive, and more than usually weak–"as weak as a child." I felt the medium's pulse, and it was very weak and very irregular.

Red Jacket's speech is often very picturesque. For example, this evening he was speaking to one in the circle who had just passed through much troubles and was discouraged. He said, **"Your boat has rocked and your oars are fallen out."** Of a public character who was known somewhat for his bitterness of speech, he said, **"He shot his words like arrows, and they wounded people. We should give health, not hurt. This is right. Say, friends, it is right."**

During the last sitting or two we have directed our attention more to the thoughts uttered by the voices, and have sought to compare them with the thoughts expressed by Mrs. French when not in the circle, striving to judge of the mental caliber of the medium and mental caliber of the individualities as revealed through these voices. There seems to be as great a difference between the mentality of the medium and the mentality of Red Jacket, Dr. Hossack, and two or three others of the individualities revealed through these strange phenomena, as there is in the voices.

It is well constantly to bear in mind that a quick, accurate ear is rare. A close observer is not a personage we meet every day. An investigator of phenomena of this kind should studiously avoid coming to any conclusions during his series of sitting, for an opinion is sure to bias his physical senses.

And let me just here whisper to the critic, we should all learn to judge leniently the opinions of others, knowing that our own are sometimes in error.

The moral quality of the talks at these seances is an element that is to be considered. Not once at the sittings this week has there been uttered a word of hate, an unclean word, or even a silly word. In fact experiences at a great majority of the seances I have attended with different mediums justify the testimony of Frederick Myers that the "spirit" talks are as a whole of an exceptionally exalted character. I find in my notebook this sentence which I jotted down from a prayer of Mrs. Pepper given at one of her meetings in Brooklyn, she supposed to be at that time in a trance: **"We thank Thee for that divine and wonderful blessing men call birth, and we thank Thee for that equally divine and still more wonderful blessing which men have misnamed death."**

With dozens of sentences of this kind come from the same individual under various circumstances it becomes increasingly difficult to believe that the soul that utters them is unclean or unspiritual.

### Sixth Sitting, Saturday, June 3, 1905:

We made many efforts at the meeting to-night to have talking by the medium at the same time the "voices" spoke. The medium seemed very weak, having had, Mrs. Blank reported, a severe attack of heart trouble during the day, which was treated, she declared, by Dr. Hossack, the spirit doctor, they having "a seance in the dark closet in the boarding-house." Mrs. Blank assured us that it is usual in these attacks of faintness and paroxysms of pain "to consult the spirit, Dr. Hossack," and his prescriptions are followed.

The sincerity of both these women, and their innate refinement and nobility of character have steadily become more and more factors in the problem that we have in hand. There has never been the slightest evidence of evasion or deceit. Whatever doubts we have of these ladies in their absence is wholly occasioned by the strangeness of the phenomena, and is dissipated in their presence, so straightforward are they, and simple, and perfectly ladylike in all their manners and talks.

Red jacket to-night gave us a talk on mediumship. Among other things, he said: **"Most mediums are mere playthings of their imagination; others, a smaller number, are the dupes of the intelligences, tricky, sometimes sportive, at other times malignant. It is a terribly dangerous mistake to think that there**

**are no evil spirits. There are great hosts of them. They come at times without formal invitation of the medium or of the circle, and control to the hurt of the members of the circle and to the hurt of the medium."**

To revert to Sir William Crooke's vibration theory of the universe: If it be true that we are living in the midst of vibrations from both sides of the grave, then it is not hard to believe that those spirits on the other side who are nearest the earth, that is those who are most earthly, would find it easier to return, and may give us false communications although the medium be altogether honest. Who then is safe? It is well to remember the words of the prophet: "The angel of the Lord encompasseth round about them that revere him, to deliver them." God Almighty is not dead, nor does He sleep. It is quite easy to believe that no mother ever so tenderly cared for her child as He for His children. But remember those words "that revere him"—this attitude of soul may make us recipients of help which otherwise could not possibly reach us.

At our request the laughing voice came again. He spoke for the first time. He said that when he died he was certain his family was glad, for they thought they could get the insurance money that was on his life, and that their grief was hypocritical. He laughed bitterly at their deceit. When he looked at himself in the coffin and saw that he looked so natural he could not believe he was dead. He felt so deeply the wrong done him by his wife and family that he did not speak, and if any spirit talked to him he just laughed. But he said that he now begins to feel that he was wrong in this, and that we must forgive, and, **"now I feel that my heart grows warm again and I now talk."** Then he broke out again into a good-natured laugh, very loud, but free from the bitterness that marked it heretofore. At our request, which we made for test purposes, he laughed again and again, and the medium laughed in a natural, low voice. Mrs. Z. had both hands of the medium in hers on the table, and reported that she could recognize distinctly that the medium was laughing at the same time that the voice laughed. At times her laughing was so loud we could all hear it. The contrast between the two voices was very great—the one loud, vibrant, and even coarsely masculine, so loud that it could have been heard a hundred feet distant; the other feeble, ladylike, that could be heard by us only by close attention, and then not at distance of more than a few feet. Suddenly an explosive laugh, unusually loud, came seemingly immediately from behind the medium. She jumped and cried aloud—we were all startled. The medium faintly called for water. I found that her pulse was beating very feebly, and exceedingly irregular. It seemed for a while that we might have a corpse on our hands and our medium go to the beyond. If this was all acted, it was supreme acting and wholly inconsistent with the reputation of Mrs. French and seemed vastly beyond her physical strength.

After awhile the seance continued. Dr. Hossack's voice assured us that the test was given to show how impossible was the assumption that the medium could produce the voice. And again he assured us that the experiment was extremely dangerous to the medium, and asked that this suffice, because of the medium's condition of extreme weakness, telling us that anxious as they are to satisfy us and satisfy the scientists, they must not risk further injury to the medium, and that as to this danger we must trust their superior experience and judgment.

Mrs. Z. again assured us that in all these laughter seances, when she held the medium's two hands, she did not feel the slightest vibration from the great lung effort required to produce these vocal explosive noises, but that she could feel the vibrations when Mrs. French either spoke or laughed naturally as she frequently did.

It was decided to give the medium perfect rest on Sunday, and hence no sittings were held until the following Monday.

## Seventh Sitting, Monday, June 5, 1905

Before the arrival of the medium and her escort we reviewed our past week's work.

1. Confederates outside the circle.

2. Confederates from inside the circle.

3. Collective hallucination without hypnotic suggestion.

4. General hallucination through hypnotic suggestion.

5. Intentional fraud on part of medium through use of megaphone.

6. False voices through use of various mouth devices.

7. Ventriloquism.

8. Unintentional fraud by the medium through trance as by alternating personalities.

9. Outside intelligences making use of the vocal organs of the medium without the medium being conscious of the fact, or through vocal organs extemporized by the spirits.

The following seems to be a reasonable summing up:

1. Confederates from the outside during this entire series of sittings are absolutely excluded by the conditions.

2. The only possible confederate from the *inside* is Mrs. Blank. Against this theory are:

   a. Mrs. Blank's well-known character.

   b. The fact that she always sits wedged in between Mr. Z and myself, our hands being joined.

   c. Conversation is carried on with her frequently while the voices are speaking.

3.,4. Any one after reading the descriptions given of conditions, and of what has taken place during the past week and who yet can believe the theory of collective hallucination or hypnotism of the entire circle, I am quite sure would be capable of believing anything, and given the proper mental twist toward Spiritualism he would, quite likely, become the most credulous of Spiritualists. The belief or disbelief of persons of this class does not rest on reason or fact, but on preconceived ideas.

5. All in the circle are sure that the megaphone theory has been absolutely excluded by the tests already made.

6.,7. The possibility of the medium either through the trick of ventriloquism or by the use of mouth devices producing the various voices we determined further to test.

8. The possibility of the medium, in trance, speaking in these different voices, and this without intentional fraud, we thought needed further testing.

As to this last theory including that of secondary personalities, the rapidity with which these changes take place and the naturalness of the medium at all times seems to exclude this hypothesis, and yet it deserves further investigation. After many of the sittings I talk with the medium about what has taken place, and she remembers all perfectly, commenting intelligently upon the incidents. Also during the sittings, Mrs. French often comments on what has been said and done, in a perfectly natural way, the same as the rest of us. Frequently I and other members of the circle ask her questions, and her answers are wholly natural. The reader must bear in mind that she is hard of hearing and each evening, frequently, we have occasion to talk to the outside intelligences, and often we do not raise our voices for them to hear us, but talk in our natural tones of voice, and sometimes purposely in lower tones, and are always understood by the intelligences. If we desire Mrs. French to know what we have asked, we are compelled to repeat in much louder tones of voice.

As to intentional fraud of any kind we must bear in mind that there is no money motive for fraud. The medium was paid nothing for her trip to New York on this occasion. If there is deception on her part, there can be no motive for it except that of the gratification of vanity or a sense of power which is effective in many people. Otherwise the motive must be pure cussedness. But a morbid vanity is often a very strong motive in leading people to commit fraud along the mediumistic line, and should not be ignored. All of the appearances are against this theory, but still it should be borne in mind, for human nature is at times exceedingly untrustworthy, hence tests for supernormal powers should be insisted upon along the lines that involve something more than the good faith of the medium.

I asked Red Jacket this evening how he could account for the unfavorable opinion of the friend I sent to Buffalo to investigate this medium, he believing fraud a likely explanation.

**"What is it,"** said Red Jacket, **"that your friend says took place?"**

"He says at one of these sittings he had with Mrs. French no voices came for a long time, and that when finally a voice did come it explained the delay by saying that the band were helping a doctor at a certain distant prison who was "passing out" [dying]. The next day this friend in talking with a gentleman in Buffalo told him what the voice said. This gentleman remarked that Mrs. French knew all about the case, for she had told him about it prior to that meeting. Now this friend says that this was proof of deception on the part of Mrs. French."

Red Jacket replied, **"In what way? Is this fair? Mrs. French did not say one word at that time. We spirits did not get our** knowledge from her of the sickness of the doctor. We told at that seance simply a fact. We did not give the name of the doctor because some doctors do not like it known that they are sick. Is this the reasoning of science: because Mrs. French knew of this case—saying nothing about it—that therefore she is a cheat? I told you we did not get our information from her, and if we had got if from her mind, how would that have affected her honesty? What we said was true. We do not lie. But your friend is not fair, and does a great wrong by these guesses, and guesses are surely not science.

"You say the woman, Miss H., is sick. We did not know until you told us. Sometimes we get this knowledge from the minds of those who are in the circle and sometimes from their words, sometimes from the mind of the medium, and sometimes from the spirit friends of the person who is sick. How is it right to say because we tell something the medium already knows that the medium is not honest? This kind of treatment grieves us when we are trying to do good."

"Now, Red Jacket," I said, "we do not mean to wrong you, nor the medium, but are trying to get the exact facts. My friend does not mean to wrong the medium, but there are a great many cheats in the so-called medium business, and he was trying to get evidence that would shut out all possibility of fraud, even if the medium should desire to commit fraud. The evidence that is to convince the world must be of a nature that will not depend upon the honesty of the medium. You know what I mean."

"Yes, I think I do, and we are trying to give you such evidence, and we tried to give such evidence to your friend, but he did not help us. He was hard to us and to the medium in his thought. The influences that came from him were not helpful. He had no intention to hinder, but he did. Some people give out help, but your friend did not. We will see what we can do for you."

"Would you tell us whether, in speaking, you make any use of the organs of the medium, or whether you organize your own vocal organs?"

Red Jacket: "We make our own vocal organs. How is it possible for her organs to speak as I speak? Science and common sense should make that clear. How is it possible for her organs to laugh as that laughing voice laughs? You must use your reason as you do in other matters. The medium has come a great distance and she gets nothing for it; but she comes to help you and we come to help you. Now, you must be fair. You

**have had hold of the medium's hands while I talk, and we talk often at the same time she talks, although this is dangerous to her. This we do to give you proof that it is not she who talks, and yet will you say the medium does it?"**

"No, Red Jacket, we do not say the medium does it. What we wish is to get proof, not to convince ourselves, who now have met the medium, that she is honest, but proof that will convince those who have never met the medium."

**"What do you ask us to do?"**

"Would it be possible for the medium to talk if she put both of her hands in one of Mrs. Z.'s hands, and then permit Mrs. Z. to put her other hand over the medium's mouth?"

**"Now, this may seem easy to you, and I do not know how to make you understand that any act of suspicion like that increases manifold the difficulty that we have of holding the medium's strength. We can try this test to-night. It would not be safe. We will see if whether we can do it tomorrow night. You don't seem to understand that the medium is exceedingly sensitive, and putting her under that kind of test implies that she is a cheat, and this necessarily excites her nerves and affects her heart; but we will do what we can."**

Curious that unbelief should hinder the manifestation of psychic powers, but can we be sure it does not? Even the great Master, Christ, insisted upon the condition, *believe*. He could not do any mighty work in Galilee, why? *Because* of the unbelief of the people. Note the words *could not*.

During this evening we had a singing voice which sang very pleasingly, and other new voices spoke.

One voice reproved the thought that the spirits are to blame if in a circle errors are made or communications do not come readily.

This seemed just. I do not find it well in a circle to dispute with the intelligences as it is apt to interfere with the results, just for what reason I am not altogether sure. Quite likely it affects the passivity of the medium. A spirit in another circle explained the imperfection in communication after this manner—

**Mediumship is not like a phonograph that Edison has so wonderfully invented, and that carries a message on it that is indelibly there, and repeats itself to you again and again. This is not so with the medium. You call up a friend on the telephone, and you ask him a question, and he speaks to you, and you say, "I can not understand a word you are saying." You finally call up "central," and then you may not be able to hear**

**any better. You do not think of blaming your friend, but you blame the medium, that is, the telephone machine and wire. Your friend is all right, but the medium is imperfect.**

## Eighth Sitting, Tuesday, June 6, 1905

The voices were numerous to-night. The laughing voice again came at our request, and gave us much evidence to prove that it was independent of the medium. This lasted perhaps fifteen minutes. It was a natural human laugh, but the laugh of a physically powerful man. The laughing voice always arouses the risibilities of the medium, and she laughed at it heartily, so that it afforded us a constant opportunity of contrasting the *timbre* of the two voices. It is as hard to think that the weak delicate voice organs of the medium could produce that laugh as to believe that a lark could imitate the bellowing of a bull. If we heard the barking of a dog in a room in which we were convinced that there was no other living thing than a canary bird, it might puzzle us to account for the phenomenon; but we would not hesitate to say that the canary's vocal organs did not produce that sound.

There was evidently a supreme effort of the intelligences in control to convince us that the medium's vocal organs did not produce these independent voices. But if not the medium's, whose vocal organs did produce these sounds loud enough to fill a large hall? I thought of every possible explanation. The only other persons present were Mr. and Mrs. and Miss Z. and Mrs. Blank, myself, and the medium. As I have already repeated several times, Mrs. Blank was always wedged in between Mr. Z. and myself, and all in the circled had hands joined, and Mrs. Blank was laughing and talking with the rest of us. Then, she is a woman whose history is well known, and she is deeply interested in investigating theses phenomena, as deeply interested as are the rest of us. Had the phenomena taken place in the medium's home or in the house of any friend of hers or of a professed and easily fooled Spiritualist, we might conclude that in some manner a confederate had slipped in, but here a confederate was simply impossible—utterly, absolutely impossible. The performance under the circumstances was a very puzzling demonstration.

Against accepting the spirit hypothesis, spring up to the mind a score of difficulties. Of course, that threadbare one, why should spirits be engaged in a work of this kind? Why not help us to solve some great practical social problem, as a government problem, a great invention? The same old stone wall against which many of us have often before butted our heads. It is evident, if these are spirits, their ways are not our ways. Possibly it is true, as Professor James of Harvard says, they may be under some tremendous inhibitions. At any rate, we do not know enough to dogmatize for or against the spirit hypothesis. Let us keep gathering facts and keep our heads level and our feet within a reasonable distance of the earth, and largely let the research be carried on by experienced investigators.

In answer to questions, the voices talked much about the dwellings, occupations, etc., in the spirit-world, and then told how to live "in the life that now is" in order that our progress in the beyond may be rapid. The burden of the talk was that we should avoid selfishness in its many forms on earth, that we should live lives of self-denial and of service. These talks were of an ennobling character and the philosophy behind them all indicated clear logical thinking of no mean order.

### Ninth Sitting, Wednesday, June 7, 1905

This evening Mrs. Z. asked the control whether her father was present. **"No,"** was the reply, **"we will send a message for him if you so desire."**

"Yes, do."

"How can you send a message to a distant spirit?"

**"Do you think that you in your world can send messages to a distant one, and we can not? Believe me, the spirit-world is far ahead of your world in the arts and sciences and in all manner of conveniences. Why, my friends, yours is the shadow, and this is the real world."**

Mrs. Z. said she felt a hand on her head. She asked if any on in the circle had touched her. The medium put both of her hands on Mrs. Z's hands. Red Jacket said, **"That was your father who touched you."** Mrs. Z. said, "Father, are you here?" A voice different from any we had yet heard replied, **"Yes, my child, I am so glad to have you hear me and talk to you and know that I talk once more. We know all you think and feel and do, and are helping you every way we can."** Then the voice indicated certain help to be given to a sick relative at a distance. There are many curious elements in this psychic problem, and that of receiving help from the dead is not the least curious.

I listened attentively to the voice, that claimed to be Mrs. Z.'s father, to see if I could detect any resemblance to the medium's voice, especially as this voice was mild and was within the capacity of her vocal organs and her physical strength. If the medium had so desired she, it is reasonable to believe, under the circumstances, could have produced this voice had she sufficient cunning and deceit, and the much practice necessary.

I, this evening, urged upon the control what I call the water-test, that is, that the medium should hold a measured quantity of liquid in her mouth, and then have the spirit talking to continue. The medium was to take from a measuring-glass which I brought with me two tablespoonfuls of water, colored by a coloring-matter known only to myself, and her hands were to be held and we were to note whether any independent talking took place. If such talking would take place, then a light was to be struck and the water emptied from the medium's mouth into the measuring-glass. This, of course, if carefully done, would be strong proof of the presence of outside intelligences.

We were told that, unfortunately, the medium during the day had had a bad turn with her heart, suffering very much, so that the controls reported to us that it would not be safe to make the test, but that they would be glad to do it at some time later if the medium would rally sufficiently to make sure it wise to take the risk.

I assured Red Jacket that I was very anxious to make the test. To help allay any fear that might be in the mind of the medium I said: "As to the coloring-matter which I have here, I will drink some water thus colored before the medium takes it, so that she may know that it is safe. I will tell her immediately before the test what is in the water, and I will see that she takes only two tablespoonfuls. Now, if this can be done with both hands of the medium held, and it be made known to scientists, it can not but be regarded as a test having evidential value."

**"We will do it if we can,"** replied Red Jacket, **"but not to-night—we dare not try it on account of the medium's condition. Even this talk of a test makes her heart beat irregularly. We must talk of something else."** I was sorry we had not carried on the conversation in a low tone of voice-lower than the medium's ability to hear.

The after-talk was mainly on the mission-work of spirits in helping, as the control claimed, feebly developed souls that come over to the spirit side of life.

There was the usual variety of voices. The medium talked considerably in her natural voice—as before, seemingly at the same time the other voices were speaking.

## Tenth Sitting, Thursday, June 8, 1905

The medium was said to be sick and conditions unfavorable.

### Eleventh Sitting, Friday, June 9, 1905

Red Jacket spoke eloquently of the wrongs of the Redman, but claiming that notwithstanding these wrongs, a powerful band of his people were seeking to do the Palefaces in this country only good. **"We know,"** he said, **"that no other work is worthwhile either to your world or in the spirit-world—nothing but good to others. This is the only way spirits can grow from one state to a higher."** Red Jacket greatly deplored the terrible war raging between Russia and Japan, as it sent over to the spirit-world so many who were violently forced out of life and hence immature as spirits. He was asked if he had ever seen Washington in spirit-life. **"Oh, yes,"** he replied, **"many times. I have often been in his home here. He has a beautiful dwelling, and he is a lofty spirit, doing a great work in teaching."**

Red Jacket abruptly asked me, **"What is imagination?"** After my answer, he continued, **"Much of what you call imagination is the result of spirit influence, good or evil. A large proportion of your thoughts and impressions come from above."** I urged again that we have tests of two voices speaking at the same time. This was done apparently in a number of cases, but only briefly and not absolutely satisfactorily. Again Red Jacket protested against these tests, insisting that such tests compelled "cross-currents" in the medium. He gave an exhibition of the power of his voice in contrast with that of the medium, by suddenly speaking unusually loud. I have seldom heard a more powerful male voice than this exhibition revealed. As quickly as the light was turned up I felt Mrs. French's pulse. It marked forty-eight and was extremely irregular.

### Twelfth Sitting, Saturday, June 10, 1905

The medium was weak, seemingly exhausted. Mr. M. and his wife were guests this evening—invited by myself. They sat between Miss Z. and Mrs. Z.; the rest of us sat as on previous evenings.

The voices were of a considerable variety.

This evening we gave the water-test, but nothing satisfactory resulted. The controls suggested that when the medium grew strong another effort would be made. They assured us they fully understood the importance of the test for evidential purposes.

This concluded this remarkable series of sittings in New York.

### A Supplemental Sitting at Rochester

Some weeks after Mrs. French and Mrs. Blank returned from New York to their home in Rochester, I arranged for a seance in

Rochester. My object was, if possible, to try again the water-test. This arrangement was made through a prominent lawyer in that city, a man well known, but not a Spiritualist. This friend is deeply interested in the investigation of these mysterious phenomena.

We met Mrs. French at a private house of my friend's selecting. I required Mrs. Blank, who was to be present, to coach Mrs. French in holding two tablespoonfuls of water in her mouth and breathing at the same time through her nostrils. We hoped in this way to allay her nervous excitement which in our previous tests in New York was said to have been largely the cause of the fluttering of her heart during the trial. The conditions were wholly under my control the same as they were in New York.

The room was on the second floor, and the keys, after locking the two doors, I placed in my pocket. I bought the matter for coloring the water on my way to the house, and brought with me my own measuring-glass. No one but myself knew the color of the liquid I would use. I took into the seance-room the glass container containing the two tablespoonfuls of water, and then placed in the glass the coloring matter and permitted the medium to taste it, so as to relieve her mind as to any thought or any fear of it being unpleasant.

The plan to be pursued by us, I outlined as follows:

A candlestick with a candle in it was placed on a table at the side of one of the members of the circle, and when the control gave the word, that gentleman, who is a dentist in Rochester, was to light the candle; then I was to give to the medium the liquid in the presence of all the members of the circle. Holding the glass in my hands, the medium was to take all the liquid in her mouth; I was to place the empty glass on the floor between my feet; the light was then to be extinguished, and immediately thereafter Red Jacket, if possible, was to speak in his natural voice, and then the candle was to be relit, and the colored water was to be ejected from the mouth of the medium into the measuring glass which I was to hold, and we were all to see whether the same amount of liquid had been emptied from the medium's mouth into the glass as was in it at the beginning of the seance, and whether it was of the same color.

The four persons—besides my friend, Mrs. Blank, Mrs. French and myself—who made up the circle were all intimately known to my friend.

The plan of procedure as described above was carried out to the letter, and Red Jacket spoke *within a minute after the liquid had been taken into the medium's mouth and the light extinguished.* It should be remembered that I held the glass to her mouth before the light was extinguished, and after the voice came the candle was relit and the medium emptied the liquid from her mouth into the measuring-glass which I held in my hand. The liquid emptied into the glass I found to be of the exact amount that I gave her, and was in the judgment of us all the same color.

This test was a perfect one with only a single *drawback* which did not occur to me, I am sorry to say, until after I left the house. A very sly, tricky person might have had an empty bottle or glass concealed about her person and, as soon as the light was extinguished, emptied the liquid into this glass and then, after the speaking and before the light was relit, put the liquid back into her mouth. Had one of our number held both of the medium's hands while the room was in darkness, the test would have been complete in every part as far as I can see. This concealed-glass theory is an exceedingly unlikely one under all of the conditions. But it must be regarded as a *possible* one, and should be guarded against in any future tests. At some future sitting I will try to guard against this unlikely, but possible hypothesis.

## Affidavit of A.W. Moore, Secretary of the Rochester Art Club

"I have attended the sittings with Mrs. French of this city from time to time during the past twenty years. I am positively convinced of the genuineness of the manifestations of spirit voices which occur through her mediumship.

"I have, during years, tried, by every device that human ingenuity could suggest, to discover fraud on the part of Mrs. French, but without avail.

"I have known Mrs. French, during some of her seances, when I happened to sit next to her, to place her mouth on the back of my hand and keep it there while Red Jacket, her principal control was speaking.

"And I have many times heard Mrs. French conversing while Red Jacket's or some other control's voices, have been addressing the circle."

A.W. Moore
Sworn to, before me, this 19th day of April 1906
Mary Jeanette Ballantyne
Notary Public

## The Return of Dr. Isaac K. Funk

Dr. Isaac J. Funk, a man of much learning, spent forty years in psychic research. (He was also the director and principal proprietor of the publishing house of Funk and Wagnalls, New York and London. —Ed.) He published the result of his investigation and many of his conclusions, but he always lived in awe of the criticism of science. I spent many hours with Dr. Funk going over the details of my own work, and I discussed with him many of the problems with which we had to deal. He was much interested in the investigation that I was making with Mrs. French, and for that reason I arranged for her to go to New York where she spent eleven days with him and his associates. There, under conditions that he desired, she demonstrated the work she was doing with me. The result he published in his "Psychic Riddle." He was always anxious for proof that the voices which he heard were independent, and he wanted evidence of the identity of those with whom I had speech. These points he regarded as important to prove the continuity of life, and in his work he was unable to satisfy himself concerning them. His method was to attempt to prove a fact by the process of elimination, that is, to prove truths by demonstrating their opposite. He, like all other scientific men, attempted to rear a structure by tearing the structure down. This process has impeded the progress of nearly all psychic investigators, and I often said to him that one should seek what he wanted to find with open and receptive mind, always having in his thoughts that conditions cannot be changed to satisfy any one's particular notion; that we must accept conditions as we find them and make them better, to enable us to gain the end desired. In all of Dr. Funk's published works he left a loophole in his conclusions, that he might avoid criticism should he be found in error.

Some time ago the doctor left his physical body, and one night soon after, during one of the last sessions I had with Mrs. French, a man's voice spoke my name. The tone was familiar, but I could not associate the voice with any one whom I had known in the earth-life, although I knew a spirit was speaking.

I replied, "Your voice is familiar, but I do not recognize it."

He replied, **"I am Dr. Isaac Funk. I have been out of the body but a short time and being interested in your work, I have been permitted to come."**

I then said: "You may be Dr. Funk, as you claim, but we cannot permit you to consume our time unless you establish your identity. This is one of the rules that we adopted sometime since, for the reason that, knowing the person, we can form some judgment as to the value of what he may say. If you are Dr. Funk and desire to continue this conversation, you must establish that fact."

He quickly responded: **"You are entirely right about that; what you ask is fair. I ought to be able to establish my identity."**

I said: "Certainly, if you are Dr. Funk you can give us some proof of your identity. During your earth life you always made a great point of establishing identity."

Then he inquired: **"How shall it be done?"**

I answered: "That is not for me to suggest. You know how technical the body of scientific gentlemen to which you belong always is. If you are going to have a test here, we want it to be evidential. If you are going to prove your identity, you must do it without suggestion from me."

He replied, after a pause: **"Identity was what I invariably wanted satisfactorily proved. I recall a conversation I had with you in my private office at which no one was present but ourselves."**

"Yes," I suggested, "we had many such interviews."

He then said: **"I refer to one at which I asked you to make a special test at one of your meetings with Mrs. French. I asked that when someone with an independent voice was speaking, you put you hand upon the table and have Mrs. French put her mouth upon your hand; you were then to place your free hand over her head, holding it firmly, and in that situation see if you could hear the independent voice. I wanted such evidence to demonstrate that Mrs. French did not do the talking. No one knew of that conversation but ourselves, and that ought to be proof to you that I am Dr. Funk."**

I replied: "Yes, I do recall that conversation at the time and place. I now recognize your voice, and your proof is satisfactory."

I then put my hand on the table. Mrs. French, at my suggestion, put her mouth upon the back of my hand, I put my free hand over the back of her head, holding it firmly, and then I said:

"Is this what you asked me to do?"

Dr. Funk replied: "Yes."

I immediately said: "Dr. Funk, you do the talking, and we will demonstrate that your voice is independent."

Afterward there was a general talk between Dr. Funk, certain of my group of co-workers upon his side of life, and me, and some plain things were said. I told Dr. Funk that because of his prominence, and as one who had investigated this important subject for many years, he could have been a great force for good; that many people in this world of men were interested in him and his writings and were guided by his conclusions, but that he never published them in full, for which reason his readers could not reach a better conclusion than he did. I told him that he had failed at the crucial moment, and had nullified the good he could have done. I added that I regarded this as a great misfortune not only to him, but to the world at large.

He replied: **"I realize that now more than ever. It is a fact that I was afraid of the criticism of men of science. I now regret very much that I did not fully publish my conclusions. In my own mind there was no doubt."**

A spirit answered and said to him: **"You were the custodian of much knowledge. Through your investigations you learned many things. By reason of your position you could have done much good. That was your stumbling block, and before you can progress, you must become strong where you were weak."**

# PART IV

**Epilogue**

# CHAPTER 12
## Rational Deductions

*Cast aside that which is merely legendary, mythical, or traditional, and dare to walk alone, untrammeled by any bonds and unfettered by dread of any conclusion at which you may arrive. Dare to trust God, and seek for truth. Dare to think soberly, calmly, about revelation. To such a seeker shall come a knowledge of which he little dreams; a comfort which no creed of tradition can afford. He will know of God and His truth as none can know who has not trodden the path of personal investigation.*

+ Imperator, "Spirit Teachings," M.A. Oxon

There is not in the universe a single great problem that man can truthfully say he has mastered, that nothing remains to be found out concerning it. The laws that control this world are universal and in force in other spheres as well as in this; they control all solar systems and worlds in space; therefore, a complete comprehension of those laws and their application requires more than mortal life. If this were not so, perfection would be practically immediate and without process, and men would become Gods here and now. The most brilliant men who ever lived, knew but little of natural laws and of the origin and destiny of man. Until now little effort has been made to find them out.

The earth is yet so crude, our senses so dull and our vision so limited, that we fail to realize those emanations and movements of refined matter about us, or the subtle and incessant play of forces around us. From a single ray of light shoot millions of electrons and corpuscles, the basic constituents of matter, smaller than the atom of hydrogen; these, striking blow upon blow, pass by and through us in their incessant warfare with the night, but we feel them not.

We do not realize the quivering and bending of the earth's crust under our feet, caused by changes of temperature or the pressure of atmospheric waves, nor do we hear the fermentations and oxidations of the soil in the changing seasons. We do not even yet know the exact nature of that ether which a recent investigator considers omnipresent and omnipotent. We see the action of gravitation, but we know nothing of the medium through which it operates. We hear the wind soughing among the trees; but we do not hear the roar of sap up trunk and branch, the bursting of the buds as they bombard the air, or the speech of growing trees and flowers and grass among themselves; yet life, where found, has language.

The vibrations from out the abyss of space would reach our ears if they had more and higher octaves, or if our capacity for catching sound were immeasurably intensified; we do not hear the clang of the planets as they ring down through their orbits, the explosive detonations of the sun, the wild dance and chant of the Nebulae, the comets' note of warning, or the rush of wandering matter of which worlds are made, which must send out impulses and tremblings through the ether to this planet of ours. We are at all times in a great sea of intensely active forces and potentialities governed by a law of which we have little conception.

About us, but invisible to most, a nation, or rather many nations, of spirit-people, "live and move and have their being," more industrious, more active, more intellectual, and more energetic, than we; so intense is their vibration that we do not ordinarily feel their touch, hear their voices, or see their forms; but conditions can be made, and have been made, whereby, not withstanding our limitations, we may have speech with them, and know at least something of how and where they live, and what they are doing.

There is so much in nature that we do not understand, is it any wonder that, having kept our eyes so close to the ground, we have not discovered this spirit world before? We have made conditions in which it became possible for us to know a little of those other people, and, even though many have not had this evidence, that does not derogate from the truth of the discovery, which must forever stand as another fact added to the sum total of human knowledge. The possibility of communication between mortals and those in the world of spirits, has been proven beyond doubt; and it now remains for men of genius to discover new methods, and to bring into this new field of research, the same intelligent action that is applied to the lower sciences, thereby increasing our knowledge of the spirit as they have of the material world.

Those who, through ignorance or prejudice, decry a new discovery, and so prevent fair consideration, are enemies of civilization. The time has come for man to be free and to think alone. Neither the teachings of the so-called dead, nor the conclusions of the living, can change facts or nullify a single natural law. Truth has neither youth nor age; it is, and ever has been, a brother to reason; it does not need the assistance of fame or science; it has never been in the keeping of any particular class of men; it is the heritage of all who live.

## Looking Into the Future

The idea of immortality, like the sea, has ebbed and flowed in the human heart, beating with endless waves, since time began. All hope that they may reach the shore, but the words hope and faith concede that the fact is unknown. Uncertainty and ignorance breed fear. If one must rest his salvation on belief alone, let it be the gospel of help; a kind act is better than a theory.

This life is designed to fit us for a greater work. I do not criticize Nature, or the Master Intelligence that planned our progression. I have not arrived at the state of mind where I feel competent to criticize any natural law. All others are conceded for our good. Why not the last? And if that be true, why weep and shed bitter tears, when in this change we advance to another and higher existence?

The microscope discovered a new world, the telescope millions more. Everywhere has been found infinite life. In all explorations there has been found nothing independent of, or superior to, Nature, and in that presence I find God.

Common notions about death are all wrong. Nothing ever dies. None who have gone ever want to come back. Must not that life be most engaging and fair?'When a good man goes, his soul is filled with light, for his good deeds shine like stars. A noble life enriches itself and all the world. But all lives are not lived worthily. Think of the vast multitude, the endless procession, that hourly pass, leaving no thought, no truth, as a legacy of mankind.

From the frontiers of the afterlife, from that belt or zone where spirit people live, they send us cheering messages, they speak in full-toned voice and write, as when they lived among us. And so we come to know the dead have never died.

And then again we are told, that in the next plane, the continuation of this, the basest soul will find its way and have the everlasting chance of doing right, and that the better souls, the finer men and women, pass at once to opportunity and happiness.

In these chapters I have stated facts and narrated incidents as I have come to know them from those actually living in the after life. With all the strength that I possess, with all the personality that lies behind a life of effort, I vouch for the truth of what I have written. I sought in the beginning to bring to the understanding propositions of vital importance, though practically new to every thinking mind. I restate them as follows:

1. Here and now, within our physical and visible bodies, is an invisible, living, active, inner body, composed and made up of substance or material which we term ether; it is this body that is permanent, holding form, feature and expression, while the outer flesh covering with which it is clothed, changes from hour to hour; death or dissolution is but the final separation of the inner body, which is invisible before as well as after, from the physical body. The spirit body passes into the next etheric plane of existence, vibrating in harmony with all that is there, where all is just as tangible and material to them as this plane is to us who are still in the physical. This change is Nature's process for advancing our plane of activity, and is not to be feared any more than birth.

2. The next fact that I would bring to human consciousness is the location of this after life, where spirit people live. No subject is so little known and so vital to our understanding. Let me restate this condition as follows:

Around and about the earth are belts or zones of exceedingly fine matter, a substance called ether, varying in character or density, very similar to those belts or zones that the telescope has discovered about the planets Jupiter and Saturn. They are all just as much substance as the earth itself, the outer belts or zones being higher in vibration and lighter than those that touch and really blend with the earth itself. In those zones, from the substance that composes them, all structures and things are builded and formed naturally, as here. They have fields and meadowland, rugged mountains and deep forests, homes, buildings, books, paintings, music, sculpture and institutions of learning. What we have are imperfect imitations of what exists, and first existed, there.

Too long we have held the thought that the universe was specially created for us. The infinite mind which formed and fashioned this planet, who fixed its pathways and made the definite law through which mankind should obtain his development, had the wisdom, power and intelligence to create and provide conditions and a place in nature for man to finish what was here begun. Because we have not heretofore discovered and located the boundaries of the next life, should not lead us to the conclusion that such place or condition has not existed from the beginning. Men did not know of the continent of America until 1492, but it had been here millions of years before. We have not had actual knowledge of the after life until of late, but it too has existed for all time.

If this work serves the purpose for which it was designed, it will bring to the consciousness of those who reason, the two propositions, if nothing more.

In the last analysis, there comes to each the question of where, at the journey's end, he will find himself. Many never permit themselves to think about it, hoping, possibly, by so doing, that they may escape something, ignoring the fact that earth life is designed to fit us for that most important event, and that each is accountable for the opportunities that have been his.

This is a matter of scientific fact. Faith will not take the place of acts, belief will not help, confession will not change conditions that a lifetime has made, for it will take as long to change what we have created for ourselves as it did to build.

Dissolution will not add to or subtract from the conditions we have made. If we have been criminal or debased, the great law of attraction will draw us with those of similar character, separate and apart from others. If we have lived immoral lives, we shall find ourselves herded among those of like kind. If we have been idle and have not improved our minds, we shall find ourselves among the indolent. If we have been selfish, then the dark, with only selfish companions, *for the only light one carries radiates from his own etheric body.* If we have lived cleanly and fairly, been charitable and helpful to those less fortunate than we, and have done right according to our understanding, our souls become spiritualized; they will radiate light, by which we may see the glories of the after life as we enter into the fullness thereof. Nature metes out exact justice to everyone. We inherit what we have created, and nothing more.

I see good in every act of kindness, in all the words of tenderness that fall from human lips, and to me the sum of all the good in all the world is God.

# CHAPTER 13
## Emeline Sophia French

*There shall be a mourning*
*When I shall be removed,*
*And men shall be on with their tasks.*
*The same sun shall lick the paves,*
*And the same shadows fill them.*
*The very winds which now*
*Encircle me, shall dance the earth—*
*And I shall be removed.*

*The hand which is the tool of love*
*Shall be still, and my tongue*
*No longer left to sing.*
*There shall be a morning,*
*When I shall be removed,*
*When men shall behold me singing forth*
*From the script which idly blows apart,*
*Or is turned by a listless finger.*
*And they shall hark—and I shall smile*
*In understanding of God's mercy.*

"When the Door Closes" by Patience Worth

On June 22, 1912, at her home in Rochester, New York, Emily S. French, the most perfect psychic of modern times, left this world of ours. She had passed on life's highway the stone that marked four score and more, and weary with the burden of good deeds and many years, she crossed the golden bridge from life to life.

On that June day as I stood where all that was mortal of my friend was being put away, memory flashed back to a previous time. I saw the open grave of my mother, I felt again the biting winds, and the chill of another death, —a sensation born of ignorance, —and I recalled my early resolution to solve the problem of dissolution. Again I stood apart, about me hills and valleys crowned and carpeted with green, winding roads, lakes and streams, trees and shrubs and flowers, and when the casket was lowered, the sun's rays, rich and warm, fell upon it, and birds sang merrily in the trees. With joy in our hearts, we among the many who came to bid Mrs. French God—speed, turned homeward, for this good woman—one among millions—had gone to the next life with absolute knowledge of what conditions were to come. She knew that death was not the end, but the open door.

"Glad," one asks, "that she was gone?" Yes, for it is the most glorious privilege possessed by mankind, after a long and eventful career, when the shadows lengthen, to pass to more intense and comprehensive life.

Mrs. French was born possessed, of what Crookes has termed, "Psychic Force"; from infancy she had unusual abilities. She could not remember a time when she was unable to see people and hear voices which were neither seen nor heard by others; for this reason she was in childhood thought peculiar. There came a period in her young womanhood when, with a pencil in each hand, she could write on different subjects simultaneously, easily conversing at the same time. Automatic writing was not then known or understood, and the suggestion that the beyond was inhabited by people, just as this world is, had not dawned upon our mentality. Afterward there came in her presence under certain conditions, independent voices, that is, a way was found by which the vocal organs of the dead, so-called, could be and were clothed, so that they spoke audibly in our atmosphere, and in this manner came the discovery of another plane inhabited by all the countless dead, where individuality is actually continued—a world as real and tangible as this.

It was my good fortune to meet Mrs. French early, and the compact then formed was faithfully kept to the end. She was as anxious as I was to understand the play of forces in her presence, and without payment she freely gave her time and strength that through her instrumentality good might come, not only to those living here but also to those in the great beyond. The idea of accepting money for such services was abhorrent to her, and she devoted her life to the liberation of the mind, that the mental bonds of superstition might be broken, and that mankind might become better by living more intelligently.

Her work gave the world a new discovery, and her labor opened the door to the Unknown Land. Her love went out to those in sorrow—to the unfortunate, the rich, the poor, and the ignorant, and yet with her great power she was a child, sincere and frank and full of hope as Spring, and she ever borrowed sunshine of tomorrow to make the present glad. She saw into the great beyond where the modes of motion were too rapid for physical sight; she knew the needs of others, and her charities encompassed them, and as the years passed, and the results became more apparent, the censure of this little world failed to sting. Her span of earth's life was exceedingly long. For many years her physical ears failed to catch sounds; she grew refined and delicate as her life force ebbed. Some years before her dissolution she became blind, and all the beauty of the physical world was shut out, but still our wonderful work went on. Toward the end she became weary with well-doing, and met the change with confidence and courage.

Mrs. French passed into the next world gladly, for her psychic sight had already beheld the glories of her new home; she had more friends there than here, and she had often heard the voices of the husband, who gave his life that the Union might be preserved, and of her son who passed just as manhood touched the noon of life. She went not as a stranger into an unknown land, but as one familiar with the way, for just across the border, there waited with outstretched hands and words of welcome countless thousands who had been helped through her effort.

The memory of Emily S. French comes like a benediction. Over every cradle Nature bends and smiles, and at this second birth it does the same. She made me her friend by being fair, and so we worked for twenty years and more to learn how to expel the fear of death from the human heart. She grew old as we count time, feeble in body and blind; yet her courage and devotion never waned, and at the end she smiled and met the dawn of everlasting life.

She was an instrument through which a great group worked. In her presence with the necessary conditions the people in the next plane spoke, and never again can it be said, "The dead know not anything."

I cannot give out the knowledge gained through Mrs. French's instrumentality without paying this tribute to her. She was the noblest woman I have known; she was both honest and brave; she enriched herself by aiding others. She helped to stay the tears that fell from furrowed cheeks and looked with pity on ignorance and superstition. She came to know that all wretchedness and pomp lose distinction in the democracy of death and that only character survives. To her in the great beyond where she now resides I send my love. —We shall meet again.

Edward C. Randall

# CHAPTER 14

## "To That Mortal Would I Speak"

*It shall come to pass afterwards that I will pour out my spirit upon all flesh; and your sons and your daughters shall prophesy, your old men shall dream dreams, your young men shall see visions; and also upon the servants and upon the handmaids in those days I will pour out my spirit."* —Joel 2: 28-29

The gentleman who opened the discussion on the "Attitude of Science" (Chapter 9) was himself, while, in earth life, a great thinker, and has evidently made much progress a a chemist in the sphere where he now lives. He is fearless in speech, and has the courage born of knowledge. It is a privilege that I prize greatly to discuss philosophy with him, and many of his discourses have found place in this work. After speaking on the subject above mentioned, I asked permission to use what he had said. With his consent, I give, in his answer, perhaps the most remarkable message that ever came from the spirit-world:

**"In so far as you are impressed with the thought that my simple words will enable you to give to the people of earth a clear and honest statement of the facts with reference to the change from one sphere to another sphere of usefulness, everything which is in perfect accord with, and which carries out the intent of that whole, which it so perfectly controls, you are welcome to use. If anything I have said, or may say, can, in any degree, bring to the people of earth an appreciation of the future that awaits them, I am deeply grateful.**

"One, older in spirit-life, and far—oh so very far beyond me bids me say:

"'Upward and onward! Always lead the way, for climb ye must, whether ye would or nay! That omnipotent force that has fixed the destiny of all things, has so willed, and, struggle though ye do and will, to follow your self-impulse, and journey to and fro, yet shall your course lay onward and upward. In all that has been, in all there is, and in all you shall know as you journey on, that one intent is the manifest purpose. The one supreme intent ye of earth-life shall not and cannot know, and that is wise and just. But this ye may know, for your very peace and comfort: every change that shall overtake you, is but to prepare you for the next, and further knowledge is but a dream of your own fancy, that springs from the speculative intensity of your desire to know.

"'Knowing all, would ye not be that ALL? And knowing all, yet having the wisdom to make use of that knowledge, what blundering fools would ye be! Only as ye shall have wisdom to exercise just and proper care of such things as be, shall ye know the meaning of those things. The servant must ever be able to do intelligently the master's bidding, that he may be worthy of trust; and if he faileth, then must the master bid him begone, and another shall enter into his stewardship until he who hath failed shall be worthy, once more, of his master's trust; and, should he fail scores of times without number, yet shall he be set aside until he hath become his own master; and then only may he be a worthy servant to his master. And so I say unto you, that ye may learn concerning the future, that shall help you in the time that is; but beyond the simple knowledge of the fact that ye shall have answered unto you the great question of Job—asked by every son of woman from all time—'Though I die, shall I live again?' I answer unto you, saying to all in earth-life, Yea! You shall! Let that, then, suffice for I say once more to all men, through you, that no mortal can obtain knowledge of what lies beyond save through the sphere above that wherein he dwells, for all must pass from earth before reaching the spirit-sphere; those in the earth-plane must receive all knowledge of the after life from those who have progressed into spirit-life.

"'Upward and onward ye must go; and only by such a ladder, as ye shall have built, can ye mount. So it is well that ye build wisely and with care. Let the rungs be of good deeds, and ye shall mount quickly and joyously to great and splendid heights; but if ye are careless and slothful in the building, and heed not nature's laws, —and they are writ that all may read, —your advancement will be delayed by your failure, for each rotten rung must be replaced; and O ye of earth! If ye could but know the weariness of such undoing and redoing, more heed would ye give as ye rush onward through life.

"'And so I say to you this: to know that ye live again, though ye die, is all ye need to know to fit you for the future; and if ye knew too much of that future state that ye shall enter into, it would unfit you for that state in which ye now live. Take ye no heed of the morrow, but see that ye so live, each day, that the morrow may find you prepared. True honesty, like charity, begins in one's own heart. It is far better to have committed an honest error and reaped no profit, than to have great profit and to have honestly gone from your own heart.'

"This spirit gives me no name. He says it has been lost so long from his memory that he scarce heeded its going. As you respect a worthy man of much learning and honesty of heart, without regard to his name, so I reverence this other spirit; and I am indebted to you for the privilege of knowing him, as he came to me saying; 'To that mortal would I speak.'"

# Appendices

# *Appendix A*
## *Edward Caleb Randall (1860-1935)*

## Men of New York — Western Section — 1898

EDWARD C. RANDALL has impressed himself upon the community in which he lives as a man of unusual force and energy. He is a well-known lawyer, and since his admission to the bar thirteen years ago, he has figured as counsel in many important legal controversies. He is still so young that the success already achieved may fairly be regarded as the forerunner of higher achievements.

Mr. Randall was born thirty-six years ago in the town of Ripley, N.Y., and had the usual experience of a country boy seeking a liberal education. He received his preliminary training in the district school and academy of his native place, and was prepared for college under private tuition. He pursued his classical studies at Allegheny College, Meadville, Penn. In 1879 he entered the office of Morris & Lambert at Fredonia, N.Y., and commenced a course of legal study. He subsequently moved to Dunkirk, and completed his preparation for the bar in the office of Holt & Holt. After four years spent in maturing the theory and practice of the law, Mr. Randall was admitted to the bar by the Supreme Court April 3, 1883, at Rochester. He at once opened an office in Dunkirk, and met with unusual success from the start. The professional field there was limited, however, and he decided to seek a larger sphere of labor. Turning over his office and business to Eugene Cary, a local attorney, in the fall of 1884 he moved to Buffalo, in whose future growth and development he had great faith, and formed a partnership with Joseph P. Carr, under the firm name of Carr & Randall. Mr. Carr retired from the profession two years later, and Mr. Randall continued to practice alone for the next ten years. He formed a partnership with Jeremiah J. Hurley on January 1, 1896, becoming senior member of the firm of Randall & Hurley.

Mr. Randall first became prominent in Buffalo for his celebrated defense of Frank Curcio, who was tried for murder in 1887. For five years Mr. Randall was counsel for the receivers of the Tonawanda Valley & Cuba Railroad; and he acted in a similar capacity for the supply creditors of the New York, Lake Erie & Western Railroad, and participated in the reorganization of that company.

In politics Mr. Randall has been an active Republican. A graceful and earnest speaker, he has taken the stump in behalf of his party in the various campaigns of the last twelve years. He has never accepted a nomination for political office, preferring to devote his entire attention to the building up of a legal clientage. Believing in the great destiny in store for Buffalo, he has invested largely and successfully in real estate in that city. He is a loyal citizen, interested in many charities, and an earnest promoter of every measure that tends to the permanent welfare of the Queen City. He is member of the Masonic Order, and is widely known in social circles.

## Municipality of Buffalo History / 1923

EDWARD CALEB RANDALL — After two years in the practice of law in Dunkirk, New York, Mr. Randall located in the city of Buffalo, where he has attained distinction both as a lawyer and businessman. He has acquired not only high professional honor, but of late has organized and financed various industrial enterprises. As a writer and lecturer on psychic subjects, he stands in America's front rank; his books are published and sold around the Globe. He is a son of Nelson Randall, a farmer of Ripley, New York, who later engaged in private banking and became one of the influential men of his town.

Edward C. Randall was born in Ripley, New York, July 19, 1860, and there until 1870 attended the district school. He then became a pupil in a private preparatory school, taught by Alanson Wedge, later entering Allegheny College at Meadville, Pennsylvania. He did not graduate, but left to take up the study of law. He was admitted to the bar at Rochester, New York, April 3, 1883, and for the following two years followed his profession successfully in Dunkirk. In 1885, seeking a broader field, he located in Buffalo and there has continued in active practice during the last thirty-seven years. He has also acquired large business interests. He is now one of the leading men of the industrial world, and is the executive head of various companies in addition to being president of the following corporations: American Super-Power

Corporation, Super Power Syndicate, Inc., South Buffalo Terminals, Inc., and Niagara Terminal Buildings Corporation.

A lawyer of learning and ability, and a businessman of successful achievement, Mr. Randall since 1890, has also devoted a great deal of time to scientific psychic research, with the result that he has become one of the leading American authorities. In 1906 he published his first book *"Life's Progression,"* a work which has had a large sale and has been translated into foreign languages. This was followed, in 1908, by *"The Future of Man,"* and in 1914 by *"Psychic Truths,"* published in Australia. *"The Dead Have Never Died,"* now in its sixth edition, was brought out both in England and America in 1918. His latest work, *"Frontiers of the Afterlife,"* was published in 1922. In addition to his literary work, Mr. Randall has delivered many lectures in different parts of the United States. In the near future, when business affairs are arranged, he will devote his entire time to lecturing and psychic research. Mr. Randall is a member of Ellicott Club, Buffalo Chamber of Commerce, New York State Bar Association, and Erie County Bar Association.

Mr. Randall married, in Buffalo, New York, October 6, 1897, Maria Louise Howard, a granddaughter of the late General Rufus L. Howard. Mrs. and Mrs. Randall have two daughters, Virginia and Marian, both graduates of Misses Master's School at Dobbs Ferry, New York. The summer homes of the Randalls are "Crown Hill," Eden, New York, and "Ladnar Lodge," in the Canadian wilderness on Blackstone Lake.

## Buffalo News, 1923

Niagara Falls Company Rival Seeking Permit.

*Corporation headed by financiers proposes to spend three hundred millions. Plan Two Big Projects. Development at Niagara and on the St. Lawrence to give power to many cities.*

Announcement was made yesterday that Henry L. Doherty and A.B. Leach, leading New York utility magnates, had become associated with American Super Power Corporation, with headquarters in Buffalo. Simultaneously, Edward C. Randall of Buffalo, president of the corporation, made it known that this organization plans to make a strenuous fight for the right to develop hydroelectric power at Niagara Falls and on the International reach of the St. Lawrence River . . .

The American Super Power Corporation has been incorporated in New York State for the purpose of generating and transmitting hydroelectric power in the State of New York . . . Mr. Randall, the president, is well known as a power magnate and as an attorney.

The corporation plans to offer to install at the crest of the Horseshoe Falls remedial works to stay the suicide of the cataract if the federal water power commission grants them a license to divert such waters of the Niagara . . . Mr. Randall's announcement stated that the A.S.P.C. had purchased Conner's Island in the Niagara River above the falls for an intake and nearly half a mile of river frontage in the lower gorge, where it plans to erect the largest powerhouse on the continent. The whole project, including the transmission lines it is estimated, could cost $88,000,000.

## Courier, April 18, 1926

Quarantine Bars Sister, Friends at Girl's Funeral.
*Debutante Who Headed Junior League Activities, Dies of Scarlet Fever and Meningitus—Grave Service Cut Short*

Miss Virginia Randall, twenty-one year old society girl and leader in Junior League Activities, who died Monday at her home, No. 27 Tudor Place, from scarlet fever and spinal meningitis, was buried yesterday afternoon in Forest Lawn cemetery.

The Randall home bore the yellow card of quarantine, barring friends from paying their last respects. Miss Marion Randall, who was presented to society in 1922, at the same time as Virginia, was denied opportunity of seeing her sister for a last time. She remained at Hotel Touraine while funeral arrangements were being made to meet the health law requiring burial within 24 hours following death in such cases.

Edward C. Randall, her father, who is the author of books on Spiritualism, among them *"The Dead Have Never Died,"* went to the house after hearing of her death. He was permitted to see his daughter. Mrs. Randall had remained with the girl during the illness.

## Courier, April 8, 1904

Attorney Edward C. Randall Before
International Progressive Thought League

Attorney Edward C. Randall told a room full of persons at the Iroquois last night all about what becomes of them after death. Mr. Randall is a Spiritualist or psychic philosopher and, as he explained last evening, he is an authority on such things. When stray spirits in the other world don't know just where they are at they can come to Mr. Randall and find out. He has put many of them right acting as their adviser, friend and guide on things spiritual. He and Mrs. French, his medium assistant, have found thousands of spirit wandering around in a sort of spirit daze and have comforted and cheered them and told them who they were and have given them such other information as is good for spirits befuddled by their new surroundings.

It was a meeting of the International Progressive Thought League that Mr. Randall addressed. The progressive thinkers listened to Mr. Randall for an hour and a half and then asked questions for a while. They seemed much interested. The speaker said Buffalo is a great psychic center and then told about the Independent-Voice phenomena; voices of spirits speaking, apart from the medium, without her going into a trance or anything of the sort. Sir William Crookes sent Admiral Moore all the way from England to Buffalo to hear the voices. Admiral Moore heard them and went back to England.

"Dissolution at so-called death is simply separation," said Mr. Randall. "No mental change takes place. No more than we do spirit people know the mysteries of God, life and eternity.

"Many spirits need help and I have, with the aid of Mrs. French, been able to help many, very many. We bring them to a realization of what and where they are. We have awakened thousands of them and we find them able to tell things that happened before they left the body and sentences begun and broken in dissolution are finished when the spirit awakens.

"When we discover one of Nature's laws we marvel at its simplicity. There is nothing in Nature that is supernatural; there

375

is no supernormal, these are but names given to conditions not understood."

Several of the very interesting chapters of Mr. Randall's book are devoted to a description of his methods of work with a medium and the conditions under which that work is carried on, and some of the things he has seen and heard and otherwise experienced not particularly germane to the general theme of his book. "The fact," he urges, "that millions of human beings have not heard or spoken to spirit people, or seen them use the hand of a sensitive to write does not even tend to prove that I have not had such experiences or that these are not facts." These chapters at least give an idea of the experiments which have led the author to speak so positively of his experiences as facts. To him they are established beyond doubt, no matter how they may strike others.

It must always be remembered that spirits are not infallible, and Mr. Randall would not have it understood by his readers that all knowledge comes with the casting off of the physical body. "They" [spirits] he says, "do not agree on many questions any more than we do. They fail to understand many of Nature's laws as mortals do, and are continually laboring to come to a better knowledge of them, just as we do here." But as their limitations are not so great, their outlook is broader, and consequently much that is theory here is fact there.

And so the doctrine of vibration is pursued through many chapters, devoted to thought and mind, to matter, to evolution, to the atom and beyond, there is a spirit explanation of the much-talked-of subconscious mind, a consideration of the influence of spirit people on our daily thought and action through suggestion; and a chapter, which will appeal to the curious, giving a spirit's description of his spirit home. One cannot fail to be interested by it all, even though he doubts or even scoffs.

## The Times — February, 1923

Spiritualism Not Religion but a Science says Randall

*Buffalo Attorney Warns Mediums Not to Try to Make Angels of Their Ghosts*

LILY DALE, NEW YORK — "Don't try to make angels of your ghosts," Edward C. Randall, Buffalo attorney, warned the Spiritualists 46th annual assembly in Lily Dale, Sunday.

"The great mistake Spiritualist have made is thinking they have a religion when they had a science," he said. "If the phenomena of Spiritualism had been treated as a matter of fact, Spiritualism would have made greater progress during the past fifty years than it has," he asserted.

Mr. Randall went on to explain that he doesn't think much of religion anyway. At least of religion as it is generally understood.

"We are all handicapped by being born into a religious state," he continued. "I personally was not so handicapped and am thankful that I was not soaked in orthodoxy. How foolish it is to believe that a single book contains all the knowledge in the world."

*Church a Bungling Friend*

Mr. Randall said that there was a time when he thought the church was blocking the path of civilization. Now he thinks that the church is not a positive enemy but a kind of bungling friend. "It has not aided civilization as it might," he said.

"But the church has the organization and the buildings," he reminded his fellow Spiritualists, "and we are slowly but surely pushing our way into their pulpits and bringing with us the knowledge they do not possess."

Mr. Randall said that he decided orthodoxy was the bunk one Sunday in Trinity Church, Buffalo. The congregation had risen to recite the creed. In the middle of it he looked out the window, saw the flowers springing and the birds singing and suddenly cut out, murmuring to himself, "I don't believe a word of it."

It was Confucius who formulated the Golden Rule hundreds of years before Christ, Mr. Randall said. And his audience applauded with enthusiasm his statement that "Robert G. Ingersoll did the greatest service to the American people of the last century when he broke the shackles from the human brain."

Mr. Randall seemed to be in agreement on this point. "I am no longer interested in phenomena," he said. "Phenomena teaches you nothing. Any thinking mind knows that nothing can be destroyed; a handful of mud contains the life force that is indestructible, and we know that the life of the human spirit is one that must go on."

Mr. Randall told his audience that his only purpose in speaking was to convince them that there are folks out of the body just as there are folks in it. Most people do not see them for they are blind, he said. They are like blind people walking among flowers and green trees.

Where are they? Well, according to Mr. Randall's belief, there are ethereal zones around the earth which they inhabit. And these places have substance; they are worlds of people and things.

The life belongs to the spirit, which is indestructible, he said. At the moment of conception the ethereal body steps into its earthly garment. And at the time most people call death, it steps out again, very much as one steps out of one's clothes at night. The spirit is there before and after: natural birth occurs as soon as it can stand the light.

*Calls Passing Out a Privilege*

Mr. Randall rewrote Longfellow's poem, "*Crossing the Bar,*" for his audience, adding a stanza of joy for the soul in being free. "It is a privilege to pass out of this life," he said. "Let us not delay our families by regrets."

Mr. Randall was introduced as the man whom Sir. Oliver Lodge referred to as the leading investigator of scientific phenomena in America. Following the meeting, Fred W. Constantine, president of the assembly said that Mr. Randall is out of step with other Spiritualists in not wishing to consider it a religion. "The religion and philosophy are the heart of Spiritualism," Mr. Constantine said. "The only use of the phenomena is to win new members to the faith."

## The Buffalo News, April 1904

Psychic Honors for E.C. Randall

*Heads of National Psychical Research Society Experiment in Buffalo Lawyer's Discoveries in Spiritual Phenomena—Believes He has Added to the Discoveries—*

Edward C. Randall, the Buffalo lawyer who did much to stir up the Boodle investigation last fall which led to the indictment of seven aldermen, is about to issue a book on psychical researches he has made for a period covering fifteen years. So determined has he been in these investigations and successful in getting results, that he has been honored within the past week of a visit from Dr. Richard Hodgson, of Boston, and Prof. James Hyslop of the same city. These men made a series of experiments at Mr. Randall's home on West Ferry Street and are said to have gone away convinced that Mr. Randall has added considerably to the knowledge of spiritual phenomena.

Mr. Randall, when asked yesterday about his experiments, admitted that Dr. Hodgson and Prof. Hyslop had been here for several days testing the truth of his statements concerning communication he had with spirits.

"My friends are aware," said he, "that I have been paying considerable attention to Spiritualism for years. I went into it first for the purpose of exposing it as a fraud, but soon became convinced that while there were many impostors calling themselves Spiritualists, there is a true Spiritualism. I can now assert that I not only believe, but I know that we can communicate with the spirits of the dead."

*Came to Make Tests*

"The gentleman mentioned here came to make certain tests of which I can say little. Both of them say they have communicated with spirits. They will accept nothing but evidence based on absolutely scientific proof. That is what their society is for. They admit that a great many fakirs are fooling the public and the difficulty is to avoid them and get at the undoubted truth."

## Courier — 1935

Services Held for E.C. Randall

*Private Funeral Rites Conducted for Lawyer and Businessman*

Private funeral services were conducted at 2:40 o'clock this afternoon in the home for Edward Caleb Randall, lawyer, businessman and leader in psychic research who, died Wednesday after a brief illness in his residence, 27 Tudor Place. Mr. Randall would have been 75 years old July 19.

Bishop Cameron J. Davis of the Episcopal diocese of Western New York officiated at the last rites this afternoon, with burial in Forest Lawn cemetery.

Alert in civic endeavor as in the legal and scientific fields, lecturer and author, Mr. Randall was widely known for various measures he sought to promote for public welfare. Outstanding among these was his proposal some five years ago for a central heating plant, which would furnish steam heat to all downtown offices at cost.

Such a plan had already proved practicable in Lockport and in certain cities of New Zealand, Mr. Randall told the Common Council at that time. His scheme was received coolly by the city legislators, who asserted it would throw many engineers and other city employees out of work.

*Collaborated with Briton*

His fame in the field of theosophic research had extended to other countries, and he had collaborated with J. Arthur Findlay, England's foremost expert of psychic research, in his work. Recently Mr. Findlay sent him a copy of the "*Unfolding Universe*" for approval before publication.

Besides his wife, the former Maria Louise Howard, he is survived by a daughter, Mrs. D. Trenchard Graham, Buffalo.

### Looking Back /J. Arthur Findlay (1883-1964)

Noted author of psychic subjects (see Reading List), economics, finance and world religions; Justice of the Peace for the counties of Essex and Ayrshire; recipient of the Order of The British Empire; researched the phenomena of Direct-Voice for many years with the Glasgow medium John C. Sloan.

"Evidence, cumulative evidence, and still more evidence will in the end win the day. With this weapon the walls of ignorance and antagonism are being brought low, and there is no stronger tool available to complete destruction than the evidence of survival of death obtained by the Direct-Independent voice. The Direct-Voice is the highest psychical phenomena yet discovered, and it is the most convincing besides being quite the most wonderful. *All of the discoveries of man fade into insignificance when compared with this great discovery.*

"Edward C. Randall of Buffalo, with whom I stayed when I was in America has, however, *been the most fortunate of all the investigators into this great subject,* as he experimented for over twenty years with one of the most highly-developed Direct-Voice mediums, Mrs. Emily S. French . . . One has only to read his books to realize that his talks went far beyond the mental capacity of the medium, who was a woman of no great learning or education, and handicapped by being deaf and very delicate. Science, philosophy and psychics were discussed between him and those who were men of learning on the other side, a revolutionary aspect of the universe being given which is quite beyond present-day scientific knowledge . . . I know of no one who has been privileged to experience the Direct-Voice at its best, who has been able to come to any other conclusion than that the voices come from those who once lived here on earth . . . "

381

# *Appendix B*
## *Mrs. Emily S. French (1831-1912)*

### Alvin A. Hubbell, M.D.
**212 Franklin St., Buffalo, NY., an Eye and Ear Specialist:**

"Mrs. Emily S. French has been a patient of mine both for her eyes and ears since May 22, 1893. She then had and still has defective hearing in both ears caused by an affection of the internal ear (auditory nerve). There was, also, and still is, defective vision due to affection—slight atrophic changes—of the optic nerves and of the choroid coat of the eye near the optic disk. She also complained of 'nerve' symptoms, shooting pains in the lower extremities, 'cramping' of muscles of the legs, feeling of a tight band around the waist, which, taken in connection with the affections of the auditory and optic nerves, suggested to me the possibility of locomotor ataxia. She had, however, an aversion to doctors and would not consult a good neurologist . . . . While Mrs. French appears to have confidence in me professionally, my skepticism along psychic lines rules me out of her seances, although she had continued to be very friendly as a patient, whose entire confidence as a specialist I seem to have. There is no doubt that Mrs. French is and has been for years a sick woman."

### Volney A. Hoard, M.D.
**691 Main Street East, Rochester, N.Y.:**

"I am a practicing physician, duly licensed as such, and have practiced my profession in the city of Rochester for the past twenty-four years. For seventeen years past I have been the physician to Mrs. Emily S. French. I knew that she was somewhat deaf from my first acquaintance with her. Her deafness has materially increased since that time, and has been specially marked since about seven years ago, at the time of a serious illness. Her deafness at the present time is marked. One sitting three feet distant from her and facing her can not make her hear ordinary conversation, but she does hear at that distance when the voice is raised about fifty percent above the ordinary conversational tone. There is no question in my mind of her entire honesty and integrity, nor is there any question as to her decided deafness. She appears to be a woman whose weight would be 120 pounds, and about seventy-two (72) years of age. I am informed that this day she was actually weighed and that her weight is 117-3/4 pounds. I have this day measured her chest and find the measurement 20-1/2 inches expiration and 30-1/2 inches inspiration . . . . I never knew that Mrs. French claimed to have any powers as a medium and have never witnessed any of her manifestations. I am not a Spiritualist myself and have never had anything to do with its manifestations."

## William A. Sutherland
### A Prominent Lawyer in Rochester, N.Y.:

"I am willing to state that I have known Mrs. French personally for five years past, and she has visited at my house and been entertained by my wife while living; that my wife was very deaf and that I procured an acousticon for my wife, which, however, she was not able to utilize very long, and after her death I presented it to Mrs. French, who has not been very successful with its use. I can certify in the strongest manner my belief in her deafness. I am not a Spiritualist, but I am one of those who are puzzled by these psychic manifestations."

## George C. Northrop
### Merchant at Lakeville, N.Y., has made the following Affidavit:
### State of New York, County of Livingston

George C. Northrop, being duly sworn, says: "I am a dealer in coal, grain, flour, etc., at the village of Lakeville in the County of Livingston, N.Y., and have been for many years; I am now 76 years of age; I have known Mrs. Emily S. French, of Rochester N.Y., ever since she was a child; I know that when she was about ten years of age she had scarlet fever and that she has been deaf ever since I have seen her since then on an average of probably three or four times each year, conversing with her. I know that her deafness has been on the increase almost ever since her childhood; I know that somewhere in the neighborhood of six years ago she had a partial stroke of paralysis, since which time her deafness has greatly increased.

(Signed) George C. Northrop
Sworn to before me, this sixth day of July, 1905.

(Signed) Frank S. Roe
Justice of the Peace

## Officer's Hospital, Libby Prison, Richmond, Virginia
### May 22, 1866

Mrs. James H. French, it becomes my painful duty to address you this letter. Your husband, Lieu't James H. French, Col. of the 100 Mt. Vol's, was wounded in the battle of the 16th of the present month on the south side of the James River, Drury's Bluff. He was wounded in the right leg, & brought to this hospital on the 17th. The surgeon amputated his leg on the 18th, from the shock to his system, he seemed never to recover.

I was an inmate of the hospital at the time and was with him until he died on this day (May 22nd), at about 12 o'clock.

Your husband will be buried here in a lot put apart for the dead of our army. Any information . . . .

You can address me here, direct to Lieu't A.M. Stark, Q.M., 110th, prisoner of war, Libby Prison in Richmond, Va.

My address when at home . . . .

Yours Truly,

(Signed) A.M. Stark

## Rochester Local Newspaper
### July 24, 1912

Died

FRENCH – in this city. Friday, June 22, 1912. Emily S.–widow of James H. French. She is survived by one daughter, Mrs. F.B. Oberst, and four granddaughters, Mrs. W.G. Augell, of Norwalk, O., and the Misses Beeale, Adele and Ruth Oberst.

The funeral will take place from the residence of the daughter, No. 227 Tremont Street, Monday at 4 P.M. Burial private. Buffalo papers please copy.

## The Courier, Buffalo, New York
### 10 January, 1909—reporter unidentified

The other day a friend of mine sneered about the absurdity of the so-called independent voices.

I don't know very far along in spiritology, but I have gotten this far in everything; I no longer ridicule, deny or abuse anything of which I am ignorant. I give everything a good bit of rope. I neither reject nor limit a new theory. A man perspiring over the 26 letters cannot weigh a problem in philosophy. I do not say this thing must be so, nor this thing cannot be so. I can wait. With vital truths a thousand years are as a day. And as for errors they are fleet of foot and take themselves out of the way.

But if I have ever heard anything, I believe I have heard the independent voices.

Through the kindness of a friend who had experimented for many years, I was invited to see an elderly and frail woman, who is regarded by many as the most wonderful medium in the country. She dined with us and she looked very fragile and attractive in her silk gown and fine old lace. She has a little weak voice like a silver thread and she is noticeably deaf. The ordinary conversation did not reach her.

After dinner we went with her up the stairway to a large bare room. There was no furniture except a square table and half a dozen chairs. The walls were red. The one window was covered with a wooden shutter. No ray of light could come through the door. It might have been nine o'clock in the evening and the night was warm with a high wind abroad. Not a good night for a test they said. Too many high vibrations against us. We sat about the table and waited.

My host, a very near, dear friend, was noticeably anxious. He was afraid the conditions were bad and we could get nothing. Within ten minutes a ribbon of light formed over our heads. The medium said, "We shall get the voices." I sat cheerfully waiting in the darkness. I had seen little of mediums or their work, and the thing was of great interest.

Suddenly out of the far upper corner of the room a great bass voice called out, **"Good evening friends!"** I was not frightened, but the power of the voice fairly raised me from the chair. Then followed one of the most remarkable half hours I have ever experienced. On kind of voice followed another. The same voices returned and were easily recognized, as we knew the voices of friends. The owner of the bass voice had a long message to deliver and he delivered it, and to tell the truth it contained information which was and which has since been of great use. An old Methodist circuit rider came, was introduced and delivered a harangue. The polished physician of Alexander Hamilton took his turn, and his conversation and manner of speech were polished and delightful. Indians talked, more than one at a time, and several loud weird voices sang a love song, a war song, and a death song at our request. There was some talking in what they explained was the original Seneca tongue.

When I came out of the room I decided that I had had a remarkable experience. Later at the home of another friend who sat with us that first evening, we spent two evenings with the same medium. My friend, who was amazed at the performance wanted to investigate further. The same results were gotten. Many of the same voices returned and brought fresh news. Even more wonderful was the singing, the speeches, the changing of voices, the deep bass, the mellow tenor, the strident Indian voices, the women's voices, a number of them familiar to the hearers. One noble voice held us bound with words of marvelous eloquence. To one another we whispered, "Only one man ever lived who spoke English like that, Robert G. Ingersoll."

388

# *Appendix C*
## The Complete Works of Edward C. Randall

*Life's Progression: Research in Metaphysics.*
Henry B. Brown Company
Buffalo, New York 1906.

*The Future of Man*
Meta-psychic
Otto Ulbrich Company
Buffalo, New York 1908.

*Psychic Truths Told in the Afterlife.* 1914.
Commonwealth of Australia
E.W. Cole, Melbourne
Sydney: George Street
Rundle Street, Adelaide

*The Dead Have Never Died*
Alfred A. Knopf
New York, N.Y. 1917.

*Frontiers of the Afterlife*
Alfred A. Knopf
New York, N.Y. 1922.

*The Living Dead and The Direct Voice*
*Harbinger of Light*
Melbourne, Australia
August-December, 1926.
January-February, 1927.

*An Hour in the Afterlife*
Psychic Book Shop
Buffalo, New York 1931.

# *Appendix D*

## Quotable Quotes of 19th Century Researchers

*We cannot but speak the things we have seen and heard.*

—Acts 4: 20

**Sir William Crookes** (1832-1919), one of the greatest physicists of the last century; discoverer of thallium; X-Ray tube; inventor of the radiometer, after witnessing phenomena through the psychic instrumentality of the American medium Daniel Dunglas Home in 1871:

> The phenomena I am prepared to attest are so extraordinary and so directly oppose the most firmly rooted articles of scientific belief—amongst others, the ubiquity and invariable action of the force of gravitation—that, even now, on recalling the details of what I witnessed, there is an antagonism in my mind between reason, which pronounces it to be scientifically impossible, and the consciousness that my senses, both of touch and sight—and these corroborated, as they were, by the senses of all who were present—are not lying witnesses when they testify against my preconceptions.

**Dr. Charles Richet** (1850-1935), founded the study of allergic disorders; awarded the Nobel Prize for Physiology in 1913:

> The fact that intelligent forces are projected from an organism that can act mechanically, can move object and make sounds, is a phenomena as certainly established as any fact in physics.

**Sir Oliver Lodge** (1851-1940), world famous physicist; wireless telegraphy; devised a detector for electromagnetic waves. In his report to the English Society of Psychological Research, concerning the phenomena he had witnessed with the Italian medium, Eusapia Palladino, Sir Oliver Wrote:

> However the facts are to be explained, the possibility of the facts I am constrained to admit. There is no further room in my mind for doubt. Any person without invincible prejudice who had the same experience would come to the same conclusion, viz: that things hitherto held impossible do actually occur....The result of my experience is to convince me that certain phenomena usually considered abnormal belong to the order of nature, and as a corrollary from this, that these phenomena ought to be investigated and recorded by persons and societies interested in natural knowledge.

**Dr. Cesar Lombroso** (1836-1909), famous Italian Psychiatrist and Criminologist:

> I am ashamed and grieved at having opposed with so much tenacity the possibility of the so-called spiritistic facts; I say the facts because I am still opposed to the theory. But the facts exist, and I boast of being a slave to facts. I am a little pebble on the beach, as yet I am uncovered, but I feel that each tide draws me a little closer to the sea.

**Sir William Barrett** (1845-1926), famous Professor of Physics at the Royal College of Science, Dublin:

> I do not hesitate to affirm that a careful and dispassionate review of my own experiments, extending over a period of forty years, together with the investigation of the evidence of competent witnesses, compels my belief in Spiritualism, as so defined.

**Alfred Russel Wallace** (1823-1903), famous naturalist, and co-discoverer, along with Charles Darwin of the principles of evolution. From his book, *"Miracles and Modern Spiritualism,"* published in 1878:

> I prefer to rest the claims of Spiritualism on its moral uses. I would point to the thousands it has convinced of the reality of another world, to the many it has led to devote their lives to works of philanthropy, to the eloquence and the poetry it has given us, and to the grand doctrines of an ever-progressive future state which

it teaches. Those who will examine its literature will acknowledge these facts.

### From *A Defense of Modern Spiritualism*, published in 1900:

The subject, of which I have here endeavored to sketch the outlines in a few pages which may perhaps be read when larger volumes would lie unopened, is far too wide and too important for this mode of treatment to do any justice to it. I have been obliged entirely to leave out all mention of the historical proofs of similar phenomena occurring in unbroken succession from the earliest ages to the present day. I could not refer to the numbers of scientific and medical men, who have been convinced of its truth, but have not made public their belief. But I claim to have shown cause for investigation; to have proved that it is not a subject that can any longer be contemptuously sneered at as unworthy of a moment's inquiry. I feel myself so confident of the truth and objective reality of many of the facts, that I would stake the whole question on the opinion of any man of science desirous of arriving at the truth, if he would only devote two or three hours a week for a few months to the examination of the phenomena, before pronouncing an opinion; for I again repeat, not a single individual that I have heard of, has done this without becoming convinced of the reality of these phenomena. I maintain, therefore, finally—that whether we consider the vast number and the high character of its converts, the immense accumulation and the authenticity of its facts, or the noble doctrine of a future state which it has elaborated—the so-called supernatural, as developed in the phenomena of modern Spiritualism, is an experimental science, the study of which must add greatly to our knowledge of man's true nature and highest interests.

"It will be seen that the phenomena of Spiritualism is no mere 'psychological' curiosity, no mere indication of some hitherto unknown 'law of nature'; but that it is a science of vast extent, having the widest, the most important, and the most practical issues, and as such should enlist the sympathies alike of moralists, philosophers, and politicians, and all who have at heart the improvement of society and the permanent elevation of human nature. I would ask all to dwell upon the long series of facts in human history that the phenomena of Spiritualism explains, and on the noble and satisfying theory of a future life that it unfolds."

# Appendix E
## The Phenomena of Direct-Independent Voice

### Suggested Reading List

Bailey, D.E. *Thoughts From The Inner Life*. Colby & Rich, 1886

Barbanell, Maurice. *The Trumpet Shall Sound*. Rider & Co. London, 1933.

Bowers, Dr. Edwin F. *The Phenomena of the Seance Room*. Rider & Co., London, 1930.

Brace, Josephine M. *The Descending Light*. John Higgins Press, Chicago, 1922.

Bradley, Dennis H. *The Wisdom of the Gods*. 1925/*Towards the Stars*. 1928. T. Werner Laurie LTD., London.

Britt, Coleen O. *Byron-Station to Station*. Dale News, Inc. Lily Dale, New York/London, 1941.

Chapman, Clive. *The Blue Room*. Psychic Book Club LTD., London, 1927.

Crane, H. Montague. *Spirit Voices*. Alex Wildey LTD., Christchurch, New Zealand. 1931.

Drouet, Bessie Clark. *Station Astral*. G.P. Putnam's Sons., New York/London, 1932.

Duncan, Rev. V.G. *Proof.* G.P. Putnam's Sons. New York/London, 1932.

Eddy, Sherwood. *You Will Survive After Death.* Clark Publishing Company., Evanston, Ill. 1950.

Findlay J. Arthur. *On the Edge of The Etheric.* 1931/*Where Two Worlds Meet.* 1951/*The Way of Life.* 1953 (all still in publication) Psychic Press Limited/The Headquarters Pub. Co. LTD., London

Flint, Leslie. *Voices in the Dark.* The Bobbs-Merrill Company., Indianapolis/New York. 1971.

Hack, Gwendolyn Kelly. *Modern Psychic Mysteries at Millesimo Castle, Italy.* Rider & Company., London. 1929.

Jebb, Robert H. *Truth of Life After Death.* Aird & Coghill., Glasgow. 1925

Jones, V. Carlton. *And The Sound of A Voice.* Ebenezer Baylis & Son LTD., Trinity Press. London 1929.

Moore, Vice-Admiral W. Usborne. *Glimpses of The Next State.* 1911. *The Voices.* 1913. Watts & Co., London.

Perriman, A.E. *Broadcasting From Beyond.* Ebenezer Baylis & Son LTD., London 1952.

Pincock, Jenny O'Hara. *The Trails of Truth.* Austin Pub. Inc., Los Angeles, CA. 1930.

Remmers, John H. *Is Death the End?.* 1928. *The Great Reality.* 1967., Ebenezer Baylis & Son LTD. London.

Robertson, F.T. *Celestial Voices.* H.H. Greaves., London. 1945.

Sewall, Mary Wright. *Neither Dead Nor Sleeping.* John M. Watkins. London. 1921.

# *Appendix F*

## *The Farewell Address of Edward C. Randall*

### FAREWELL ADDRESS

To be delivered at my funeral by minister or layman, possibly J. Boardman Scovell if the minister refuses.

Let there be just a single prayer, one not read from any book, then the Farewell, and let there be no sorrow in the home when I depart, for I go to join "Ginnie" and "Jack" and all is well.

## My Thanatopsis

Hail, and Farewell for little time. That physical body within the coffin is not me. In the death change as it is called, I emerged from that flesh garment and now stand beside the casket functioning in my own inner Etheric body as in earth life, and this moment have the same form with feature, expression and intellect as before. Nothing gained but opportunity, and nothing lost, not even memory, and I come in this manner in hope of changing the character of funeral services from gloom and sorrow, to thanksgiving and joy for a soul has passed into the reality as planned in the beginning.

Before my dissolution I became satisfied beyond question that life continues on, that in the democracy of death the rags of wretchedness and the purple robes of power lose distinction, and that personality survives and functions in the same inner body as in Earth Life.

From the beginning, generation after generation have lived a day on this earth and passed through the death change, as many of the present generation are doing, yet but few in all the ages past have made any efforts to solve the problem or inquired whither they have gone.

The hope of life beyond was not born of any book or creed. That idea like the sea has ebbed and flowed its waves beating on the shores of time, since men came up out of savagery, all wish for happiness beyond earth life—to meet again the loved and lost. Immortality is a word that Hope has whispered through the ages to all.

For over forty years I have worked to ascertain the fact and come to know that those who have gone from the physical plane are alive today as when they lived on earth and wore a flesh garment. Dissolution is natural, and comes to every expression and form of life, just a step in life's progression. There is no sorrow at birth, there should be none in this great change and would not be if dissolution advantages were known, and there was less thought of self. The creative intelligence planned both and both are good. Out of the invisible we came and back to that source we go.

I have also learned that thoughts are things, and from day to day woven like tapestries in patterns involved and strangely interlaced with dreams, hopes and fancies concerning life's great theme, as wonderous as traceries in frost wrought on glass, by winter's subtle art, all visible to those in the afterlife.

When the gold of evening meets the dusk beneath the Western Skies the tired worker should rest. One cannot live on the earth when the flame lacks oil. When an old tree is visited by rain in spring, when the sun no longer thrills, it is not meant to stand leafless and alone. It is far better to fall where nature will softly cover its outer garment with woven moss and creeping vines, and so with man. No life of any character ever has been destroyed.

When age creeps on with half-remembered things, over sightless eyes death presses down the lids to rest. As the inner body which alone is alive, throws off the flesh garment in the death change and leaves the world of men, you see it not, no physical sound is made and you cannot hear the words of welcome that greet the newborn soul.

That something you call death is a great inheritance. When one can scarcely read the blurred and faded pages of the past, enters the open door, sees another world beautiful beyond comparison, hears words of greeting fall from the lips of the living dead, they realize how a great privilege is theirs for then will come from the center of space music of the spheres, for all was planned in the beginning by the God Force for our good, and such should be a time of rejoicing among those left as well as those who have gone before. To challenge the necessity of the death change, is to challenge the wisdom of God.

When the afternoon grows short like mine, the twilight falls like a benediction at the close of day, and it was time to go. I knew the end was near and I went gladly knowing that those I loved, who had preceded me, and thousands of earthbound souls I had helped in my secret mission work on the other side would welcome and help me, even as I had helped them.

Earth life is one of the preparations for the reality into which I have entered. A thousand years is but yesterday when it is past, for in that domain there is no time, and knowing something of the plan and purpose of the creative intelligence I was prepared in a measure, and do not I pray, enter the next state with empty hands. The universe is governed by law, and of that law, without bias or preconceived notions I became a student, which led me into the psychic field.

For a long period of time I have talked voice to voice with the living dead and know something of conditions into which I have entered. No soul is ever lost. On by one in the years that I have lived, those I have loved and who have loved me and nearly all my friends have crossed the great divide, but I have kept in touch with them and know where and how they live, how they labor and serve and continue to progress, and that through such service earn their advancement.

I would leave as a heritage to this poor world, the idea or thought that the funeral ceremony should be changed from tears and sorrow, to laughter and joy, for the greatest privilege after birth is dissolution, and among earth people should be a period of rejoicing, and would be if those that are left could forget self and their personal loss and think of the advantage a loved one has gained, as they go on to higher progression and greater happiness and opportunity, and I ask you who have gathered her to have no sorrow or regret on my account, but give or send thoughts and love, words of congratulation and good cheer for my work on earth was done, and youth and strength and new courage is now mine to carry on.

Had Tennyson when he wrote "*Crossing the Bar*" known that to die and live again was the greatest blessing the God force has provided for mankind he would have made that great poem read:

> Sun and Evening Star
> As the call comes for me
> Let there be no mourning in the home
> When I go out to sea
>
> Twilight and Evening Bells
> And after that the dark
> Let there be no sorrow
> In the heart when I embark
>
> Day break and morning light
> Bring renewed life force to me
> The dawn of everlasting life,
> Has come and I am free.

As you come across the border one by one, I will mingle with your friends and bid you welcome, and possibly in some measure aid in your adjustment and understanding.

I have told but little of the knowledge that I have gained, for the public as well as my friends were not ready to receive it. Perhaps these words from a living dead man may impress you and help you understand the change of conditions, for there is no death, there are no dead, and it is well to know something of the journey's end.

Again, Hail and Farewell for little time, we shall meet again.

And now as an evidence of my sincerity, and to illustrate what a funeral service should be like, I ask you in passing out to join me in a glass of wine, and toast "the living and the living dead."

*Edward C. Randall.*

"We are leaves tossed on the broad river of life, sometimes lying in the small dark shallows near the shore until a breeze or ripple quickens us to action, and then we are carried toward the ultimate end of all, the great Ocean of Exaltation. Wise are they who seek the faster current, avoiding all stagnant pools. The great force of the universe sweeps us on and on, and in the end we become a part of the power that speeds all life."